Continuity and Change in Sub-Saharan African Demography

This book offers an in-depth African perspective to the major issues in demographic discourse in sub-Saharan Africa. It provides comprehensive analysis of sub-Saharan African censuses, profiling demographic changes, trends, patterns and consequences in the region. Interdisciplinary, comprehensive, accessible, simple and topical, this volume is perfectly suited to researchers, students and lecturers who are interested in understanding sub-Saharan African population dynamics and issues.

Clifford O. Odimegwu is the head of Demography and Population Studies Programme at the University of the Witwatersrand, Johannesburg, South Africa.

John Kekovole is currently an Executive Manager in charge of Census Inputs and Outputs at Statistics South Africa.

Routledge African Studies

1 **Facts, Fiction, and African Creative Imaginations**
Edited by Toyin Falola and Fallou Ngom

2 **The Darfur Conflict**
Geography or Institutions?
Osman Suliman

3 **Music, Performance and African Identities**
Edited by Toyin Falola and Tyler Fleming

4 **Environment and Economics in Nigeria**
Edited by Toyin Falola and Adam Paddock

5 **Close to the Sources**
Essays on Contemporary African Culture, Politics and Academy
Abebe Zegeye and Maurice Vambe

6 **Landscape and Environment in Colonial and Postcolonial Africa**
Edited by Toyin Falola and Emily Brownell

7 **Development, Modernism and Modernity in Africa**
Edited by Augustine Agwuele

8 **Natural Resources, Conflict, and Sustainable Development**
Lessons from the Niger Delta
Edited by Okechukwu Ukaga, Ukoha O. Ukiwo and Ibaba Samuel Ibaba

9 **Regime Change and Succession Politics in Africa**
Five Decades of Misrule
Edited by Maurice Nyamanga Amutabi and Shadrack Wanjala Nasong'o

10 **The Political Economy of Development and Underdevelopment in Africa**
Edited by Toyin Falola and Jessica Achberger

11 **Pan-Africanism, and the Politics of African Citizenship and Identity**
Edited by Toyin Falola and Kwame Essien

12 **Securing Africa**
Local Crises and Foreign Interventions
Edited by Toyin Falola and Charles Thomas

13 **African Youth in Contemporary Literature and Popular Culture**
Identity Quest
Edited by Vivian Yenika-Agbaw and Lindah Mhando

14 **Indigenous Discourses on Knowledge and Development in Africa**
Edited by Edward Shizha and Ali A. Abdi

15 **African Culture and Global Politics**
Language, Philosophies, and Expressive Culture in Africa and the Diaspora
Edited by Toyin Falola and Danielle Porter Sanchez

16 **Urbanization and Socio-Economic Development in Africa**
Challenges and Opportunities
Edited by Steve Kayizzi-Mugerwa, Abebe Shimeles and Nadège Désirée Yameogo

17 **Continuity and Change in Sub-Saharan African Demography**
Edited by Clifford O. Odimegwu and John Kekovole

Continuity and Change in Sub-Saharan African Demography

Edited by
Clifford O. Odimegwu and
John Kekovole

Routledge
Taylor & Francis Group
NEW YORK   LONDON

First published 2014
by Routledge
711 Third Avenue, New York, NY 10017

and by Routledge
2 Park Square, Milton Park, Abingdon, Oxfordshire OX14 4RN

First issued in paperback 2016

Routledge is an imprint of the Taylor & Francis Group, an informa business

© 2014 Taylor & Francis

The right of Clifford O. Odimegwu and John Kekovole to be identified as the authors of the editorial material, and of the authors for their individual chapters, has been asserted in accordance with sections 77 and 78 of the Copyright, Designs and Patents Act 1988.

All rights reserved. No part of this book may be reprinted or reproduced or utilised in any form or by any electronic, mechanical, or other means, now known or hereafter invented, including photocopying and recording, or in any information storage or retrieval system, without permission in writing from the publishers.

Trademark Notice: Product or corporate names may be trademarks or registered trademarks, and are used only for identification and explanation without intent to infringe.

Library of Congress Cataloging-in-Publication Data
Continuity and change in Sub-Saharan African demography / edited by
  Clifford O. Odimegwu and John Kekovole. — 1st Edition.
    pages cm. — (Routledge african studies ; 17)
  Includes bibliographical references and index.
  1. Africa, Sub-Saharan—Population. 2. Demography—Africa, Sub-Saharan. I. Odimegwu, C. O., editor of compilation. II. Kekovole, John, editor of compilation. III. Series: Routledge African studies ; 17.
    HB3661.A3C686 2014
    304.60967—dc23
    2013051006

ISBN 13: 978-1-138-68722-6 (pbk)
ISBN 13: 978-0-415-71194-4 (hbk)

Typeset in Sabon
by IBT Global.

This book is dedicated to scholarship in African demography, which has come of age by the production of this work.

Contents

List of Figures xiii
List of Tables xvii
Foreword xxi
Acknowledgments xxiii

1 Introduction and Organization 1
CLIFFORD O. ODIMEGWU AND JOHN KEKOVOLE

2 Examining the Accuracy of Age-Sex Data: An Evaluation of Recent Sub-Saharan African Population Censuses 12
CHUKS J. MBA

3 Analysis of Mortality Using Census and Household Data: A Practical Bayesian Multilevel Spatial Modeling Approach 36
LAWRENCE KAZEMBE AND N.B. KANDALA

4 Child Health and Mortality in Sub-Saharan Africa: Trends, Causes, and Forecasts 60
YOHANNES KINFU, COLLINS OPIYO, AND MARILYN WAMUKOYA

5 Indirect Estimation of Levels of Adult Mortality in Sub-Saharan Africa 78
STEPHEN AYO ADEBOWALE AND SUNDAY ADEPOJU ADEDINI

6 Fertility Transition in Sub-Saharan Africa: Evidence from Census Data 97
SUNDAY ADEPOJU ADEDINI

Contents

7 Nuptiality Patterns and Differentials in Sub-Saharan Africa: Analysis of African Census Data — 113
GIDEON RUTAREMWA

8 Population Distribution in Sub-Saharan Africa: Internal and International Migrations in Sub-Saharan Africa — 130
AKANNI AKINYEMI AND SUNDAY OMOYENI

9 Demography of Labor Force in Sub-Saharan African Censuses — 158
CLIFFORD O. ODIMEGWU

10 The Dynamics of Household Structure in Sub-Saharan Africa — 173
LATIFAT D.G. IBISOMI AND NICOLE DE WET

11 Sub-Saharan African Children and Adolescents: Economic Gain or Burden? — 192
ONIPEDE WUSU AND EMMANUEL OLAGUNJU AMOO

12 Orphaned Children in Sub-Saharan Africa: What Can We Learn from Census Data? — 210
BRUNO MASQUELIER AND ABDRAMANE B. SOURA

13 Profiling the Elderly: Understanding Recent Trends in Acceleration of Sub-Saharan African Population Aging — 234
HENRY VICTOR DOCTOR

14 Sex Profile in Education and Educational Attainment in Sub-Saharan Africa — 251
SERAI DANIEL RAKGOASI

15 Living Arrangements of Children in Sub-Saharan Africa and Their Implications on Schooling — 268
ESTHER W. DUNGUMARO

16 Armed Conflict and Demographic Outcomes in Mozambique and Rwanda: What Can Censuses Tell Us? — 284
CARLOS ARNALDO

17 Population Policies in Sub-Saharan Africa: Evolution,
   Achievements and Challenges   303
   JOHN KEKOVOLE AND CLIFFORD O. ODIMEGWU

   Contributors   319
   Index   327

Figures

3.1 Left panel: posterior means of the structured spatial effects of child survival at district level in Rwanda based on model *M3b*. Right panel: posterior probabilities at 80 percent nominal level in Rwanda.   47

3.2 Left panel: posterior means of the unstructured spatial effects of child survival at district level in Senegal based on model *M3b*. Right panel: posterior probabilities at 80 percent nominal level in Senegal.   49

3.3 Left panel: posterior means of the structured spatial effects of child survival at district level in Uganda based on model *M3b*. Right panel: posterior probabilities at 80 percent nominal level in Uganda.   51

3.4 Unstructured spatial effects, at the province level in Rwanda and Senegal and at the county level in Uganda, of child survival (model *M3b*).   52

4.1 Trends in under-five mortality in sub-Saharan Africa, 1965–2005.   66

4.2 Trends in under-five mortality by country, 1965–2005.   68

4.3 Relationship between under-five mortality and estimated broad causes of death in eighteen countries.   70

5.1 Graphs of probability of surviving to age x using census survival method for males for Kenya, 1989–1999.   90

5.2 Graphs of life expectancy at age x (ex) using census survival method for males for Kenya, 1989–1999.   91

5.3 Males estimates of probability of dying at age 60 having survived to age 15 (15q45) using INDEPTH and census survival method for Kenya.   91

6.1 Estimates of TFR by place of residence, based on Arriaga Method (using two census waves).   103

6.2 Estimates of TFR by educational attainment, based on Brass P/F ratio technique (using two census waves).   104

6.3	Gompertz Relational implied TFR by educational attainment (using two census waves).	105
6.4	Estimates of TFR by employment status, based on Brass P/F ratio technique (using 2 census waves).	106
6.5	Gompertz Relational implied TFR by employment status (using two census waves).	107
8.1	Map showing the flow of international migrants by source and destination from two waves of censuses.	136
8.2	Map showing the flow of international migrants by source and destination from two waves of censuses.	137
8.3	Map showing West Africa migrants by country of origin to Guinea, 1983 census.	138
8.4	Map showing West Africa migrants by country of origin to Guinea, 1996 census.	138
8.5	Map showing West Africa migrants by country of origin to Mali, 1987 census.	139
8.6	Map showing West Africa migrants by country of origin to Mali, 1998 census.	139
8.7	Map showing West Africa migrants by country of origin to Senegal, 1988 census.	140
8.8	Map showing West Africa migrants by country of origin to Senegal, 2002 census.	140
8.9	Map showing South African migrants by country of origin to South Africa, 1996 census.	141
8.10	Map showing South African migrants by country of origin to South Africa, 2001 census.	142
8.11	Map showing East Africa migrants by country of origin to Kenya, 1989 census.	142
8.12	Map showing East Africa migrants by country of origin to Kenya, 1999 census.	143
8.13	Map showing East Africa migrants by country of origin to Rwanda, 1991 census.	144
8.14	Map showing East Africa migrants by country of origin to Rwanda, 2002 census.	145
8.15	Map showing East Africa migrants by country of origin to Uganda, 1991 census.	145
8.16	Map showing East Africa migrants by country of origin to Uganda, 2002 census.	146
8.17	Map showing East Africa migrants by country of origin to Tanzania, 1998 census.	146
8.18	Map showing East Africa migrants by country of origin to Tanzania, census.	
9.1	Age-sex activity rates of labor force by 1990 round of censuses.	163

9.2	Age-sex activity rates of labor force by 2000 round of censuses.	164
9.3	Rwandan length of working life, 1991–2002.	165
9.4	Length of working life Senegal, 1988–2002.	166
9.5	Length of working life South Africa, 1996–2001.	167
11.1	Classic phases of demographic transition.	194
11.2	Population pyramid for Kenya, Senegal, and South Africa.	199
11.3	Education attainment by age-group across selected countries.	202
11.4	Projected dependency levels across the selected regions.	204
12.1	Percentage of children aged 5–9 who have lost their mother or father; West, Middle, East and Southern Africa, 1970–2010.	214
12.2	Comparison of the percentage of children aged 5–9 who have lost their mother or father, as estimated by Spectrum and reported in censuses.	216
12.3	Proportions of maternal orphans at age 7 estimated from mixed-effects Poisson regression models from IPUMS data.	219
13.1	Projected changes in the levels of aging for Africa for four indicators of aging.	243
13.2	The changing decadal speed of increase in Africa's selected indicators of aging.	244
16.1	Age-sex distributions, Mozambique, 1980 and 1997, and Rwanda, 1991 and 2002.	291
16.2	Under-five mortality over time, Mozambique.	293
16.3	Under-five mortality over time, Rwanda.	294
16.4	Trends in total fertility rate, Mozambique, 1983–2007.	296
16.5	Trends in total fertility rate, Rwanda, 1977–2002.	296

Tables

2.1	Evaluation Indexes for Age in Single Years	19
2.2	Age Ratios by Country and Census Year	25
2.3	Summary Indexes by Country and Census Year	29
3.1	Summary of Covariates Used in the Analyses Given in the Table Are the Counts (and Proportion Dead) across Covariates	42
3.2	Model Comparison Values Based on Deviance Information Criterion (DIC) for the Models	45
3.3	Fixed Effects for Rwanda Child Survival	46
3.4	Fixed Effects for Senegal Child Survival	48
3.5	Fixed Effects for Uganda Child Survival	50
4.1	Estimated and Predicted Under-Five Mortality Rates for Selected African Countries, 1965–2015	69
4.2	Indirect Estimates of Causes of Death for Various African Countries	70
5.1	Census Survival Method for Ten-Year Intercensal Intervals Applied to Kenya: Males and Females, 1989–1999	84
5.2	Coale-Demeny Model Life Tables (West Family) Using Probability of Surviving to Age 1 (1q0) and Age 5 (5q0) from DHS and Life Expectancy at Age 20 (e20) Estimates from Census Survival Methods Males: Kenya, Rwanda, Senegal, Tanzania, and South Africa	86
5.3	INDEPTH MLTs (Pattern 1) and Coale-Demeny (West Family) Estimates of the Female Survival Function for Kenya Using Only Values of l1 and l5 for the Year 2010 KDHS	88
6.1	Estimates of Total Fertility Rate from Census Data Using Arriaga Method (AM), Brass Relational Gompertz Model (RGM), and Brass P/F Ratio (P/F ratio) Technique	102
7.1	Percentage Distribution of Population Aged 15–54 Years Ever Married by Country and Year of Census	118
7.2	Singulate Mean Age at First Marriage by Residence and Sex of Individual	119

7.3	Multinomial Logistic Regression Model Predicting the Odds of Being Currently and Previously Married in Uganda in 1991 and 2002	121
7.4	Multinomial Logistic Regression Model Predicting the Odds of Being Currently and Previously Married in Tanzania in 1988 and 2002	123
8.1	Volume of Rural–Urban Migration in African Regions, 1985–2005	133
8.2	Estimated Number of International Migrants in Africa by Region at Midyear Population	133
8.3	Interregional Migration Matrix in Sub-Saharan Africa 1983–2002 by Citizenship and Country of Birth	136
8.4	Intercountry Migration Matrix for Countries with the Highest Migration Stock within the Three African Regions	147
8.5	Age-Sex Distribution of Migrants by Source, Round of Censuses across Three African Regions	151
8.6	Education-Employment Status Distribution of Migrants by Source, Round of Censuses across Three African Regions	154
10.1	Trend in Total Number of Households ('000) and the Percentage Change in Number of Households between the Two Censuses by Type of Household	178
10.2	Trend in Average Household Size and Percentage Change in Average Household Size between the Two Censuses by Type of Household	179
10.3	Percentage and Change in Distribution of Types of Households	181
10.4	Percentage of Households Headed by Females by Type of Households	183
10.5	Average Household Size by Sex of Household Head and Type of Household	184
10.6	Percentage of Employed Heads of Household and Heads of Households with Secondary or Higher Level of Education	186
11.1	Children and Adolescent Dependency Ratio versus Total Dependency Ratio by Selected Countries	201
11.2	Percentage Distribution of Children and Adolescents by Employment Status by Selected Countries	206
12.1	Relationship to the Household Head by Parental Survival Status (7- to 17-Year-Olds, Row Percentages)	221
12.2	Percentage of Girls in Union at Age 17 According to Parental Survival Status, and Percentage of Children (Aged 7–17) According to Parental Survival Status and Selected Characteristics of Households	224
12.3	School Attendance of 7- to 17-Year-Olds, School Attainment of 15- to 17-Year-Olds, and percentage of children (7- to 17-years-olds) in Employment, by Parental Survival Status	226

13.1	Brief Demographic and Socioeconomic Profile of Selected Countries as at Mid-2011	238
13.2	Basic Description of Selected African Census Raw Data	239
13.3	Indicators of Aging for Selected African Countries for Both Sexes	241
13.4	Indicators of Aging for Selected African Countries for Both Sexes (Continuation of Table 13.3)	242
13.5	Some Notes on Measures of Aging for Selected African Countries	247
14.1	Primary Education Gross Enrollment Rates and Gender Parity Index (Population 7–13 years) in Selected Sub-Saharan African Countries	257
14.2	Gross Enrollment Ratios and Comparison with UN Estimates	257
14.3	Secondary Education Gross Enrollment Rates and Gender Parity Index (Population 14–18 Years) in Selected Sub-Saharan African Countries	258
14.4	Tertiary Education Gross Enrollment Rates and Gender Parity Index (Population 19–23 Years) in Selected Sub-Saharan African Countries	260
14.5	Educational Attainment and Gender Parity in Educational Attainment (Population 25+ Years) in Selected Sub-Saharan Countries	261
14.6	Binary Logistic Regression Coefficients of the Likelihood of Being Enrolled in Formal Education	262
15.1	Trends in Percentage of Children by Survival Status of Parents	272
15.2	Multinomial Logistic Regression Model of Predictors of Living Arrangements of Children Aged 5–17 Years in Uganda in 2002	275
15.3	Multinomial Logistic Regression Model of Predictors of Living Arrangements of Children Aged 5–17 Years in Rwanda in 2002	277
15.4	Multivariate Logistic Regression of Predictors of School Attendance in Rwanda and Uganda, 2002	279
16.1	Population Growth Rate, Mozambique, 1940–2007	290
17.1	Rounds of Population and Housing Census in Sub-Saharan Africa	306
17.2	Demographic Indicators for Major Subregions of Africa, 1997–2025	311
17.3	Population Indicators for Some Selected African Countries Pre- and Post-Cairo ICPD of 1994	313

Foreword

The origin of this ongoing work dates back to 1998 when Statistics South Africa convened a meeting to strategize on how to enhance the in-depth analysis and utilization of data collected in African censuses under the auspices of the African Census Analysis Project (ACAP) situated at the University of Pennsylvania. The meeting noted the paucity of archiving data collected in various countries as well as inadequate analysis of the data. The project succeeded in getting African governments to provide the requisite data and published two volumes: *A General Demography of South Africa* in 2005 and *African Households—Censuses and Surveys* in 2006.

Most countries in the subregion have participated in all the four United Nations rounds of census, from 1980 to 2010 Round of Population and Housing Censuses. Once these exercises were completed, aggregate results were released. In almost all the countries, the story ends here. No further attempt was made to critically interrogate the huge data sets with a view to understanding demographic processes in the subregion. One consequence of this inability is that what we know of sub-Saharan African demography is mostly based on surveys that are undertaken internationally for comparability purposes mainly by outside agencies. We, stakeholders in the national statistical systems, watch as our demographic stories are told by outsiders who in most cases do not understand sub-Saharan African's sociocultural milieu. It is therefore of paramount importance that data collected in our censuses be availed to African scholars to enable them to undertake in-depth analysis to provide the requisite insights into what is happening in the continent. Africa can no longer continue to be a generator of data while foreign scholars become the users and disseminators of such data.

This book, *Continuity and Change in Sub-Saharan African Demography*, presents a unique opportunity for African scholars to dig deep into African census datasets that are in the public domain with a view to telling the demographic story of the subregion. The book tries to capture the dynamics of sub-Saharan African demography with a view to identifying any patterns of change and continuity in demographic dynamics of the region. Understanding the subregion's past, present, and future demographic dynamics is central to the fulfillment of development objectives of poverty eradication, achievement of equality, and sustainable development. It is also central to deepening democratic reforms in the subregion.

This book is a follow-up of the work done by ACAP. It has been conceptualized, initiated, led, and driven solely by African scholars to gain a better understanding of demographic processes and other emerging population issues in the subregion. It describes demographic trends, patterns, determinants, and consequences in the subregion. It also provides comparable, reliable cross-national comparisons of critical population issues confronting the subregion, including those that arose from the International Conference on Population and Development (ICPD) and epitomizes a commitment to the ideals of New Partnership for Africa's Development (NEPAD), which encourages African-led initiatives to solve problems of the continent.

The book has adopted an interdisciplinary approach in the analysis and presentation of the results, and, hence, it should serve as a guide to students of both technical and substantive demography. As I have observed elsewhere, "a regional approach in the analysis of population processes will further enhance the capability of African scholars to make positive intellectual contribution to Africa and the rest of the world." Despite the positives of this intellectual exercise, it is sad to note that most notable countries in the region are not mentioned in this book simply because there are no census data from these countries. This is a good opportunity to call on my colleagues in this business of national statistical management to make at least 5 percent or 10 percent of their census data sets available to researchers in the public domain. What is the value of spending huge amounts of resources both human and financial in a national census exercise if it is only to generate aggregate data without rigorous in-depth analysis? How can we understand African or sub-Saharan African demography and development if stakeholders hoard census data sets?

I wish to use this opportunity to thank all the contributors for their dedication in completing the project. My special thanks go to Clifford Obby Odimegwu of the Demography and Population Studies Programme of the University of the Witwatersrand, South Africa, and John Kekovole of Statistics South Africa for the able leadership they demonstrated in getting this project completed. We note with gratitude the bold step taken by ACAP in initiating this important endeavor in 1998.

Pali J. Lehohla
Statistician-General
South Africa

Acknowledgments

The editors of this seminal book by young African scholars in the field of population studies are highly indebted to the following organizations, individuals, and colleagues for their immense contribution and support for the completion of this work.

1. Statistics South Africa for the vision of African capacity building in census analysis; initiating this work, providing all the logistics for the analysis and writing workshops. The role of the Statistician-General of South Africa and his management team cannot be quantified.
2. Brown University Population Studies and Training Center (PSTC) for Visiting Scholarship appointment to the principal editor, which provided a conducive intellectual environment for the final editing of the book. We also appreciate the positive contributions of colleagues at PSTC to this project.
3. International Statistical Institute (ISI) 57th Conference Presentations in Dublin, Ireland, for the opportunity to disseminate some of the chapters at the conference where the authors benefited from comments and feedback from conference participants.
4. African Development Bank (AfDB) and United Nations Fund for Population Activities (UNFPA) for financial support: AfDB for sponsoring some of the authors participation at the ISI 57th conference in Dublin, Ireland; the UNFPA Africa Region Office for facilitating the purchase of the analytical software used by the authors during the analysis workshops.
5. Reviewers: We acknowledge the immense contribution of the internal, external, and publishers' reviewers, whose critical reviews of all the chapters helped in no small measure to improve the quality.
6. Administrative and institutional support: Many people assisted in one way or the other for this project to be completed. We hereby acknowledge the role of such individuals as Noma Mbhele of Statistics South Africa for being the administrative anchor of this project; Alfons Fanoe of Statistics South Africa for his passionate and intellectual

commitment to this project; Julia Mamabolo, our second administrative anchor at the Programme in Demography and Population Studies at the University of the Witwatersrand, Johannesburg; Max Novick and Jennifer Morrow at Routledge, Taylor and Francis, New York, for their patience, guidance, understanding, and encouragement throughout the arduous task of editorial and production processing. Other individuals whose contributions in one way or the other are deeply appreciated are Leonard Ahuejere, Mojisola Oguntosin, Kefiloe Masiteng, and all the graduate students of the Programme in Demography and Population Studies at the University of the Witwatersrand, Johannesburg, South Africa.

1 Introduction and Organization

Clifford O. Odimegwu and John Kekovole

Since the publication of two volumes of R.R. Kuczynski's study on the demographic survey of the British Colonial Empire, more than sixty-five years ago, several other attempts have been made to describe the population dynamics of what is known as sub-Saharan Africa (Martin, Hill, and Foote 1993; Kuczynski 1948, 1949). In 1961, two books by Galeoti (1961) and Lorimer (1961) were published to summarize what was known about the demography of tropical Africa (Garenne 2011). Seven years later, William Brass et al. (1968), noting prior efforts at providing demographic information about Africa, focused their work on the critical evaluation and analysis of the then existing data sets. Their focus was on data availability, quality, and adjustments of poor-quality data. Through this effort they were able to compile estimates of demographic parameters and provided valuable tools for estimation of demographic parameters of countries with inadequate data and weak statistical bases. Tarver (1996) in his book, *The Demography of Africa*, claimed to provide basic understanding of the major aspects of demography in (sub-Saharan) Africa, its past, present, and future. Martin, Hill, and Foote (1993), in the National Academy of Science work on demographic change in sub-Saharan Africa, attempted to describe and explain demographic changes in the region using demographic and health survey data. There have been various UN estimates and projections on the subcontinent (UN 1983). These efforts made use of survey samples and estimates from various UN sources. Tabutin and Schoumaker (2004) conducted a statistical assessment and changes in sub-Saharan African demography. They used data from United Nations agencies to reconstruct the major changes since 1950 and the Demographic and Health Surveys or similar surveys. The purpose of this work was to present data that are as comparable, reliable, and 'recent' as possible on the evolution of sub-Saharan African demography since 1950 and present demographic characteristics of the population of each country. They also aimed to provide a synthetic view of the major components of population change and differences in the region. The highlight of these early publications is the fact the demography of sub-Saharan Africa was characterized by early marriage, high fertility, excessive mortality, and rapid population growth. They have also noted emerging changes in demographic patterns of the region (Martin, Hill, and Foote 1993; Tabutin and Schoumaker 2004).

However, recent events in Africa and the world tend to redefine what should be the focus of any discourse on sub-Saharan African demographic landscape and have challenged the old assumptions about African population issues. Leading in these new developments is the 1994 International Conference on Population and Development (ICPD) held in Cairo, Egypt, which marked a major paradigm shift in the issues that demography tends to pursue. The conference outcome, exemplified by the popular ICPD Program of Action, has impacted on many demographic projects, activities, and population discourse (UN 1994). Many sub-Saharan African countries have embraced the institutionalization of population policies and programs (UNECA 1995). Almost all countries in the subregion have population policies and programs rooted in the 1994 ICPD and other international agreements.

There have been many rounds of censuses in many sub-Saharan African countries, coupled with national surveys that are used for socioeconomic planning in several countries. Since the establishment of African Census Program in the 1970s, there have been the following rounds of censuses in Africa: the 1980 round (1975–1984), which witnessed many countries undertaking population censuses, except Chad, Nigeria, and Sierra Leone; the 1990 round, which covers the period 1985–1994; the 2000 round covering the period 1995–2004; and the most current, the 2010 round, which extends from 2005 to 2014. Added to specific national surveys, the quantity, quality, and availability of data on demographic processes in sub-Saharan Africa have improved and are readily available to profile the continent's population dynamics. But these census data sets remain unexplored. There are geopolitical developments that could have impact on population and development issues. These include conflict in many countries, refugees, the ravaging effect of HIV/AIDS, women empowerment issues, increasing urbanization, and international migration. There is a huge growth in the number of sub-Saharan African scholars and institutions interested in demography and population issues who would like to make significant contributions to the global understanding of African censuses and surveys. The ability and expertise of these young African scholars have not been explored and tested.

Analysis of existing survey data sets in the subregion has indicated the onset of fertility decline even in the face of increasing child mortality attributable to the combined effects of wars, conflicts, the AIDS pandemic, corruption, and negative cultural practices. Cities are growing rapidly because of increasing rural–urban migration, which has led to rapid urbanization. This has led to congested urban centers with limited infrastructure to provide social services. These have added greater dimension to the need to understand the implications as far as sub-Saharan African demography and population studies are concerned.

While these features are taking place, many sub-Saharan African countries have participated in the 2000 and 2010 rounds of population and housing censuses and other national household surveys, such as demographic and health surveys, and special surveys, such as AIS, MIS, and so on (Garenne 2011). Analyses of these data sets have been descriptive to give the general impression of the population characteristics without rigorous technical analysis of these data sets. With multiple data sets, comparative analysis between countries in the subcontinent can be conducted. The need therefore exists to utilize the avalanche of census data sets to describe and explain demographic trends, patterns, determinants, and consequences in the continent over the past fifty years, especially from the ICPD perspective.

Generally there is a noticeable lack in the skill of African scholars to analyze huge sub-Saharan African data sets. The result of this is that the analysis of sub-Saharan African census data sets, and therefore telling the story of sub-Saharan African demography, has been the exclusive preserve of Western scholars and institutions. Thus while countries in the subregion are the generators of census data, the capacity to analyze and interpret the demographic pathways of the subcontinent reside elsewhere.

Overall this book is intended to provide comprehensive analysis of census data collected in sub-Saharan African censuses. It profiles emerging demographic changes, trends, patterns, and consequences in the region. It is expected that a holistic analysis of this sort will either verify or challenge existing theoretical frameworks and raise fundamental methodological issues relevant to the conduct of censuses in Africa. The demography of sub-Saharan Africa will be better understood and enriched. The uniqueness of this book is the fact that it is initiated, implemented, and wholly driven by African and Africanist scholars who have firsthand experience of day-to-day demographic interactions and dynamics in sub-Saharan Africa. This is one major contribution to building the capacity of young and emerging scholars from the subcontinent in the analysis of census data. It has an authentic sub-Saharan African perspective. For the first time, sub-Saharan African scholars in population studies have analyzed and interpreted sub-Saharan African demographic parameters from African perspectives.

The book adopts both technical and descriptive approaches in its presentation. The various demographic events were subjected to serious technical analysis to provide information on the levels and trends in demographic process, while the descriptive approach was used to provide explanation of the observed trends and their impact on sub-Saharan African demography and development.

The authors, drawn from different academic and research institutions in sub-Saharan Africa, participated in the rigorous scientific activities that facilitated the production of this book. Emerging from the different chapters is the fact that there are demographic changes and commonalities in this subcontinent, similar characteristics and extremes in the region. The various chapters also show that the subregion is a place of continuity and change. While in some parameters, the demographic profile is changing, there is continuity in others. Marriage remains key to family building and fertility, although there is an increasing trend in age at marriage. The fertility level imposes a youthful age structure with a high dependency ratio, although this is declining in some of the countries, especially in East and Southern Africa. Mortality decline is contributing to a high population growth rate. Another feature is the demographic effect of internecine conflicts in most of the countries in the region. The need for a policy of data collection, analysis, and for training and research of fertility reduction, population aging, mortality, and health and population distribution cannot be overemphasized.

Chuks J. Mba in Chapter 2 attempts to find out irregularities in age-sex statistics and quantifies the quality of age and sex data. Censuses from thirteen African countries are used. For the single-year age distributions, graphical method and three conventional indexes (Whipple's, Myers's, and the Bachi's) are used. The United Nations joint score is applied to five-year age-groups. Census data from these countries are generally inaccurate. The greatest concentration of digits 0 and 5 could be found in Guinea, while the sex ratios at birth varied from 97 in Guinea to 108 in Sudan. Formal education is key to addressing age-sex errors. Africa needs accurate demographic information for effective development planning.

In Chapter 3, Lawrence Kazembe and N.B. Kandala apply a Bayesian approach to analyze child mortality. The authors review the main implications of adopting survival analysis in the census and highlight the practical application of appropriate analytical techniques by merging census and household survey data. The contribution of this chapter is threefold. First, through the use of empirical methods, the authors are able to investigate determinants of under-five mortality more flexibly than most previous work. Second, the methods also allow for the investigation of the spatial pattern of under-five mortality, prior to and after controlling for the socioeconomic covariates. This enables the authors to determine to what extent the substantial spatial pattern of mortality is driven by socioeconomic factors. Third, by using data from recent census and household data from three sub-Saharan Africa countries (Rwanda, Senegal, and Uganda), the authors are able to investigate the relative importance of country-specific socioeconomic factors and government policies vis-à-vis geographical factors that aim to estimate the effect of area of residence (environmental and cultural practices) and further covariates on under-five mortality. Results provide clear evidence of considerable geographical variation of under-five mortality that is unexplained by socioeconomic factors. Even if the causes of the spatial effects in each country are not fully explained, one can use this spatial information for planning purposes, which is gaining increasing importance in policy circles that attempt to focus the allocation of public resources to the most affected sections of the population. The resulting under-five mortality maps can also be used as a practical tool for monitoring progress within and countries for the achievement of Millenium Development Goal Number 4.

In Chapter 4, Yohannes Kinfu, Collins Opiyo, and Marilyn Wamukoya focus on trends and causes of child mortality and health in sub-Saharan Africa. The authors argue that while achieving optimal human welfare and survival remains a key challenge for social and economic development in sub-Saharan Africa, where many children die of preventable causes, the study of child mortality has been hindered by shortcomings in availability, accuracy, and timeliness of appropriate data. Using thirty-two national censuses from nineteen countries and applying new version of the Brass technique, the authors examine trends in under-five mortality rates in selected sub-Saharan African countries from the early 1970s until the first half of 2000s. As for the most recent years, the trend analysis is supplemented by estimates on the cause-structure of under-five mortality, both to compare the African experience with that of the classical epidemiologic transition model. The results show that child mortality transition in Africa has passed through three distinct phases since the late 1960s and four distinct regional patterns of mortality transitions. Intervention strategies for further mortality reductions are intractably linked with the stage in which a country finds itself in this transition continuum. There was a close correspondence between the cause-structure estimates for the countries in the region and those of the classical epidemiologic transition models. As levels of under-five mortality fall below sixty, increased attention should be given to improving skilled newborn care, including the availability of referral services for adequate clinical management. This way it may then be possible to accelerate the child mortality transition in Africa. If current patterns prevail, among the countries investigated, only Ethiopia, Kenya, and South Africa are most likely to meet the millennium development target for under-five mortality.

Steve Adebowale and Sunday Adepoju Adedini, in Chapter 5, estimate levels of adult mortality in sub-Saharan Africa. Census survival and model life tables are applied to data for Kenya, Rwanda, Senegal, Tanzania, and South Africa. Mortality is in most cases lower among females than males. The probability of dying between ages 15 and 60 ($_{45}q_{15}$) is highest in South Africa (males = 794/1000 and females = 817/1000). The estimated $_{45}q_{15}$ is high compared with what is the case in advanced nations. Policy and methodological implications of the study are discussed.

In Chapter 6, Adedini estimates fertility levels of countries with two census data points in sub-Saharan Africa using different census data sets from sub-Saharan African countries. Two census data points from Kenya, Rwanda, Senegal, and South Africa are considered in the analyses. The three indirect estimation techniques employed are Arriaga's method, Trussell variant of Brass P/F ratio technique, and the Brass Relational Gompertz model. Results from the three estimating procedures indicate fertility decline in the selected countries, while a stall in fertility transition in Senegal is noticed. Fertility is approaching the replacement level in South Africa, although it remains high in other countries in sub-Saharan Africa. Differentials in fertility patterns are observed. Findings suggest that policies that would lead to substantial reduction in fertility levels in the region must include strategies that ensure women have up to secondary or higher education.

Gideon Rutaremwa, in Chapter 7, presents results pertaining to nuptiality patterns and differentials in sub-Saharan Africa. The inclination to study nuptiality in relation to other phenomena is that a lot of analyses have focused on fertility, mortality, and migration as key determinants of population change with minimal focus on nuptiality. Data from nine countries, namely, Guinea, Mali, Senegal, Mozambique, South Africa, Kenya, Rwanda, Uganda, and Tanzania, are used. Assessment of Singulate Mean Age at Marriage (SMAM) and multinomial logistic regression are applied. The study shows that there are wide variations in the SMAM for males and females in all countries studied. However, the least male–female margin in SMAM estimates is for South Africa at both the 1996 and 2007 censuses. It is also worth noting that the SMAM estimates increased at the later census for nearly all the countries, implying that age at marriage is increasing among the population of all countries studied. The findings indicate that females continue to get married at a lower age compared with males. In Uganda, the proportion of men who were ever married was highest compared with other African countries studied. The results from regression analysis show that the employed, women, those in rural areas, and with less education are more likely to be in the currently married category compared with other population groups. The study improves our understanding of marriage patterns and dynamics in sub-Saharan Africa. The study provides insights into some simple empirical approaches for using available census data to inform research and policy.

In Chapter 8, Akanni Akinyemi and Sunday Omoyeni discuss the patterns of population distribution, migration, and urbanization. The result shows the volume (both in flow and stock) of migration within Africa is quite enormous with a great potential for economic development in the continent. The demographic profile of migrants shows an increasing trend in the proportion of underage (minors) in intraregional movement as well as an increasing trend in female autonomous migration. Information on the education–employment issue also shows that there is a sharp decrease in proportion of those in employment of migrants outside each of the three regions. The chapter concludes by advocating for a review of labor-restrictive laws as well as harnessing the economic and developmental potential of huge migration volume in the region.

Clifford O. Odimegwu in Chapter 9 examines the levels and patterns of labor force participation in the subcontinent in a period of HIV/AIDS pandemic. The chapter extends the frontier of the use of African censuses in the analysis of African labor force by providing analytical approaches to (a) studying the structure of labor force in selected African countries, (b) examining changes in the labor force structure of these countries, and (c) computing African tables of economically active life or labor force life tables. The sources of data include: Rwandan 1991 and 2002 census data (to represent East Africa), Senegalese 1988 and 2002 census data (representing the West African region), and South African 1996 and 2001 census data (to represent the Southern African region). The South African and Rwandan census data are utilized to track the effect of HIV/AIDS on the length of working life in the continent. The rationale behind the choice of these countries lies in the fact that the two countries have at least two census waves and the HIV prevalence rates for the two countries are higher than 10 percent (INDEPTH Network 2004), Also, the INDEPTH model life table is used for the analysis in order to take care of the effect of fluctuating fertility and the impact of HIV/AIDS.

While the South African two censuses showed that the proportion of male and female population in the labor force increased between 1996 and 2001, Rwanda witnessed a drastic fall in male (and female) labor force population from 81 percent in 1991 to 66 percent in 2002 (and 82 percent to 71 percent for females). Also, Senegal witnessed slight decline in male labor force population over the period 1988–2002 from 78.4 percent to 76.3 percent, while that of females had a remarkable increase from 23 percent to 31 percent. Results also showed that except for South Africa, activity rates among young men and women aged 15–19 were high in Africa. In addition, male and female activity rates mostly peaked around age categories 30–34 and 35–39 for all the selected countries. Length of working life is shorter for women than for men. It is also highest for Senegalese men and women compared with Rwanda (perhaps attributable to the effect of genocide) and South Africa (a result of HIV/AIDS), but men and women in Senegal spent a high proportion of their lifetimes in economically inactive pursuits. The observed trend indicates that the gaps between male and female labor force participation would get closer because the study suggests that female participation in the labor force would increase and get better in the continent. The study concludes that the generally low level of life expectancy in sub-Saharan Africa has had the effect of lowering the length of economically active life in the region.

In Chapter 10, Latifat Ibisomi and Nicole De Wet focus their analysis on the dynamics of households in sub-Saharan African. The authors present the findings pertaining to levels and pattern of number of households, average household size, and household types over time, across sub-Saharan Africa, with a special focus on female-headed households. The study used a 5 percent sample of Mali, Rwanda, Kenya, Tanzania, Uganda, Malawi, and South Africa integrated census data at two time points. The household is the unit of analysis. The findings show that the average household size is declining but there is a greater proportional increase in the total number of households. Results further show that the percentage of female-headed households is increasing, even in the nuclear household type. The observed high level and increasing percentage in female-headed households in the face of great disparities in access to socioeconomic opportunities between the two sexes certainly has implications for the well-being of persons that reside in female-headed households. This calls for a reappraisal of the effectiveness of the various measures taken by countries to promote the empowerment of women.

Onipede Wusu and Emmanuel Olagunju Amoo in Chapter 11 examine the issue of sub-Saharan African children and adolescents, whether they are dividend or debt. Using census data from Kenya, Senegal, and South Africa and applying sundry descriptive analytical techniques, they note that the majority of the children and adolescents in the region are dependants owing to the predominance of a youthful population structure. Consistent with various age structure economic frameworks adopted for the study, the present proportion of children and adolescents are more of economic burden at both micro (individual families) and macro (governments) levels. Nevertheless, if reductionist population policies are vigorously implemented now and birthrates begin to decline in a sustainable way, the current large proportion of children and adolescents would graduate into the working age population in about a decade or so while dependency ratio would begin to fall. If appropriate economic, social, and legal frameworks are put in place, this situation is most likely to propel rapid economic growth and social welfare. Thus, children and adolescents in Sub-Saharan Africa are more debt presently, but, all things being equal, they are a potential great source of economic miracles.

In Chapter 12, Bruno Masquelier and Abdramane B. Soura demonstrate the use of census data to investigate the issues of orphaned and vulnerable children. Despite a renewed interest in the situation of orphans in Africa spurred by the HIV-TB epidemic, census data on parental survival remain hardly exploited. Many censuses conducted in Sub-Saharan Africa contain information on parental deaths, which can complement what is being learned from sample surveys. Using published reports and samples of individual-level records, the authors provide three illustrations of the value of census data to research on orphanhood. First, census estimates are useful to reconstruct past trends in orphanhood rates at the national level. Second, they allow for the mapping of the orphan prevalence at small geographical scales. Third, along with household surveys, census data permit the study of the vulnerability of orphans, in terms of school attendance, living arrangements, and labor force participation.

Henry Victor Doctor, in Chapter 13, profiles the demography of the elderly in the subcontinent. Recently, the world's population has experienced a remarkable transition from a stage of high birthrates and death rates to one characterized by low death rates. The core of this transition has been the growth in the number and proportion of older persons. Considering the rapid pace of aging in Africa over the past few years, and using census data to assess the recent paths of population aging, report on future levels of indicators of aging and the speed at which they change, results show that despite the slow pace, generally all the measures indicate that aging will continue in the next four decades. The proportion of the African population 60-plus years increases from 5 percent in 1990 to 11 percent in 2050. The two rapidly increasing indicators (proportion aged 60-plus years and median age) suggest the need for institutional adjustment to cope with the expected increases. These findings call for African governments to respond to the needs of an aging population in a timely manner. We hope that this study will contribute to the knowledge of past and future acceleration of African population aging and call attention of policy makers to address issues that affect the elderly.

In Chapter 14, Serai Daniel Rakgoasi examines sex differentials in educational attainment in sub-Saharan Africa. Human development, through education, is a key to sustaining social and economic development. This chapter uses census data from selected sub-Saharan African countries to examine access to formal education and educational attainment in Africa. The results of the analysis show that access to primary and secondary education has increased for all countries during their respective intercensal periods. However, access to secondary and tertiary education, while significantly lower than access to basic primary education, is also found to be highly inequitable, with males being disproportionately likely to have attained higher levels of education than females. For most of the countries studied, investment in improved access to basic formal education beyond the primary level is an important development imperative, and such an investment should necessarily involve addressing the sometimes pervasive social, cultural, and other norms and beliefs that impede girls' access to formal education.

In Chapter 15, Esther W. Dungumaro examines the living arrangements of children in selected African countries and their implications on schooling. Selected measures are used to assess living arrangements and schooling using 5 percent census data sample. Results show that age of the child, survival status of parents, and marital status are predictors of living arrangements. Type of households, wealth index, and age of the child are important predictors of children schooling. Changing living arrangements of children raise concerns about the long-term investment in education. The study recommends that in order to broaden our understanding of the challenges children face, studies on changes in living arrangements of children should not focus only on orphans but also on non-orphans. Policy efforts may be effective if they are designed to expand social and economic security for poor families to enable them to invest in children's education. Public policy should therefore focus on children residing with older persons and siblings to enable them to invest in children's education.

Carlos Arnaldo, in Chapter 16, assesses the impact of armed conflict on demographic outcomes (age-sex structure, fertility, and under-five mortality) in Mozambique and Rwanda. Indirect estimation techniques were applied to pre- and post-conflict census data, to trace demographic changes that may be related to conflict. There was a rise in under-five mortality and a fall of fertility during the period of conflict. However, this pattern is much clearer in Rwanda than in Mozambique. The author concludes by noting that the nature, duration, and characteristics of societal conflict are important factors in shaping the magnitude of the demographic impact.

John Kekovole and Odimegwu, in Chapter 17, examine the evolutionary patterns, implementation, achievements, and challenges of population policies and programs in sub-Saharan Africa. The authors note that sub-Saharan African population policies have experienced a global paradigm shift in population policies and programs with a focus on reproductive health care. It is observed that there is an emerging declining trend in sub-Saharan African demography as far as fertility and mortality rates are concerned as a result of huge investments in population programs. However, in order to accelerate various demographic and development objectives, countries in the subcontinent have to review their population policies and programs and intensify actions on specific targets with a view to benefiting from the demographic dividend, especially in the post-2015 development era. The post-2015 development agenda should account for a progressively and rapidly sub-Saharan Africa by promoting healthy aging and economic well-being in old age. A reinvigorated population policy should prioritize planning for future urban growth, including appropriate infrastructure and access to basic education and health, including reproductive health, and geriatric and other services so that countries in the region can reap the benefits of economies of scale and greater efficiency. It can also specify how to manage and incorporate demographic dynamics in national sustainable development policies. The issue of data quality and availability, provision of scientific evidence for policy dialogue and development, and, clearly, robust and defined policy relevant indicators should be given due attention.

REFERENCES

Brass, William, Ansley J. Coale, Paul Demeny, Don F. Heisel, Frank Lorimer, Anatole Romaniuk and Etienne van de Walle. (1968) *The Demography of Tropical Africa*. Princeton, NJ: Princeton University Press.

Galeoti, G. (1961) *Problemi demografici dei paesi sotttosviluppati e solidarieta internazionale*. Bologna: G. Malipiero.

Garenne, M. (2011) "Fifty Years of Research in African Demography: Progress and Challenges." *African Population Studies 25th Year Commemorative Edition* 25 (2): 151–167.

INDEPTH Network (2004): Indepth Model Life Table for sub-Saharan Africa. Ashgate.

Kuczynski, R.R. (1948) *Demographic Survey of British Colonial Empire, Vol. 1 (West Africa)*. Oxford: Oxford University Press.

Kuczynski, R.R. (1949) *Demographic Survey of British Colonial Empire, Vol. 1 (East Africa)*. Oxford: Oxford University Press.

Lorimer, F. (1961) *Demographic Information on Tropical Africa*. Boston: Boston University Press.

Martin, L., Kenneth H. Hill, and Karen A. Foote (1993) *Demographic Change in Sub-Saharan Africa*. National Academy Press, Washington DC.

Tabutin, Dominique, and Bruno Schoumaker. (2004) "The Demography of Sub-Saharan Africa from the 1950s to the 2000s: A Survey of Changes and a Statistical Assessment." *Population-E* 59 (3–4): 457–556.

Tarver, James. (1996) *The Demography of Africa*. Westport, CT: Praeger Publishers.

UNECA. (1995) "Experts and NGOs Workshop on the Implementation of the DAKAR/NGOR Declaration and the ICPD Programme of Action" (Abidjan, June 6–9). Conference Proceedings.

United Nations. (1983) *Manual X: Indirect Techniques for Demographic Estimation*. New York: United Nations.

United Nations. (1994) "Report of International Conference on Population and Development" (Cairo, September 5–13).

2 Examining the Accuracy of Age-Sex Data
An Evaluation of Recent Sub-Saharan African Population Censuses

Chuks J. Mba

1 INTRODUCTION AND RATIONALE

Good governance under a democratic dispensation must be data driven. Indeed, quality data from censuses and nationally representative sample surveys are key to decision making and developmental planning.

The age-sex structure of a population is important both for demographic analysis and development planning. Research on such population dynamics as fertility, mortality, migration, nuptiality, and so on, utilizes the age-sex distribution as an indispensable tool. Similarly, in planning for educational programs, military recruitment, job creation, health facilities, and geopolitical considerations, accurate empirical statistics with respect to age and sex are of paramount importance. However, the literature is replete with problems associated with the collection of reliable age-sex data in the African context (Siegel and Swanson 2004; Obonyo and Bauni 1999; Ewbank, 1981) and has failed to address how errors in such data could be detected before use. This part of the book was designed to fill the gap.

The results of censuses of most African countries are bedeviled by gross errors and deficiencies in age data classified by sex. It has been found, for example, that there were biases from age misreporting and recording between 1973 and 1993 in Gambia (Mba 2004), and that there is a tendency to digit preference, particularly the even numbers and those ending in zero, in census enumeration in Lesotho (Mba 2003). Also, Gibril (1979) has noted that the ages of a substantial number of respondents were provided by either the enumerators themselves or heads of households.

The problem of demographic data scarcity and quality in Africa has been noted in previous studies (Udjo 2005; Mba 2004, 2003; Onsembe 2003; Myers 1940). Even with the recent progress in assembling data and promoting survey efforts, notably under the World Fertility Survey (WFS) and its replacement, the Demographic and Health Survey (DHS) programs, gaps still remain (El-Attar 1998; Cleland 1996; Krotki 1978). A few countries have not had regular censuses and surveys, but the good news is that most countries have conducted censuses and nationally representative sample surveys. However, the coverage of demographic variables during enumerations has not been entire and adequate, and, more often than not, very little is known regarding the data quality. It is common knowledge that content as well as enumeration errors mar the quality and reliability of data for planning purposes (Cleland 1996; Sembajwe 1990). In fact, one of the key questions that confront the social scientist using a particular data set for research is the nature and magnitude of errors inherent in the data collected with specific reference to the variables of interest.

Nevertheless, there has been a pronounced upsurge in demographic data availability in Africa in recent years. What is not clear, however, is whether there has been improvement in the quality of data accumulated over the years. Very little is known about the reliability of the data collected with reference to specific variables of interest. One of the fundamental precautions that must be taken before embarking on demographic data analysis and interpretation is ascertaining the quality of the observed data.

It is important to determine whether there are irregularities in the most recent age-sex statistics from Africa, as a primary step following which further demographic analyses could be justified. Furthermore, it is not known whether the quality of age-sex data has improved in parts of Africa in recent years. Consequently, the thrust of this chapter is to examine the quality of age-sex data using the 2000 and 2010 rounds of African population censuses with a view to establishing patterns and trends in the quality of age-sex data for possible policy and research interventions.

Consequently, the objective is to examine the age-sex data of national populations with a view to determining the quality of the reported age-sex structures of these populations.

2 REVIEW OF RELEVANT LITERATURE

Census taking in parts of Africa is of colonial origin and dates back to the nineteenth century (Mba 2003; Ewbank 1981; Lorimer 1961; Kucsynski 1948). There has been growing interest in conducting regular censuses in post-independence Africa. About 50 countries in the region took part in the 1990 round of census (Onsembe 2003). For example, subsequent to independence, Ghana conducted four censuses (1960, 1970, 1984, and 2000), while Nigeria carried out three censuses (1960, 1991, and 2006). Census results are not only useful as the major source of data for overall social and economic planning; they also provide the frame for sample survey design and the denominator for calculating vital rates from the registration of births and deaths.

In sampling procedures such as those of the DHS program, errors include those relating to coverage and content (Siegel and Swanson 2004). In theory, everybody is expected to be covered in a census exercise, but in practice, achieving 100 percent coverage is a huge challenge to the international community, particularly in the developing world. Consequently, it can be argued that coverage error, which occurs when individuals or households are excluded from a survey, or as a result of overcounting or multiple counting, also applies to a census exercise. Content error, on the other hand, refers to inaccurate reporting or tabulation of information on age, sex, and other demographic variables during the census enumeration exercise. Researchers have argued that these errors characterize census exercises in African countries (Mba 2006; El-Attar 1998; Makannah 1990).

It is common knowledge that a respondent may be ignorant of facts pertaining to his/her age or may deliberately misinform the enumerator. Most censuses and demographic survey reports from parts of Africa indicate that a substantial number of individuals do not know their exact ages. In such circumstances, ages are estimated by the enumerators or interviewers. Thus, knowledge of the exact age of household members is still a major challenge in the African context. This situation must be addressed because the age-sex distribution of any population is indeed a crosscutting issue in planning since it is directly or indirectly associated with all aspects of life (Udjo 2005). People do exaggerate their ages when some benefits such as rationing, old age benefits, medical aid, voting rights, and so on, are involved. But none of these factors inform the basis of recent African population censuses.

The quality of an enumeration exercise also depends on the selection and adequate training of enumerators. For example, an enumerator may incorrectly record the age or other characteristics of household members, even when given the correct information. Lack of formal education and the absence of birth registration statistics have also been noted as major contributors to age falsification (Mba 2004; Makannah 1990). The Nigeria Demographic and Health Survey (NDHS) and other data from parts of Africa show that the majority of women who do not know their dates of birth have little or no formal education (Mba 2002). Although age falsification is common everywhere, there is evidence that it is more prevalent in societies with low literacy levels.

Mba (2006, 2003) argues that an important aspect of any demographic and socioeconomic data collection exercise is the ultimate use of the information for planning, policy formulation, and implementation of programs. Thus, not only are data needed in quantity; they should also be of an acceptable quality. Biased or defective data would lead to wrong decisions, resulting in wastage of time and resources, as well as in the suffering of the people for whom wrong planning decisions are made on the basis of wrong empirical information.

3 METHODOLOGY

3.1 Data Sources

Much of the data for this chapter emanated from the most recent censuses of various African countries whose data have been made available to the IPUMS International project of the Minnesota Population Center, University of Minnesota. The other census data for this chapter, which are not yet archived by IPUMS, have been obtained from other sources (highly placed government functionaries, researchers, and colleagues).

3.2 Techniques

One of the principal methods of identifying errors in age data is to examine the single-year age distributions. In this regard, the single-year age distributions of the censuses will be represented graphically to see whether they conform to standard. Three conventional indexes of appraising single-year age data, namely, the Whipple's index, the Myers's blended index, and the Bachi's index, will be applied to the census data sets (Siegel and Swanson 2004; Bachi 1951; Myers 1940). The Whipple's index is used to measure age preferences for digits ending in 0 and 5 as compared with other digits. The index varies between a minimum of 100, indicating no concentration at all at digits 0 and 5, and a maximum of 500, if only digits 0 and 5 were selected. Between these extreme values, the data quality is regarded as highly accurate if the Whipple's index is less than 105; fairly accurate if the index lies between 105 and 109.9; approximate if it falls between 110 and 124.9; rough if it is located in the range of 125–174.9; and, finally, the data are seen as very rough if the index is 175 or more. The Whipple's index (WI) equation for assessing digit preference for terminal digits 0 and 5 which utilizes data for 23–62 ages is given below.

(i) $WI_0 = (P_{30} + P_{40} + P_{50} + P_{60}) \times 100 / \frac{1}{10}(\sum_{i=23}^{62} P_i)$

It should be noted that WI_0 measures heaping on terminal digit 0 over a ten-year range.

(ii) $WI_5 = (P_{25} + P_{35} + P_{45} + P_{55}) \times 100 / \frac{1}{10}(\sum_{i=23}^{62} P_i)$

It should be noted that WI_5 measures heaping on terminal digit 5 over a ten-year range.

3.2.1 Ranges

WI_0 or WI_5: the index ranges from 100 for no preference to 1,000 for complete or total preference.

It should be noted that the WI (and the Myers's index that follows) is based on the assumption of rectangularity, that is that the ages are evenly distributed.

The Myers's blended index is the most widely used test of age accuracy for single-year distributions. It helps to identify whether there is a preference for ages ending in certain digits over others in the census enumeration. The index shows the preference for, or avoidance of, each of the ten digits between 0 and 9 inclusive. One could take the successive sums of numbers that end in each of these digits to determine preferences. However, this is not appropriate since with advancing terminal digits of age, the sum would tend to increase. The Myers's index circumvents this problem by blending the population in such a way that each digit has almost an equal sum. The blended totals for each of the ten digits are expected to be nearly 10 percent of the grand total. The extent, therefore, of the overselection or avoidance of a particular digit shows up in the deviation from 10 percent of the proportion of the total population reporting on the given digit. The deviations of each sum from 10 percent of the grand total are added together, ignoring the signs. Their sum is the Myers's index. A summary index of preference for all terminal digits is derived as one-half of the sum of deviations from 10 percent. The index is 0 where all terminal digits are equally chosen and 90 where a single terminal digit is chosen by everyone.

3.2.2 Steps for Calculating the Myers' Blended Index

1. Select the age range for which the digital preference has to be measured, for instance, age 10–89 years.
2. This range is then divided into two overlapping age ranges: 10–89 years, 20–89 years.
3. Population totals are calculated for ages ending in each of the 10 digits and then recorded.
4. Apply weights to each digit selected, for example, weights for 0 digit are 1 and 9, for digit 1 weights are 2 and 8, and so on. Note that the sum of the weights should yield 10, and convert the distribution into percent.
5. Find the deviations from 10 percent. The deviations from 10 percent indicate the preference or nonpreference of digits.
6. A summary index of deviations for all ages is calculated by dividing the sum of the deviations by 2, or it is one-half of the sum of the deviations from 10 percent.

The method yields a reference index for each terminal digit as well as a summary index of preference for terminal digits. The theoretical range of Myers's blended index is from 0 to 90. An index of 0 represents no heaping and an index of 90 represents a heaping of all reported ages at a single digit, say, 5.

The Bachi's index is another technique that is used to test accuracy in the reported single-year age data. This procedure is similar to the Myers's approach. Whereas the Myers's index is based on the sum of the absolute deviations of the values, the Bachi's index is based on the sum of the positive deviations only.

In assessing the accuracy of reporting by sex and five-year age-groups, the age ratio score, the sex ratio score, and the United Nations age-sex accuracy index were used (Siegel and Swanson 2004; United Nations 1952). The United Nations joint score or the age-sex accuracy index quantifies the accuracy of the overall age-sex data, when the data are arranged in five-year age-groups. It uses both age and sex ratios to identify deviations from what might be expected. The index not only identifies digital preferences but it is also sensitive to the omission of changes in the vital rates (Arriaga, Johnson, and Jamison 1994). The index is computed by simply adding the sum of the male age ratio score and the female age ratio score to three times the sex ratio score. In defining criteria for data quality, the United Nations (1983) stipulates that if the index is less than 20, then data are accurate; if the index lies between 20 and 40, then data are inaccurate; and if the index is above 40, then the data are highly inaccurate.

Sex ratio is defined as the number of males per 100 females. It is symbolically given as:

$$SR = P_m \times 100/P_f$$

where: SR = Sex Ratio; P_m = male population; P_f = female population.

The sex ration score is defined as the sum of the absolute deviations of successive sex ratio divided by the number of deviations.

$$SRS = \frac{1}{n} \Sigma \left| SR_{(i)} - SR_{(i-1)} \right|$$

The age ratio is the ratio of the population in an age-group P(i) to the average of population in the two adjacent age-groups P(i-1) and P(i+1).

$$\text{Age Ratio (AR)} = \frac{P(i)}{\frac{1}{2}[P(i_{-1}) + P(i_{+1})]} \times 100$$

Age ratio score (ARS) is an index derived from the age ratios. This is the sum of the absolute deviation of age ratios from 100 divided by the number of deviations.

$$ARS = \frac{1}{n} \sum_{i=1} \left| AR(i) - 100 \right|$$

UN joint score = $ARS^m + ARS^f + 3SRS$,

where ARS^m = male age ratio score; ARS^f = female age ratio score; SRS = sex ratio score.

4 RESULTS

4.1 Single-Year Age Distributions

Theoretically, for a population that is not open to age-sex selective migration, the reported single-year age distribution of the population should indicate fewer people as one proceeds from the lower to the higher ages because of the effect of mortality; if represented graphically, the distribution should yield a smoothly declining age curve. Available information from the censuses does not conform to this expectation, but rather shows that all countries have sharp points or spikes in their single-year age distributions. For some countries, such as Guinea, Kenya, Mali, Senegal, Tanzania, and Uganda, the 'zigzag' nature of their single-year age distributions appears to be more pronounced in the recent than in earlier censuses. The spikes are likely to represent some form of age misreporting.

As a result of deliberate attempts to increase or decrease age for one reason or the other, as well as reasons bordering on ignorance of actual age, age misreporting is a common phenomenon in African censuses. It is therefore important to investigate the incidence of age misreporting further by examining preferences for or avoidance of certain terminal digits, such as 0 or 5.

4.2 Digit Preference and Avoidance

In an attempt to investigate the consistency or otherwise of the reported census age data and ascertain whether there are distortions in the single-year distributions of African censuses, patterns of digit preference and avoidance are considered. For both males and females, preference for digits 0 and 5 is more pronounced in Ghana, Guinea, Kenya, Mali, Tanzania, and Uganda. In fact, there is a general preference for these digits in Ghana, Guinea, Kenya, and Mali, while other digits are avoided. In Mozambique, digit 7 was the most preferred digit in 1997, while digit 0 was more preferred in 2007 for both males and females. Digits 1, 4, and 7 are avoided more in Mozambique, Namibia, and Rwanda. There was a massive age heaping on digit 9 in Senegal in 1988, but in 2002 the heaping was more prevalent on digit 0. The South African data indicate that there was a greater preference for digits 0 and 6 in 1996 and preference for digits 1 and 9 in 2001.

The preference for and avoidance of certain digits in parts of Africa is partly a reflection of Africa's rich and diverse cultures and traditions and partly a result of ignorance of exact age heightened by illiteracy and lack of formal education.

In order to quantify the extent of digit preference in the reported single-year age distributions, Table 2.1 indicates the evaluative indexes computed from the census data.

Table 2.1 Evaluation Indexes for Age in Single Years

Country	Index/Year	Male	Female	Both Sexes
Ghana	Whipple's			
	2000	1.76	1.91	1.84
	Myers's			
	2000	27.4	33.5	30.5
	Bachi's			
	2000	17.1	21.1	19.1
Guinea	Whipple's			
	1983	1.96	2.35	2.17
	1996	1.78	2.32	2.07
	Myers's			
	1983	35.8	47.8	42.2
	1996	30.1	46.3	38.7
	Bachi's			
	1983	20.2	28.8	24.7
	1996	17.3	28.2	22.9
Kenya	Whipple's			
	1989	1.42	1.53	1.48
	1999	1.45	1.54	1.49
	2009	1.45	1.48	1.47
	Myers's			
	1989	13.5	17.7	15.6
	1999	13.5	16.7	15.1
	2009	13.7	15.7	14.7
	Bachi's			
	1989	9.3	11.9	10.6
	1999	9.2	11.5	10.4
	2009	9.5	10.6	10.1

(continued)

Table 2.1 (continued)

Country	Index/Year		Male	Female	Both Sexes
Malawi	Whipple's				
		1987	1.39	1.38	1.39
		1998	1.50	1.46	1.48
		2008	1.21	1.20	1.21
	Myers's				
		1987	13.2	15.3	14.3
		1998	21.1	22.4	21.8
		2008	10.7	10.5	10.5
	Bachi's				
		1987	9.6	10.3	9.8
		1998	13.3	13.6	13.5
		2008	7.5	7.2	7.4
Mali	Whipple's				
		1987	1.74	1.96	1.86
		1998	1.67	1.94	1.81
	Myers's				
		1987	26.0	33.3	29.8
		1998	26.4	35.4	30.9
	Bachi's				
		1987	15.7	20.5	18.2
		1998	15.6	21.4	18.6
Mozambique	Whipple's				
		1997	1.18	1.19	1.19
		2007	1.26	1.26	1.26
	Myers's				
		1997	13.1	15.6	14.4
		2007	14.1	15.6	14.9
	Bachi's				
		1997	7.2	8.7	7.8
		2007	8.7	9.2	8.9
Namibia	Whipple's				
		2001	1.05	1.03	1.04
	Myers's				
		2001	3.7	3.3	3.5

(continued)

Table 2.1 (continued)

Country	Index/Year		Male	Female	Both Sexes
Namibia (continued)	Bachi's				
		2001	2.7	2.3	2.5
Rwanda	Whipple's				
		1991	1.01	1.00	1.01
		2002	1.08	1.06	1.07
	Myers's				
		1991	2.6	3.7	3.0
		2002	5.0	4.6	4.8
	Bachi's				
		1991	1.9	2.5	2.2
		2002	2.9	2.5	2.7
Senegal	Whipple's				
		1988	1.02	1.01	1.01
		2002	1.73	1.97	1.85
	Myers's				
		1988	16.2	22.0	19.2
		2002	27.1	34.0	30.7
	Bachi's				
		1988	9.7	13.6	11.7
		2002	16.6	21.5	19.1
SouthAfrica	Whipple's				
		1996	1.01	1.01	1.01
		2001	0.97	0.97	0.97
	Myers's				
		1996	4.4	4.9	4.6
		2001	2.8	2.8	2.8
	Bachi's				
		1996	2.9	3.0	2.9
		2001	1.6	1.7	1.6
Sudan	Whipple's				
		2008	2.39	2.45	2.42
	Myers's				
		2008	45.4	48.0	46.7

(continued)

Table 2.1 (continued)

Country	Index/Year	Male	Female	Both Sexes
Sudan (continued)	Bachi's			
	2008	30.1	31.2	30.7
Tanzania	Whipple's			
	1988	1.75	2.02	1.90
	2002	1.53	1.62	1.58
	Myers's			
	1988	29.5	37.7	33.8
	2002	24.6	27.6	26.2
	Bachi's			
	1988	19.3	25.7	22.6
	2002	15.1	17.1	16.2
Uganda	Whipple's			
	1991	1.35	1.52	1.44
	2002	1.45	1.54	1.50
	Myers's			
	1991	14.2	20.3	17.3
	2002	19.6	22.9	21.3
	Bachi's			
	1991	9.0	13.4	11.3
	2002	12.2	14.2	13.2

The WI results indicate that there was a slight improvement in data quality between the earlier and more recent census years for both males and females in Guinea, Mali, South Africa, and Tanzania. On the other hand, the previous census recorded better-quality data than the recent ones in Kenya, Mozambique, Rwanda, Senegal, and Uganda. For all countries in general, male data are of better quality than those of the females. Furthermore, with an index of 101 in 1996 and 97 in 2001 for both sexes, South African data are of better quality than those of other countries, while the greatest concentration of digits 0 and 5 can be found in Guinea (WI value of 217 in 1983 and 207 in 1996 for both sexes).

Similarly, the Myers's and Bachi's index results paint the same picture as the WI values. Both Myers's and Bachi's index values were lowest in South Africa and highest in Guinea. For example, in South Africa the Myers's index value declined from 4.4 in 1996 to 2.8 in 2001 for males and from 4.9 in 1996 to 2.8 in 2001 for females, while in Guinea the value reduced from 35.8 in 1983 to 30.1 in 1996 for males and from 47.8 in 1983 to 46.3 in 1996 for females. Employing the conventional evaluative scheme highlighted above, these findings point to a substantial amount of age misreporting by sex in the Guinean censuses, as well as those of countries such as Mali, Senegal, and Tanzania. The findings further show that the incidence of age misreporting in Africa tends to be slightly more pronounced for females than for their male counterparts.

By African standards, however, these indexes compare favorably with what obtains in some settings. For example, it has been found that that Myers's index of preference for Gambia was around 50 in 1973, but declined mildly to 48 in 1983 and further fell to 44 in 1993, representing a decline of 12 percent over the period, while both the Bachi's index and WI have remained around 28 and 230, respectively, in twenty years (Mba 2004). Additionally, an evaluation of the 1991 population census of Nigeria revealed that the Myers's index, Bachi's index, and WI for the country (both sexes) were 62, 41, and 293, respectively (National Population Commission 1998). The situation is not very different in some other African countries.

It should be noted that because of distortions arising from an unusually large number of persons (affecting both males and females) reporting ages ending in 0 or 5, and relatively small numbers at other ages, as has been found in parts of Africa, use of data classified by single years is usually not recommended for most demographic analyses.

4.3 Investigating National Population Pyramids

National population pyramids by country and census year were produced (not shown) with a view to providing additional insights into the quality of the reported age-sex data. Partly because of the very clear image these pyramids present, population pyramids are often viewed as the most effective way to depict a population's age and sex structure graphically and help in understanding the population dynamics of the society in question.

The triangular shapes of the pyramids indicate that these populations are youthful or experiencing rapid growth. Assuming reproductive trends remain the same, most of these populations will still be growing in the future, implying that resources have to be spent on basic needs of young people, including education, health, and nutrition.

For Africa's youthful populations, one should expect children aged 0–4 years to have the largest population. But the pyramids for Namibia, Mali, and Senegal do not reflect that pattern, which may be indicative of errors in the reported data. South Africa's population bulges at the 10–19 age-group, which partly shows the effect of sustained contraceptive use over time that has reduced birthrates. It should be noticed that the percentage of males and females within each age class is not equal. This is more pronounced in Guinea (1983 and 1996), Mali (1998), and Mozambique (1997).

Generally, the national population pyramids show a wide base and steep sides indicating that Africa still has high birthrates and low life expectancy. Barring drastic changes brought about by wars, famines, pestilence, or natural disasters, one should expect more people at younger than at older age-groups. Deviation from this pattern could be indicative of errors in age-sex reporting. While the population pyramids reflect the expectation for a developing region, it is apparent that the consistent slow decline in population with advancing age has not been witnessed in some of the countries.

When a particular country is investigated, the pyramids show that not much has changed in the intercensal period. The shapes of national pyramids from one census to another in Kenya and Senegal have remained largely similar, for example, while the noticeable difference in the age-sex structure in Rwanda between 1991 and 2002 may be attributable to the 1994 Rwanda Genocide in which an estimated eight hundred thousand people, or as much as 20 percent of the country's total population, were killed.

4.4 Sex Ratios by Country and Census Year

Variations in sex ratios provide an opportunity for appraising the extent of age falsification in a population by five-year age-groups. Under normal circumstances, it is a valid expectation in all populations to get a slightly higher number of males at younger ages and a consistently greater number of females at older ages since females live longer than males (Siegel and Swanson 2004; United Nations 1973). Also, the larger the departure of the sex ratio from 100, the larger the possibility of errors in the data.

The sex ratios for the countries under review, however, indicate fluctuating sex ratios in all the census data files for all countries. The sex ratios at birth varied from 97 in Mozambique (in 1997 and 2007) to 103 in Guinea (in 1983 and 1996) and then to 108 in Sudan (in 2008). The sex ratios at birth for the other countries fall within these two extreme values.

In Ghana, Guinea, Senegal, and Tanzania (for 1988), sex ratios were generally higher than 100 at age 50-plus years, which should not be expected if the data were error-free. It is common knowledge that as a result of genetic, biological, environmental, and occupational factors, as well as general lifestyle and sociocultural considerations, women tend to live longer than men (United Nations 2011; Mbamaonyeukwu 2001; Apt 1996; Kane 1991; Treas and Logue 1986). Moreover, overall sex ratios ranged from 90 in 2001 in South Africa to 97 in Kenya (1999) and Malawi (1998) and then to 107 in Namibia (2001) and Sudan (2008). Only Namibia and Sudan fell within the model sex ratio range of 100–107 for Africa (United Nations 1983).

It is remarkable that the sex ratio is generally lower than 100 for all age-groups in both census years in Rwanda, and this is more pronounced in the productive ages, with the lowest sex ratio of 77 at age-group 50–54 in 1991 and 69 at age-group 60–64 in 2002. This could be attributable to the Rwandan Civil War, which was a conflict between the government of President Juvénal Habyarimana and the rebel Rwandan Patriotic Front (RPF). The conflict began on October 2, 1990, when the RPF invaded, and ostensibly ended on August 4, 1993, with the signing of the Arusha Accords to create a power-sharing government. The assassination of President Habyarimana in April 1994 proved to be the catalyst for the Rwandan Genocide, in which, according to a Human Rights Watch estimate, more than five hundred thousand people were killed and many more displaced.[1] Most of the people who were killed or forced into exile were able-bodied men.

Such deficiencies in Africa's age-sex data are generally traceable to the high rate of illiteracy, especially among elderly people, which is responsible for their inability to keep accurate records of their dates of birth. There is also the problem of underreporting of females coupled with cases of selective male emigration in search of economic prospects. When unusual sex ratios at any age are observed, it is important to examine misreporting, misrecording, or underregistration of births or deaths as possible explanatory factors. For instance, some studies have attributed the high masculine sex ratios observed in mainland China in the past twenty-five years partly to the people's refusal to report the births of female children, especially after the implementation of the one-child policy (see, for example, Greenhalgh 2003). The low report of births or deaths is usually sex selective, and it affects demographic and health surveys, as well as censuses, thus inaccurately reflecting the actual sex ratios.

4.5 Age Ratios by Country and Census Year

All age ratios should be close to 100 where fertility has not fluctuated considerably during the past and international migration has not been significant. According to the conventional evaluation scheme, the point of balance in age ratios is 100 (Siegel and Swanson 2004; United Nations 1952). Age ratios higher than 100 indicate an overenumeration at that particular age-group, while an age-group is deemed underenumerated if its age ratio falls below 100.

Table 2.2 Age Ratios by Country and Census Year

	Ghana		Kenya					
	2000		1989		1999		2009	
Age	Male	Female	Male	Female	Male	Female	Male	Female
5–9	109.9	110.1	102.1	102.0	95.0	94.6	102.3	102.3
10–14	97.9	96.5	103.2	102.1	109.9	108.3	103.6	103.1
15–19	100.6	95.3	97.5	95.7	100.5	97.9	98.5	91.0
20–24	92.2	97.3	91.8	99.2	94.0	102.9	95.7	108.2
25–29	104.3	106.5	105.4	106.4	104.3	102.8	101.2	102.2
30–34	95.4	96.8	93.9	88.7	92.3	88.0	99.5	94.6

(continued)

Table 2.2 (continued)

	Ghana		Kenya					
	2000		1989		1999		2009	
Age	Male	Female	Male	Female	Male	Female	Male	Female
35–39	97.0	99.3	96.9	96.3	102.2	106.0	100.7	100.2
40–44	103.1	100.7	100.0	97.7	93.3	90.9	90.2	89.5
45–49	103.9	94.2	92.0	96.7	97.1	96.6	104.5	104.8
50–54	99.3	110.7	103.8	101.6	106.3	105.1	95.8	97.2
55–59	80.3	73.2	91.7	89.1	83.5	85.0	92.7	90.9
60–64	114.5	124.5	103.5	111.7	108.1	108.7	109.2	105.9
65–69	90.5	83.4	97.2	91.8	89.0	89.4	80.7	87.8

	Mali				Mozambique			
	1987		1998		1997		2007	
Age	Male	Female	Male	Female	Male	Female	Male	Female
5–9	111.8	112.2	111.3	112.9	97.0	98.3	100.9	102.9
10–14	91.7	83.5	97.3	88.3	100.2	89.4	97.6	91.2
15–19	98.8	105.0	97.6	107.8	98.0	100.1	92.8	91.3
20–24	89.4	92.6	93.3	91.8	98.7	109.3	95.7	107.9
25–29	102.1	109.1	93.0	98.8	98.1	101.0	103.0	101.5
30–34	98.4	95.7	100.4	102.3	92.9	87.5	98.8	95.5
35–39	98.2	97.2	102.2	96.2	109.0	110.7	100.6	105.8
40–44	101.0	102.9	99.9	104.4	86.1	84.2	91.6	86.8
45–49	96.2	89.7	93.4	85.0	113.7	110.8	107.5	98.6
50–54	103.8	110.1	104.4	117.1	86.8	92.6	89.6	104.5
55–59	91.3	81.9	90.5	78.9	108.6	103.6	104.0	96.2
60–64	117.1	130.0	113.2	128.8	87.8	87.5	92.1	93.7
65–69	90.2	81.4	89.2	78.7	124.3	125.5	106.3	106.6

	Rwanda				Senegal			
	1991		2002		1988		2002	
Age	Male	Female	Male	Female	Male	Female	Male	Female
5–9	106.3	107.2	94.4	94.3	102.8	107.4	106.7	107.1
10–14	97.5	97.8	98.7	99.3	91.8	86.0	100.7	95.9
15–19	95.4	94.7	114.6	112.6	98.7	107.2	101.1	108.6

(continued)

Table 2.2 (continued)

	Rwanda				Senegal			
	1991		2002		1988		2002	
Age	Male	Female	Male	Female	Male	Female	Male	Female
20–24	92.4	95.6	98.8	99.8	92.6	90.1	99.4	95.6
25–29	100.3	98.2	85.5	90.5	109.3	116.7	96.1	97.8
30–34	109.2	108.0	95.7	93.8	90.6	83.1	99.7	100.2
35–39	99.1	98.4	95.4	94.9	111.4	117.0	90.2	93.5
40–44	91.7	88.7	111.8	110.0	77.7	77.6	107.9	107.6
45–49	81.5	88.3	95.6	97.4	114.7	115.0	91.0	86.0
50–54	105.3	115.0	100.9	95.6	89.2	84.7	113.6	118.2
55–59	96.1	86.8	74.2	85.7	113.9	120.3	76.6	71.6
60–64	111.1	119.3	108.6	110.0	86.9	80.5	120.5	135.3
65–69	88.3	80.3	92.1	92.3	119.4	125.5	84.0	71.4

	South Africa				Tanzania			
	1996		2001		1988		2002	
Age	Male	Female	Male	Female	Male	Female	Male	Female
5–9	104.2	102.5	102.8	102.2	104.1	103.1	98.9	98.4
10–14	106.2	106.4	103.3	103.1	100.8	98.2	105.2	103.5
15–19	97.3	96.5	108.7	107.8	103.8	101.2	96.7	91.6
20–24	102.1	104.7	94.3	94.8	82.2	93.9	90.6	105.7
25–29	97.9	96.8	101.2	102.6	114.5	112.6	105.8	103.6
30–34	99.6	102.6	96.4	95.5	88.5	86.1	101.8	97.3
35–39	103.2	100.9	101.8	104.9	109.2	104.7	94.5	93.9
40–44	98.3	98.8	101.3	98.8	84.3	90.3	102.4	99.8
45–49	99.9	98.0	98.1	101.6	108.7	97.2	87.1	86.4
50–54	93.3	92.0	101.8	98.0	95.4	111.2	110.8	119.4
55–59	101.3	97.5	90.4	87.0	97.2	79.6	81.8	76.6
60–64	89.4	103.4	103.9	109.6	102.5	127.2	114.5	119.0
65–69	104.2	102.5	91.1	95.4	95.3	77.3	90.4	87.6

	Uganda				Namibia			
	1991		2002		2001			
Age	Male	Female	Male	Female	Male	Female	Male	Female
5–9	97.0	98.8	99.5	99.2	105.0	104.5	?	?
10–14	102.3	98.0	104.0	102.1	102.7	102.3	?	?

(continued)

Table 2.2 (continued)

	Uganda				Namibia			
	1991		2002		2001			
Age	Male	Female	Male	Female	Male	Female	Male	Female
15–19	95.5	97.3	98.8	96.7	100.3	99.6	?	?
20–24	95.4	99.9	93.0	102.7	98.2	99.5	?	?
25–29	102.5	102.1	100.4	100.3	102.3	103.6	?	?
30–34	101.9	98.2	103.0	97.2	96.1	95.7	?	?
35–39	95.5	95.1	92.5	93.6	101.4	98.8	?	?
40–44	92.2	93.3	105.3	103.6	97.1	94.9	?	?
45–49	92.8	92.1	87.5	86.5	93.8	95.9	?	?
50–54	109.0	117.2	109.9	115.1	104.3	101.0	?	?
55–59	86.5	76.6	78.6	76.8	83.5	88.4	?	?
60–64	113.5	129.7	119.8	123.9	115.8	111.2	?	?
65–69	87.7	77.6	87.2	81.9	87.9	91.6	?	?

	Malawi						Sudan	
	1987		1998		2008		2008	
Age	Male	Female	Male	Female	Male	Female	Male	Female
5–9	109.1	111.5	99.6	100.0	97.3	98.0	111.5	110.2
10–14	97.5	91.0	98.7	96.2	103.1	101.4	102.3	95.2
15–19	92.4	94.4	101.1	96.3	91.4	87.9	98.2	95.6
20–24	93.2	104.0	94.1	114.1	97.4	110.3	94.5	98.8
25–29	109.7	102.7	107.0	93.9	107.7	104.5	93.7	106.2
30–34	85.6	87.2	95.1	92.5	98.3	93.9	98.3	95.3
35–39	116.7	114.2	99.5	103.9	101.3	94.4	104.1	106.6
40–44	84.7	86.4	88.5	86.4	89.8	93.8	105.3	98.1
45–49	112.5	104.7	112.2	113.4	96.1	95.7	84.3	85.3
50–54	84.6	95.1	92.7	92.0	87.9	93.0	117.8	101.6
55–59	112.8	95.9	93.3	86.1	113.4	111.2	68.5	88.5
60–64	82.9	100.8	92.9	102.3	88.8	89.1	144.9	125.5
65–69	126.0	111.8	112.8	111.2	110.7	106.7	68.1	63.8

A closer look at Table 2.2 reveals a substantial departure from this theoretical expectation in the census data for the countries under investigation. There is pronounced overenumeration of some age-groups and underenumeration of other age-groups in all data sets. A fluctuating pattern in age reporting is apparent in all countries. For example, the male and female age ratios for Senegal in 2002 for the 60–64 age-group were 121 and 135, respectively, while the corresponding figures for the age-group 65–69 were 84 and 71, respectively. Similarly, in Tanzania the male and female age ratios in 2002 for 60–64 age-group were 115 and 119, respectively, while the corresponding figures for age-group 65–69 were 90 and 88, respectively. A similar picture emerges when age ratios from other countries are examined. The table shows that age estimation errors were more pronounced at older ages in all the countries, a situation that is undoubtedly linked to low educational attainment.

Errors that occur in age reporting may be attributable to a general tendency to state age in figures ending in certain preferred digits; an exaggeration of ages by older people for sociocultural reasons; ignorance of exact dates of birth; carelessness in reporting and recording age; and deliberate falsification arising from social, political, economic, or personal reasons (Siegel and Swanson 2004; Mba 2003).

4.6   Summary Indexes by Country and Census Year

Table 2.3   Summary Indexes by Country and Census Year

Ghana				
2000	6.4	6.4	8.9	34.7
Guinea				
1983	16.9	7.5	17.5	75.7
1996	13.9	7.3	17.3	66.4
Kenya				
1989	3.9	4.4	5.3	21.4
1999	3.4	6.7	7.0	23.9
2009	3.7	5.3	5.8	22.2
Malawi				
1987	7.2	12.8	7.7	41.9
1998	5.3	6.1	7.8	29.9
2008	5.7	6.9	6.8	30.7

(continued)

Table 2.3 (continued)

Mozambique				
1997	4.8	8.5	9.3	32.3
2007	5.7	4.9	5.8	27.8
Namibia				
2001	3.9	5.8	4.5	21.9
Rwanda				
1991	4.7	6.9	9.3	30.4
2002	3.7	8.1	6.8	26.0
Senegal				
1988	5.9	11.1	15.9	44.8
2002	6.0	8.7	12.7	39.5
South Africa				
1996	3.3	4.1	4.0	18.1
2001	3.7	4.2	4.8	20.0
Sudan				
2008	12.0	13.9	10.0	59.9
Tanzania				
1988	10.3	7.7	10.6	49.2
2002	5.0	7.7	9.2	31.8
Uganda				
1991	5.6	6.7	9.4	32.7
2002	4.0	8.1	8.9	28.9

Note: UN age-sex accuracy index = male age ratio score + female age ratio score + 3 (sex ratio score).

Table 2.3 shows the UN joint score results for the continent. Using the United Nations (1983) recommended criteria for evaluating data quality, only the South African data can be judged to be accurate because, as stated previously, if the UN summary index is less than 20, then data are accurate; if the index lies between 20 and 40, then data are inaccurate; and if the index is above 40, then the data are highly inaccurate (United Nations 1983). Nevertheless, the results indicate that there is no apparent improvement in the quality of data collected in the country over the years because the age-sex accuracy index increased from 18 in 1996 to 20 in 2001. Most countries in the African region fall within an age-sex accuracy index of 20–40, implying that their data are inaccurate. The data from Guinea (with age-sex accuracy index of 76 in 1983 and 66 in 1996), Malawi (with age-sex accuracy index of 42 in 1987), Senegal (with age-sex accuracy index of 45 in 1988), and Sudan (with age-sex accuracy index of 60 in 2008) are highly inaccurate, according to the United Nations (1983) criteria for evaluation.

The findings show that, though most of the data are inaccurate, subsequent censuses over time point to a modest improvement in quality in the majority of the countries. For instance, the UN joint score declined from 76 in 1983 to 66 in 1996 in Guinea, representing a 13 percent improvement, while the corresponding figures for Uganda were 33 in 1991 and 29 in 2002, representing a 12 percent improvement.

4.7 Comparing Age Distributions with a Standard Population

In comparing the reported age distributions of national populations with a standard population, use is made of the WHO (2001) World Standard Population as the reference standard age distribution. Because of Africa's growing populations, one should be expected to use a standard population with higher proportions in the younger age-groups. However, choosing a standard population with higher proportions in the younger age-groups tends to weight events at these ages disproportionately. Similarly, choosing an older standard does the opposite. Hence, rather than selecting a standard to match the current age structure of some populations, the WHO adopted a standard based on the average age structure of populations to be compared (in the world) over the likely period of time that a new standard will be used (some 25–30 years), using the latest United Nations statistics.

The WHO approach recommends that instead of selecting a standard to match the current age structure of some population(s), the standard must be chosen to reflect the average age structure of all populations to be compared over the period of use. This is to base the standard on the average age structure of populations to be compared over the likely period of time that a new standard will be used (some twenty-five to thirty years). The use of an average world population, as well as a time series of observations, removes the effects of historical events such as war and famine on population age composition.

The percentage of the population in each five-year age-group in the new WHO World Standard population is widely available in the literature. In an attempt to establish whether anything has changed over time, the comparison is done at two levels. The reference standard population is compared with the reported age distributions of national populations separately for the two census years for all countries reporting more than one census.

National population distributions are similar among themselves but different from the reference standard population. The variation is more pronounced in previous than in recent censuses, implying that there has been some modest improvement in data quality over the years. It may therefore be necessary, as shown in Section 4.6, to adjust the age-sex data before further demographic analysis is carried out. For example, age adjustment, using the direct method, is the application of observed age-specific rates to a standard age distribution to eliminate differences in crude rates in populations of interest that result from differences in the populations' age distributions.

It should be noted, however, that the choice of a particular reference standard population determines the results one obtains. Different reference standard populations will yield different results. As there is no such thing as an ideal reference standard population, interpretation of results should be treated with caution.

5 CONCLUSION

Demographic transition allows for the comparison of national demographic trends, such as an increase or decrease in fertility and mortality rates, or its divergence, convergence, or relative stability. The materials for such investigations are readily available in published statistics. While early analyses by the forebears of demography and population studies had access only to limited and mostly defective data, it is expected that contemporary sources of population statistics should be more comprehensive and, more importantly, reliable. The reliability of empirical information is a product of its accuracy.

Clearly, population census is a complex, large-scale operation, and a perfect census is unattainable anywhere in the world. However, because census data are used extensively for policy and research purposes, it is essential to evaluate data. The foregoing analysis was confined to age-sex data assessment because of their centrality in all demographic inquiries.

The examination of the overall accuracy of population data by age and sex revealed that census data from these countries are generally inaccurate. The good news, though, is that there is a slight improvement in data quality when censuses for particular countries are analyzed over time. In other words, there has been a modest improvement in the quality of age-sex data in Africa.

With world attention focused on achieving the Millennium Development Goals (MDGs) by 2015, the availability of consistent and comparable statistical information has become even more crucial and plays an even more prominent role not only in monitoring progress but also in the assessment and realignment of the MDG plans and strategies. This is because each of the MDGs is associated with measurable targets and indicators to gauge progress and evaluate the efficacy of different approaches. The reliability of these indicators, in turn, depends on collecting, disaggregating, and analyzing data according to international standards, which enable cross-country comparisons and analyses of trends over time.

However, errors in age-sex data are not peculiar to the countries under review. Africa needs accurate statistical information for effective development planning especially of basic societal needs in all sectors: education, employment, health, housing, transportation, and agriculture and food supply. Indeed, adequate statistical data for planning is lacking for many countries in Africa. In these countries, a significant amount of collected data lags unduly behind and the universal coverage is generally incomplete. Development planning, as well as policies and programs that promote good democratic governance and accountability, should be evidence based. If statistics on which decisions are made are faulty, the decisions themselves will be faulty. The importance of collecting accurate age and sex data cannot be overemphasized. Planning is essentially predicated on the collection of accurate age and sex data.

Africa has benefited immensely from technical support to implement census-related activities from various development partners over several decades. It appears that the support and the advancement in demographic training and research have not kept pace with formal educational uptake that is critical to accurate age reporting. Consequently, uptake in educational levels is likely to reduce age misstatement in the region.

It has been argued that differences in the degree of age falsification in censuses in Africa can be traced *inter alia* to levels of adult literacy and birth registration coverage (see, for example, Mba 2006; Makannah 1990). The preceding analysis suggests that respondents in the older population are more likely to report incorrect ages than the younger respondents, a situation directly related to lack of education. African governments should therefore promote better education for males and females. The benefits of education are enormous. Making education more accessible to the people, at least to the secondary school level, will not only improve birth registration coverage and substantially minimize age falsification but will also enable men and women to achieve greater self-fulfillment and increase the social and economic development of the continent.

NOTES

1. Human Rights Watch (2007).

REFERENCES

Apt, N.A. (1996) *Coping with Old Age in a Changing Africa: Social Change and the Elderly Ghanaian.* Averbury dershot: Brookfield.

Arriaga, E.E., P.D. Johnson, and E. Jamison. (1994) *Population Analysis with Microcomputers: Presentation of Techniques. Vol. 1.* Washington, DC: US Bureau of the Census.

Bachi, R. (1951) "The Tendency to Round Off Age Returns: Measurement and Corrections." *Bulletin of the International Statistical Institute* 33 (4): 195–222.

Cleland, J. (1996) "Demographic Data Collection in Less Developed Countries 1946—19%." *Population Studies* 50 (3): 433–450.

El-Attar, M. (1998) "Population and Rural Development: A New Approach to an Old Problem with Special Attention to Developing Nations." *Demography India* 27:1147–1153.

Ewbank, D.C. (1981) *Age Misreporting and Age-Selective Under-Enumeration: Sources, Patterns and Consequences for Demographic Analysis*. Washington, DC: National Academy Press.

Gibril, M.A. (1979) *Evaluating Census Response Errors: A Case Study of the Gambia*, Paris: OECD.

Greenhalgh, S. (2003) "Science, Modernity, and the Making of China's One-Child Policy." *Population and Development Review* 29 (June): 163–196.

Human Rights Watch. (2007) *Leave No One to Tell the Story: Genocide in Rwanda*. http://www.hrw.org/reports/1999/rwanda.

Kane, P. (1991) *Women's Health: From Womb to Tomb*. London: St. Martin's Press.

Krotki, K.J., ed. (1978) *Developments in Dual System Estimation of Population Size and Growth*. Edmonton: University of Alberta Press.

Kuczynski, R.R. (1948) *Demographic Survey of the British Colonial Empire Vol. 1*. Oxford: Oxford University Press.

Lorimer, F. (1961).*Demographic Information on Tropical Africa*. Boston: Boston University Press.

Makannah, T.J. (1990) "An Evaluation of the Age-Sex Data of Recent African Censuses." Paper presented at the Sixth Session of the Joint Conference of African Planners, Statisticians and Demographers, United Nations Economic Commission for Africa, Addis Ababa, Ethiopia.

Mba, C.J. (2003) "Assessing the Reliability of the 1986 and 1996 Lesotho Census Data." *Journal of Social Development in Africa* 18 (1): 111–127.

Mba, C.J. (2004) "Challenges of Population Census Enumeration in Africa: An Illustration with the Age-Sex Data of The Gambia." *Research Review* 20 (1): 9–19.

Mba, C.J. (2006) "Reliability of Age-Sex Data in Demographic Analysis: An Assessment of Nigeria's Empirical Evidence." Ibadan Journal of the Social Sciences 4 (2): 89–102.

Mbamaonyeukwu, C.J. (2001) "Africa's Ageing Populations." *Quarterly Journal of the International Institute on Ageing* 11 (4): 2–7.

Myers, R.J. (1940) "Errors and Biases in the Reporting of Ages in Census Data." *Transactions of the Actuarial Society of America* 41:395–415.

Obonyo, B J., and E.K. Bauni. (1999) "Civil Registration Systems in Africa: Present and Future." *Union for African Population Studies* 463–472.

Onsembe, J. (2003) *Improving Data Quality in the 2000 Round of Population and Housing Censuses*. Addis Ababa: UNFPA Country Technical Services Team.

Sembajwe, I. (1990) "The Evaluation of the Vital Registration System in Lesotho: The Case of Mantsebo." Working Papers in Demography, Department of Statistics, Demography Unit, Maseru, National University of Lesotho.

Siegel, J.S., and D.A. Swanson, eds. (2004) *The Methods and Materials of Demography*. 2nd ed. Washington, DC: Census Bureau.

Treas, J., and B. Logue. (1986) "Economic Development and the Older Population." *Population and Development Review* 12 (4): 645–673.

Udjo, E.O. (2005) "An Examination of Recent Census and Survey Data on Mortality within the Context of HIV/AIDS." In *The Demography of South Africa*, ed. T. Zuberi, S. Sibanda, and E. Udjo, 90–113. New York: M.E. Sharpe.

United Nations. (1952) "Accuracy Tests for Census Age Distributions Tabulated in Five-Year and Ten-Year Groups." *Population Bulletin. United Nations Population Division* 2 (October).

United Nations. (1970) *Principles and Recommendations of 1970 Census. Statistical Paper, Series M. No. 44.* New York: United Nations.

United Nations. (1983) *Manual X: Indirect Techniques for Demographic Estimation.* New York: Population Division, ST/ESA/SER.A/81.

United Nations. (2011) *World Population Prospects, the 2010 Revision Vol. I: Comprehensive Tables.* New York: Department of Economic and Social Affairs, Population Division, ST/ESA/SER.A/222.

3 Analysis of Mortality Using Census and Household Data
A Practical Bayesian Multilevel Spatial Modeling Approach

Lawrence Kazembe and N.B. Kandala

1 INTRODUCTION

There have been considerable gains in child survival in the world over the past ten years. Recent reports on the State of the World's Children indicate an overall decline in child mortality from 100 to 72 per 1,000 children, and in some cases even by half, between 1999 and 2010 (UNICEF 2012). Despite such gains, significant disparities between countries and across regions exist, with remarkably high rates and "top-ranked" worst performers in the reduction of child mortality being found in the sub-Saharan Africa (SSA) region. Very few countries in this region are making progress, while the majority are experiencing no change or a reversal in gains made some ten or so years before. For instance, in Ethiopia, Malawi, and Namibia, the decline has been substantial despite meager resources, while in other SSA countries these have remained the same. A case in point is DR Congo, which posted an under-five mortality of 199 per 1,000 children in 1999 and the same in 2009. In countries such as Chad, there was a reversal in gains from 201 to 209 per 1,000 children born from 1999 to 2009 (UNICEF 2012). In short, even with the best solutions and international assistance being made available to the SSA region, the transition from high mortality to low mortality is highly uneven.

The International Conference on Population and Development Program of Action (ICPD-PA) recommended concerted action to reduce disparities in child mortality. The ICPD-PA proposed that by 2005 the following targets should be reached: 50 deaths per 1,000 births for infants, and 60 deaths per 1,000 births for under-fives. By 2015, an infant rate of below 35 per 1,000 and an under-five mortality rate of below 45 per 1,000 should be achieved (UNFPA 1995). The same framework called for a holistic assessment of underlying causes of child mortality.

Several studies have shown that child survival in the first five years of life is influenced by a myriad of risk factors. For instance, studies in

Burkina Faso, Ghana, Tanzania, and Malawi showed that child mortality depicted rural–urban disparities (Kazembe, Kleinschmidt, and Sharp 2007; Kazembe and Mpeketula 2010), varied with socioeconomic inequalities (Becher et al. 2004), and was influenced by disproportionate coverage of interventions (Binka, Indome, and Smith 1998). The general picture is that major causes of childhood mortality, summarized as diseases and malnutrition, are exacerbated by socioeconomic differences and varied intervention coverage (Johnson et al. 2010); these risk factors apply at both the individual and community level (Magadi 2011). Many of these studies have been conducted at the subnational or national level. Our search showed that relatively few studies have considered cross-national analyses of childhood health and associated determinants. Magadi (2011) examined the risk factors of malnutrition among children whose mothers are infected with HIV in SSA by applying a multilevel logistic regression to the Demographic and Health Survey (DHS) data from eighteen countries for the period 2003–2008. Another cross-countries study was conducted by Kandala et al. (2009) in which they considered the geographical and socioeconomic determinants of child undernutrition in Malawi, Zambia, and Tanzania. This identified regional patterns that transcend national boundaries. In a similar study, Wang (2003), using data from sixty countries, explored the global pattern of child mortality and investigated the determinants both at national and subnational level.

While tackling the issue of determinants of child mortality, mostly survey data has been used. Only a few studies have considered using mostly census data to analyze demographic indicators such as fertility, and then only with very limited statistical modeling of childhood mortality (Haines and Preston 1997). Census data provide a large cross-sectional database that permits investigating the association between health outcomes and risk factors. Because census data are a complete enumeration of all individuals in a country, statistical analysis has more power than data derived from a small survey. Further, it provides a complete picture of a country at any given time, allowing a better understanding of risk factors critical to explaining variations in child mortality, and is thus crucial for implementing interventions.

1.1 Theoretical Frameworks for Studying the Determinants of Child Survival

Our study on small-scale geographical variability in child mortality is guided by Mosley and Chen's analytical framework which outlined proximate determinants on child survival (Mosley and Chen 1984). Extending the ideas of Davis and Blake (1946), who first introduced the concept of proximate determinants in fertility, Mosley and Chen argued that any social factors influencing the level of child health operate through intermediate or proximate determinants. Because not all determinants are measurable, they create unobservable heterogeneity. These may include background social, economic, cultural, and health systems variables that collectively and parsimoniously influence a single health outcome, manifested as morbidity or eventually mortality.

According to Sastry (1996, 1997), the unobserved heterogeneity referred to as *frailty* represents an individual's susceptibility to risk of death. Some of these frailties are spatially correlated, mainly because of shared characteristics of individuals. The Mosley–Chen analytical framework begins with individual variables and the proximate determinants. Arguably these determinants are manifested or captured as frailties. A growing body of evidence suggest that these factors are spatially correlated or geographically vary within a country on a small scale (Balk et al. 2004). However, in many sub-Saharan countries, geospatial analysis to explain spatial variation and clustering in under-five mortality is inconclusive. To guide further hypotheses on program or intervention targeting in child care, a small area analysis will be vital. This is in line with demographic thinking that aims at explaining variations in mortality at different levels, either over time or across subgroups (e.g., regions). See Weeks (2004) and Voss (2007) and references therein.

Spatial analysis has increased its role in hypothesis development and validation of theoretical constructs and incorporates and estimates the importance of location and interaction (Anselin 1999). This has been of interest among demographers; concepts such as social norms, neighborhood effects, peer group effects, social capital, and strategic interactions have collective behavior and aggregate patterns. In these conceptualizations, the role of location, space, and spatial interaction is central (Anselin 1999). Increasingly, quantification of such processes in demography is gaining ground. A few examples exist that relate individual behavior to that of context and thus estimate neighborhood effects (Weeks 2004). The expansion of spatial demography is supported by the recent availability of spatial data linking geographical coordinates to demographic, social, and economic variables for analysis (Voss 2007).

Our modeling considered two issues. First, the concept and role of space, which answered the question: do spatial effects provide the means to discover and understand the underlying demographic processes and outcomes? Second, a Bayesian analysis was used, which attempted to incorporate the demographer's uncertainty about child mortality and the ability to offer proper inference in a statistical modeling of mortality.

The Bayesian approach expresses uncertainty in terms of probability distributions. These distributions generally reflect empirical evidence or some expert opinion viewed to governing demographic processes. It makes one's beliefs explicit using probability distributions. Furthermore, the use of Bayesian analysis extends flexibility in demographic analysis by allowing probability inputs in probability outputs. One thing to note is that there is uncertainty in data that are adjusted for under- or overestimation or age misreporting or heaping. Demographers rely on scientific knowledge and experience to make proper adjustments to raw data. Examples of the use of expert opinion exist in population projections; however, this adjustment is largely subjective and an appropriate approach is necessary. Applying Bayesian inference in the analysis of child mortality fits into this line of thinking.

The analysis therefore builds complex models basically because of the presence of complicated processes and the hierarchical nature of the data, compounded by uncertainty in parameter estimation. Such complex models are tackled using conditional or joint approaches. In principle this builds a hierarchical model that is again best tackled using the Bayesian paradigm. Adopting Wikle's (2010) approach, the Bayesian approach to the hierarchical model is broken down to three primary stages:

Stage 1: Data model, summarized as data, given some process and parameters
Stage 2: Process model, summarized as the process given parameters
Stage 3: Parameters model

Accordingly, the first stage is concerned with the observational process or "data," which describes the distribution of the data, followed by the process model, then the parameters model.

1.2 Overview of the Analysis of Mortality Data

A number of statistical models have been proposed when analyzing the risk of child mortality in the first five years of life and its determinants. Most popular have been logistic regression models that assume child survival as a binary response (either the child lived beyond five years or died before the fifth birthday). These models, nevertheless, ignore the time to the event (death), and therefore fail to capture exposure to the risk of dying or hide the evolution of the subject's state over time (Box-Steffensmeier and Jones 2004). More appropriately, survival models can be used to analyze the hazards of child survival. Both the logistic and survival analysis can be implemented within the basic generalized linear models (GLM) framework.

Research on survival analysis in demography and related fields has increased since the seminal work by Cox in the 1970s (Cox 1972), with applications to child mortality or survival appearing in the 1990s and 2000s (Sastry 1996, 1997; Kandala and Ghilagaber 2006), involving both standard proportional hazard models (Haines and Preston 1997) and complex models (Adebayo and Fahrmeir 2005). Two important extensions in survival regression models that have received considerable attention recently are the inclusion of random effects and flexible modeling through semi-parametric and nonparametric approaches (Wienke 2010). Such analyses have an added advantage compared with ordinary GLM. Models that incorporate random effects are commonly called generalized linear mixed models (GLMM), and those that account for nonlinearity are referred to as generalized additive models (GAM); when extended to include random effects, they are known as generalized additive mixed models (GAMM).

The inclusion of random effects permits modeling of unmeasured and unobserved contextual factors in the models. These may act at the family, community, district, regional, or national levels since the underlying causes of neonatal mortality are multisectoral and interwoven (Magadi 2011; Kandala and Ghilagaber 2006). In essence, frailties are group-specific factors acting on child survival, together with individual factors that may protect or accelerate death (Vaupel, Manton, and Stallard 1979). Recent studies have assumed that such unobserved factors are spatially varying, to achieve what are considered spatial frailty survival models (Banerjee, Carlin, and Gelfand 2004). The application of such models to study child health in SSA showed that child mortality varies in space (Kazembe, Kleinschmidt, and Sharp 2007; Adebayo and Fahrmeir 2005), with well-documented space-time interactions (Escaramis et al. 2011). Again, none of these considered the census data.

The main objective of this study is to analyze small-scale geographical variability in under-five mortality in the sub-Saharan region, by applying existing spatial statistical methodology (Fahrmeir and Lang 2001) to census data. Our aim is to extend the standard Cox regression model to random-effects model to permit spatial clustering and heterogeneity using census data from a number of countries. Specifically, we apply generalized linear mixed models (GLMM) with spatially correlated random effects proposed by Hennerfeind, Brezger, and Fahrmeir (2006), and used it to analyze factors associated with the child survival in the first five years of life. This modeling approach falls within what are termed structured additive regression (STAR) models (Fahrmeir and Lang 2001). STAR models are a comprehensive class of models that permit the simultaneous estimation of nonlinear effects of continuous covariates, spatially unstructured and structured components together with the usual fixed effects in the predictor. A detailed description of the statistical methodology used is published in the appendix. In this study, we apply the techniques to 2000–2010 census data from selected SSA countries.

2 DATA AND METHODS

2.1 Data

Data analyzed were from three countries, Rwanda, Uganda, and Senegal,[1] purposively selected because of availability of relevant variables to carry out survival analyses. All three countries have made considerable gains in reducing infant and under-five mortality. Rwanda and Uganda lie in the Great Lakes Region in East Africa, while Senegal is located in West Africa. All the countries are experiencing an under-five mortality rate (U5MR) of between 40 and 99 per 1,000 births, and they lie in the lower quartile as best-performing countries. Between 1990 and 2010, the U5MR decreased from 163 to 91 per 1,000 live births in Rwanda, with a rank of thirty-one in the world. At the same time, infant mortality rate (IMR) dropped from 99 to 59 per 1,000 births between 1990 and 2010. As part of its health sector strategic plan for 2009 to 2012, Rwanda has recognized the need for deeper interventions for maternal and child health. Neighboring Uganda is ranked twenty-seventh in U5MR. The U5MR was 175 per 1,000 in 1990 and 99 per 1,000 in 2010, while IMR declined from 106 to 63 deaths per 1,000 live births over the same period. Senegal is ranked slightly higher with respect to U5MR, standing at forty-two. The reduction in U5MR has been slowest, reduced from 139 to 75 per 1,000 births between 1990 and 2010. Over the same period, infant mortality rate changed from 70 to 50 per 1,000 births (UNICEF 2012).

Census data used in this study include the 2001 data for Rwanda, while for Uganda and Senegal we used data from the 2002 round of the census. While the censuses have a limited number of variables, each child record, which was derived from self-reported information given by the household head, consisted of age at time of death, whether a child was alive or deceased at the time of census, as well as other covariates that may influence child mortality. As no information was available as to whether the child was alive at the last census prior to the current enumeration, the survival information was right-censored. Factors influencing child mortality varied from country to country, as questions were not uniform across the three countries. However, to enable comparability of the results, we tried to select similar covariates. We considered a number of sociodemographic variables in the analysis as determinants of child mortality. These are summarized in Table 3.1. Further, we constructed two indexes: (a) shelter—for the following characteristics, specifically the type of dwelling unit: permanent, semipermanent, traditional, type of roof, wall, and floor and type of toilet; (b) electronics—for the following electronic assets: radio, cell phone, television, phone, iron, and fridge. For spatial analysis, we used provinces and districts as units of analysis. Again Table 3.1 provides the summaries.

Table 3.1 Summary of Covariates Used in the Analyses Given in the Table Are the Counts (and Proportion Dead) across Covariates

	Country		
	Rwanda	Senegal	Uganda
Covariate			
Residence			
Rural	38,154 (8.1)	23,490 (10.6)	29,410 (4.4)
Urban	6,215 (5.5)	10,036 (6.5)	4,028 (3.3)
Religion			
Christian	40,650 (7.9)	977 (6.9)	28,567 (4.4)
Muslim	837 (8.2)	32,378 (9.4)	4,167 (4.0)
Others	4,369 (7.1)	171 (10.5)	689 (2.7)
Age of child			
< 1 year	10,516 (16.1)	4,806 (15.5)	94,440 (10.1)
1 year	7,710 (11.1)	5,276 (16.1)	9,307 (1.8)
2 years	7,853 (5.0)	6,278 (11.5)	6,937 (0.8)
3 years	6,128 (3.7)	5,628 (6.4)	3,613 (0.4)
4 years	5,701 (2.6)	5,780 (4.5)	2,303 (0.5)
5 years	6,461 (2.1)	5,811 (3.4)	1,553 (9.8)
Sex of child			
Male	22,189 (8.5)	16,722 (8.2)	17,056 (4.4)
Female	22,147 (6.9)	16,793 (10.2)	16,382 (4.2)
Electronic Index			
Least	763 (3.0)	10,004 (9.8)	2,373 (2.3)
Less	22,250 (8.7)	3,261 (10.8)	15,881 (4.9)
Medium	619 (2.9)	8,789 (11.2)	173 (1.7)
More	19,249 (7.3)	4,753 (8.5)	14,104 (4.1)
Most	1,489 (5.0)	6,719 (6.2)	907 (3.0)
Shelter Index			
Least	8,168 (7.0)	6,688 (5.4)	6,644 (3.2)
Less	10,904 (7.3)	6,785 (9.2)	6,647 (3.9)
Medium	7,706 (8.3)	6,743 (10.5)	7,461 (4.0)
More	8,434 (8.9)	6,162 (10.9)	5,571 (5.7)

(continued)

Table 3.1 (continued)

	Country		
	Rwanda	Senegal	Uganda
Most	9,157 (7.5)	7,248 (10.8)	7,169 (4.9)
Mother Alive			
Yes	39,687 (1.0)		25,501 (1.1)
No	1,247 (10.1)		7,937 (5.0)
Father Alive			
Yes	37,133 (0.7)		19,637 (4.0)
No	3,201 (8.5)		13,801 (4.7)

2.2 Statistical Analysis

We examine spatial variation in under-five mortality with a flexible geo-additive semi-parametric mixed model while simultaneously controlling for spatial dependence and possibly nonlinear effects of covariates within a simultaneous, coherent regression framework. Individual data records were constructed for children in each country. We proposed the use of a spatial Cox regression model (Hennerfeind, Brezger, and Fahrmeir 2006) to quantify factors associated with the risk of early childhood mortality. We apply a fully Bayesian approach and used Markov Chain Monte Carlo (MCMC) techniques for inference. Model selection was based on Deviance Information Criterion (DIC) (Spiegelhalter et al. 2002).

The analysis was carried out using version 1.4 of the BayesX software package (Brezger, Kneib, and Lang 2005). For all models fitted, twenty-five thousand iterations were run with the initial five thousand discarded and every twentieth sample stored to give a final sample of one thousand for parameter estimation. Convergence was evaluated by inspecting trace and autocorrelation plots of samples for each chain, as well as through numerical summaries, such as the R diagnostic statistic of Brooks and Gelman (1998). After five thousand iterations, all parameters showed signs of convergence in the trace plots. The values of R also quickly approached 1 and were all below the value of 1.12, which indicated convergence of both the pooled and within interval widths to stability. The statistical methods are discussed in more detail in the appendix.

3 RESULTS

Table 3.1 gives a summary of the selected covariates across the three countries. There are evident disparities by place of residence for all the three countries, with rural children being slightly disadvantaged in terms of mortality. The same picture was observed in data by age, with children less than 1 year old being disadvantaged compared with older children, and the proportion diminished by increasing age. Children without a living mother or father were likely to die in their first five years of life. However, there was no clear pattern in data regarding indexes for shelter and electronics or the religion and sex of the child.

3.1 Model Selection

In Table 3.2, model selection values are given for the discrete-time survival models with different specifications of the covariates for the three countries. For all three data sets, the model that combined fixed and random effects was much better than those that did not, which indicates the importance of both factors at explaining child survival. For Rwandan data, the best model was model $M3b$, which combines fixed effects at individual and household levels and random effects at district and provincial levels. The DIC for model $M3b$ was 7,756.1, compared with the nearest model, $M1b$, with DIC = 10,240.3. Moving to Senegal's data, again the model that combines fixed and random effects produces a best fit (model $M3b$). Evidently, model $M3b$ has DIC = 14,711.1, which is smaller than DIC = 15,361.5 of model $M3a$ (Table 3.2). Similar results are obtained for the Ugandan data, with model $M3b$ emerging as a best fit, although model $M2d$ was undistinguishable (see Table 3.2).

3.2 Model Estimates

Turning to the best-fitting models, Tables 3.3–3.5 present estimates of fixed risk factors resulting from these models. For Rwanda (Table 3.3), the overall the risk of a child dying in the first five years of life is lower (mean =–3.14, 95 percent CI:–3.86,–2.36). Children in urban areas were less likely to die than those in rural areas (mean =–0.24, 95 percent CI:–0.31,–0.19), whereas children from households that owned their own dwelling units have a reduced hazard compared with those who do not (mean =–0.06, 95 percent CI:–0.12,–0.01). In relation to the age of the child, we observed that children of up to 1 year of age were at increased hazard relative to those aged 5 years or more. At less than 1 year of age the hazard was 0.77 (95 percent CI: 0.71, 0.83), while for those at 1 year the hazard was 0.48 (95 percent CI: 0.42, 0.55). As age increased, the hazard reduced. For example, for those aged 2 to 4 years, the hazard was–0.02,–0.22, and–0.46, respectively. The relationship of a child dying and a household owning some electronic assets was nonlinear. At level 2 compared with level 1, the risk is higher with mean = 0.26 (95 percent CI: 0.15, 041), while at level 3 we observed a lower risk with mean =–044 (95 percent CI:–0.77,–0.11). This is reversed at level 4 with

Table 3.2 Model Comparison Values Based on Deviance Information Criterion (DIC) for the Models

Model	Description	$\bar{D}$	P_D	DIC
Rwanda				
M0	Province (random effects)	24,060.2	12.4	24,084.9
M1a	Fixed effects only	10,256.7	21.9	10,300.7
M1b	Fixed+province (random effects)	10,184.8	29.3	10,240.3
M2a	Unstructured random effects (district)	19,911.4	25.7	19,956.2
M2b	Structured spatial effects (districts) only	19,212.3	25.7	19,963.5
M3a	Structured effects (district)+unstructured effects (province)	19,870.3	24.9	19,920.3
M3b	Fixed+structured effects (district)+unstructured effects (province)	7,667.2	44.9	7,756.1
Senegal				
M0	Province (random effects)	20,536.7	10.4	20,557.5
M1a	Fixed effects only	19,361.8	28.4	19,418.7
M1b	Fixed+province (random effects)	19,362.7	28.4	19,419.1
M2a	Unstructured random effects (district)	15,284.5	54.2	15,356.8
M3a	Structured effects (district)+unstructured effects (province)	15,284.6	56.4	15,361.5
M3b	Fixed+structured effects (district)+unstructured effects (province)	14,574.2	68.6	14,711.1
Uganda				
M0	Province (random effects)	11,681.1	63.3	11,807.5
M1a	Fixed effects only	10,613.0	20.1	10,653.1
M1b	Fixed+province (random effects)	10,425.9	76.8	10,606.6
M2a	Unstructured random effects (district)	11,735.7	30.0	11,795.7
M2b	Structured spatial effects (districts) only	10,484.6	49.5	10,58.5
M3a	Structured effects (district)+unstructured effects (province)	11,691.7	48.5	11,788.7
M3b	Fixed+structured effects (district)+unstructured effects (province)	10,468.9	59.6	10,588.1

mean = 0.27, 95 percent CI: 0.15–0.41. When compared with shelter index, the risk is reduced at lower levels and increased at higher levels of the index, although this relationship is not significant at $p < 0.05$. It is interesting to note that a child with a living mother and father had a reduced risk of dying (Table 3.3).

Table 3.3 Fixed Effects for Rwanda Child Survival

Variable	Estimate	Standard Error	95%CI.
Intercept	−3.14	0.39	(−3.86, −2.36)
Place of residence			
urban	−0.24	0.03	(−0.31, −0.19)
rural	0		
Dwelling ownership			
yes	−0.06	0.03	(−0.12, −0.01)
no	0		
Religion			
Christian	0.13	0.04	(0.05, 0.24)
Muslim	−0.04	0.08	(−0.21, 0.11)
others	0		
Sex of child			
male	0.06	0.03	(0.023, 0.08)
female	0		
Age of child			
< 1 year	0.77	0.03	(0.71, 0.83)
1 year	0.48	0.03	(0.42, 0.55)
2 years	−0.02	0.03	(−0.11, 0.05)
3 years	−0.12	0.05	(−0.22, −0.04)
4 years	−0.46	0.06	(−0.56, −0.36)
5 years	0		
Electronic Index			
Least	0		
Less	0.26	0.07	(0.15, 0.41)
Medium	−0.44	0.18	(−0.77, −0.11)
More	0.27	0.06	(0.15, 0.41)
Most	0.14	0.09	(−0.01, 0.30)
Shelter Index			
Lowest	0		
Low	−0.04	0.03	(−0.13, 0.01)
Medium	−0.02	0.03	(−0.08, 0.05)
High	0.05	0.03	(−0.02, 0.12)
Highest	0.09	0.03	(0.03, 0.17)

(continued)

Table 3.3 (continued)

Variable	Estimate	Standard Error	95%CI.
Mother alive			
yes	−1.84	0.05	(−1.88, −1.79)
no	0		
Father alive			
yes	−0.97	0.02	(−1.02, −0.93)
no	0		

The spatial variability of risk of dying is shown in Figure 3.1, ranging between −8.23 and 3.14. There were a number of areas that were associated with an increased risk of death higher than the overall mean. These areas are identified by the right map, with a white color and appear in the south, west, and at the center of the country. There were also areas of reduced risk shown by a black color, and the figure does indicate there were a few such areas.

In Table 3.4 we present results for Senegal. Overall the risk of death was lower, with mean =−3.72 (95 percent CI:−4.21,−3.11). The risk significantly varied with ownership of the dwelling unit, electronic assets, sex, and age of the child. Owning a dwelling unit was associated with an increased risk (mean = 0.17, 95 percent CI: 0.09, 0.25) compared with households without

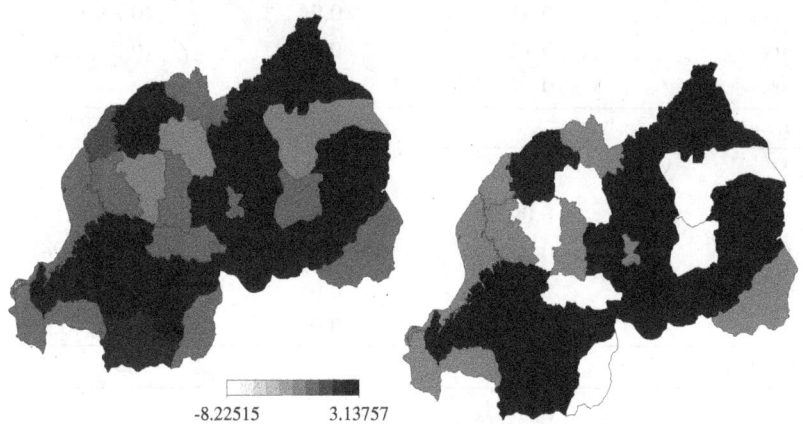

Figure 3.1 Left panel: posterior means of the structured spatial effects of child survival at district level in Rwanda based on model M3b. Right panel: posterior probabilities at 80 percent nominal level in Rwanda with white denoting districts with strictly negative credible intervals, black denoting regions with strictly positive credible intervals, and gray depicting regions of nonsignificant effects.

Table 3.4 Fixed Effects for Senegal Child Survival

Variable	Estimate	Standard Error	95% CI
Intercept	−3.72	0.27	(−4.21, −3.11)
Place of residence			
urban	0.01	0.02	(−0.03, 0.05)
rural	0		
Dwelling ownership			
yes	0.17	0.04	(0.09, 0.25)
no	0		
Religion			
Christian	−0.18	0.18	(−0.58, 0.17)
Muslim	−0.01	0.18	(−0.34, 0.35)
others	0		
Sex of child			
male	−0.13	0.02	(−0.16, −0.09)
female	0		
Age of child			
<1 year	0.91	0.04	(0.81, 1.01)
1 year	0.88	0.04	(0.80, 0.94)
2 years	0.66	0.04	(0.58, 0.73)
3 years	0.31	0.04	(0.24, 0.39)
4 years	0.12	0.05	(0.03, 0.22)
5 years	0		
Electronic Index			
Least	0		
Less	0.04	0.03	(−0.01, 0.11)
Medium	0.02	0.02	(−0.02, 0.06)
More	0.001	0.04	(−0.06, 0.05)
Most	−0.07	0.03	(−0.14, −0.01)
Shelter Index			
Lowest	0		
Low	0.01	0.03	(−0.05, 0.07)
Medium	0.01	0.03	(−0.05, 0.06)
High	−0.01	0.03	(−0.07, 0.04)
Highest	0.04	0.03	(−0.04, 0.09)

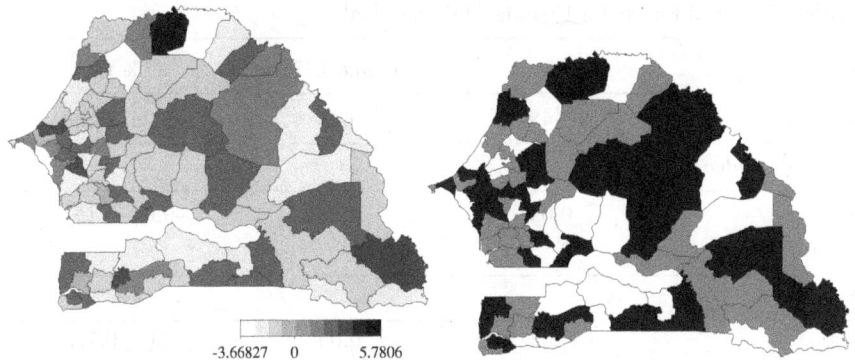

Figure 3.2 Left panel: posterior means of the unstructured spatial effects of child survival at district level in Senegal based on model M3b. Right panel: posterior probabilities at 80 percent nominal level in Senegal with white denoting districts with strictly negative credible intervals, black denoting regions with strictly positive credible intervals, and gray depicting regions of non-significant effects.

a dwelling unit. Male children were more likely to survive the first five years than female children (mean $=-0.13$, 95 percent CI:$-0.16,-0.09$). The risk of dying was positively associated with all ages; however, this risk decreased with age, ranging from 0.91 at age less that 1 year to 0.12 at age of 4 compared with those aged 5 years or more. This pattern is also observed with ownership of electronic assets. The risk is higher for those at level 1 and decreases with increasing levels, although this relationship is marginally significant at $p < 0.1$ (results not shown). Nevertheless, the results are significant, at $p < 0.05$ for the level 5 category when compared with those at level 1 (mean $=-0.07$, 95 percent CI:$-0.14,-0.01$). Turning to the spatial distribution of risk in Figure 3.2, there is substantial variation, with estimates ranging from -3.44 to 5.87 (left map). The right map defined areas associated with significantly high risk (here shaded white) as well as those of significantly low risk (black shading). Evidently, there is no clear patterning of risk as all regions are equally disposed to high and low risk of dying.

Results for Ugandan data are given in Table 3.5. Again, the overall risk of death was lower (mean $=-4.49$, 95 percent CI:$-5.06,-4.04$). Risk factors associated with under-five mortality were identified to be the number of under-five children in the household, marital status, education level of mother, ownership of electronic assets, and shelter characteristics. Families with no under-five children predisposed the children to a high mortality risk compared with those with four or more children (mean $= 1.43$, 95 percent CI: 1.07, 1.76), while those with one to three children predisposed a reduced risk (mean $=-0.62$, 95 percent CI:$-0.95,-0.32$). Being married also increased the risk of a child dying compared with those with children of single mothers (mean $= 0.74$, 95 percent CI: 0.57, 0.88). Our results also showed that the education level of the mother matters when it comes to child survival. Children of mothers with no formal education were more likely to die than those with tertiary education

Table 3.5 Fixed Effects for Uganda Child Survival

Variable	Estimate	Standard Error	95% CI.
Intercept	−4.49	0.26	(−5.06, −4.04)
Place of residence			
urban	0.04	0.06	(−0.08, 0.15)
rural	0		
Employed			
yes	0.01	0.05	(−0.09, 0.12)
no			
Children under 5			
None	1.43	0.17	(1.07, 1.76)
1–3 children	−0.62	0.17	(−0.95, −0.32)
4	0		
Married			
yes	0.74	0.08	(0.57, 0.88)
no	0		
Polygamy			
yes	0.02	0.04	(−0.05, 0.11)
no	0		
Sex of last birth			
male	0.02	0.06	(−0.08, 0.15)
female	0		
Education			
none	0.39	0.07	(0.25, 0.53)
lower primary	0.19	0.07	(0.05, 0.37)
upper primary	−0.17	0.11	(−0.35, 0.05)
secondary	−0.57	0.21	(−1.01, −0.21)
tertiary	0		
Electronic Index			
Least	0		
Less	0.46	0.15	(0.14, 0.77)
Medium	−0.63	0.53	(−1.86, 0.24)
More	0.31	0.14	(0.01, 0.64)
Most	0.13	0.20	(−0.17, 0.52)

(continued)

Table 3.5 (continued)

Variable	Estimate	Standard Error	95% CI.
Shelter Index			
Lowest	0		
Low	−0.08	0.06	(−0.19, 0.03)
Medium	−0.13	0.05	(−0.21, −0.01)
High	0.28	0.06	(0.14, 0.41)
Highest	0.11	0.06	(−0.03, 0.22)

(mean = 0.39, 95 percent CI: 0.25, 0.53), and similarly than those of lower primary mothers (mean = 0.19, 95 percent CI: 0.05, 0.37). For those with secondary education, the risk was lower relative to those with tertiary education (mean =−0.57, 95 percent CI:−1.01,−0.21). In relation to electronic assets, the risk was nonlinear, with an increasing risk at level 2 and then reduced risk at level 3, increased again at levels 4 and 5 compared with level 1 (Table 3.5). When comparing across shelter index, we observed that the risk was lower at levels 2 and 3 and increased at levels 4 and 5 relative to level 1. Nevertheless, the only significant difference was observed at levels 3 and 4 (−0.13 and 0.28, respectively).

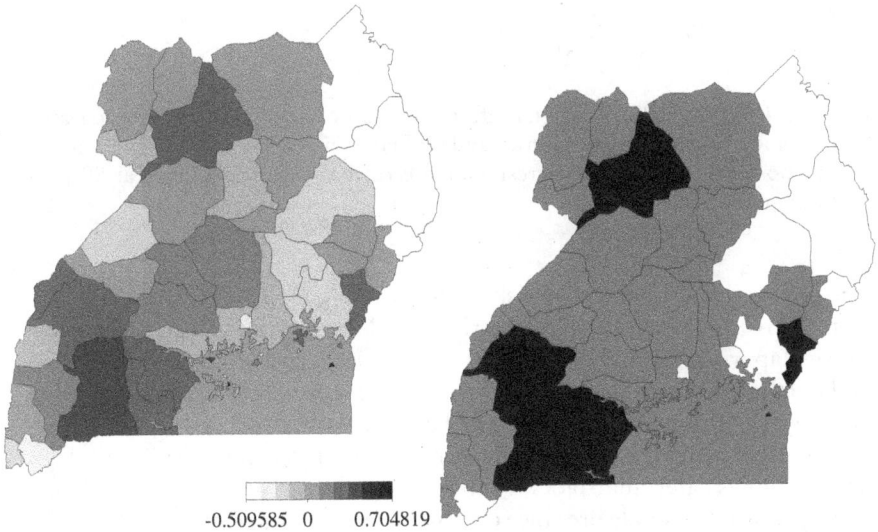

Figure 3.3 Left panel: posterior means of the structured spatial effects of child survival at district level in Uganda based on model M3b. Right panel: posterior probabilities at 80 percent nominal level in Uganda with white denoting districts with strictly negative credible intervals, black denoting regions with strictly positive credible intervals, and gray depicting regions of nonsignificant effects.

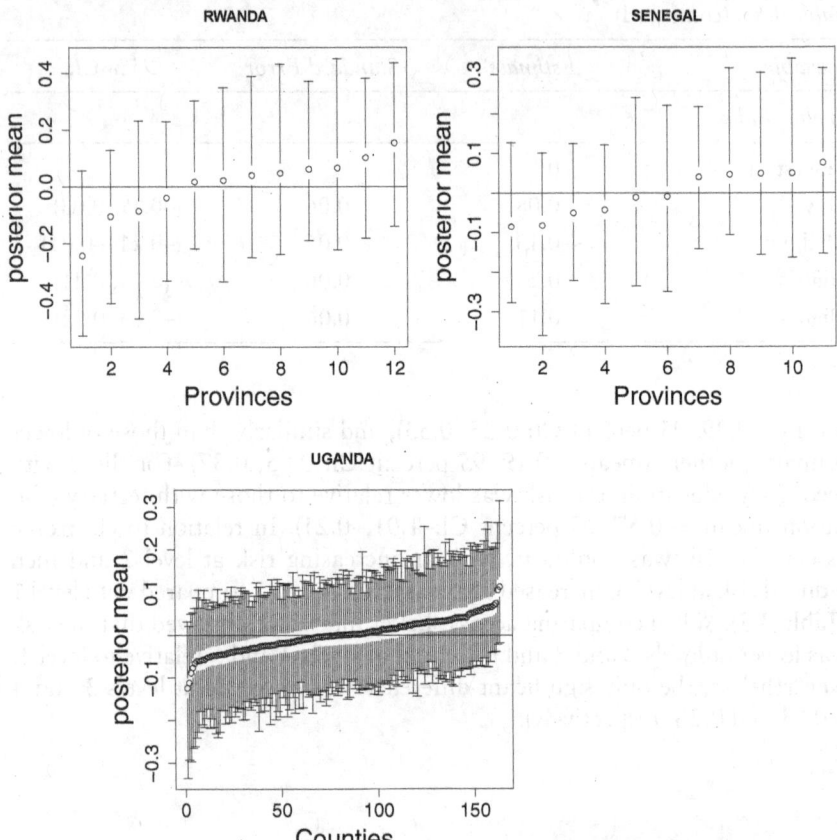

Figure 3.4 Unstructured spatial effects, at the province level in Rwanda and Senegal and at the county level in Uganda, of child survival (model M3b). Shown are the posterior means and corresponding error bars at probabilities at 80 percent nominal level.

The geographical variation in risk is shown in Figure 3.3. Estimates ranged from –0.61 (low risk) to 0.73 (high risk) (see left plot). However, the significance map (right map) indicates that areas of high risk are in the southwest and northwest, while those of low risk are in the northeast and center-east. Notably, the Kampala district showed a significantly reduced risk.

The unstructured spatial effects at provincial level were also fitted. Figure 3.4 shows caterpillar plots for the three countries at the provincial and county levels. No single province or county residual was significantly above or below zero, indicating no difference in risk of death between provinces or counties in the three countries. However, there was a variation in the risk of death; for example, in Rwanda there are four provinces with an estimated negative risk of death, while six provinces have an estimated risk in the positive direction. For Senegal, we have four provinces with a reduced risk and eight regions of estimated high risk. In Uganda, about a hundred counties were estimated to have a lower risk of child mortality, while another seventy had a high risk (Figure 3.4).

4 DISCUSSION AND CONCLUSION

The central question of this study was to identify risk factors associated with child mortality, mainly going beyond individual factors by including other unobserved factors, such as the geographic location where the child lives. These factors were assumed to vary in space and were best captured by assuming spatially varying processes. Our approach adopted the Mosley–Chen (1984) analytical framework, which deployed proximate determinants to child survival. We further expanded Sastry's approach and embraced spatially correlated frailties. Further, because of the uncertainty in the data, we applied a novel Bayesian framework that permitted the estimation of risk at the individual, household, and area levels in a unified framework. Our modeling approach can be considered as an extension of the GLM and can be classified as a spatial GLM. These models have a complex structure, which is easily exploited using the Bayesian approach.

Despite the complexity of our approach (i.e., by estimating individual factors, nonlinear, time-varying effects in addition to spatial factors in the same model), results of fixed effects obtained from our approach are consistent with what have been reported in the literature. Thus it is, in fact, an internal validity check of our approach confirming that we were able to estimate the effect of unobserved factors, such as the geographic location where the child lives, in addition to estimating individual and household factors. Nevertheless, the degree of association between fixed effects and child mortality varied per country (Tables 3.3–3.5).

The significance of spatial effects indicates that unobserved community factors have an important influence on child survival in the three countries. These represent many factors, some spatially varying, with similar effects across areas, while others are confined to a particular area only. These spatial effects are surrogates of factors not captured by the survey instruments and include distal factors, such as access to health care, availability of a health care center, reproductive health behavior, cultural practices (including nutrition habits) specific to certain areas that put children at risk of mortality, high disease prevalence in certain areas, and general quality of life (food prices, sanitation, etc.). Understanding the geographical variability of a demographic phenomenon such as mortality is an increasingly important research problem (Weeks 2004; Voss 2007). However, this has often been done implicitly and often at gross scale using categorical variables to measure geographic effects (Voss 2007). In our approach, we explicitly introduced spatial effects and modeled them at the local level.

Our analysis of child mortality shows evident continuity in African demography, with persistent cross-country heterogeneity, which is a salient feature in the global demographic profile. For example, the U5MR ranking shows that although child survival is improving, the reduction rates are quite different, slowest in Senegal and fastest in Rwanda. Demographic heterogeneity is considerable not just across countries but between groups and regions within a country (Figures 3.3, 3.4, and 3.5). For example, rural–urban differences in Rwanda demonstrate continuity, while the nonsignificant differences between rural and urban areas reveal that some changes are being observed in Senegal and Uganda; however, it is still debatable if such a change is permanent.

This study is not without limitations. The main issue concerns data quality in that age at death, which is reported in months, shows considerable recall bias or heaping at twelve months. This may result in the underestimation of infant mortality or overestimation of child mortality (i.e., in the 1 to 4 age-group). The baseline survival shows that this may not the case in the three countries. Evidence from an assessment of DHS data carried out in these countries shows that in most recent surveys in children, birth data were substantially better reported and have improved over the years (Pullum 2008). In Uganda, age displacement in children appeared to be downward than in preceding surveys, and more apparent in rural areas. However such a bias evens out when socioeconomic factors are taken into account. The statistical techniques used here, which permitted the incorporation of uncertainty and smoothing of spatial effects, ensured accuracy in the estimates.

In summary, the primary objective of this chapter was to illustrate a novel application of a recently developed structured additive regression model to analyze census and demographic data in SSA. The approach is data driven and has rarely been applied in the SSA region using census data. The results emphasize the fact that a clear understanding of complex social and demographic processes in under-five mortality can be reached using adequate statistical modeling. Such models should go beyond identifying individual child risk factors and should incorporate distal factors, such as the area where the child lives (spatial effects) at the time of the survey. This has implications in terms of policy and planning for the achievement of Millennium Development Goal (MDG 4) to reduce under-five mortality by half by 2015, as well as implementation of the ICPD program of action.

APPENDIX 3.1

Statistical Methodology

In studying the survival of a child, we assume T as time to event or survival time with t as the actual realization. The probability that a survival time T is less than or equal to some value t is thus $F(t) = P[\text{Child dies at time} \leq t]$. An important approach is to consider the duration analysis through the hazard rate. The hazard rate, which links the survival and failure functions, is equivalent to $h(t) = -logS'(t)$, where $S(t) = 1-F(t)$ is the survivor function. The hazard rate describes the risk or event of "failure" given that the individual has survived all along up to point t.

In the analysis of child mortality, our interest is to answer this question: given that the child has survived up to month t, what is the likelihood it will survive in the subsequent months? Further, one is interested in how the hazard rate varies with respect to some covariates; for instance, will the hazard be the same for children living in urban and rural areas?

We proposed using a more general Cox model that captures a wide range of issues, including spatial frailties. Thus, a spatial Cox regression model (Hennerfeind, Brezger, and Fahrmeir 2006) was applied to determine factors associated with the risk of early childhood mortality. Assume that T_{ij} is the observed number of months lived or the censoring time for j-th child in area i. Under Cox's model, the hazard function at time $T = t$ is given by

$$h(t|\beta,v_{ij}) = h_0(t)\exp(\beta v_{ij}) \qquad (1)$$

where $h_0(t)$ is the baseline hazard at time t, and the βs are a vector of regression coefficients for the fixed and time-invariant variables (v_{ij}). Since individuals are clustered in geographical regions, group-specific random frailty term, ψ_i, was introduced to augment the Cox model, that is,

$$h(t|\beta,v_{ij},\psi_i) = h_0(t)\exp(\beta v_{ij} + \psi_i) \qquad (2)$$

The above model indicated that childhood survival was influenced by both individual-specific factors (v_{ij}) and group-specific environmental factors ψ_i. Here it was assumed that the environmental factors were approximated by geographical locations. In the case of geographical regions, spatially distributed random effects s_i were assumed, while for the other unstructured heterogeneity a random effect, u_i, was specified such that $\psi_i = s_i + u_i$ (Besag et al. 1991). Fitting model (2) assumed a semiparametric additive predictor, which is known as geo-additive survival model (Hennerfeind, Brezger, and Fahrmeir 2006),

$$\eta_{ij}(t) = f_0(t) + \beta v_{ij} + u_i + s_i \qquad (3)$$

where η_{ij} is the log-additive predictor at time t for child j in area i. The term $f_0(t) = \log(h_0(t))$ is the log baseline hazard effect at time t. The other terms are as defined above.

ESTIMATION: FULLY BAYESIAN APPROACH

Modeling and inference uses the fully Bayesian approach. In the Bayesian formulation, the specification of the proposed model (equation 3) is complete by assigning priors to all unknown parameters. For the fixed regression parameters, a suitable choice is the diffuse prior, but a weakly informative Gaussian prior is also possible. The baseline hazard effect, $f_0(t)$, was assigned a penalized spline with a second order random walk prior. Similarly, the time and continuous covariates were estimated non-parametrically through smoothness priors. We use the second-order Gaussian random walk prior to allow enough flexibility, while penalizing abrupt changes in the function, as suggested by Fahrmeir and Lang (2001). For the unstructured spatial heterogeneity term, i is assumed to follow an exchangeable Gaussian prior with zero mean and variance. Finally, for the spatial components s_j, we assign a Markov random field (MRF) prior. See for details, Fahrmeir and Lang (2001) and Kazembe and Mpeketula (2010).

Fully Bayesian inference is based on the analysis of posterior distribution of the model parameters. In general, the posterior is highly dimensional and analytically intractable, which makes direct inference almost impossible. This problem is circumvented by using MCMC simulation techniques, in which samples are drawn from the full conditional of parameters given the rest of the data.

DATA ANALYSIS

A number of models were fitted. The first model ($M0$) explored unstructured variation in child i at provincial level k.

$$M0: \eta_{ik} = \gamma_{const} const + f_{unstr}(PROVINCE)$$

The second set of models estimated fixed effects only ($M1a$) and then we adjusted for unstructured random effects at province level ($M1b$).

$$M1a: \eta_{ijk} = x'_{ijk}\gamma$$

$$M1b: \eta_{ijk} = x'_{ijk}\gamma + f_{unstr}(PROVINCE)$$

We also investigated geographical variation at district level. We fitted both unstructured ($M2a$) and structured random effects ($M2b$) using districts as variables.

$$M2a: \eta = \gamma_{const} const + f_{unstr}(DISTRICT)$$

$$M2b: \eta = \gamma_{const} const + f_{str}(DISTRICT)$$

The last set of models combined fixed and random effects at district and province levels. In model $M3a$ we estimated structured spatial effects at district level and unstructured effects at province level, and model (M3b) improved model M3a by combining with fixed effects.

$$M3a: \eta = \gamma_{const} const + f_{DISTRW}(DISTRW) + f_{PROVRW}(PROVRW)$$

$$M3b: \eta = \gamma_{const} const + x'_{ijk}\gamma + f_{str}(DISTRICT) + f_{unstr}(PROVINCE)$$

Model comparison was based on the DIC (Spiegelhalter et al. 2002). Small values of DIC indicate a better model. Models with differences in DIC of less than 3 compared with the best model cannot be distinguished, while those between 3 and 7 can be weakly differentiated (Spiegelhalter et al. 2002, 613).

ACKNOWLEDGMENTS

The authors gratefully acknowledge the Minnesota Population Center, for permission to access IPUMS–International database, and all the reviewers whose comments helped to improve the quality of this chapter.

NOTES

1. Data for the selected countries were accessed from the IPUMS International database archived by Minnesota Population Center (2011).

REFERENCES

Adebayo, S.B., and L. Fahrmeir. (2005) "Analysing Child Mortality in Nigeria with Geo-Additive Discrete-Time Survival Models." *Statistics in Medicine* 24:709–728.
Anselin, L. (1999) "The Future of Spatial Analysis in the Social Sciences." *Geographic Information Sciences* 5:67–76.
Balk, D., T. Pullman, A. Storeygard, F. Greenwell, and M.A. Neuman. (2004) "Spatial Analysis of Childhood Mortality in West Africa." *Population, Space and Place* 10:175–216.
Banerjee, S., B.P. Carlin, and A.E. Gelfand. (2004) *Hierarchical Modeling and Analysis for Spatial Data*. London: Chapman and Hall/CRC.
Becher, H., O. Muller, A. Jahn, A. Gbangou, G. Kynast-Wolf, and B. Kouyate. (2004) "Risk Factors of Infant and Child Mortality in Rural Burkina Faso." *Bulletin of World Health Organization* 82:265–273.
Besag, J., J. York, and A. Mollie. (1991) "Bayesian image restoration with two applications in spatial statistics." *Annals of the Institute of Statistical Mathematics* 43:1–20.
Binka, F.N., F. Indome, and T. Smith. (1998) "Impact of Spatial Distribution of Permethrin-Impregnated Bednets on Childhood Mortality in Rural Northern Ghana." *American Journal of Tropical Medicine and Hygiene* 59:80–85.

Box-Steffensmeier, J.M., and B.S. Jones. (2004) *Event History Modeling: A Guide for Social Scientists*. Cambridge: Cambridge University Press.

Brezger, A., T. Kneib, and S. Lang. (2005) "BayesX: Software for Bayesian Inference Based on Markov Chain Monte Carlo Simulation Techniques." *Journal of Statistical Software* 14:11.

Brooks, S.P., and A. Gelman. (1998) "General Methods for Monitoring Convergence of Iterative Simulations." *Journal of Computational and Graphical Statistics* 7:434–455.

Cox, D.R. (1972) "Regression Models and Life-Tables." *Journal of the Royal Statistical Society* 34:187–220.

Davis, K., and J. Blake. (1946) "Social Structure and Fertility." *Economic Development and Cultural Change* 4:211–235.

Escarams, G., J.L. Carrasco, J.J. Aponte, D. Nhalungo, A. Nhacolo, P. Alonso, and A. Carlos. (2011) "Spatio-Temporal Analysis of Mortality among Children under the age of Five in Manhia (Mozambique) during the Period 1997–2005." *International Journal of Health Geographics* 10: 14.

Fahrmeir, L., and S. Lang. (2001) "Bayesian Inference for Generalized Additive Mixed Models Based on Markov Random Field Priors." *Journal of the Royal Statistical Society* C 50:201–220.

Haines, M.R., and S.H. Preston. (1997) "The Use of the Census to Estimate Childhood Mortality: Comparisons from the 1900 and 1910 United States Census Public Use Samples." *Historical Methods* 30:77–96.

Hennerfeind, A., A. Brezger, and L. Fahrmeir. (2006) "Geo-Additive Survival Models." *Journal of the American Statistical Association* 101:1065–1075.

Johnson, H.L., L. Liu, C. Fischer-Walker, and R.E. Black. (2010) "Estimating the Distribution of Causes of Death among Children Age 1–59 Months in High Mortality Countries with Incomplete Death Certification." *International Journal of Epidemiology* 39:1103–1114.

Kandala, N.B., and G. Ghilagaber. (2006) "A Geo-Additive Bayesian Discrete-Time Survival Model and Its Application to Spatial Analysis of Childhood Mortality in Malawi. Quality & Quantity." *International Journal of Methodology* 40:935–957.

Kandala, N.G., L. Fahrmeir, S. Klasen, and J. Priebe. (2009) "Geo-Additive Models of Childhood Undernutrition in Three Sub-Saharan African Countries." *Population Space Place* 15:119–126.

Kazembe, L., I. Kleinschmidt, and B. Sharp. (2007) "Spatial Analysis of the Relationship between Malaria Endemicity and Early Child Mortality." *Geospatial Health* 13:183–212.

Kazembe, L., and P.M.G. Mpeketula. (2010) "Quantifying Spatial Disparities in Neonatal Mortality Using a Structured Additive Regression Model." *PLoS ONE* 5:11–180.

Magadi, M.A. (2011) "Household and Community HIV/AIDS Status and Child Malnutrition in Sub-Saharan Africa: Evidence from the Demographic and Health Surveys." *Social Science and Medicine* 73:436–446.

Minnesota Population Center. (2011) *Integrated Public Use Microdata Series International: Version 6.1 [Machine-Readable Database]*. Minneapolis: University of Minnesota.

Mosley, W.H., and L.C. Chen. (1984) "An Analytical Framework for the Study of Child Survival in Developing World." *Population and Development Review* 10:25–45.

Pullum, T.W. *An Assessment of the Quality of Data on Health and Nutrition in the DHS Surveys, 1993–2003*. Methodological Reports No. 6. Calverton, MD: Macro International.

Sastry N. (1996) "Community Characteristics, Individual and Household Attributes, and Child Survival in Brazil." *Demography* 33:211–229.

Sastry, N. (1997) "A Nested Frailty Model for Survival Data, with an Application to the Study of Child Survival in Northeast Brazil." *Journal of the American Statistical Association* 92:426–435.

Spiegelhalter, D.J., N.G. Best, B.P. Carlin, and A. van der Linde. (2002) "Bayesian Measures of Model Complexity and Fit (with Discussion)." *Journal of the Royal Statistical Society B* 64: 583–616.

UNFPA. (1995) *International Conference on Population and Development.* ICPD-Program of Action. New York: United Nations.

UNICEF. (2012) *Levels and Trends in Child Mortality.* UNICEF Annual Report. New York: UNICEF.

Vaupel, J.W., K.G. Manton, and E. Stallard. (1979) "The Impact of Heterogeneity in Individual Frailty on the Dynamics of Mortality." *Demography* 16:439–454.

Voss, P.R. (2007) "Demography as a Spatial Social Science." *Population Research and Policy Reviews* 26:457–476.

Wang, L. (2003) "Determinants of Child Mortality in LDCs: Empirical Findings from Demographic and Health Surveys." *Health Policy* 65:277–299.

Weeks, J.R. (2004) "The Role of Spatial Analysis in Demographic Research." In *Spatially Integrated Social Science: Examples in Best Practice*, ed. M.F. Goodchild and D.G. Janelle, 381–399. New York: Oxford University Press.

Wienke, A. (2010) *Frailty Models in Survival Analysis.* Boca Raton, FL: Chapman and Hall/CRC.

Wikle, C. (2010) "Hierarchical Modelling with Spatial Data." In *Handbook of Spatial Statistics*, ed. A. Gelfand, P. Diggle, M. Fuentes, and P. Guttorp, 89–106. Boca Raton, FL: Chapman and Hall.

4 Child Health and Mortality in Sub-Saharan Africa
Trends, Causes, and Forecasts

Yohannes Kinfu, Collins Opiyo, and Marilyn Wamukoya

1 INTRODUCTION

The world population reached seven billion people on October 31, 2011 (UNFPA 2011). While this reflects an extraordinary period in human demographic history, population and development scientists celebrated it cautiously, declaring that it presented achievements, setbacks, and paradoxes for different regions and countries of the world. On the whole, whereas most regions of the world have experienced a dramatic transition to low fertility and mortality regimes during the decades leading to this extraordinary demographic milestone, large parts of sub-Saharan Africa (SSA) has continued to experience moderately high fertility and mortality rates, with adult and child mortality remaining at stubbornly high levels (UNICEF 2011; WHO 2011).

Child health and mortality are of particular interest in SSA for a number of reasons. First, SSA's child mortality level is one of the highest of any major region of the world, and progress to meet the Millennium Development Goal (MDG) target of a two-thirds decline by 2015 remains elusive in the region (UNSD 2006). Second, levels of child health and mortality are important indicators of the health and well-being of nations. Thus, trends in under-five mortality provide an indication of the success or failure of government social development policies in the region. Finally, the loss of human life at an early age represents both a tragedy for families and a capital investment loss for nations. Hence, their well-being is worthy of study.

This chapter, therefore, seeks to gain further insights into the continuities and changes in child health and mortality in Africa. In particular, it seeks to find answers to the following key scientific and policy relevant questions. What are the recent trends in child health and mortality in SSA? Is SSA likely to achieve child-health-related MDGs? What factors will trigger the change? Will there be similarities—at least across nations—in the direction and speed of child mortality transition in the region? And, more broadly, will SSA's health and mortality transitions follow the tenets of the classical epidemiologic transition models?

Conceivably, answers to these questions require an in-depth study of levels, trends, and causes of under-five mortality and ill health in the region. However, in the absence of reliable vital registration systems, which is common in the region, such a study must first effectively navigate the challenges relating to data paucity and the use of methods whose fundamental assumptions now stand violated owing to recent changes in population and health dynamics in the region. Above all, researchers must develop or adopt methods or techniques that overcome the data deficiencies and other measurement challenges in order to provide up-to-date and reliable information on child mortality in the region.

To this end we use data never before used in a similar exercise and apply a new indirect technique to provide reliable estimates of the levels and trends of childhood mortality in the region since the early 1970s (Rajaratnam et al. 2010). Along the way, we also produce broad causes of under-five mortality in the region by making use of a recently developed indirect method that links under-five mortality and related mortality ratios to broad cause categories (Rao, Adair, and Kinfu 2011). It is hoped that the resulting estimates will be of interest both to scientists interested in understanding the continuities and changes in child health and mortality in SSA and to policy makers and planners who need such information to guide, formulate, plan, and implement effective and targeted intervention programs.

The remaining sections of the chapter are structured as follows. Section 2 summarizes the current state of knowledge on child health and mortality in SSA and provides the rationale for the current study. In Section 3 we describe the sources and nature of data and the methods of analysis used in the study. This is followed by a discussion on the levels and trends in under-five mortality estimated using indirect methods from census data assembled for various countries. The findings on causes of under-five mortality are discussed in Section 4.2, while some concluding remarks appear in Section 5.

2 CURRENT STATE OF KNOWLEDGE: A BRIEF OVERVIEW

The attainment of a long and better life is a universal goal of humanity. However, translating this goal into a reality remains a key challenge in most parts of the world, including SSA, where many children die of preventable causes. Current estimates show that of the nearly eight million children who died before reaching the age of 5 in 2010, about half were from the region, although SSA accounts for not more than a fifth of the world's young children (UNICEF 2011). Yet the study of child mortality in SSA has for a long time been hindered by shortcomings in the availability, accuracy, and timeliness of appropriate data. Until the publication of the *Demography of Tropical Africa* in the second half of the 1960s, mortality statistics for the region—and childhood mortality in particular—were mostly based on small-scale studies, speculations, and/or expert opinions (Brass et al. 1968). However, in subsequent years, attributable largely to the availability of relevant data and partly to improvements in estimation methods, child mortality estimates are now available for almost all countries in the region.

The evidence adduced from these studies has shown that both the levels of childhood mortality and the speed of decline were markedly different between countries and subregions of the continent (Ahmad, Lopez, and Inoue 2000; Hill 1989, 1991, 1992, 1993; Adegbola 1977). The period from the late 1940s to the late 1970s generally showed higher childhood mortality rates in middle and Western Africa than in countries in Eastern and Southern Africa regions, creating an overall pattern of a rough gradient running from higher mortality in the northwest to lower mortality in the southeast corner of the continent (Hill 1989, 1991, 1992, 1993). However, within this broad regional pattern, the decline in childhood mortality was rather pervasive. For the region as a whole, while in the 1950s 30–40 percent of newborn children died before reaching age 5, this had declined to about 277 per 1,000 in the 1960–1964 period and to a further 250 by the late 1960s (Ahmad, Lopez, and Inoue 2000). By the second half of the 1970s, there was no single country in the region where the under-five mortality rate (U5MR) was not substantially lower than pre–World War II levels.

However, the optimism of a possible child survival revolution in the region was suddenly muted after the mid-1980s when the rate of childhood mortality decline decelerated in many countries, stalled in some, and even reversed in others (Hill 1993; Hill and Pebley 1989; Zuberi et al. 2003). The deterioration has been observed mainly in countries with a relatively high prevalence of HIV/AIDS (Adetunji 2000; Amouzou and Hill 2005) and among those that experienced major economic reversals (National Research Council 1993). Consequently, many studies have suggested that the high prevalence of HIV/AIDS and falling living standards, which were responsible for these patterns, will continue to influence future trends in child mortality in the region (Adetunji 2000; Amouzou and Hill 2005; Garenne and Gakusi 2005; Hill, Bicego, and Mahy 2001; Hill et al. 2004; Mahy 2003; Timaeus 1998; United Nations 2003; Zuberi et al. 2003). Yet others challenge this popular notion, cautioning that the impact of HIV/AIDS on childhood mortality can be minute and ambiguous (Mahy 2003), often with tenuous causal pathways (Zaba, Marston, and Floyd 2003). On the other hand, others noted that the demographic impact of economic reversals in SSA—especially on childhood mortality—is inconsistent across countries, although there is a general notion that it is negative (National Research Council 1993). Since the publication of these studies, new data have become available and Brass's technique has been further refined. These now make it possible for us to generate more recent and consistent estimates for a larger number of countries and examine both the continuities and changes in child health and mortality in the region.

3 DATA AND METHODS

Since the last multicountry study on child survival in SSA was undertaken in the early 1990s, a number of countries have carried out national censuses and made their data available for public use (Foote, Hill and Martin 1993; Hill 1993). In this chapter, we use thirty-one national censuses,[1] which were carried out between the late 1980s and the first half of 2000s in eighteen African countries. Of the eighteen countries under study, three (Ethiopia, Kenya, and Malawi) had three censuses each; seven (Botswana, Mali, Mozambique, Rwanda, South Africa, Tanzania, and Uganda) had two censuses; and eight (Burkina Faso, Cape Verde, Guinea, Namibia, Senegal, Sierra Leone, Sudan and Zimbabwe) had one census each. In terms of regional distribution, six of these countries were from East and the Horn of Africa, and six each from West and Southern Africa. Five of the thirty-one censuses were from the 1980s round of censuses, ten were from the 1990s round, and the remaining sixteen were part of the 2000s round. This enables us to examine U5MRs for some of these countries from the early 1970s until the first half of the 2000s and reach conclusions about the extent to which the conclusions reached in the foregoing section still hold both at the country and at the continental level.

In order to generate U5MRs from the available data, an indirect approach, belonging to the family of the Brass-type technique was used. The basic idea behind the original Brass method is that, given the age pattern of fertility, it is possible to deduce a relation between the age of mothers and the distribution in time of the births they have experienced, and, assuming a standard age pattern of mortality, to calculate the proportion of children surviving (lx function of the life table) from birth to certain specific ages from information on the proportion of dead children to women in each age-group and age-specific correction factors related to a set of model fertility schedules (see Sullivan 1972; Trussell 1975; Preston and Palloni 1977; Coale and Trussell 1977; Feeney 1980; Zlotnik and Hill 1981; Hill 1991).

The original method has since been modified by various scholars (see Sullivan 1972; Trussell 1975; Preston and Palloni 1977; Coale and Trussell 1977, 1978; Feeney 1980; Zlotnik and Hill 1981; Hill and David 1988; Hill and Figueroa 2000). However, a number of assumptions fundamental to the application of the various variants of the method continue to pose challenges in the application of the technique to contemporary African data, primarily owing to changes in population and health dynamics in the region (Ward and Zaba 2008; INDEPTH 2004). In this present chapter, we make use of a new variant of Brass's indirect method, recently proposed by Rajaratnam and colleagues (2010), which circumvents some of the key contemporary challenges to the application of the technique. First, unlike previous approaches, the coefficients of the new method were developed entirely based on data from developing countries. Second, in the new approach, country-specific differences in mortality patterns are explicitly captured by the use of country-specific random effects, hence overcoming the need for assuming model age patterns of mortality that are often based on the experience of developed countries (which has always been a moot point among mortality researchers in the region). Third, the new procedure also provides indirect estimates that are closer to the years of enumeration than comparable estimates generated using previous methods, hence making it more appealing for detecting the impact of recent interventions on child survival in the region. Finally, in the new method, the final mortality estimates corresponding to each of the seven age-groups of women are provided in terms of U5MRs rather than of early age mortality rates corresponding to various ages. This in turn is particularly significant in two respects. First, it enables researchers to get away with using model life tables for translating the resulting mortality indexes into a common denominator. Second, it allows researchers to obtain mortality trends directly from the data.

Once under-five mortality estimates were generated for each country and census year using the new technique, we then applied *lowess regression* procedure for long-term pattern identification and an autoregressive integrated moving average (ARIMA) model for predicting child mortality rates to 2015, the target year for attaining MDGs (Chatfield 2004; Enders 2004; Harvey 1989, 1993). We used the *lowess regression* procedure also to identify patterns of under-five causes of death, once the latter was estimated for each of the eighteen countries using the indirect method developed by Rao, Adair, and Kinfu (2011). Rao, Adair, and Kinfu's indirect cause-specific mortality model is a proportionate predictive model that enables the estimation of underlying broad causes of deaths among under-fives for any population using only information on levels of under-five mortality and related mortality indexes. Such data can easily be derived either directly, from maternity history, or indirectly, from a summary birth history data, using the Brass-type techniques as is the case in the present study (for more details, see Rao, Adair, and Kinfu 2011).

4 RESULTS

4.1 Levels and Trends in Child Mortality

Before the data were used for mortality estimation, we assessed the quality of the parity data and the data on the proportion of children who died by the age of women—the two key pieces of information required for the indirect estimation of the U5MR—graphically for each census and country year to identify possible errors. The results for proportion of children dead and average parity (not shown here) suggest that the data were—by and large—of acceptable quality. As expected mean parity increased progressively with the age of women, which is suggestive of the absence of any substantial omission of births attributable to memory lapse in these data. For the majority of countries and census years, the proportion of dead children by the age of women (result not shown here) either shows a linear trend or a J-shape pattern with the age of the mother, both of which suggest no significant error in the source data. However, in some cases, such as Botswana, Cape Verde, Kenya (1999), Mozambique (1997), and South Africa, the patterns by age were irregular, ranging from one that is U shaped in countries such as Cape Verde to a 'spoon'-like feature for most of the data for the Southern African countries. It is not evident at this stage whether the latter is the result of a reporting error or a reflection of an elevated risk of death among children of HIV/AIDS infected women.

Only six censuses—three from Ethiopia, two from Mozambique, and one from Kenya (2009)—had sex-specific data on children ever born, hence the patterns of sex ratio of ever born and dead children were examined only for these groups of census-country years. Our analysis (results not presented here) showed no evidence of sex-selective omission errors in these data. As a further consistency check, our indirect estimates from the summary birth history data were also compared with both direct and indirect estimates from complete birth history data from Demographic and Health Survey (DHS) and other related surveys for each country for comparable years to assess the consistency of the results from the census data. However, despite the consistency checks that we have applied on the source data, it should be noted that the estimates discussed below remain imperfect. It should also be noted that neither the analyses nor the countries included in this chapter are comprehensive or even representative of the region as a whole, as both were largely guided by the availability of data and methods used in the study. However, given that they are current and cover all regions of the continent, we believe that the resulting estimates still provide sufficient indications for making generalizations about mortality and health transitions in Africa.

This notwithstanding, the overall picture emerging from the available data suggests three distinct phases of child mortality transition in Africa since the late 1960s. As can be seen from Figure 4.1, the first phase is the trend that prevailed throughout the 1970s and mid-1980s. This is characterized by an overall and rapid decline in under-five mortality, continuing from the child survival revolutions of the 1940s, 1950s, and 1960s noted in the review section. During this phase, the region experienced extreme diversity in terms of child mortality levels, but generally mortality remained high across the board with about 15–30 percent of children dying before reaching age 5.

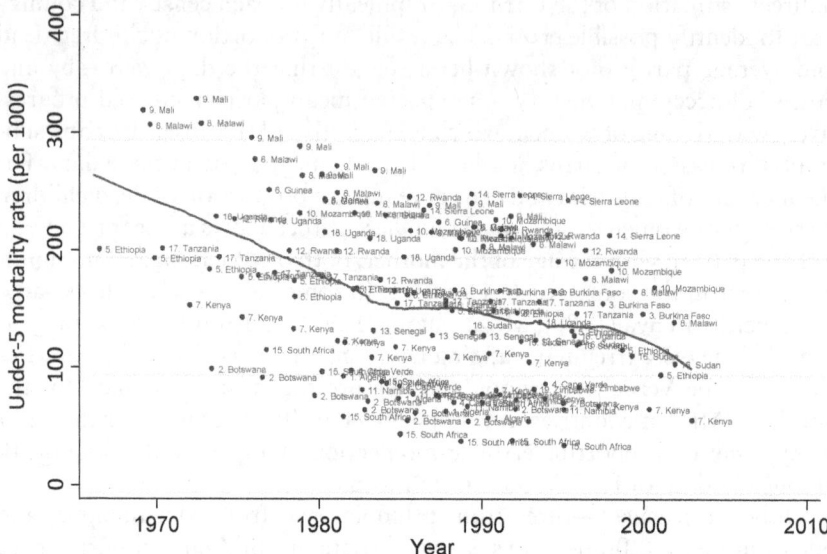

Figure 4.1 Trends in under-five mortality in sub-Saharan Africa, 1965–2005.

However, the pace of decline slowed down considerably from the mid-1980s through the early 1990s in the majority of countries represented in the study, introducing the second phase of child mortality transition in the region. In this phase, countries became rather more diverse in terms of the direction and speed of mortality change, while between-country differences in mortality levels became less pronounced. In almost half the countries under study, the gains in child mortality recorded in the previous decades were either lost or, at best, stalled altogether. On the other hand, even in countries where child mortality rates continued to decline during this period, the rate of decline became flatter and slower than observed during the previous two decades. In some of the countries where a rise (or a stall) in child mortality was observed, the trend coincided with either periods of economic stagnation (or reversals) resulting mainly from structural adjustment programs or with increased rates of HIV/AIDS observed from the late 1980s or both.

Evidence presented in the same figure, however, showed that the decline has resumed since the late 1990s, representing the beginning of a third (and probably final) stage of the child mortality transition in the region. As in phase I, this phase is characterized by a rapid decline in child mortality levels, but, unlike in phase I, it also shows an emerging pattern of increased convergence and homogeneity in mortality levels across the region. The bold trend line, representing the average pattern obtained through the *lowess regression* procedure, vividly depicts these three phases of mortality change in the region.

Our analysis also revealed four distinct regional patterns, each representing West, East, and Southern African subregions, respectively, and one representing the unique pattern of Malawi and Mozambique. The West African pattern comprises West and Northwest African countries. These countries had the highest childhood mortality rates in the 1970s and 1980s, and have shown faster and consistent decline toward lower mortality in the most recent periods. Evidence adduced elsewhere indicates that these countries have exhibited the lowest HIV prevalence rates in SSA (UNAIDS 2010).

The East African pattern, comprising countries such as Ethiopia, Kenya, Rwanda, Tanzania, and Uganda, on the other hand, exhibits moderate levels of childhood mortality in the 1970s and the early 1980s, but a stall in the decline (and in some cases a tendency to increase) in the mid-1980s and early 1990s, thereby converging at the levels portrayed by the Western pattern for the most recent periods. Evidence from other sources indicates that these countries either experienced slower growth (or a decline in economic conditions) in the 1980s or were under civil conflict or exhibited high HIV prevalence rates, but lower than Southern African countries (National Research Council 1993; UNAIDS 2010). This pattern also included Sudan.

The Southern African pattern is characterized by relatively lower childhood mortality in the 1970s and early 1980s, with a considerable slowing down of pace of decline and/or significant increase in the mid-1980s and 1990s. Thus they show a tendency toward higher mortality for the most recent periods. Evidence shows that these countries posted the highest HIV prevalence rates in SSA (UNAIDS 2010).

The last pattern is the hybrid case of Malawi and Mozambique, two countries from Southern Africa, with a West-Eastern mortality pattern. Generally, these two countries, belonging to the Southern Africa region, have an Eastern Africa mortality pattern but with Western Africa levels. In these countries, mortality levels have remained extremely high as in the west and northwestern parts of Africa, but, unlike in countries in that region, their mortality levels increased slightly during the 1980s, a pattern that mirrors those of countries belonging to the East African regional pattern. However, most recently, mortality rates in both Malawi and Mozambique have shown considerable and consistent decline toward lower mortality; their mortality rates for the early 2000s are now only marginally higher than the average for the Africa region as a whole, represented by the bold-trend line in Figure 4.3.

Long-term trends in under-five mortality for individual countries are presented in Figure 4.2 and Table 4.1. These show that for almost all countries, with the exception of countries in western and northwestern regions of the continent, child mortality rates generally increased in the mid-1980s and early 1990s or remained at the same level as those of the early 1980s. However, this does not mean that the trends in these countries were governed by

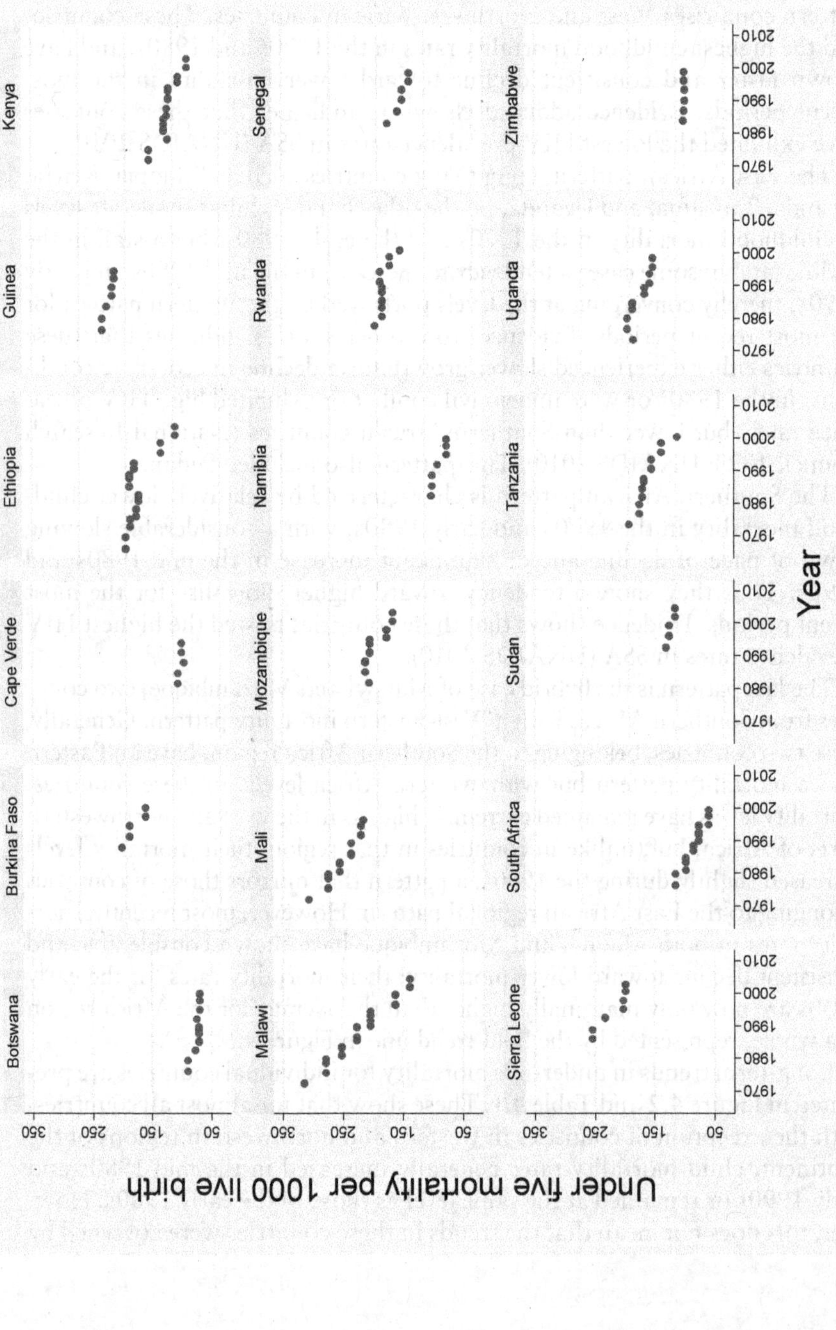

Figure 4.2 Trends in under-five mortality by country, 1965–2005.

similar forces. For instance, the increase in (or near stable) rates of mortality for Ethiopia, Rwanda, Mozambique, and the Sudan in the second half of the 1980s most likely resulted from either civil war or the consequences of the war on the economy of these countries. On the other hand, the trends in countries such as Kenya and Tanzania may largely stem from a combination of the effects of structural adjustment programs and the high prevalence of HIV experienced by these countries. In countries such as Botswana and Namibia, the latter factor may have been more important.

Table 4.1 Estimated and Predicted Under-Five Mortality Rates for Selected African Countries, 1965–2015

	1965–1969	1970–1974	1975–1979	1980–1984	1985–1989	1990–1994	1995–1999	2000–2004	Predicted Mortality by 2015	Level to be Attained by 2015 to Achieve MDG Target
Botswana			90	78	71	75	70		53	25
Burkina Faso			232	232	209	194	161		76	65
Cape Verde				91	77	82			36	27
Ethiopia	200	190	177	174	193	182	126	94	55	61
Guinea			249	240	228	224	224		162	75
Kenya		149	108	109	111	117	117	69	31	39
Malawi		314	278	262	227	205	205	139	78	68
Mali		344	304	278	256	234	234		156	78
Mozambique				217	224	215	215	169	118	72
Namibia			116	85	84	73	63	54	34	24
Rwanda			204	188	188	193	172	150	103	64
Senegal		257	214	178	155	145	132		75	48
Sierra Leone					255	234	203	200	156	78
South Africa			103	80	65	54	34		14	18
Sudan			143	151	153	123	116	103	79	41
Tanzania	200	177	171	168	153	132	98		62	51
Uganda		190	204	191	166	156	149		119	52
Zimbabwe		111	97	83	82	81	83		61	27

Note: Estimates represent arithmetic averages of point estimates for countries that have more than one estimate during the period.
Source: Compiled by authors.

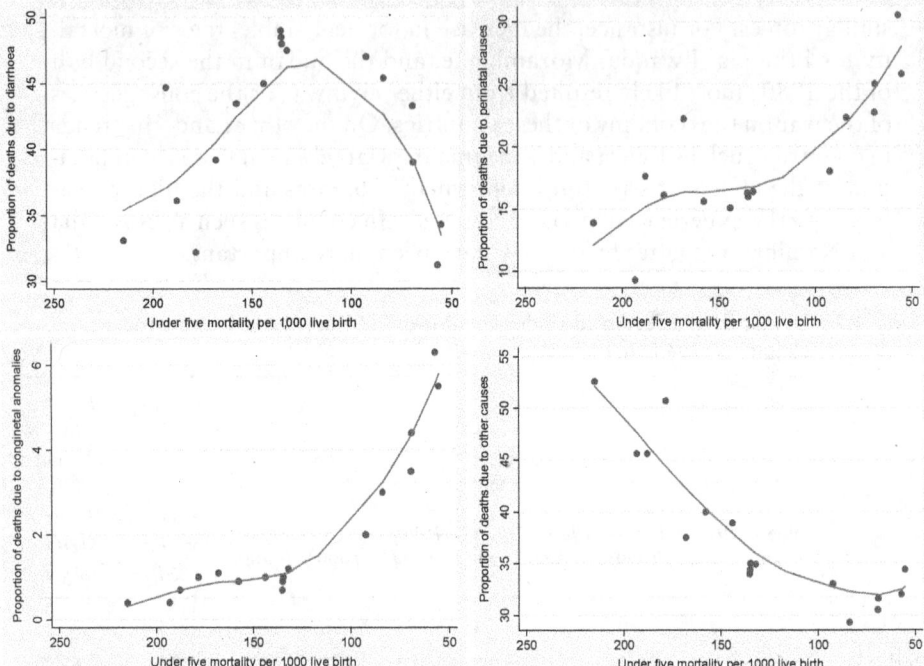

Figure 4.3 Relationship between under-five mortality and estimated broad causes of death in eighteen countries.

Table 4.2 Indirect Estimates of Causes of Death for Various African Countries

PANEL A: Comparison of Causes of Death with Inputs Obtained from Census and DHS Data

Country	Year	Diarrhea & Country LRI		Perinatal		Congenital Anomalies		Others	
		Census	DHS	Census	DHS	Census	DHS	Census	DHS
Ethiopia	2000	41	39.7	14.2	15.1	1.5	1.3	43.3	43.9
Kenya	2000	45.5	48.6	19.2	18.9	3.3	1.8	32	30.6
Mozambique	2000	39	32.2	23.8	26.2	1.2	1	35.9	40.7

PANEL B: Estimated Causes of Death with Inputs Obtained from Latest DHS Data

Country	Year	Diarrhea & LRI	Perinatal	Congenital Anomalies	Others
Botswana	1998	34.3	25.8	5.5	34.5
Burkina Faso	2003	44.7	9.3	0.4	45.6
Ethiopia	2005	47.2	15.9	1.2	35.7
Guinea	2005	36.1	17.6	0.7	45.6
Kenya	2008	45.4	22.3	3	29.3

(continued)

Table 4.2 (continued)

PANEL B: Estimated Causes of Death with Inputs Obtained from Latest DHS Data (continued)

		Diarrhea & LRI	Perinatal	Congenital Anomalies	Others
Malawi	2004	43.5	15.6	0.9	40
Mali	2006	33.1	13.9	0.4	52.5
Mozambique	2007	32.2	26.2	1	40.7
Namibia	2006	39	25	4.4	31.6
Rwanda	2007	49.3	13.5	1	36.2
Senegal	2005	53.8	9.9	0.7	35.5
Sierra Leone	2008	39.2	22.2	1.1	37.5
South Africa	1998	31.2	30.5	6.3	32
Sudan	1989	50.5	12.8	0.9	35.8
Tanzania	2010	47	18	2	32.9
Uganda	2006	45	15.1	1	38.8
Zimbabwe	2005	43.3	22.7	3.5	30.5

Source: Compiled by authors.

How then do the patterns and transition phases identified in this chapter compare with the broad conclusions from previous studies reviewed in an earlier section? Notwithstanding the differences in methods and sources of data between these studies, there is a good level of agreement on the general features identified for the period until the mid-1980s—namely, the near-universal nature of the mortality decline of the 1970s and early 1980s, the great diversity in levels as well as speed of mortality decline between countries, and marked differentials on the same between different regions of the continent (Hill 1993). However, unlike the then widely prevailing pessimistic view of an extended period of a stall in mortality decline in the region beyond the late 1980s, our analysis based on more recent data showed that mortality rates were changing faster than anticipated earlier. Wherever new data were available for the 1990s and beyond, mortality rates declined dramatically in all countries irrespective of the economic level of the country or the level of mortality that prevailed in the late 1980s. There is now also a noticeable clustering and overlap in regional mortality patterns, with the mortality gradients observed for the decades before 1990s becoming less clear and fading quickly over time.

However, between-country differences in child mortality still remain wide. As shown in the country-specific mortality estimates presented in Table 4.1, there is almost a fourfold difference in under-five mortality between the countries with the lowest and highest mortality rates for the period 2000–2004. Countries also differ in their likelihood of meeting the target for under-five mortality by 2015. Of the eighteen countries under study, our prediction shows that only three countries—Ethiopia, Kenya, and South Africa[2]—are most likely to meet the target, while countries such as Guinea, Mali, Rwanda, Sierra Leone, and Uganda have a long way to go before meeting the millennium target.

4.2 Broad Causes of Under-Five Mortality

Cause-specific mortality data is essential for planning intervention programs and reorienting health sector policies aimed at reducing U5MRs. However, in most countries of the developing world where mortality remains unacceptably high and progress toward meeting the millennium target remains slow, such data are either unavailable or limited to health facilities, which may be subject to selectivity biases because of differential access to health services in these countries. Rao, Adair, and Kinfu (2011) have developed a simple but robust proportional model that enables the estimation of four broad causes of death among under-fives, using only data on levels of under-five mortality, the ratio of infant to under-five mortality, the ratio of child to under-five mortality, and sex differentials in under-five mortality rates as inputs. Figure 4.3 and Table 4.2 present cause-specific distributions of under-five mortality for eighteen African countries estimated using this model. To enable us to identify the overall pattern of relationship between under-five mortality and the four broad causes, we have also fitted *lowess regression* for each cause and plotted the result in the same figure (see the bold-trend line).

Figure 4.3 shows that where U5MR is up to 200 per 1,000 or more, up to 45 percent of all deaths will come from causes designated as 'others,' such as malaria and other infectious diseases. As mortality declines to between 100–150 per 1,000 live births, the proportion of deaths attributable to 'other causes' declines to less than a third and is progressively replaced by diarrhea and lower respiratory infections (LRIs). At this level of mortality, up to half of all deaths will be attributable to diarrhea and LRIs. However, as mortality declines further to below 100 deaths per 1,000 live births, diarrhea and LRIs will in turn progressively be replaced by perinatal causes. At levels of mortality between 50 and 100 per 1,000 live births, a fourth of all deaths among under-fives will be attributable to perinatal causes. As countries move along the mortality transition continuum, they also experience a relative increase in the contribution of congenital causes to total under-five deaths.

Panel B in Table 4.2 shows estimated causes of death for individual countries based on input data obtained from the latest available years. Where the available census data are either outdated or do not contain the required information, the input data used for Panel B were sourced either from the DHS or other relevant household data for each country.

However, before using these noncensus data for further exploration, we have compared in panel A the results of cause distributions estimated alternatively using DHS and census data for the three countries where all the required inputs for the application of the indirect method are available from the two sources. These results show that the cause distributions obtained using census and survey data for the three countries are well comparable to each other, which heightens our confidence in the results presented in panel B.

The estimates show that the contribution of 'other causes' is relatively higher in Mali, Burkina Faso, and Malawi, all of which have U5MRs of 188–215 per 1,000 live births. On the other hand, in countries such as Kenya and Namibia, where U5MR is between 75–100 per 1,000 live births, deaths attributable to diarrhea and LRIs are relatively higher than those from 'other causes.' On the other hand, as compared with other countries, deaths attributable to perinatal causes are relatively higher in South Africa, where the U5MR is also the lowest in the region.

5 CONCLUSION

Achieving optimal human welfare and survival remains a key challenge for social and economic development in SSA, where many children die of preventable causes. Current estimates on child deaths show that, of the more than seven million children who died before reaching their fifth birthday in the world in 2010, about half were from the region, although SSA accounts for only about a fifth of the world's young children (UNFPA 2011). Yet the study of child mortality in the region has for a long time been hindered by shortcomings in availability, accuracy, and timeliness of appropriate data and relevant analyses in the region. Using thirty-one national censuses from eighteen countries, in this chapter we looked at U5MRs in selected African countries from the early 1970s until the first half of 2000s.

As we did this, we used a new indirect technique that circumvents some of the key limitations of the original Brass method and its later alternatives, and also produced broad causes of under-five mortality in the region by making use of a recently developed indirect method that links under-five mortality and related mortality ratios to broad cause categories. Our results showed that child mortality transition in SA passed through three phases since the late 1960s: a period of rapid decline that lasted until early 1980s, followed by a stage of stagnation (or even reversal in some cases) during the mid-1980s and early 1990s, and finally a rebound that started from the late-1990s. We also identified four distinct regional patterns of child mortality transition in the region: Western, Eastern, and Southern Africa patterns that more or less corresponded with the geographic location of countries, and a fourth and hybrid pattern, West-Eastern, which was represented by Malawi and Mozambique, two countries geographically belonging to the Southern Africa region, but that have an Eastern Africa mortality pattern with a Western Africa levels.

The findings of this study, by and large, corroborate those of earlier studies. They portray the near-universal nature of child mortality decline in the 1970s and 1980s, a great diversity in levels as well as pace of decline between countries, and marked differentials between subregions. However, instead of the expert prediction of an extended stall or reversal following the 'mortality crisis' of the mid-1980s and early 1990s, our analysis indicates faster and consistent transition to lower mortality—for all countries where more recent data were available—in recent years. The convergence happens for both levels in individual countries and subregional patterns, with the mortality gradients observed for the decades before the 1990s becoming less pronounced and quickly fading over time. However, between-country differences in mortality regimes (levels) still remain wide and so, perhaps similarly, do the factors underlying the broad causes and patterns.

So, is SSA's mortality and health transition following on the tenets of the classical epidemiologic transition models (Omran 1971)? The answer is yes and no. Yes, in the sense that the earlier phases of the transition had all the hallmarks of the classical model. And the patterns identified broadly reflect the diversity observed among countries as captured in the classical model. However, the theory of the classical epidemiologic transition that stipulates a downward trend in mortality once it started to drop from its peak levels seems to have been disproved by the SSA experience. We have shown that the penultimate phase of the African child mortality transition was largely perturbed by economic reversals (crises), a high HIV/AIDS prevalence, and/or conflicts. These "unforeseen" forces affected countries differently, both in magnitude and nature of government response, which, ultimately, disrupted the classical transition pattern (which predicts consistent decline in mortality once the transition starts). The final phase of the African transition is clearly tending to the final phase of the classical model. However, it cannot be guaranteed that the same or other forces will allow a smooth ride to the end of the transition. In any event, between country differences in mortality levels still remain wide, while the majority of the countries continue to choke under a double burden of disease (dealing with both infectious and degenerative diseases at the same time) compounded by bleak economic outlooks. But there is hope—for some countries more than others.

Our cause of death analysis also closely mirrors those of the classical epidemiologic transition models. As in the classical model, we observed that diarrhea, LRIs, and other infectious diseases still dominate as major causes of death in the region, and these become less prominent and replaced by perinatal causes for countries where under-five mortality has declined to below the 100 mark. The analyses clearly suggest different types of clinical interventions that policy makers may want to consider. At levels of U5MRs of 100 or more, the focus should be on the Integrated Management of

Childhood Illness (IMCI) strategy, particularly on developing interventions to prevent, detect, and treat diarrhea, pneumonia, and other infectious causes of death. As the U5MR further declines to levels between 60–100 deaths per 1,000 live births, there is a need to intensify efforts to extend existing IMCI strategies into the neonatal period, including the first week of life. Finally, as levels of under-five mortality fall below 60, increased attention should be given to improving skilled newborn care, including the availability of referral services for adequate clinical management. This way it may then be possible to accelerate the child mortality transition in SSA. In fact, our prediction indicates that, if current patterns prevail in the coming three to four years, only three of the eighteen countries under study—Ethiopia, Kenya, and South Africa—are most likely to meet the target, while countries such as Guinea, Mali, Rwanda, Sierra Leone, and Uganda have a long way to go in meeting the millennium target.

ACKNOWLEDGMENTS

The authors would like to acknowledge the Minnesota Population Center for permission to access IPUMS–International database, and also the reviewers whose comments helped to improve the quality of this chapter.

NOTES

1. Census data were accessed from the IPUMS–International database archived by Minnesota Population Center (2011).
2. The predicted U5MR for South Africa seems to be on the lower side, particularly given the considered adverse impact of a high HIV/AIDS prevalence on recent childhood mortality rates. However, our analysis and the prediction for this country are based on trends from old data that may not accurately capture the current scenario.

REFERENCES

Adegbola, O. (1977) "New Estimates of Fertility and Child Mortality in Africa, South of the Sahara." *Population Studies* 31 (3): 467–486.

Adetunji, J. (2000) "Trends in Under-5 Mortality Rates and the HIV/AIDS Epidemic." *Bulletin of the World Health Organization* 78 (10): 1200–1206.

Ahmad, O., A. Lopez, and M. Inoue. (2000) "The Decline in Child Mortality: A Reappraisal." *Bulletin of the World Health Organization* 78 (10): 1175–1191.

Amouzou, A., and K. Hill. (2005) "Child Mortality and Socioeconomic Status in Sub-Saharan Africa." *African Population Studies* 19 (1): 1–12.

Brass, W., Ansley .J. Coale, and Paul. Demeny. (1968) *The Demography of Tropical Africa*. Princeton, NJ: Princeton University Press.

Chatfield, C. (2004) *The Analysis of Time Series: An Introduction*. 6th ed. Boca Raton, FL: Chapman and Hall/CRC.

Coale, A., and J. Trussell. (1977) "Estimating the Time to Which Brass Estimates Apply." *United Nations Population Bulletin* 10:87–89.
Coale, A.J., and J. Trussell. (1978) "Annex I Estimating the Time to Which Brass Estimates Apply." *United Nations Population Bulletin* 10:87–89.
Enders, W. (2004) *Applied Econometric Time Series*. 2nd ed. New York: Wiley.
Feeney, G. (1980) "Estimating Infant Mortality Trends from Child Survivorship Data." *Population Studies* 34 (1): 109–128.
Foote, K.A., K.H. Hill, and L.G. Martin. (1993) *Demographic Change in Sub-Saharan Africa*. Washington, DC: National Academy Press.
Garenne, Michel, and E. Gakusi (2005) "Under-Five Mortality Trends in Africa: Reconstruction from Demographic Sample Surveys." *Demographic and Health Surveys Working Papers Number 26*. Washington, DC: USAID.
Harvey, A.C. (1989) *Forecasting, Structural Time Series Models and Kalman Filter*. Cambridge: Cambridge University Press.
Harvey, A.C. (1993) *Time Series Models*. 2nd ed. Cambridge, MA: MIT Press.
Hill, A.G., and P.H. David. (1988) "Monitoring Changes in Child Mortality: New Methods for Use in Developing Countries." *Health Policy and Planning* 3 (3): 214–226.
Hill, A.L.L. (1989) "La mortaliite' des enfants: Niveau actuel et evolution depuis 1945." In *Mortalite' et Societe' en Afrique au Sud du Sahara. Cahier No 24*, ed. G. Pison van de Walle and M. Sala-Diakanda. 13–34. Paris: Presses Univesitaires de France.
Hill, A.L.L. (1991) "Infant and Child Mortality: Levels, Trends and Data Deficiencies." In *Disease and Mortality in Sub-Saharan Africa*, ed. R. Feachem and D.T. Jamison, 37–70. Oxford: Oxford University Press for the World Bank.
Hill, A.L.L. (1992) "Trends in Childhood Mortality in Sub-Saharan Mainland Africa." In *Mortality and Society in Sub-Saharan Africa*, 10–31, ed. van de Walle, G. Pison and M Sala-Diakanda. Oxford: Clarendon Press.
Hill, A.L.L. (1993) "Trends in Childhood Mortality." In *Demographic Change in Sub-Saharan Africa*, 153–217, ed. K.A. Foote, K.H. Hill, and L.G. Martin. Washington, DC: National Research Council. National Academy Press.
Hill, K. (1991) "Approaches to the Measurement of Childhood Mortality: A Comparative Review." *Population Index* 57 (3): 368–382.
Hill, K., B. Cheluget, S. Curtis, G. Bicego, and M. Mahy. (2004) "HIV and Increases in
Childhood Mortality in Kenya in the Late 1980s to the Mid 1990s". Measure Evaluation Special Report 04–26, Chapel Hill, NC: University of North Carolina.
Hill, K., G. Bicego, and M. Mahy. (2001) "Childhood Mortality in Kenya: An Examination of Trends and Determinants in the Late 1980s to Mid-1990s." Johns Hopkins Population Center Working Paper.
Hill, K., and M-E. Figueroa. (2000) "Child Mortality Estimation by Time since First Birth." In *Brass Tacks: Essays in Medical Demography*, 9–19. ed. Zaba, B and J. Blacker. London: The Athlone Press.
Hill, K., and A.R. Pebley. (1989) "Child Mortality in the Developing World." *Population and Development Review* 15 (4): 657–687.
INDEPTH. (2004) *INDEPTH Model Life Tables for Sub-Saharan Africa. INDEPTH Network*. Aldershot, England: Ashgate Publishing Limited.
Mahy, M. (2003) "Measuring Child Mortality in AIDS-Affected Countries." Paper prepared for the Training Workshop on HIV/AIDS and Adult Mortality in Developing Countries, organized by the Population Division, Department of Economic and Social Affairs, United Nations, New York.
Minnesota Population Center. (2011) *Integrated Public Use Microdata Series International: Version 6.1 [Machine-Readable Database]*. Minneapolis: University of Minnesota.

National Research Council. (1993) *Demographic Effects of Economic Reversals in Sub-Saharan Africa.* Washington, DC: National Academy Press.

Omran, A. (1971) "The Epidemiologic Transition: A Theory of the Epidemiology of Population Change." *Milbank Memorial Fund Quarterly* 49 (4): 509–538.

Preston, S.H., and A. Palloni. (1977) "Fine-Tuning Brass-Type Mortality Estimates with Data on Ages of Surviving Children." *United Nations Population Bulletin* 10:72–91.

Rajaratnam, J., L. Tran, A. Lopez, and C. Murray. (2010) "Measuring Under-Five Mortality: Validation of New Low-Cost Methods." *PLOS Medicine* 7 (4): 1–24.

Rao, C., T. Adair, and Y. Kinfu. (2011) "Using Historical Vital Statistics to Predict the Distribution of Under-Five Mortality by Cause." *Clinical Medicine & Research* 9 (2): 66–74.

Sullivan, J. (1972) "Models for the Estimation of the Probability of Dying between Birth and Exact Ages of Early Childhood." *Population Studies* 26 (1): 79–97.

Timaeus, I. (1998) "Impact of the HIV Epidemic on Mortality in Sub-Saharan Africa: Evidence from National Surveys and Censuses." *AIDS* 12 (1): S15–S27.

Trussell, J. (1975) "A Re-Estimation of the Multiplying Factors from the Brass Technique for Determining Childhood Survivorship Rates." *Population Studies* 29 (1): 97–107.

UNAIDS. (2010) *UNAIDS Report on the Global AIDS Epidemic: HIV Estimates with Uncertainty Bounds, 1990–2009.* Geneva: UNAIDS.

UNFPA. (2011) *State of the World Population 2011.* New York: UNFPA.

UNICEF. (2011) *Levels & Trends in Child Mortality: 2011 Report.* New York: UNICEF.

United Nations. (2003) "The Impact of HIV/AIDS on Mortality." Workshop on HIV/AIDS and Adult Mortality in Developing Countries. Population Division, Department of Economic and Social Affairs, New York.

UNSD. (2006) *Progress towards the Millennium Development Goals: 1990–2005.* Department of Economic and Social Affairs, United Nations, New York.

Ward, P., and B. Zaba. (2008) "The Effect of HIV on the Estimation of Child Mortality Using the Children Surviving/Ever Born Technique." *Demography* 11 (1): 39–73.

World Health Organization (2011) *World Health Statistics 2011.* Geneva: WHO.

Zaba, B., M. Marston, and S. Floyd. (2003) "The Effect of HIV on Child Mortality Trends in Sub-Saharan Africa." Paper Prepared for the Training Workshop on HIV/AIDS and Adult Mortality in Developing Countries organized by the Population Division, Department of Economic and Social Affairs, United Nations, New York.

Zlotnik, H., and K. Hill. (1981) "The Use of Hypothetical Cohorts in Estimating Demographic Parameters under Conditions of Changing Fertility and Mortality." *Demography* 18 (1): 103–122.

Zuberi, T., A. Sibanda, A. Bawah, and A. Noumbissi. (2003) "Population and African Society." *Annual Review of Sociology* 29:465–486.

5 Indirect Estimation of Levels of Adult Mortality in Sub-Saharan Africa

Stephen Ayo Adebowale and Sunday Adepoju Adedini

1 INTRODUCTION

The mortality level of a society is a fundamental indicator of health and development. This is why governments watch the mortality rate of their countries with keen interest to see what has been achieved over a period of time. Death is inevitable and marks the end of human life. In ideal situations, where diseases, infections, and isolated social disruptions and disorder are minimal and there is an adequate food supply, while affordable modern health facilities and social infrastructures are available, individuals tend to live longer. The wide differential in the aforementioned conditions makes the timing of deaths vary regionally, nationally, and at the level of the individual. This is the reason for higher life expectancy among more developed than less developed countries (WHO 2000).

Among all mortality indexes, childhood and maternal mortality have been given much attention in the past, whereas adult mortality has been neglected, particularly in sub-Saharan Africa (SSA) (Bradshaw and Timaeus 2006). However, the emergence of communicable (e.g., HIV/AIDS) and noncommunicable diseases (cancer, stroke, etc.) and poor health conditions associated with poverty and poor infrastructural development that threaten adult survival are changing population health researchers' interest in childhood mortality alone to include adult mortality (Akachi and Canning 2008). SSA countries carry high burdens of these diseases; therefore, the soaring adult mortality in the SSA has been given more attention in recent times (Timaeus and Jasseh 2004; Timaeus 1999). In this region, different policies and strategies have been designed to curtail the upsurge of diseases; the efforts have resulted in a slight improvement in population health in SSA, improving the survival chances of adults.

A review of the adult population in Africa shows that in the later part of the last century, about half of the African population consisted of adults; an increasing proportion of adults is also envisaged in decades ahead (Setel et al. 1998). The predicted changes in the adult population might alter the future mortality pattern among adult populations in Africa (Setel *et al.* 1998). Therefore, monitoring the pace of adult mortality in Africa through the use of adequate data should be of interest to population health researchers, but such data are lacking in SSA countries (Hill 2001). Imperfect vital registration, inaccurate censuses, and misreporting of age at death are among the problems often encountered by researchers wishing to use mortality data sets (United Nations 1983, 2002; United Nations 2005; ECA/ADB 2012).On this basis, researchers have suggested the use of indirect method for the provision of better estimates of adult mortality in SSA countries using census and survey data (UN 1983, 2002; Hill 2000; Bradshaw and Timaeus 2006).

Our study was designed to contribute to existing knowledge on the use of indirect method for estimation of adult mortality indexes in SSA. The estimated indexes include: survival probability (l_x), age-specific mortality rate (ASMR), crude death rate (CDR), life expectancy at birth (e_0), life expectancy at age 20 (e_{20}), and life expectancy at age x (e_x). These indexes will reveal the patterns of adult mortality in the selected countries and show how the adult age structure and size will evolve over time. In the actualization of these goals, we adopted the census survival method (CSM) and INDEPTH model life tables (IMLT), which were specifically designed for SSA countries. CSM was based on two-point census data, whereas IMLT relied on the Demographic and Health Survey (DHS) data set.

2 THEORETICAL BACKGROUND

One of the earliest theories of mortality is the demographic transition theory, which was proposed to explain how changes in mortality and fertility influence population growth. This theory describes a three-stage process during which slow population growth gives way to a period of rapid population growth, before reverting back to slow growth (Thompson 1929). In most parts of SSA today, fertility and mortality have been reduced, although they are still high and the gain in mortality reduction is being threatened by an upsurge in diseases, infections, and poverty (PRB 2012).

In parallel to the stages of the mortality component of the demographic transition model, Omran developed the epidemiological transition theory. He recognized that the shift in patterns of mortality in the developed world as indicated by the demographic transition is defined by a number of successive phases. He stated that there is possibility of a cessation in the decline in mortality, or even a temporal reversal, acknowledged that communicable diseases had not totally disappeared, and said that new communicable diseases might appear (Omran 1971). The conclusion drawn from this theory is manifesting itself in SSA, today where HIV/AIDS, cancer, and other life-threatening diseases constitute serious challenge to human health, particularly among adult populations (WHO 2010).

The modernization theory of mortality supports the belief that industrialization reduces mortality through an increased economic output. It is agreed that economic growth has a mechanism that fosters improvements in education, housing, health care, nutrition, sanitation, and various public services that reduce mortality. When the economy is improved, the morale and energy of the populace are positive. Positive energy therefore translates into healthy individuals and families, and thus people live longer (Hussain and Tribe 1981). The theory suggests that an early stage of social and economic development corresponds to a high level of mortality. Most of the countries in SSA are still striving to improve their economies, but the gain in economic development is being made by a small section of the population to the detriment of the larger segment of the population. The majority of people living in SSA countries at the moment earn below a dollar per day; thus deaths attributable to poverty, hunger, and malnutrition account for a substantial proportion of total deaths among adult populations in the region.

The dependency theory is of the view that, as the dependent country extracts goods from the alpha country, the dependent country keeps losing while the alpha country keeps gaining. The relations between the dependent and alpha countries are thought to retard human well-being in the dependent countries because such relations promote resource and surplus extraction that could have been invested in economic growth and public programs designed to increase human well-being. The majority of countries in SSA depend on one developed country or the other for things that could have been produced in their countries if their resources had been channeled to human development and programs that could improve the economy and the populations' health. Good health care services are lacking; the few that are available are overstretched and services are not affordable for the poor segment of the population, which constitutes the majority. The rich and leaders seek health care in advanced countries, while the poor who cannot afford such health care die untimely deaths.

The economic disarticulation theory emphasizes that a country's disarray is based on the disjointed economy and uneven development. Public funds are channeled away from humanitarian efforts. In effect, economic disarticulation reduces human well-being and increases mortality because of economic stagnation and unequal economic development. The influx of resources into the economy creates a strain between the rich and the poor; the rich get richer and the poor get poorer. Unfortunately, the poor constitute a huge proportion of people living in SSA. Their access to good health care, a balanced diet, and good living conditions is compromised. Thus their survival chances tend to be much lower than that of their rich counterparts. Obviously, the economic disarticulation theory explains why life expectancy remains low and adult mortality is still high in SSA countries.

2.1 Levels and Trends of Adult Mortality in Sub-Saharan Africa

The level of adult mortality is the probability of dying at age 15–60 years. This has declined substantially from a global average of 354/1,000 in 1955 to 207/1,000 in 2002 (Hill 2001; WHO 2004). In recent times, the rate of decline has been slow, an indication that achieving a continuing reduction in adult mortality might be unfeasible, particularly in developing countries.

Nevertheless, there has been regional variation in the probability of adult death. For instance, in some parts of SSA, the probability of adult death is nearly four times higher than that observed in low-mortality countries of the Western Pacific Region (WHO 2003).

Since the middle of the last century, tremendous success has been achieved in population health in terms of the reduction in death rates across countries, including those of SSA. The improvements that continue globally are associated with better nutrition and public health strategies aimed at sustaining good health among populations (Akachi and Canning 2008). The onset of HIV/AIDS in the early 1980s reversed the trend and turned previous gains in life expectancy into a continuous decline until 1990 (Family Health International 1996). The reversal has caused wide differentials in the level of adult mortality among countries, particularly in SSA, which carries a high burden of the disease (Hill 2003; Timaeus and Jasseh 2004). Research shows that without HIV/AIDS, the expectation of life at the time of birth in the African region would have been almost 6.1 years higher in 2002 (WHO 2002).

In most regions of the world, life expectancy at age 15 has slightly increased in the last twenty years. The notable exceptions are the high-mortality countries in Africa, where life expectancy at age 15 decreased by nearly seven years between 1980 and 2002 (WHO 2002). The level of adult mortality rises in SSA as a result of a resurgence of other diseases, such as cancer and gastrointestinal problems, which in the past were known to be peculiar to the Western world. These diseases have caused a shift in mortality since 1990 from a steady decline into a rapidly escalating mortality. The reversal in parts of SSA has been so drastic that current adult mortality rates exceed the levels of three decades ago (WHO 2002). In this part of Africa, it has been estimated that around 40 percent (or more) of people who reach the age of 15 will not survive to the age of 60 ($_{45}q_{15}$), given the current mortality rates (Bradshaw and Timaeus 2006).

The Eastern and Southern African regions have been the hardest hit by the HIV/AIDS plague (UNAIDS 2012); the available data show high adult mortality incidence in these regions (Timaeus 1998). In South Africa and Zambia, for instance, $_{45}q_{15}$ was estimated to be as high as 57 percent and 72 percent, respectively (WHO 2003). In Botswana, Lesotho, Swaziland, and Zimbabwe, HIV/AIDS has reduced male and female life expectancies by more than twenty years (WHO 2003). In Zimbabwe, upturns in reported adult deaths were significantly greater in 1991–1995 than in 1986–1990. In some of the worst affected countries, HIV/AIDS can affect certain age segments of the population, decreasing the number of adults available to reproduce and contribute economically to the development of the country (Ngom and Clark 2003).However the high prevalence of HIV/AIDS may not result in increasing mortality, as found in countries like Kenya, Tanzania, and Burkina-Faso (Timaeus and Jasseh 2004).

Despite what is often argued, a decline in mortality is underway in SSA. The high prevalence of HIV/AIDS in the region and the emergence of some noncommunicable diseases that pervasively affect the region are major contributory factors in this regard. Governments of some countries in SSA are doing everything possible through population health programs to reduce the prevalence of noncommunicable diseases and the spread of HIV/AIDS, which are a threat to population health, particularly the adult population. To monitor the success of such programs requires the estimation of appropriate mortality indexes as evidenced in the current study.

3 DATA SOURCES AND METHODS

3.1 A Brief Description of the Selected Countries

3.1.1 Kenya

Basic demographic profiles of Kenya's total population estimates include: 2012 population estimate 43,013,341; sex ratio at birth 1.02; population growth rate 2.4 percent; death rate 7.26 deaths per 1,000 of the population. In addition, the life expectancy at birth is 63.07 years (male: 61.62 years; female: 64.55 years) and adult HIV prevalence is 6.3 percent (PRB 2012).

3.1.2 Rwanda

Rwandan's population estimate is 11,689,696; sex ratio at birth 1.03; population growth rate 2.75 percent; death rate 9.64 deaths per 1,000 of the population. The life expectancy at birth for the total population is 58.44 years (male: 56.96 years; female: 59.96 years) and adult HIV prevalence is 2.9 percent (PRB 2012).

3.1.3 Senegal

The estimated population of Senegal is 12,969,606, sex ratio at birth 1.03; population growth rate 2.53 percent; death rate 9.05 deaths per 1,000 of the population. The life expectancy at birth for the total population is 60.18 years (male: 58.22 years; female: 62.19 years) and adult HIV prevalence is 0.9 percent (PRB 2012).

3.1.4 Tanzania

Tanzania has a population estimate of about 43,601,796; sex ratio at birth 1.03; population growth rate 1.96 percent; death rate 11.92 deaths per 1,000 of the population. The life expectancy at birth for the total population is 53.14 years (male: 51.62 years; female: 54.7 years) and adult HIV prevalence is 5.6 percent (PRB 2012).

3.1.5 South Africa

The population of South Africa was estimated to be 48,810,427; sex ratio at birth 1.02; population growth rate 0.412 percent; death rate 17.23 deaths per 1,000 of the population. The life expectancy at birth for the total population is 49.41 years (male: 50.34 years; female: 48.45 years) and adult HIV prevalence is 17.8 percent (PRB 2012).

3.2 Data Justification and Extraction

Death as one of the vital events is relatively rare; therefore, any reliable study on mortality must involve a large data set. The current study involves the comparison of adult mortality indexes among nations; thus there is a need for nationally representative data. Reliable data sources for such information are scarce except censuses, household surveys, and vital registration. A combination of these data sources presents the best approach for analyzing adult mortality. But of all the SSA countries, only South Africa has a reasonably good record of vital registration data that extends for many years. But even this has some shortcomings, as the data exclude former homeland populations (Timaeus and Nunn 1997). This limits us to the use of only the most recent available censuses and DHS data set in the subregion.

The data utilized for this study were extracted from Integrated Public Use Microdata Series (IPUMs) (http://www.ipums.org/) archived by Minnesota Population Center (2011) and measure DHS database (http://www.measuredhs.com/). Five countries were purposefully selected from SSA. The selection was based on the availability of DHS and two rounds of census recently conducted in these countries; as such, the adult mortality indexes estimates in this study may not reflect the true situation in SSA. The selected census rounds for the countries are: Kenya (1989–1999), Rwanda (1991–2002), Senegal (1988–2002), South Africa (1996–2001), and Tanzania (1988–2002). The DHS data utilized are: Senegal (1999 and 2010), Tanzania (1999 and 2010), Kenya (1998 and 2010), Rwanda (2000 and 2010), and South Africa (1999 and 2003). The focus is on the census and DHS data sets because of their availability, large capacity, and credibility of the collection procedures when compared with other sources.

3.3 Analysis Method

Data were analyzed using Stata version 12.0, MortPak-Lite version 4.1 (United Nations 1988) and Excel software packages. The aim of this study was to provide estimates of adult mortality indexes such as: survival probabilities (l_x), total person-years lived (T_x), life expectancies (e_x, e_0, e_{20}), CDRs, and ASMRs for the selected countries by gender. To achieve this, CSM, IMLT, and Coale-Demeny life tables (west family) were used. The CSM is one of the techniques designed by the United Nations for estimation of adult mortality (United Nations 2002), whereas IMLT was specifically designed for SSA countries in order to account for HIV prevalence and other mortality causative factors peculiar to the region. The description and utilization of the methods are discussed below.

Table 5.1 Census Survival Method for Ten-Year Intercensal Intervals Applied to Kenya: Males and Females, 1989–1999

Age group	1989 $P_1(x,5)$	1999 $P_2(x,5)$	Age (x)	CSR	POS2.5 $l_x/l_{2.5}$	POS7.5 $l_x/l_{7.5}$	MPOS $l_{x1}/l_{2.5}$	Age (x)	POSx $l_x/l_{2.5}$	PYL $_5L_x/l_{2.5}$	TPYL $T_x/l_{2.5}$	e_x
(1)	(2)	(3)	(4)	(5)	(6)	(7)	(8)	(9)	(10)	(11)	(12)	(13)
MALES												
0–4	96,073	108,828	2.5	1.0418	1.0000	N.A	1.0000*	N.A	N.A	N.A	N.A	N.A
5–9	87,601	99,245	7.5	0.9473	N.A	1.0000	1.0209*	5	1.0105*	5.1048	54.9011	54.33
10–14	75,470	100,090	12.5	0.8629	1.0418*	N.A	1.0418*	10	1.0314*	5.0895	49.7963	48.28
15–19	58,652	82,980	17.5	0.9479	N.A	0.9473	0.9671	15	1.0044*	4.8437	44.7068	44.51
20–24	44,817	65,119	22.5	0.9255	0.8990	N.A	0.8990	20	0.9330	4.6023	39.8631	42.72
25–29	39,014	55,596	27.5	0.8788	N.A	0.8980	0.9168	25	0.9079	4.4557	35.2608	38.84
30–34	29,203	41,476	32.5	0.8767	0.8320	N.A	0.8320	30	0.8744	4.2331	30.8051	35.23
35–39	23,176	34,285	37.5	0.8898	N.A	0.7892	0.8057	35	0.8188	3.9660	26.5720	32.45
40–44	18,621	25,601	42.5	0.9056	0.7294	N.A	0.7294	40	0.7675	3.7267	22.6060	29.45
45–49	14,070	20,621	47.5	0.7892	N.A	0.7022	0.7169	45	0.7231	3.5297	18.8793	26.11
50–54	11,958	16,864	52.5	0.8151	0.6606	N.A	0.6606	50	0.6887	3.2548	15.3496	22.29
55–59	8,975	11,104	57.5	0.7729	N.A	0.5542	0.5658	55	0.6132	2.9133	12.0948	19.72
60–64	7,603	9,747	62.5	0.7694	0.5385	N.A	0.5385	60	0.5521	2.5508	9.1815	16.63
65–69	5,728	6,937	67.5	0.7032	N.A	0.3897	0.3978	65	0.4682	2.1856	6.6307	14.16
70–74	4,185	5,850	72.5	0.4855	0.4143	N.A	0.4143	70	0.4061	1.8827	4.4451	10.95
75–79	3,260	4,028	77.5	N.A	N.A	0.2740	0.2797	75	0.3470	1.4686	2.5624	7.38
80–84	1,915	2,032	82.5	N.A	0.2011	N.A	0.2011	80	0.2404	N.A	1.0938	4.55
85+	2,050	2,627	2.5	N.A	N.A	N.A	N.A	N.A	N.A	N.A	N.A	N.A

Indirect Estimation of Levels of Adult Mortality   85

FEMALES

Age											
0–4	94,548	107,451	2.5	1.0455	1.0000	N.A	1.0000	N.A	N.A	N.A	N.A
5–9	86,419	97,578	7.5	0.9836	N.A	1.0000	1.0228	5	1.0114	5.1133	61.2943	60.60
10–14	74,834	98,851	12.5	0.9990	1.0450	N.A	1.0450	10	1.0339	5.1485	56.1810	54.34
15–19	60,165	85,003	17.5	1.0015	N.A	0.9836	1.0060	15	1.0255	5.1263	51.0325	49.76
20–24	50,910	74,759	22.5	0.8344	1.0440	N.A	1.0440	20	1.0250	5.1270	45.9062	44.79
25–29	42,497	60,253	27.5	0.8539	N.A	0.9851	1.0076	25	1.0258	4.9130	40.7792	39.75
30–34	28,947	42,481	32.5	0.8977	0.8711	N.A	0.8711	30	0.9394	4.5130	35.8662	38.18
35–39	22,744	36,289	37.5	0.9178	N.A	0.8412	0.8604	35	0.8658	4.2175	31.3532	36.21
40–44	18,297	25,987	42.5	0.9414	0.7820	N.A	0.7820	40	0.8212	4.0178	27.1357	33.04
45–49	14,709	20,875	47.5	0.8094	N.A	0.7721	0.7897	45	0.7859	3.8723	23.1179	29.42
50–54	12,110	17,224	52.5	0.8906	0.7362	N.A	0.7362	50	0.7630	3.6268	19.2456	25.22
55–59	9,131	11,905	57.5	0.8686	N.A	0.6249	0.6391	55	0.6877	3.3378	15.6188	22.71
60–64	8,394	10,785	62.5	0.8280	0.6557	N.A	0.6557	60	0.6474	3.1323	12.2810	18.97
65–69	5,904	7,931	67.5	0.7022	N.A	0.5428	0.5552	65	0.6055	2.8865	9.1487	15.11
70–74	4,466	6,951	72.5	0.5901	0.5429	N.A	0.5429	70	0.5491	2.5388	6.2622	11.40
75–79	2,971	4,146	77.5	N.A	N.A	0.3812	0.3899	75	0.4664	2.0540	3.7234	7.98
80–84	2,211	2,635	82.5	N.A	0.3204	N.A	0.3204	80	0.3552	N.A	1.6694	4.70
85+	94,548	107,451	2.5	N.A	1.0000	N.A	1.0000	N.A	N.A	N.A	N.A

*Unusual probability estimates mainly because of age misreporting in the earlier census or effect of migration; NA: Not Available; CSR: census survival ratio; $POS_{2,5}$: probability of survival from age 2.5 years; $POS_{7,5}$: probability of survival from age 7.5 years; MPOS: merged probability of survival; POS_x: probability of survival to age x; PYL: person years lived above age x; TPYL: total person years lived above age x; e_x: estimated life expectancy at age x.

Table 5.2 Coale-Demeny Model Life Tables (West Family) Using Probability of Surviving To Age 1 ($_1q_0$) and Age 5e ($_5q_0$) from DHS and Life Expectancy at Age 20 (e_{20}) Estimates from Census Survival Methods Males: Kenya, Rwanda, Senegal, Tanzania, and South Africa

	Kenya			Rwanda			Senegal			Tanzania			South Africa		
Age	l_x	$_nM_x$	e_x	l_x	$_nM_x$	*ex	lx	$_nM_x$	e_x	l_x	$_nM_x$	e_x	l_x	$_nM_x$	e_x
(1)	(2)	(3)	(4)	(5)	(6)	(7)	(8)	(9)	(10)	(11)	(12)	(13)	(14)	(15)	(16)
0	100,000	0.078867	53.79	100,000	0.134284	33.93	100,000	0.078316	52.77	100,000	0.12813	64.07	100,000	0.051042	39.76
1	92,550	0.009208	57.10	87,680	0.028223	37.65	92,600	0.02157	55.96	88,200	0.015891	71.59	95,100	0.004492	40.80
5	89,220	0.003436	55.18	78,470	0.010893	37.91	85,030	0.003064	56.81	82,820	0.000187	72.16	93,410	0.009643	37.50
10	87,700	0.002654	51.09	74,309	0.008810	34.89	83,737	0.002256	52.65	82,743	0.000119	67.22	89,012	0.009001	34.24
15	86,544	0.004399	46.74	71,107	0.015014	31.35	82,798	0.003462	48.22	82,695	0.000137	62.26	85,095	0.019550	30.70
20	84,660	0.005612	42.72	65,954	0.016866	28.60	81,377	0.004884	44.02	82,637	0.000386	57.30	77,151	0.016881	28.59
25	82,316	0.006131	38.86	60,616	0.01899	25.89	79,412	0.005296	40.04	82,478	0.000358	52.41	70,907	0.018990	25.89
30	79,831	0.007021	34.99	55,120	0.022086	23.22	77,337	0.006055	36.05	82,330	0.000400	47.50	64,477	0.022086	23.22
35	77,075	0.008426	31.15	49,349	0.025972	20.64	75,029	0.00731	32.08	82,165	0.000556	42.59	57,727	0.025972	20.64
40	73,893	0.010589	27.38	43,329	0.031445	18.16	72,335	0.009312	28.18	81,937	0.000975	37.70	50,684	0.031445	18.16
45	70,079	0.013449	23.73	37,012	0.036264	15.84	69,041	0.012094	24.40	81,539	0.002002	32.87	43,296	0.036264	15.84

Indirect Estimation of Levels of Adult Mortality

Age	l_x	nM_x	e_x	l_x	nM_x	e_x	l_x	nM_x	e_x	l_x	nM_x	e_x	l_x	nM_x	e_x
50	65,515	0.018293	20.21	30,858	0.045871	13.49	64,984	0.016718	20.76	80,726	0.003830	28.17	36,097	0.045871	13.49
55	59,776	0.024939	16.90	24,511	0.055511	11.34	59,761	0.023228	17.35	79,194	0.007474	23.66	28,672	0.055511	11.34
60	52,744	0.036169	13.81	18,540	0.076081	9.19	53,187	0.033999	14.17	76,283	0.012931	19.46	21,687	0.076081	9.19
65	43,974	0.052184	11.05	12,626	0.101853	7.35	44,831	0.049571	11.33	71,494	0.022611	15.58	14,770	0.101853	7.35
70	33,801	0.077662	8.60	7,535	0.142125	5.67	34,918	0.074396	8.82	63,813	0.039154	12.13	8,814	0.142125	5.67
75	22,804	0.118246	6.54	3,643	0.210407	4.22	23,954	0.113919	6.71	52,376	0.066430	9.207	4,262	0.210407	4.22
80	12,469	0.201649	4.96	1,227	0.315385	3.17	13,394	0.196793	5.08	37,383	0.145711	6.86	1,436	0.315385	3.17
85	4,599	0.272602	3.35	80	0.440888	2.20	5,506	0.265135	3.43	26,115	0.175647	4.70	173	0.411152	2.35
90	1,097	0.414202	2.33	7	0.636040	1.57	1,368	0.404331	2.38	10,504	0.283650	3.22	20	0.592977	1.67
95	117	0.624847	1.58	N.A	N.A	N.A	155	0.612011	1.62	2,333	0.453109	2.14	1	0.855046	1.17

*Estimates are based on $e_{20} = 28.6$, since the census survival method computed value is less than the least value that is obtainable in Coale-Demeny model life tables (west family); l_x: probability of survival to age x; nM_x: age-specific mortality rate; e_x: life expectancy at age x; DHS: Demographic and Health Survey; NA: not available in the Coale-Demeny model life tables (west family).

Table 5.3 INDEPTH MLTs (Pattern 1) and Coale-Demeny (West Family) Estimates of the Female Survival Function for Kenya Using Only Values of 11 and 15 for the Year 2010 KDHS

(1)	(2)	(3)	(4)	(5)	(6)	(7)	(8)	(9)	(10)	(11)	(12)	(13)	(14)	(15)	(16)	(17)	(18)	(19)
Age	l^s_x	γ_x	$1^s_x/\gamma_x$	$Logit(l^s_x/\gamma_x)$	lx	$logit(l_x)$	INDEPTH l_x	l_x	n	${}_nd_x$	${}_na_x$	${}_nm_x$	${}_nL_x$	T_x	e_x	l_x	${}_nm_x$	e_x
			INDEPTH ESTIMATION PROCEDURES									INDEPTH					Coale-Demeny	
0	1.000000	1.0	1.000000		1.0000		1.000000	100,000	1	2,758	0.21	0.02819	97,822	6,075,841	60.76	100,000	0.028256	60.29
1	0.930389	1.0	0.930389	−1.296344	0.9146	−1.185570	0.962735	97,242	4	4,600	0.36	0.012194	377,195	5,978,019	61.48	97,242	0.012187	61.00
5	0.907049	1.0	0.907049	−1.139064	0.8353	−0.811833	0.914837	92,643	5	1,204	0.50	0.002616	460,204	5,600,824	60.46	92,643	0.002858	59.95
10	0.902277	1.0	0.902277	−1.111390	0.8164	−0.746072	0.902012	91,439	5	680	0.50	0.001493	455,495	5,140,620	56.22	91,329	0.002103	55.78
15	0.899582	1.0	0.899582	−1.096292	0.8054	−0.710196	0.894310	90,759	5	833	0.50	0.001843	451,713	4,685,125	51.62	90,374	0.003008	51.34
20	0.897129	1.0	0.897129	−1.082861	0.7952	−0.678280	0.887014	89,926	5	1,160	0.50	0.002597	446,731	4,233,412	47.08	89,023	0.004132	47.08
25	0.893942	1.0	0.893942	−1.065826	0.7817	−0.637800	0.877133	88,766	5	1,584	0.50	0.003602	439,870	3,786,681	42.66	87,203	0.004743	43.01
30	0.889073	1.0	0.889073	−1.040654	0.7606	−0.577986	0.861178	87,182	5	1,972	0.50	0.004575	430,980	3,346,811	38.39	85,158	0.005416	38.98
35	0.882575	1.0	0.882575	−1.008522	0.7317	−0.501632	0.838327	85,210	5	1,841	0.50	0.004368	421,449	2,915,831	34.22	82,882	0.006206	34.98
40	0.874815	1.2	0.729012	−0.494809	0.6964	−0.415107	0.808868	83,369	5	2,472	0.50	0.006021	410,665	2,494,382	29.92	80,348	0.007204	31.00
45	0.865771	1.1	0.787064	−0.653660	0.6547	−0.319882	0.771902	80,897	5	3,089	0.50	0.007786	396,761	2,083,717	25.76	77,505	0.008785	27.05
50	0.855117	1.1	0.777379	−0.625230	0.6056	−0.214427	0.725413	77,808	5	4,810	0.50	0.012757	377,014	1,686,956	21.68	74,171	0.012057	23.15
55	0.842878	1.1	0.766253	−0.593635	0.5503	−0.100941	0.669298	72,998	5	7,027	0.50	0.020226	347,423	1,309,942	17.94	69,825	0.016651	19.43
60	0.827267	1.3	0.636359	−0.279799	0.4831	0.033813	0.595947	65,971	5	8,824	0.50	0.028668	307,796	962,519	14.59	64,233	0.025308	15.89
65	0.808336	1.8	0.449076	0.102203	0.4086	0.184878	0.508476	57,147	5	12,335	0.50	0.04839	254,900	654,723	11.46	56,567	0.038169	12.69
70	0.782079	2.1	0.372419	0.260927	0.3201	0.376656	0.397381	44,813	5	14,521	0.50	0.077337	187,761	399,823	8.92	46,676	0.060726	9.82

3.4 Census Survival Method

The CSM is one of the methods designed for estimating adult mortality. It has been applied widely across countries. It requires age distributions, specifically five-year age-groups for a population at two different points in a time interval. The method is based on the assumptions that the population is closed to migration and that survival ratios for each age cohort over the interval can be used to estimate the mortality levels during the period. The method works well if the intercensal interval is five years. However, provision was made for its utilization in arbitrary intervals (intervals more or less than five years) (United Nations 2002; Table 5.2).

3.5 INDEPTH Model Life Tables

Mortality data in Africa and other parts of developing world have been proved by researchers to be either nonexistent or inadequate; therefore, data underlying the construction of most of the existing model life tables did not involve those from SSA countries. However, most of their applications are found in Africa (INDEPTH Network 2004). This informed the construction of IMLT, which was based on pulling together data from numerous research sites in SSA. It principally captures the current mortality pattern in SSA countries, which is changing profoundly because of the impact of the HIV/AIDS (INDEPTH Network 2004).

3.6 Coale-Demeny Model Life Tables

The Coale-Demeny model life table was designed to provide means of estimating population parameters for tropical Africa. In this study, we used MortPak-Lite to generate the Coale-Demeny model life table, as shown in Table 5.2.

4 RESULTS

Using two points' census age distribution and $_1q_0$ and $_5q_0$, the data show that among males, at ages 5–60, 10–60, and 15–60 years, CDRs were highest among South Africans, while Tanzanians had the lowest at the same age intervals.

An important observation in the results shown in Table 5.1 is that some of the probabilities of survival (l_x) are greater than 1. This is unfeasible, as probability cannot be greater than 1. One significant thing about this result is that it reveals levels of error in the age data. As an example, the l_x to ages 30 and 35 for males and females in Kenya were slightly above 1 (Table 5.1). The high value of the l_x might reflect substantial underenumeration of early years of life in this age-group in the 1988 census. These unexpected results of l_x being greater than 1 may be interpreted to mean either that the

1988 census enumerated the population somewhat more completely than the 2002 census, or that there was net immigration into the affected age-groups during the intercensal period.

The maximum probability lines were drawn to ascertain the level of errors in age data for the countries. Any part of the graph exceeding these lines signifies a probability higher than 1, which is not feasible and shows a certainty of errors of either age misreporting in the two censuses or most recent census, or gross migration into such ages at the recent census. These situations tend to overestimate l_x as seen in some of the countries, particularly Tanzania.

Also, in all the analyzed countries, e_x was higher among females than males across all adult ages (Table 5.1). As expected, the total person-years lived above age x also reduces down the age points, it reduces from 39.86 to 1.094 and 45.91 to 1.67 for males and females, respectively, and the estimated values were higher among females than males across all ages.

The data as shown in Figure 5.1 using CSM is evidence that across all ages l_x was highest in Tanzania and lowest in Rwanda for males and females. At early adulthood, say, ages 20–27, the l_x clusters around 0.9 and 1.0 for males and females except in Rwanda, where lower estimates were observed. For Senegal and Kenya, the l_x were at par across all ages, although at ages below 45 years, males in Kenya have slight higher l_x than their Senegalese counterparts and vice versa for older age cohorts. Among females, this pattern was observed between Senegal and South Africa, with Kenyan women having highest l_x at all age cohorts when compared with countries such as South Africa, Senegal, and Rwanda.

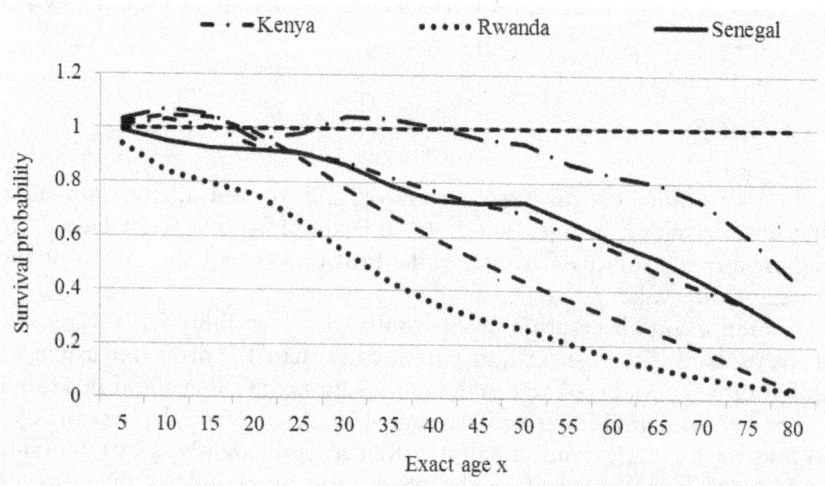

Figure 5.1 Graphs of probability of surviving to age x using census survival method for males for Kenya, 1989–1999.

In male and female populations, the ASMR as estimated using Coale-Demeny model life table on CSM and IM increases steadily at ages 20 through 50 years with a sharp increase at older ages. In both CSM and IM, among males, the ASMRs at all ages were highest among Rwandans.

Using IM, the l_x estimates were highest in South Africa for both males and females, while the values for Kenya, Senegal, Tanzania, and Rwanda form almost a single path on the survival curve. With slight variations, the Brass model life table (African standard) underestimates the l_x at all ages for all countries.

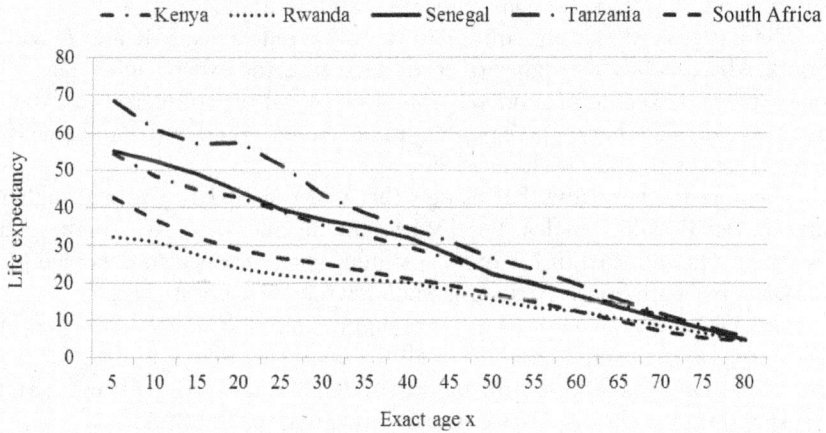

Figure 5.2 Graphs of life expectancy at age x (e_x) using census survival method for males for Kenya, 1989–1999.

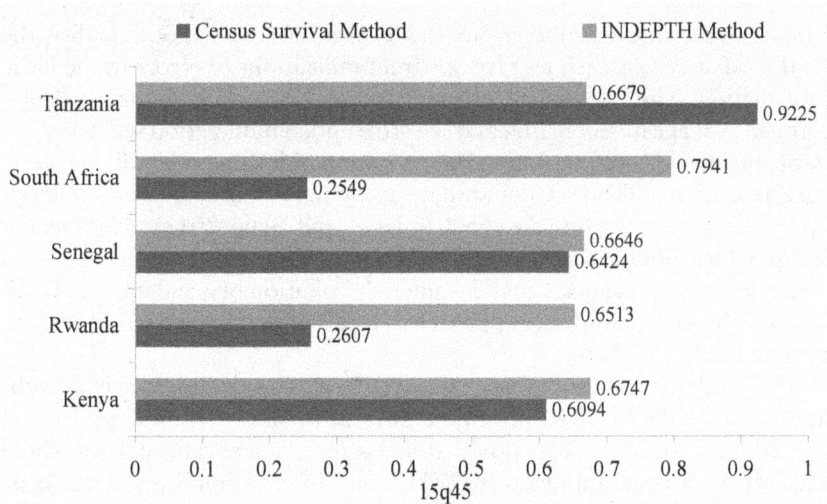

Figure 5.3 Males estimates of probability of dying at age 60 having survived to age 15 ($_{15}q_{45}$) using INDEPTH and census survival method for Kenya.

From the estimates of IM, the data are evidence that l_x estimates were higher at all ages for females than males. For instance, in Kenya, l_x at ages 0 to 45 and 75 plus were almost equal for both sexes, whereas a clear disparity exists between ages 45 and 75. A similar pattern to that seen for Kenya was observed for other countries.

The IM of ASMR as found in this study depicts that ASMR reduces from age 0 to 1, almost remains constant from ages 5 and 40, and increases steadily at higher ages. The patterns of ASMR for all countries were similar for males and females but consistently lower among South Africans, particularly between ages 50 and 80. However, slight variation exists in ASMR among Kenya, Senegal, Tanzania, and Rwanda.

The patterns of e_x were similar to the observed for ASMR and l_x with South Africans having higher e_x at all ages with the exception of ages 85 plus, where e_x were approximately the same for all the countries. The data are also evidence that e_x increases slightly between ages 0 and 5 and consistently reduces steadily with increasing age.

The data further show that using either CSM or IMLT, $_{45}q_{15}$ was higher among females than males. For IMLT, among males $_{45}q_{15}$ was highest in South Africa and least in Rwanda. A similar pattern was also observed for females, but with South African women having the highest $_{45}q_{15}$.

The data depict that e_0 and e_{20} were higher among females than males at ages ranging between 20 and 50 in all the countries. The e_0 and e_{20} form a single path at ages 50 to 60 for males and females in Kenya, Rwanda, and Senegal, but a slight disparity exists in Tanzania and South Africa.

5 DISCUSSION

In spite of the care taken to ensure that census data are of good quality, the final tabulations sometimes give apparent indications of errors in the basic information. More often, the errors can only be inferred. Ewbank (1981) claimed that age misreporting and selective underenumeration will continue to plague demographic studies. The revelation of his opinion still manifests itself in census and survey data today, particularly those obtained in developing countries (Adebowale, Fagbamigbe, and Bello 2012). The current study, which provides estimates of adult mortality indexes in five selected countries in SSA, suggests that despite the limitation of age data, much can be done through an indirect approach in terms of making it useful for planners and policy makers.

The adult mortality indexes presented in this study are: survival probability (l_x), ASMR, CDR, life expectancy at birth (e_0), life expectancy at age 20 (e_{20}), and life expectancy at age x (e_x). Where data permit, these indexes have been adjudged by WHO and international agencies to be useful indicators for measuring overall level of mortality of a country (UN 2002).

Comparing the estimates of e_x produced by the CSM with those made by the IMLT, it is obvious that the CSM estimates tend to be lower at all ages for both men and women. The discrepancies are especially large for women. However, the comparison of the two approaches might not carry great weight since different methodologies and data sets were used in the estimation produced by the two methods. But this can provide a valuable insight into the patterns of adult mortality in SSA. In contemporary times, SSA countries are experiencing increasing adult mortality as a result of the HIV/AIDS epidemic, which is ravaging some of the countries in the region. HIV/AIDS is not the only life-threatening disease in the region at adult ages; however, it contributes significantly to high mortality currently experienced in the region.

The study has further revealed that the CSM estimates of the level of adult mortality indexes vary across the countries. This is in line with the estimates of mortality obtained by WHO, which show that variations exist in the level of adult mortality across African countries (WHO 2002). Going by these estimates as generated using CSM, Rwanda and South Africa had particularly high adult mortality, whereas mortality in Tanzania, Senegal, and Kenya was lower. This is consistent with the study conducted previously in the region, where it was found that Southern and Eastern Africa have particularly high adult mortality (Timaeus et al. 2001). High adult mortality in South Africa and Rwanda could be traced to the HIV/AIDS epidemic, which severely affects South Africa as the country has the highest burden of the disease in SSA (PRB 2012). The occurrence of genocide in the past decade in Rwanda may also explain its estimated high adult mortality. However, the trend was reversed by IMLT, with South Africa having the highest e_x and l_x, while few variations exist for other countries. The reversal was the result of a wide variation in input parameters (infant and under-5 mortality probabilities) needed for the estimation of life table functions between South Africa and other selected countries. The infant and under-5 mortality in South Africa is much lower than that of other countries, and higher life expectancy is associated with lower infant and under-5 mortality as designed by IMLT.

The estimates also suggest that adult men have a consistently lower probability of surviving and life expectancies (e_0, e_{20} and e_x) than adult women in the selected countries. The finding of higher mortality among men than women is in agreement with what obtains in different nations across the globe (Conn and Diefenbach 2007). Higher ASMRs among men than women at adult ages in this study can be explained by the higher exposure of men to the risk of death than women. Biologically, the likelihood of surviving through life is higher in females than males except during reproductive years, where pregnancy-related deaths reduce the survival chances of women (Klein and Schoenborn 2001).

We also found that using either CSM or IMLT the probability of dying at age 60 years, having survived to age 15 ($_{45}q_{15}$), was higher among females than males. For IMLT, among males $_{45}q_{15}$ was highest in South Africa and lowest in Rwanda. A similar pattern was observed for females, but with South African women having highest $_{45}q_{15}$ and Tanzanian women having the lowest. Comparing the $_{45}q_{15}$ estimates from the two methods, a striking distinction exists between the estimates, with IMLT having higher values than CSM among males and females for all the countries, except Tanzania, where the values were lower.

The limitations of the estimates of adult mortality indexes as found in this study are that CSM can only work perfectly if migration is negligible and errors in age distribution are minimal, which are features peculiar to census and survey data in SSA countries. The census information failed to include information on the number of deaths during the intercensal period; therefore, the conventional growth balance method was not applicable. The choice of the CSM was based on the available information provided by census data and DHS data were used to supplement the data requirement where necessary. It must be noted, however, that the CSM might not give an accurate picture of the actual estimates of adult mortality indexes because of distribution of errors in age structure as observed in Tanzania, but it will give an insight into likely estimates and patterns in reality.

Age-reporting errors can result in large variations in calculated survival ratios, so generating inconsistent estimates of mortality indexes. They may also produce biased estimates of these indexes if the completeness of censuses is lacking. Therefore, some of the challenges mentioned above cannot be completely ruled out in our findings.

6 CONCLUSION

The life expectancy established is low if compared with what obtains in some advanced nations; the hardest hit country is Rwanda. However, IMLTs tend to produce more reliable estimates of other adult mortality indexes having taking into consideration the influence of HIV/AIDS in the region. Consequently, it is worthwhile to construe these estimates in the light of other relevant information, including typical errors in the data used and each country's demographic condition. The estimates should always be interpreted with caution, bearing in mind limitations in data used, including questions on household deaths in a national census questionnaire, which can also be an acceptable substitute to death registration data, as this will improve the reliability of mortality indexes estimates using mathematical models.

ACKNOWLEDGMENTS

The authors gratefully acknowledge the Minnesota Population Center for permission to access census data from IPUMS–International database, and all the reviewers whose comments helped to improve the quality of this chapter.

REFERENCES

Adebowale, A.S., A.F. Fagbamigbe, and S.A. Bello. (2012) "Refined Age Distribution and Demographic Parameters Estimation in Nigeria: An Indirect Approach." *Journal of Statistics and Management Systems* 15 (1): 29–48.

Akachi, Y., and D. Canning. (2008) "The Mortality and Morbidity Transitions in Sub-Saharan Africa: Evidence from Adult Heights." Program on the Global Demography and Aging. Working Paper Series, PGDA Working Paper No. 33.

Bradshaw, D., and I.M. Timaeus. (2006) *Levels and Trends of Adult Mortality In: Disease and Mortality in Sub-Saharan Africa*. Washington, DC: World Bank.

Conn, P.B., and D.R. Diefenbach. (2007) "Adjusting Age and Stage Distributions for Misclassification Errors." *Ecology* 88:1977–1983.

ECA/ADB. (2012) *Reforming and Improving Civil Registration and Vital Statistics Systems in Africa Regional Medium-Term Plan: 2010–2015* Durban, Republic of South Africa: Economic Commission for Africa.

Ewbank, D.C. (1981) *Age Misreporting and Age Structure Under-Enumeration: Sources, Patterns and Consequences for Demographic Analysis*. Washington, DC: National Academy Press.

Family Health International. (1996) "The Status and Trends of the Global HIV/AIDS Pandemic: Final Report." Summary of the proceedings of a satellite symposium of the XI International Conference on AIDS, Vancouver, Canada.

Hill, K. (2000) "Methods for Measuring Adult Mortality in Developing Countries: A Comparative Review. The Global Burden of Disease 2000." Aging Populations Research Paper No. 01 13.

Hill, K. (2001) "Methods for Measuring Adult Mortality in Developing Countries: A Comparative Review." Paper presented to the International Population Conference, Salvador, Brazil.

Hill, K. (2003) "Adult Mortality in the Developing World; What We Know and How We Know It." Training workshop on HIV/AIDS and adult mortality in developing countries, Population Division, Department of Economic and Social Affairs, United Nations Secretariat, New York, September 8–13.

Hussain, A., and K. Tribe. (1981) *Marxism and the Agrarian Question: German Social Democracy and the Peasantry 1890–1907*. Hong Kong: MacMillan Press.

INDEPTH Network. (2004) *INDEPTH Model Life Tables for Sub-Saharan Africa*. Padstow: T.J. International.

Klein, R.J., and C.A. Schoenborn. (2001) *Age Adjustment Using the 2000 Projected US Population. Healthy People 2010. Statistical Notes. Saharan Africa*. New York: Population Division, United Nations.

Ngom, Pierre, and Samuel Clark. (2003) *Adult Mortality in the Era of HIV/AIDS: Sub-Saharan Africa*. New York: Population Division, United Nations.

Minnesota Population Center. (2011) *Integrated Public Use Microdata Series International: Version 6.1 [Machine-Readable Database]*. Minneapolis: University of Minnesota.

Omran, A.R. (1971) *The Epidemiologic Transition: A Theory of the Epidemiology of Population Change. The Millbank Memorial Fund Quarterly*, 49 (4), 509–539.

PRB. (2012) *Population Reference Bureau. World Population Data Sheet*. United States Agency for International Development: Washington, DC, USA.

Setel, P., H. Kitange, K. Alberti, and C. Mashiro. (1998) "The Policy Implications of Adult Morbidity and Mortality in Tanzania: From Data Analysis to Health Policy—Preliminary Experiences." Paper presented to Global Forum for Health Research (Forum 2), Geneva, June 25–26.

Timaeus, I.M. (1998) "Impact of the HIV Epidemic on Mortality in Sub-Saharan Africa, Evidence from National Surveys and Censuses." *AIDS* 12 (1): S12–S27.

Timaeus, I.M. (1999) "Mortality in Sub-Saharan Africa." In *Health and Mortality: Issues of Global Concern,* ed. J. Chamie and R.L. Cliquet. New York: United Nations Population Division and Population and Family Study Centre, Flemish Scientific Institute: 108–131

Timaeus, I.M., R.E. Dorrington, D. Bradshaw, N. Nannan, and D. Bourne. (2001) "Adult Mortality in South Africa, 1980–2000: From Apartheid to AIDS." Paper presented at the Population Association of America's annual meeting, Washington, DC, March 29–31.

Timaeus, I.M., and M. Jasseh. (2004) "Adult Mortality in Sub-Saharan Africa: Evidence from Demographic and Health Surveys." *Demography* 41 (4): 757–772.

Timaeus, I.M., and A.J. Nunn. (1997) "Measurement of Adult Mortality in Populations Affected by AIDS: An Assessment of the Orphanhood Method." *Health Transition Review,* :7(2), 23–43.

UNAIDS. (2012) *Report on the Global AIDS Epidemic.* World Health Organization, Switzerland.

United Nations. (1983) "Manual X: Indirect Techniques for Demographic Estimation. Department of International Economic and Social Affairs." *Population Studies* 81: 1–9

United Nations. (1988) *MortPak-Lite. The United Nations Software Package for Mortality Measurement. An Interactive Software for the IBC-PC and Compatibles.* New York: United Nations Secretariat.

United Nations. (2002) *Methods for Estimating Adult Mortality.* New York: Department of Economic and Social Affairs, Population Division.

United Nations. (2005) *World Population Prospects: The 2004 Revision.* New York: Department of Economic and Social Affairs, Population Division.

Thompson, Warren. (1929) "Encyclopedia of Population." In *Macmillan Reference,* Macmillan Publishers, United States of America: 939–940.

WHO. (2000) *The World Health Report 2000—Health Systems: Improving Performance. World Health Report by World Health Organization.* Geneva: World Health Organization.

WHO. (2002) *The World Health Report, 2002. Global Health: Today's Challenges Adult Health at Risk: Slowing Gains and Widening Gaps.* Geneva: World Health Organization.

WHO. (2003) *The World Health Report 2003: Shaping the Future.* Geneva: World Health Organization.

WHO. (2004) *The Global Burden of Disease: 2004 Update.* Geneva: World Health Organization.

WHO. (2010) *Global Status Report on Non-Communicable Diseases. World Health Organization Action Plan for the Global Strategy for the Prevention and Control of Non-Communicable Diseases. 2008–2010.* Geneva: World Health Organization.

6 Fertility Transition in Sub-Saharan Africa
Evidence from Census Data

Sunday Adepoju Adedini

1 INTRODUCTION

Over the last two centuries of human history, fertility transition had taken place in most countries of the world from an initial high level to a low level, and now even to the replacement level of 2.1 or lower in many parts of the developed world (Strulik & Vollmer, 2010). Toward the end of the twentieth century, fertility decline had also spread through many parts of the developing world. Declines have been particularly rapid in the regions of the developing world where socioeconomic development has been relatively rapid (Bongaarts, 2008). Such regions include Latin America, Asia, and North Africa.

Evidence also shows that fertility has started and continued to fall in many countries in the sub-Saharan Africa (SSA) (Bongaarts, 2003; Ezeh et al., 2009; Gaisie, 1995; Odimegwu & Adedini, 2013; Ortega, 2008; Shapiro & Gebreselassie, 2008; Sneeringer, 2009). Although fertility level in the SSA has remained the highest in the world, a number of countries in the region have experienced considerable fertility decline (Shapiro & Gebreselassie, 2008). These include South Africa, Kenya, Botswana, Zimbabwe, and so on. The decline has been attributed to socioeconomic development with attendant increase in female education and female labor force participation (Bongaarts, 2009; Poston, 2000; Tien, 1984), as well as decline in infant mortality leading to fertility decline (El-Ghannam, 2005). Other contributing factors to fertility transition include increase in contraceptive use, as well as the effect of HIV/AIDS pandemic. For instance, the use of contraceptive methods has markedly increased in most parts of the developing world (Kocourková & Fait, 2011; Sacci et al., 2008).

While numerous studies have established declines in fertility level in SSA, others have established a stalled or delayed fertility transition in the region (Bongaarts, 2008; Ezeh, et al., 2009; Garenn, 2008; Moultrie et al., 2008; Schoumaker, 2009; Shapiro & Gebreselassie, 2008). Bongaarts (2008) noted that the pace of decline in the fertility level in SSA was slower around year 2000 compared with the 1990s.

Considering that the discussion on African fertility transition has been inconclusive, this chapter aims to use the available census data to examine the fertility levels and trends in the region with the aids of indirect estimation techniques. Although many studies have been conducted to establish the levels and trends of fertility in many countries in SSA (Ezeh, et al., 2009; Gaisie, 1995; Garenn, 2008; Gould & Brown, 1996; Kalipeni, 1995; Ortega, 2008; Shapiro & Gebreselassie, 2008), most of them have utilized survey data such as World Fertility Surveys, Demographic and Health Surveys (DHS), and other forms of specialized surveys. Population censuses are the major source of information for the study of population dynamics (ECA/RIPS, 1988; Stats SA, 2010). Population censuses remain the main source of comprehensive data for the computation of vital rates particularly in SSA, where vital registration system has had a very poor performance (Adedini & Odimegwu, 2011). This chapter utilizes census data to provide fertility estimates at national level and according to selected socioeconomic variables, such as place of residence, level of education, and employment status, thereby assessing fertility trends and socioeconomic differentials in selected countries with two census data points.

2 DATA SOURCES AND METHODS

Data for the analyses in this chapter came from the available census data for Kenya (1989 and 1999), Rwanda (1991 and 2002), Senegal (1988 and 2002), and South Africa (1996 and 2001). These data sets were obtained with permission from the Minnesota Population Center (2011), which archived the harmonized census data available on the Integrated Public Use Microdata Series program (IPUMS). A 10 percent randomly chosen sample of the census data was made available for downloads and analytical weights were provided along with data applied where necessary. One of the major shortcomings of census data is comparability of the questions asked. The census data contain a limited number of questions about the socioeconomic characteristics of the respondents. There is information on age, education, rural–urban residence, and employment status.

2.1 Fertility Measures

Total fertility rate is a widely used measure that adjusts for age distribution differentials. It is a synthetic cohort measures representing current situation. It is calculated by summing the age-specific fertility rates for five-year age-groups and multiplying by five. It is interpreted as the mean number of births that a woman would have if she survived all her reproductive years and experienced the age-specific fertility rate schedule prevailing in a given period. Age-specific fertility rates are calculated by dividing the number of births to women in a specific age-group during a specific period by the number of women in that age–group.

2.2 Indirect Measures

In this chapter, three indirect estimating procedures were employed in data analysis. As a result of little experience in census taking coupled with a high illiteracy rate in Africa, most enumeration exercises on the continent have produced data that are of poor quality (ECA/RIPS, 1988). Hence, because of difficulty in obtaining accurate information through the direct questions in many countries on the continent, indirect techniques of inferring fertility estimates from information that is not collected for the purpose of estimating fertility levels are frequently being employed by demographers. The indirect estimating techniques employed in this chapter are: Trussell variant of Brass P/F ratio technique, Arriaga's method, and the Brass Relational Gompertz model.

2.3 Brass P/F Ratio Technique

P/F ratio technique is a fertility estimation technique based on data about children ever born, and it is easy to collect information on the number of children ever born through a simple question, that is, "How many children have you ever borne alive?" (United Nations, 1983). The Trussell-Coale variant of the method is used as it tends to relax the assumption of constancy in fertility trends originally proposed by Brass. The P/F ratio technique basically seeks to adjust the level of reported age-specific fertility rates essentially so it could agree with the level of fertility indicated by the average parities of women in age categories below ages 30 or 35 (United Nations 1983). The rationale behind this is that average parities for these groups of women are assumed to be accurate because they are likely to have fewer recall errors and omissions than older women. Ratios of average number of children ever born (i.e., average parities denoted by P) to the fertility rates (i.e., F) are computed by age-group and then adjusted by the ratios corresponding to the age-groups of the younger women. Average of the ratios obtained for women in the younger age-groups serves as the adjustment factor to generate a set of fertility rates that is considered more reliable than the reported level of fertility. The method is based on the formula:

$$F(i) = \emptyset(i-1) + af(i) + bf(i+1)$$

Where F is the cumulated fertility rates, $\emptyset$ is the cumulated fertility schedule for a period, a and b are constants (United Nations 1983). The Trussell variant of Brass P/F ratio technique available in the Population Analysis Spreadsheet (PAS) is used in this chapter. The data required for the use of

PAS are: age-specific fertility rates (ASFRs) and average number of children ever born per woman by five-year age-groups in the childbearing ages 15–19 to 45–49 (US Census Bureau, 2013).

2.4 Arriaga's Method

The Arriaga technique is another fertility estimating procedure like P/F ratio technique. The original P/F ratio technique assumed constancy in fertility in the past. Conversely, Arriaga method does not assume constancy in fertility rate. The Arriaga technique estimates fertility based on average number of children ever born by five-year age-groups of female population for two censuses or surveys and the pattern of ASFRs for those two periods. The technique is useful not only when information on the average number of children ever born (CEB) is available for two data points but also when information on average CEB is available for three data points.

The technique assumed that parity reports for women age 35 years or younger are of good quality and therefore number of CEB only changes linearly in a situation of declining fertility (Stats SA 2010). The method assumes that changes in fertility will produce linear change in average number of CEB per woman at each single year of age of women between the two census periods. The ASFRs and TFRs based on Arriaga method were obtained using Mortpark software (version 4.1).

2.5 Brass Relational Gompertz Model

The Relational Gompertz method proposed by Brass was designed for the evaluation and adjustment of both distributions derived from reports of births during the last twelve months and or CEB. It represents the cumulative fertility of a population by fitting the Gompertz function to reported data on average number of CEB and ASFRs by age of women (US Census Bureau, 2013).

According to ECA/RIPS (1988), the Gompertz function is of the form:

$$\frac{F(x)}{F} = A(expB^x) \quad \quad (1)$$

Where $F(x)$ is the cumulative fertility by age X and F is the total fertility rate by the end of reproductive life. A and B are constants and range between zero and unity. By taking logarithms of the above function twice, the formula can be reduced to a linear function of age as follows:

$$Y(x) = -\ln\left[-\ln\left(\frac{F(x)}{F}\right)\right] = a + bx \quad \quad (2)$$

In order to obtain a standard value and a better fit of the Gompertz function, an age scale transformation could be performed using the function:

$$Y_{(x)} = a + bY_s(x) \qquad (3)$$

Where a and b are constants that reflect the pattern of fertility of the population being considered. Detailed explanation of the computational procedure on Relational Gompertz model is available elsewhere (ECA/RIPS 1988).

All data analysis was done in this chapter using Stata (version 12.0), Microsoft Excel, Mortpark-Lite (version 4.1), and the PAS provided by the US Census Bureau.

3 RESULTS

3.1 Total Fertility Rate—Country-Level Estimates

Table 6.1 presents the estimates of total fertility rates (TFR) using the three selected indirect estimation techniques. As shown in Table 6.1, all three techniques indicate a decline in TFR in Kenya, Rwanda, and South Africa, while fertility transition seems to have stalled in Senegal. According to Table 6.1 (column 3), results from Arriaga's method indicate a decline in TFR in Kenya from 7.2 in 1989 to 6.8 in 1999; in Rwanda from 7.8 (in 1991) to 6.1 (in 2002); and in South Africa from 3.8 (in 1996) to 3.5 (in 2001). On the contrary, TFR slightly increased in Senegal from 5.4 in 1988 to 5.6 in 2002.

Results from the P/F ratio technique showed a similar pattern. For instance, while TFR declined in Kenya from 7.4 in 1989 to 6.6 in 1999, Rwanda had a decline of 1.6 in TFR over the 1991–2002 period. Similarly, the P/F ratio technique indicates a decline in TFR from 3.6 to 3.3 in South Africa over the five-year intercensal period (1996–2001), while Senegal recorded no decline in TFR over the 1988–2002 period.

Gompertz Relational implied TFR estimates for the selected countries are not so much different from the estimates derived from the Arriaga and P/F ratio techniques. The TFR declined in Kenya from 7.3 to 6.9 over the intercensal period (1989–1999). In Rwanda, there was a decline of 1.9 in TFR (i.e., 24.4 percent decline) over the 1991–2002 period, while South Africa recorded a decline of 0.3 in TFR (i.e., 8 percent decline) over the five-year period 1996–2001. Gompertz Relational implied TFR for Senegal also indicates a stall in fertility decline over the 1988–2002 period.

The recent TFR estimates, according to the Population Reference Bureau (PRB), similarly suggest a stall in fertility levels in Senegal, while the current estimates indicate a substantial decline in fertility levels in Kenya, Rwanda, and South Africa. For instance, 2012 estimates of TFR are 4.4, 4.6, and 2.4 in Kenya, Rwanda, and South Africa, respectively, while TFR was estimated to be 5.0 in 2012 in Senegal (PRB 2012). Similarly, estimates from DHS data of the selected countries indicated a slow or sluggish decline in fertility levels of Senegal compared with other countries over the twenty-five-year period from 1985 to 2009 (Department of Health *et al.*, 2007; Institut National de la Statistique du Rwanda (INSR) & ORC Macro, 2006; Kenya National Bureau of Statistics (KNBS) & ICF Macro, 2010; L'Agence Nationale de la Statistique & ICF International, 2012). For instance, as presented in Table 6.1, the fertility level of Kenya declined by 2.1 from 6.7 in 1989 to 4.6 in 2009, while TFR of Senegal recorded a decline of 1.1 from 6.4 in 1986 to 5.3 in 2005. Fertility estimates of the United Nations Population Department for the selected years, as presented in Table 6.1, also indicated a slow decline in fertility level of Senegal and Rwanda (World Factbook, 2013a, 2013b, 2013c, 2013d).

Table 6.1 Estimates of Total Fertility Rate from Census Data Using Arriaga Method (AM), Brass Relational Gompertz Model (RGM), and Brass P/F Ratio (P/F Ratio) Technique

Country	Year of Census	AM	P/F Ratio	RGM	†UN Estimates Close to the Census Year	2012# Estimate
Kenya	1989	7.2	7.4	7.3	6.7	4.4
	1999	6.8	6.6	6.9	5.4	
Rwanda	1991	7.8	7.4	7.8	6.3	4.6
	2002	6.1	5.8	5.9	5.6	
Senegal	1988	5.4	5.3	5.5	6.4	5.0
	2002	5.6	5.3	5.5	5.4	
South Africa	1996	3.8	3.6	3.9	3.3	2.4
	2001	3.5	3.3	3.6	2.9	

	Total Fertility Rate Estimates from Demographic and Health Survey data					
	1985–1989	1990–1994	1995–1999	2000–2004	2005–2009	2010–2014
Kenya*	6.7	5.4	4.7	4.9	4.6	NA
Rwanda*	NA	6.2	5.8	6.1	5.5	4.6
Senegal**	6.4	6.0	5.7	NA	5.3	5.0
South Africa***	NA	NA	2.9	2.1##	NA	NA

† *Source*: UN Population Department (World Factbook 2013a, 2013b, 2013c, 2013d).
# *Source*: Population Reference Bureau (2012).
Sources: *Kenya National Bureau of Statistics and ICF Macro (2010); **Institut National de la Statistique du Rwanda and ORC Macro (2006); ***L'Agence Nationale de la Statistique and ICF International (2012); ****Department of Health, Medical Research Council, and ORC Macro (2007).
NA = not available, ## estimate was reported to be unreliable.

3.2 Total Fertility Rate by Place of Residence

The TFR estimates by place of residence based on Arriaga method are presented in Figure 6.1. As one would expect, the figure shows that the level of TFR was generally higher in rural areas than in the urban centers in all the selected countries. TFR was estimated to be 7.8 in rural Kenya in 1989 compared with 6.5 in the urban centers. Similarly, TFR was estimated to be 6.0 for rural Kenya in 1999 as against 5.5 in urban Kenya during the same period. For South Africa, the TFR estimates derived for rural areas are 4.6 (1996) and 4.3 (2001) compared with 3.0 (1996) and 2.9 (2001) for the urban parts of South Africa. Information on place of residence was not available for Rwanda in 1991 and Senegal in 1988, but results from census wave 2 for both countries indicate a higher level of TFR for rural parts of Rwanda (7.0 vs. 5.9) and Senegal (5.9 vs. 4.9) compared with the urban parts. In addition, estimates of TFR by place of residence, according to P/F ratio technique and the Relational Gompertz model (figures not shown) yield results comparable to those obtained from the Arriaga method. Results based on P/F ratio technique indicate an estimated TFR of 7.5 for women in rural Kenya in 1989 as against 6.6 for those in urban centers, while the estimated TFR in rural South Africa in 1996 was 4.6 compared with 3.0 in urban centers. Similarly, the estimated TFR for South Africa (using Relational Gompertz model) were higher in rural areas than in urban centers in 1996 (4.8 vs. 3.3) and 2001 (4.5 vs. 3.0).

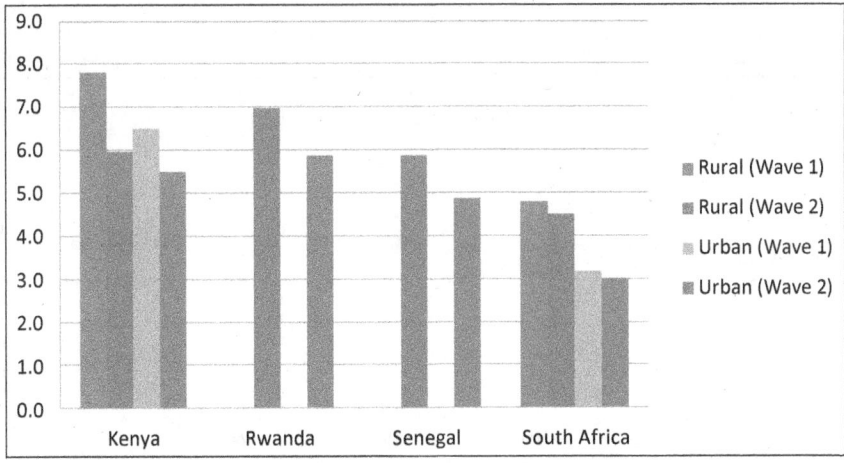

Figure 6.1 Estimates of TFR by place of residence, based on Arriaga Method (using two census waves).

3.3 Total Fertility Rate by Level of Education

Figure 6.2 presents the TFR estimates by respondents' level of education using P/F ration technique. Results from all the three estimating techniques consistently show that higher levels of fertility correspond to lower levels of education. Results based on Arriaga's technique showed that women who had no education had an estimated TFR of 7.7 (in 1989) and 7.2 (in 1999) in Kenya, compared with TFR of 3.5 (in 1989) and 3.6 (in 1999) for their counterparts who had postsecondary education. Also for Rwanda, Senegal, and South Africa, TFR estimates based on Arriaga method indicate a substantial higher level of TFR for women who had no education particularly when compared with women who had secondary or postsecondary education.

The P/F ratio technique and Relational Gompertz method yielded similar patterns of TFR estimates by level of education for all the selected countries. For instance, TFR estimates based on P/F ratio technique indicate that South African women who had no education had a TFR of 4.5 in 1996 and 4.2 in 2001, while their counterparts who had postsecondary education had a TFR of 2.4 over the 1996–2001 period. TFR estimates (using P/F ratio technique) for women who had no education in Senegal were 6.3 in 1988 and 6.2 in 2002, while Senegalese women who had postsecondary education had TFR estimates of 3.0 and 2.7 in 1988 and 2002, respectively. Although information on respondents' level of education was not available in 1991 Rwandan census data, results from the 2002 Rwandan census (using P/F ratio technique) indicate a higher level of TFR for women who had no education compared with women who had postsecondary education (5.8 vs. 3.3).

TFR estimates based on Relational Gompertz method for women who had no education in Kenya were 7.8 in 1989 and 7.2 in 1999, while their

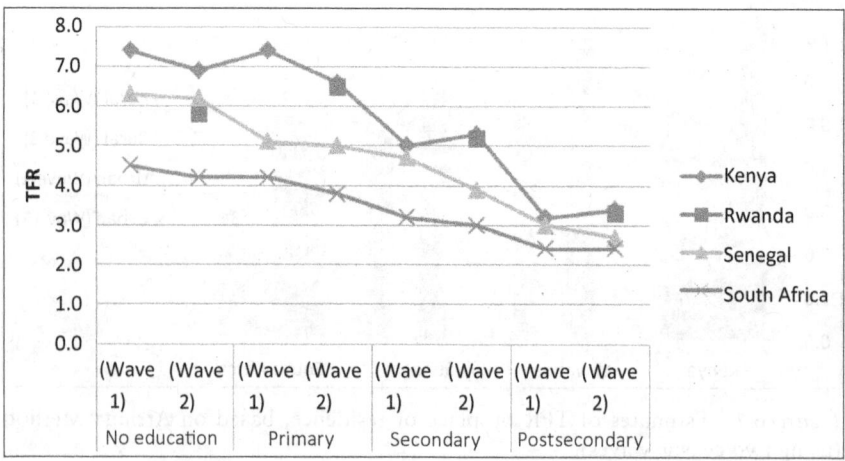

Figure 6.2 Estimates of TFR by educational attainment, based on Brass P/F ratio technique (using two census waves).

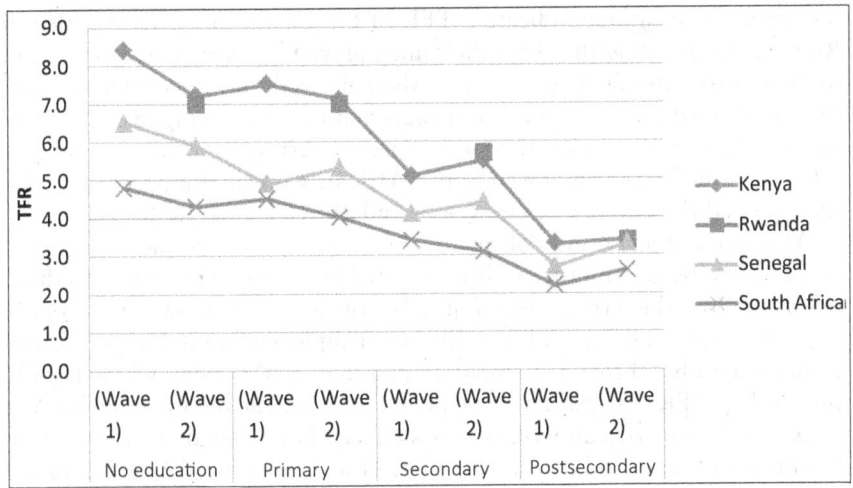

Figure 6.3 Gompertz Relational implied TFR by educational attainment (using two census waves).

counterparts who had postsecondary education had an estimated TFR of 3.3 and 3.4 in 1989 and 1999, respectively. In the same vein, estimated TFRs (based on Relational Gompertz method) for women who had no education in Senegal were 6.5 in 1988 and 5.9 in 2002, while Senegalese women who had postsecondary education had an estimated TFR of 3.3 in 1988 and 2.7 in 2001. Results from South Africa, using Relational Gompertz method, indicate that estimated TFR for South African women who had no education was 4.8 in 1996 and 4.3 in 2001, compared with 2.6 (in both 1996 and 2001) for their counterparts who had postsecondary education.

3.4 Total Fertility Rate by Employment Status

Figures 6.4 and 6.5 present the estimated TFR by respondents' employment status. Using all three techniques, estimates of TFR by employment status were found to be higher for employed women than for the unemployed in Kenya and Rwanda (and for Senegal in 2002), while the fertility level of unemployed women was higher than that of the employed women in South Africa.

Using Arriaga's method, TFR for the employed women in Kenya was 7.5 in 1989, and it was 7.2 for their unemployed counterparts. Results from the Kenyan 1999 census, based on all the estimating techniques, indicate that the gap between the fertility level of the employed and unemployed women had reduced in Kenya over the 1989–1999 intercensal period. For instance, fertility estimates from Arriaga's method indicate a TFR of 6.5 for unemployed Kenyan women compared with 6.4 for their employed counterparts. For Rwanda, all three techniques consistently showed a higher level of fertility for the employed women than for the unemployed. Estimates based on Arriaga's technique indicate a TFR of 8.0 for the employed women in Rwanda compared with 7.2 for their unemployed counterparts. For Senegal in 1988, estimates from Arriaga's method showed that the estimated TFR for the employed women was lower than that of their unemployed counterparts (4.4 vs. 5.4). Similarly, results based on Arriaga's technique indicate a lower TFR for the employed South African women compared with the unemployed in both 1996 (3.4 vs. 4.0) and 2001 (3.2 vs. 3.6).

As noted earlier, results of fertility estimation by respondents' employment status (based on other techniques) yield patterns comparable to those obtained from the Arriaga technique. For instance, estimates based on P/F ratio technique indicate a TFR of 3.8 for unemployed South African women compared with 3.3 for their employed counterparts in 1996, while in 2001 the level of TFR was estimated to be 3.4 and 3.0 for the unemployed and employed South African women, respectively. For Senegal, estimates from P/F ratio technique indicate a TFR of 4.3 for the employed and 5.2 for the unemployed. Conversely and as noted previously, results from P/F ratio technique indicate a higher level of TFR in Kenya for the employed than for the unemployed in 1989 (7.3 vs. 6.9), while the fertility gap between the two groups had reduced in 1999 (6.0 vs. 6.2).

For South Africa in 1996, results based on Relational Gompertz technique indicate a TFR of 3.4 and 4.3, respectively, for the employed and the unemployed and 3.2 and 3.9, respectively, for the employed and the unemployed (in 2001). For Senegal, Gompertz Relational implied TFR was higher for the unemployed than for the employed in 1988 (5.4 vs. 4.5) but slightly lower for the unemployed than for the employed in 2002 (5.5 vs. 5.8).

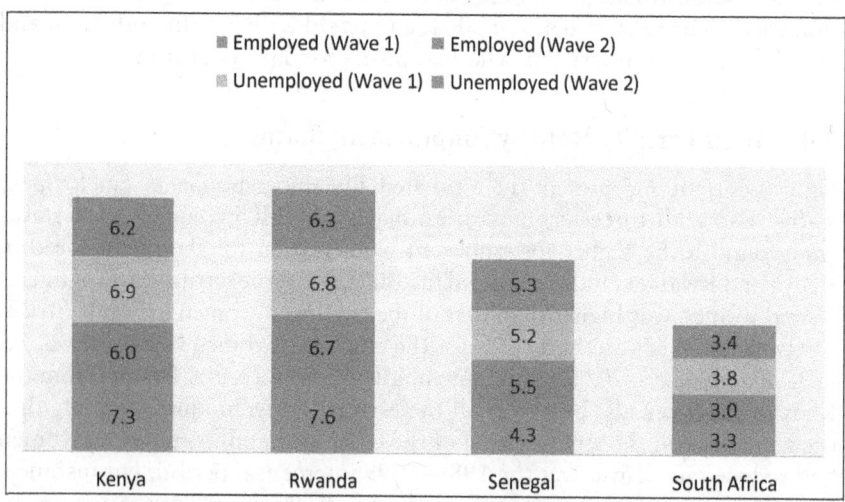

Figure 6.4 Estimates of TFR by employment status, based on Brass P/F ratio technique (using 2 census waves).

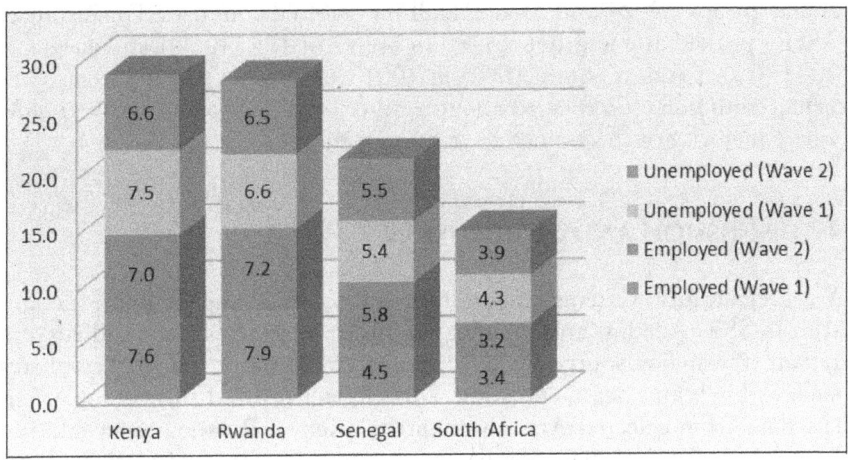

Figure 6.5 Gompertz Relational implied TFR by employment status (using two census waves).

3.5 Patterns of Age-Specific Fertility Rates (ASFRs)

The estimated ASFRs for the selected countries are computed using only Arriaga's and P/F ratio techniques. Relational Gompertz technique was not used to obtain ASFR estimates because the technique is only useful for the estimation of TFR by fitting the Gompertz function to the reported ASFRs and average number of CEB.

The ASFR estimates suggest a slightly similar pattern across the selected countries. The shapes of ASFRs obtained from Arriaga's method imply a mixture of early childbearing and late childbearing in Kenya in 1989 with women aged 20–24 (0.34) and women aged 35–39 (0.37) having the highest level of ASFRs. The pattern of ASFRs somewhat changed in Kenya in 1999 with the ASFRs peaking at age categories 25–29 (0.28) and 30–34 (0.29). This same pattern was observed for Rwanda (in 1991 and 2002) and South Africa (in 1996 and 2001). ASFR peaked at age-group 30–34 in 1991 (0.36) and 2002 (0.28) in Rwanda, while in South Africa it peaked at 25–29 (0.17) in 1996 and 25–34 (0.15) in 2001. However, while the results from the 2002 census data for Senegal followed the expected pattern, the observed patterns of ASFRs from Senegal's 1988 census data seemed to be different from those observed in other countries. The results from Senegal's 1988 data suggest a pattern of high childbearing at early age with ASFR peaking at age-group 15–19. This may be a result of data quality as the pattern seems to deviate from the expected pattern.

The observed patterns of ASFRs obtained from the application of Brass P/F ratio technique were slightly different from those obtained from Arriaga's method. ASFRs based on P/F ratio technique generally peaked at age-groups 20–24 and 25–29 in all the selected countries. For instance, ASFRs peaked at age-group 25–29 in Kenya in 1999 (0.34), in Senegal in 2002 (0.24), and in South Africa in 2001 (0.15). This pattern seems consistent with what is expected about fertility behaviors particularly in SSA, where majority of the women have no education.

4 DISCUSSION AND CONCLUSION

Vital registration systems remain inaccurate and incomplete in most countries in SSA (Adedini and Odimegwu 2011); hence, censuses and surveys remain the major source of data for the computation of vital estimates such as birth and death statistics. This chapter utilized the available census data from selected African countries (Kenya, Rwanda, Senegal, and South Africa) to estimate fertility levels based on three estimating procedures: Arriaga's method, Trussell variant of Brass P/F ratio technique, and the Relational Gompertz model. The main objective of this chapter was to examine the fertility levels and trends in these countries and to examine fertility differentials by selected characteristics.

Results based on all three estimation procedures indicate fertility transition in Kenya, Rwanda, and South Africa during the periods under study, while a stall in fertility decline was observed in Senegal. While the results based on Arriaga's method indicate a substantial decline in TFR in Kenya, Rwanda, and South Africa, a very insignificant decline was observed in Senegal over the period under study. Similarly, while results based on P/F ratio technique and Relational Gompertz model indicate a decline in the estimated TFR during the period between the two census waves in Kenya, Rwanda, and South Africa, Senegal recorded no decline in TFR over the 1988–2002 period.

The patterns of fertility trends established in this chapter seemed to be consistent with the recent evidence on fertility transition in SSA. According to the PRB (2012), a good number of countries in East Africa, such as Kenya and Rwanda, and those in Southern Africa, such as South Africa, have experienced substantial fertility decline in the last two decades. Fertility levels in South Africa are approaching the replacement level of 2.1 children per woman (Stats SA, 2010). The Southern African region is reputed to be the region with the lowest fertility levels in the SSA (Moultrie, et al., 2008). On the contrary, many countries in the Central and West African subregions, including Senegal, still have a TFR level of five children per woman or higher (Population Reference Bureau, 2012).

In most of the countries in SSA, including those considered in this chapter, national estimates of total fertility rates tend to mask the variations in fertility level by subpopulation groups. One of the objectives of this chapter was to examine fertility levels and trends by subpopulation groups. This chapter showed that the fertility level was generally higher in the rural areas than in the urban areas in all the selected countries. Although results from the analysis of Kenyan data, for instance, suggest a 23 percent decline in TFR levels of rural Kenya during the 1989–1999 period, findings revealed that the fertility levels of rural areas in Kenya and other selected countries are responsible for the high TFR at the national level.

Further, it is shown that the level of fertility tends to consistently reduce with increased levels of education. Results from all three estimation procedures indicate that as the level of education increases, the level of fertility reduces. In all the selected countries, the estimated TFR of women who had no education was more than double the TFR of women who had postsecondary education.

Comparing the fertility levels of women who had no education and women who had primary education, our findings suggest a similar level or pattern, thereby suggesting no difference between the fertility level of women who had no education and women who had primary education. Results from these analyses revealed that a substantial proportion of women must have at least secondary education if a significant decline is to be achieved in fertility levels in SSA. It is remarkable to note that the results from the census wave 2 of all the countries included in this chapter showed that the fertility level of women who had postsecondary education is approaching the fertility replacement level. This shows that education is a key driver of fertility levels of the selected countries. As observed by Bongaarts (2003), educational attainment is a key determinant of fertility level, and low levels of education can significantly lead to stalling in fertility transition.

Findings on the level of TFR by employment status did not yield a similar pattern in all the selected countries. The fertility patterns by employment status as observed in Kenya and Senegal could be regarded as inconsistent. For instance, while the fertility level was higher for the employed than for the unemployed in 1989, the opposite was the case in 1999. Our analyses indicate that the fertility level was consistently higher for the employed women in Rwanda than for the unemployed. Conversely, findings indicate a consistently lower level of fertility for the employed women in South Africa compared with the unemployed. This follows the patterns observed in most countries that are in an advanced stage of socioeconomic development where a negative relationship is established between women's employment status and fertility levels (Kalwij, 2003; Li et al., 1997; Shuzhuo et al., 1997).

In addition, although the observed pattern of ASFRs suggests a scenario of early childbearing in most of the selected countries, it is worth noting that the pattern of ASFRs observed in this study suggests an increase in the median age at childbearing. ASFRs mostly peaked at age-group 25–29 in most of the selected countries.

In conclusion, while fertility levels are fast approaching the replacement level of 2.1 in South Africa, the findings of this study indicate a high level of fertility in other countries in SSA, although fertility transition is under way in some of the countries. This study also suggests that any government policies and programs that would bring about substantial reduction in fertility levels in the SSA region must include strategies that will ensure women have up to secondary or higher education.

4.1 Study Limitations

It is important to bear some limitations in mind when interpreting the findings in this chapter. First, most census data in Africa are of poor quality as a result of limitations attributable to undercount (and overcount in some cases), as well as recall errors. However, this should not affect the results in this chapter as the methods employed in these analyses mostly adjust for possible omissions and recall errors. Second, census data for most recent times were not available because censuses are not regularly conducted in SSA. Third, information on place of residence was not available for Rwanda in 1991 and Senegal in 1988; hence, estimates of TFR by place of residence could not be done for those periods in Rwanda and Senegal. In addition, information on respondents' level of education was not available for Rwanda in 1991. As a result, fertility estimation by level of education was not done for Rwanda in 1991.

ACKNOWLEDGMENTS

The author would like to gratefully acknowledge the Minnesota Population Center for permission to access IPUMS–International database, and all the reviewers whose comments contributed to refining the quality of this chapter.

REFERENCES

Adedini, Sunday A., & Odimegwu, Clifford O. (2011). Assessing knowledge, attitude and practice of vital system in south-west Nigeria. *Ife PsychologIA, 19*(1), 456–471.
Bongaarts, John. (2003). Completing the Fertility Transition in the Developing World: The Role of Educational Differences and Fertility Preferences. *Population Studies, 57*(3), 321–335. doi: 10.2307/3595729
Bongaarts, John. (2008). Fertility transitions in developing countries: progress or stagnation? Working paper no 7: Population Council.
Bongaarts, John. (2009). Human population growth and the demographic transition. *Philosophical Transactions of the Royal Society B: Biological Sciences, 364*(1532), 2985–2990. doi: 10.1098/rstb.2009.0137
Department of Health, Medical Research Council, & Orc Macro. (2007). South Africa Demographic and Health Survey 2003. Pretoria: Department of Health.
ECA/RIPS. (1988). *Demographic Data Evaluation and Analysis*. Ghana: United Nations Economic Commission for Africa & Regional Institute for Population Studies.
El-Ghannam, Ashraf Ragab. (2005). An examination of factors affecting fertility rate differentials as compared among women in less and more developed countries. *Journal of Human Ecology, 18*(3), 181–192.

Ezeh, Alex C., Mberu, Blessing U., & Emina, Jacques O. (2009). Stall in fertility decline in Eastern African countries: regional analysis of patterns, determinants and implications. *Philosophical Transactions of the Royal Society B: Biological Sciences, 364*(1532), 2991–3007. doi: 10.1098/rstb.2009.0166

Gaisie, S. Kwesi. (1995). Fertility transition in Bostwana: An African perspective. *Southern African Journal of Demography, 5*(1), 35–47.

Garenn, Michel. (2008). Situations of fertility stall in sub-Saharan Africa. *African Population Studies, 23*(2). doi: http://dx.doi.org/10.11564/23-2-319

Gould, W. T., & Brown, M. S. (1996). A fertility transition in Sub-Saharan Africa? *Int J Popul Geogr, 2*(1), 1–22. doi: 10.1002/(sici)1099-1220(199603)2:1 <1::aid-ijpg23>3.0.co;2-#

Institut National de la Statistique du Rwanda (INSR), & ORC Macro. (2006). Rwanda Demographic and Health Survey 2005. Calverton, Maryland, U.S.A.: INSR and ORC Macro.

Kalipeni, Ezekiel. (1995). The Fertility Transition in Africa. *Geographical Review, 85*(3), 286–300. doi: 10.2307/215274

Kalwij, Adriaan S. (2003). The Effects of Female Employment Status on The Presence and Number of Children. In Klaus F. Zimmermann & Michael Vogler (Eds.), *Family, Household And Work* (pp. 369–387): Springer Berlin Heidelberg.

Kenya National Bureau of Statistics (KNBS), & ICF Macro. (2010). Kenya Demographic and Health Survey 2008–09. Calverton, Maryland: KNBS and ICF Macro.

Kocourková, J., & Fait, T. (2011). Changes in contraceptive practice and the transition of reproduction pattern in the Czech population. *The European Journal of Contraception and Reproductive Health Care, 16*(3), 161–172.

L'Agence Nationale de la Statistique, & ICF International. (2012). Senegal 2010–11 Demographic and Health and Multiple Indicators Survey: Key Findings. Calverton, Maryland, USA: ANSD and ICF International.

Li, S., Feldman, M.W., Zhu, C., Population, Morrison Institute for, & Studies, Resource. (1997). *The Relationship Between Women's Employment Status and Fertility Behavior in Rural China: A Comparison in Three Counties*. Stanford: Morrison Institute for Population and Resource Studies.

Minnesota Population Centre. (2011). Integrated Public Use Microdata Series International: Version 6.1 [Machine-readable database], Minneapolis: University of Minnesota, 2011.

Moultrie, T. A., Hosegood, V., McGrath, N., Hill, C., Herbst, K., & Newell, M. L. (2008). Refining the criteria for stalled fertility declines: an application to rural KwaZulu-Natal, South Africa, 1990–2005. *Studies in Family Planning, 39*(1), 39–48.

Odimegwu, Clifford, & Adedini, Sunday. (2013). *Gender Equity, Fertility Intention and Transition in Sub-Saharan Africa (Forthcoming in Gender and Behaviour Journal)*.

Ortega, Jose Antonio. (2008). The fertility transition in sub-Saharan Africa: early transition rise and (slow) decline. Population Division/DESA UN. New York.

Population Reference Bureau. (2012). Total Fertiltiy Rates Estimates Retrieved 11 March, 2012, from www.prb.org

Poston, Dudley L., Jr. (2000). Social and Economic Development and the Fertility Transitions in Mainland China and Taiwan. *Population and Development Review, 26*(ArticleType: research-article / Issue Title: Supplement: Population and Economic Change in East Asia / Full publication date: 2000 / Copyright © 2000 Population Council), 40–60. doi: 10.2307/3115211

Sacci, Inna, Mkrtchyan, Zaruhi, Dolyan, Nune, & Armistad, Amy. (2008). Availability and affordability of contraceptive commodities in pharmacies and primary healthcare facilities in Armenia: Descriptive study report (pp. 1–35). Washington DC: USAID.

Schoumaker, Bruno. (2009). *Stalls in fertility transitions in sub-Saharan Africa: real or spurious?* Paper presented at the IUSSP Seminar on "Human Fertility in Africa, Trends in the Last Decade and Prospects for Change", Cape Coast, Ghana, from 16–18 September 2008.

Shapiro, David, & Gebreselassie, Tesayi. (2008). Fertility Transition in sub-Saharan Africa: Falling and Stalling. *African Population Studies, 22*(2). doi: http://dx.doi.org/10.11564/23-1-310

Shuzhuo, Li, Feldman, Marcus W., & Chuzhu, Zhu. (1997). The relationship between women's employment status and fertiltiy behaviou in rural china: a comparison in three counties. Report no 0058.

Sneeringer, Stacy E. (2009). Fertility transition in sub-Saharan Africa: a comparative analysis of cohort trends in 30 countries. DHS Comparative reports 23.

Stats SA. (2010). Estimation of fertiltiy from the 2007 Community Survey of South Africa. Pretoria: Statistics South Africa.

Strulik, Holger, & Vollmer, Sebastian. (2010). The Fertility Transition Around the World -1950–2005. PGDA Working Paper No. 57.

Tien, H. Yuan. (1984). Induced fertility transition: Impact of population planning and socio-economic change in the people's Republic of China. *Population Studies, 38*(3), 385–400. doi: 10.1080/00324728.1984.10410299

United Nations. (1983). Manual X: Indirect estimation techniques for demographic estimation. New York: Department of International Economic and Social Affairs.

US Census Bureau. (2013). Population Analysis Spreadsheet. Retrieved January 11, 2013, from https://www.census.gov

World Factbook. (2013a). Demographics of Kenya Retrieved January 11, 2013, from http://www.princeton.edu/~achaney/tmve/wiki100k/docs/Demographics_of_Kenya.html

World Factbook. (2013b). Demographics of Rwanda Retrieved January 11, 2013, from http://www.princeton.edu/~achaney/tmve/wiki100k/docs/Demographics_of_Rwanda.html

World Factbook. (2013c). Demographics of Senegal Retrieved January 11, 2013, from http://www.princeton.edu/~achaney/tmve/wiki100k/docs/Demographics_of_Senegal.html

World Factbook. (2013d). Demographics of South Africa Retrieved January 11, 2013, from http://www.princeton.edu/~achaney/tmve/wiki100k/docs/Demographics_of_South_Africa.html

7 Nuptiality Patterns and Differentials in Sub-Saharan Africa
Analysis of African Census Data

Gideon Rutaremwa

1 INTRODUCTION

Africa suffers from a registration system with incomplete vital statistics. As a result, censuses and surveys become primary sources of demographic information. The collection of information on marital status in Africa has been a feature of nearly all postcolonial censuses and surveys undertaken on the continent with the exception of South Africa, where the collection of marital information at the national level took place only after 1994. The recent surveys and censuses in Africa collect information on individual characteristics, fertility, employment, migration, mortality, and household characteristics. These African censuses also provide information on nuptiality, now readily available to researchers through IPUMS–International. Inquiry into nuptiality in the African censuses permits an estimation of patterns at the national and regional levels within countries, given that some of these data are based on samples.

Despite the regular collection of demographic data in Africa using censuses, mainly since the 1990s, little has been done in studying nuptiality patterns at the continental level. Perhaps this is because most African census data include only a simple question on the marital status of the respondent (Van de Walle 1968). Therefore, the study of nuptiality has been dominated by the period approach (Antoine 2006), such that most nuptiality research has focused on fertility, mortality, and, to a lesser extent, migration. There is a lack of nuptiality-related research, which is undoubtedly ascribed to the tendency among researchers to use marital status as a determinant of other demographic outcomes such as fertility (Palamuleni and Palamuleni 2011) and, to a lesser extent, mortality. Examples of studies using marital status as determinant of fertility include Bongaarts and Jones (1982), Pebley and Rutenburg (1986), Isiugo-Abanihe, Ebigbola, and Adewuyi (1993), Isiugo-Abanihe (1994), Harwood-Lejeune (2001), and Udjo (2001), among others. Dodoo (1998), relates marriage to reproductive decision making. Goldman (1993) provides an example of a study associating marriage with mortality. In his finding, he highlights the importance of prospective data for assessing the relative importance of selection and causal factors in accounting for the excess mortality of the unmarried. The inclination to study marital behavior in relation to other phenomenon has diminished the importance of nuptiality as an independent area of research. As a consequence, some interesting nuptiality patterns are not explored, such as the finding by Udjo (2001) that late marriage is not a phenomenon peculiar to developed countries.

A number of studies have taken on an anthropological approach to analyzing nuptiality patterns in Africa (Bledsoe and Pison 1994; Bledsoe 1990). As indicated earlier, equally in such studies nuptiality has been related to fertility and reproduction. For example, Bledsoe (1990) posits that among populations that value high fertility, marital practices often play important roles in regulating fertility. Harwood-Lejeune (2001), in a quantitative study, emphasizes the latter issue using DHS data sets for a number of countries in Southern and Eastern Africa. The key finding in the latter study was that the increases in age at marriage in the two regions of Africa accounted for between one-sixth and one-third of the fertility decline. Bledsoe's article interpreted ethnographic and demographic data to examine changes in contemporary African marriage. The study shows that female education exacerbates inequities between *de facto* polygynous women who previously would have lived together, shared household resources, and acknowledged each other as co-wives. These new forms of polygyny, however, hold an important key to explaining why polygyny and high fertility still proliferate.

Walker (2012) describes the sub-Saharan region as an area with the highest rates of early marriage in the world. The latter work also points to the harmful effects of early marriage in terms of impact on the health, education, and economic well-being of young girls (Aryee 1997). Indeed, many women in the developing world are subject to marriage at an early age (Van de Walle and Meekers, 1994). Most such women have little choice in the age at which they marry or whom they marry (Jensen and Thornton 2003). Increases in age at marriage are associated with major social-structural changes, such as increases in educational attainment, urbanization, and the emergence of new roles for single women (United Nations 1987, 1988; Lesthaeghe, Kaufmann, and Meekers 1989; Kaufman and Meekers 1998). Hertrich and Lesclingand (2012) argue that the weakening of family control over marriage and a greater involvement of young people in the choice of spouse could have also triggered this transition in nuptiality leading to increased age at marriage.

The nature of the association between education and timing of marriage has not been exhaustively investigated in Africa, particularly the relative effects of education across generations of women in light of increasing educational and career opportunities for young women. These changes have resulted in, among other things, increased participation of women in the modern economy and in salaried employment in the public sector, which has profound implications for their traditional roles as mothers and wives. Consequently, it is possible that the relation between education and marriage has also been changing over time in Africa. This chapter therefore seeks to examine, among other issues, the relative effect of education on the woman's likelihood of getting married. School attendance removes girls from the domestic environment and offers literacy and exposure to new ideas and value systems that may compete with the traditional customs, values, and beliefs that promote early marriage (Caldwell 2000, Westoff 1992; Caldwell, Reddy, and Caldwell 1983). For example, Westoff (1992) has demonstrated with the data from the recent DHS from sub-Saharan Africa (SSA) that higher education delays marriage and postpones childbearing among women in the region.

The type of place of residence may be equally important, as rural areas are generally associated with early marriage. People living in urban areas are exposed to a more diverse lifestyle and subject to weaker social control than those in rural areas. Rural areas tend to have institutional and normative structures, such as the kinship and extended family, that promote early marriage and childbearing (Goode 1963; Dixon 1971; United Nations 1988, 1990). These social structures and networks are less potent and individual responsibility in the matters of marriage is emphasized in urban areas. People in urban areas need to develop skills, gain resources, and achieve maturity to manage an independent household; thus they have to delay marriage. Furthermore, urban women tend to be more educated and engaged in salaried employment than their rural counterparts. This study will also examine the effect of religion on the age at marriage. The main denominations are Christian and Muslim. Theoretically, religious norms and beliefs affect one's orientation toward marriage and childbearing, among other things; therefore, religion is bound to affect a woman's marriage aspirations.

The purpose of this chapter, therefore, is to contribute to the understanding of nuptiality patterns on the African continent. An attempt is made to describe the patterns of marital behavior in Africa using census data. First, we examine changes in the composition of the marriageable population. Second, and specific to the married, where possible we present an overview of marriage in terms of its type, timing, and prevalence using the singulate mean age at marriage. Third, we examine the association between current marital status and a number of other covariates using a logistic regression, but this step is conducted for only two countries, Tanzania and Uganda.

2 DATA AND METHODOLOGY

All data used in this chapter are drawn from the 1990 and 2000 rounds of censuses of Africa archived by IPUMS–International (Minnesota Population Center 2011). In all the censuses, marital information was gathered by asking the respondents (or their proxies) about their current marital status. Among the married, extra information on the age at which they got married for the first time is available for some of the countries. The biggest limitation with the census micro-data is that they do not provide comprehensive information about marital behavior in Africa. For instance, with regard to the timing of marriage, the data are limited to analysis of a first marriage, thus denying researchers an opportunity to study remarriage patterns in Africa.

The measure of the timing of family formation used in this analysis is Singulate Mean Age at Marriage (SMAM). The SMAM is the average length of single life expressed in years among those who marry before age 50. This is perhaps the most commonly used measure of the mean age at which people marry for the first time (Smith, D.P. 1980; McCarthy 1982; Pebley and Rutenburg 1986), and it measures the prevalence of marriage by the percentage of men and women ever married at age 50. The SMAM is calculated from the proportions single by age as indicated in the following five steps:

Step 1. Calculation of the person-years lived in a single state, denoted by A:

$$A = 15 + \sum_{a=15-19}^{45-49} S_a * 5$$

where S_a is the proportion single in age-group a.

Step 2. Estimation of the proportion remaining single at age 50, denoted by B:

$$B = (S_{45-49} + S_{50-54})/2$$

If the proportion single in age-group 50–54, S_{50-54}, is not available, then

$$B = S_{45-49}$$

Step 3. Estimation of the proportion ever marrying by age 50, denoted by C:

$$C = 1 - B$$

Step 4. Calculation of the number of person-years lived by the proportion not marrying, denoted by D:

$$D = 50 * B$$

Step 5. Calculation of SMAM:

$$SMAM = (A-D)/C$$

We use simple frequency tables to examine the prevalence of unions and marriages across selected African countries.

At the second level of analysis, a multinomial logistic regression model is fitted to data for two countries, Uganda and Tanzania. Only members of the population aged 15 to 54 are considered in these analyses using the multinomial logistic regressions. Overall, four equations were estimated, one for each of the two census data sets of the two countries. The multinomial logistic regression is used to model nominal outcome variables. Current marital status had three categories, namely: 1 = never married, 2 = currently married, and 3 = previously married. In these regression equations, the log-odds of the outcome variable (marital status) were modeled as a linear combination of the predictor variables: residence, sex, religion, employment status, and educational level attainment. The model fitted to the data in order to explore the association between a set of independent variables explaining the likelihood of one being in the married category as opposed to being in all other categories. The form of the equation fitted to the data is as follows:

$$\ln \frac{P(Y_i = m)}{P(Y_i = 1)} = \alpha + \sum_{k=1}^{K} \beta_{xm} X_{ik} = z_{mi}$$

For a dependent variable that has three categories, this is represented by m in the equation above, and this requires the calculations for $m-1$ equations, one for each category relative to the reference category to describe the relationship between current marital status and the independent variables. For group 2 of the dependent variable (currently married), for example, the following equation derived from the latter is then estimated:

$$P(Y_i = m) = \frac{\exp(Z_{mi})}{1 + \sum_{h=2}^{M} \exp(Z_{hi})}$$

When using the multinomial logistic regression, one category of the dependent variable (never married) was chosen as the comparison category. Separate risk ratios are determined for all independent variables for each category of the dependent variable, except the comparison category, which is omitted from the analysis. The model parameter estimates and the attendant relative risk ratios for the multinomial logit model is that for a unit change in the predictor variable, the logit of outcome m relative to the reference group is expected to change by its respective parameter estimate, given fact that variables in the model are held constant.

3 RESULTS

Table 7.1 presents the distribution of the male and female population aged 15–54 in the respective censuses. The findings show certain features that characterize the marriage patterns on the continent. First, the proportion married is highest among the female relative to the male population. For example, in Guinea in 1983, the percentage of males ever married was 52.6 percent compared with 85.0 percent among the female population. This latter pattern was reflected in all the countries studied. In general, the countries that had the highest proportion married among females at their earlier census were Guinea, Mali, Uganda, and Senegal.

The least proportion married among females was recorded for South Africa. Among the males, the highest proportion ever married was recorded for Uganda; this appears to have held steady at about 60 percent over the intercensal period 1991 through 2002. Otherwise there was not much variation in the proportion of married males in other countries covered by the study. However, it is worthy to note that even among the males, South Africa had the smallest proportion of males in the married category. Table 7.1 also shows that all the countries studied exhibited some reduction in the proportion of females married at the second census, except for Guinea, whose proportion of females married increased from 85 percent in 1983 to 87 percent in 1996.

Table 7.1 Percentage Distribution of Population Aged 15–54 Years Ever Married by Country and Year of Census

Country/ Year of Census	Male			Female		
	Single/ Never Married	Ever Married	Total (N)	Single/ Never Married	Ever Married	Total (N)
Guinea 1983	47.3	52.7	101,393	15.0	85.0	121,297
Guinea 1996	47.1	52.9	143,332	13.1	86.9	169,399
Mali 1987	47.0	53.0	163,981	16.2	83.8	189,202
Mali 1998	49.5	50.5	214,185	22.5	77.5	238,577
Senegal 1988	52.0	48.0	150,818	22.3	77.7	167,770
Senegal 2002	53.3	46.7	240,022	29.9	70.1	258,464
South Africa 1996	56.9	43.1	916,521	51.2	48.8	1,013,306
South Africa 2007	62.1	37.9	258,216	56.6	43.4	287,769
Kenya 1989	49.0	51.0	235,470	31.9	68.1	247,565
Kenya 1999	48.7	51.3	342,542	33.4	66.6	362,871
Rwanda 1991	46.3	53.7	156,718	31.5	68.5	166,293
Rwanda 2002	49.4	50.6	184,203	38.4	61.6	208,182
Uganda 1991	41.4	58.6	344,325	21.6	78.4	373,310
Uganda 2002	39.7	60.3	563,056	25.5	74.5	576,733
Tanzania 1988	45.5	54.5	504,261	25.6	74.4	571,135
Tanzania 2002	44.7	55.3	858,465	28.0	72.0	960,636

3.1 Singulate Mean Age at Marriage (SMAM)

Table 7.2 presents results of the estimates of the SMAM for selected African countries. As noted earlier, SMAM is the most commonly used measure of the timing and pattern of marriage derived from censuses and surveys. According to Table 7.2, there are wide variations in SMAM estimates of the countries studied. Generally, the SMAM estimates show high values among males compared with females, with wide margins reflected in some country data sets. The highest SMAM values were estimated for South Africa at 31.1 years among the males in 1996, increasing to 32.7 years in 2007. The corresponding estimates for females were 29.7 years in 1996 and 31.4 years in 2007.

Table 7.2 shows that the lowest estimates were registered for Mozambique, where SMAM values were 22.7 years in 1997, increasing to 23.1 years in 2007 among the males. The corresponding estimates of SMAM for females were 18.3 years and 18.8 years in the 1997 and 2007 censuses, respectively. Another country with low SMAM estimates among females was Guinea.

Table 7.2 Singulate Mean Age at First Marriage by Residence and Sex of Individual

Country	Year of Census	Sex	
		Male	Female
Guinea	1983	28.6	18.4
	1996	26.9	17.3
Mali	1987	27.5	18.2
	1998	28.0	19.8
Senegal	1988	28.5	19.6
	2002	29.0	21.9
South Africa	1996	31.1	29.7
	2007	31.7	31.4
Mozambique	1997	22.7	18.3
	2007	23.1	18.8
Kenya	1989	26.4	21.3
	1999	26.6	22.5
Uganda	1991	24.8	19.3
	2002	24.2	20.1
Rwanda	1991	25.8	21.8
	2002	25.3	22.7
Tanzania	1988	26.2	21.8
	2002	26.4	22.7

Overall, the findings presented in Table 7.2 show that with the exception of South Africa, SMAM estimates for all the countries studied were very low for females and were all below twenty-three years. A look at the regional clustering of the countries under study suggests that SMAM estimates for males are lowest in Eastern Africa and are much higher for the West African countries studied. In addition, there were very wide differences between male and female SMAM estimates obtained for the three West African countries, as high as a ten-year difference in Guinea in 1983. The smallest male/female margin in SMAM estimates was recorded for South Africa at both the 1996 and 2007 censuses. It is also worth noting that the SMAM estimates increased at the later census for nearly all the countries, implying that age at marriage is increasing among the populations of all countries studied.

3.2 Logistic Regression Analysis

Table 7.3 presents results of the multinomial logistic regression predicting the odds of being in the currently married and previously married statuses, respectively, as opposed to being single for Uganda in 1991. According to Table 7.3, the results show that an increase of one year in the age of individuals aged 15–54 increased the odds of being currently married by a factor of 1.2 times. In addition, the odds of an individual being previously married increased by nearly 1.3 times for an additional increase in their age of one year. Similarly, being either married or previously married as opposed to being single significantly varied with sex of the individual. In Uganda in 1991, the odds of a female being married as opposed to being single were close to five times higher among females compared with males, while at the same time the odds of being previously married were ten times higher among females compared with their male counterparts. The rural–urban classification was equally a significant factor explaining the variations in the odds of either being married or previously married as opposed to being in the single category. The findings presented in Table 7.3 suggest that for 1991 in Uganda, the odds of being currently married were significantly lower in urban areas compared with the rural areas (RRR = 0.835; p = 0.000). On the contrary, the odds of being previously married were higher (RRR = 1.129) among those in rural areas compared with those who lived in the urban areas.

Another variable examined in the analysis (Table 7.3) was the employment status of the individual. The study's findings show that all the coefficients corresponding to the categories of this variable were significant in the regression models. Compared with those who were in the "other" category, those who were employed, unemployed, inactive, or whose employment status was unknown were less likely to be currently married and invariably were less likely to have been previously married. A further look at the relative risk of being in the currently married category shows that the smallest odds of being in the currently married category were among the unemployed compared with those in the "other" category.

Table 7.3 Multinomial Logistic Regression Model Predicting the Odds of Being Currently and Previously Married in Uganda 1991 and 2002

	1991 Census		2002 Census	
	Currently Married	Previously Married	Currently Married	Previously Married
Variable/Category	Relative Risk Ratio(RRR)	Significance	Relative Risk Ratio (RRR)	Significance
Age (continuous)	***1.210	***1.278	***1.250	***1.318
Residence				
Rural (RC)	1.000	1.000	1.000	1.000
Urban	***0.835	***1.129	***0.636	***0.881
Sex				
Male (RC)	1.000	1.000	1.000	1.000
Female	***4.576	***9.776	***3.386	***10.124
Religion				
Muslim (RC)	1.000	1.000	1.000	1.000
Christian	***0.624	***0.644	***0.730	***0.735
Other	***0.472	***0.408	***0.549	***0.279
None/Not known	–	–	***0.367	***0.250
Employment Status				
Employed (RC)	1.000	1.000	1.000	1.000
Unemployed	***0.198	***0.657	***0.444	***0.732
Inactive	***0.417	***0.292	***0.448	***0.373
Other	***0.621	***0.911	–	–
Education level attainment				
None (RC)	1.000	1.000	1.000	1.000
Primary	***0.964	***0.945	***0.913	***0.925
Secondary +	***0.472	***0.353	***0.457	***0.361

N = 718,577; p = 0.000 LR Chi-square = 345,460.6 (20 df)

Finally, the findings in Table 7.3 show that the educational level of attainment was a significant factor predicting the odds of being currently married as opposed to being single in 1991. The relative risk of being in the currently married category reduced from 0.964 for individuals with a primary education to 0.472 among those with a secondary and higher education level. Concerning the category previously married, education was equally a significant factor. The odds of being previously married decreased from 0.945 among those with a primary education to 0.353 among those with a secondary and higher education. Whether the pattern of relationships exhibited by the findings from the 1991 Uganda census persisted with the later census (2002) is revealed in further analysis based on the 2002 census and is also presented in Table 7.3.

The findings in Table 7.3 from Uganda's 2002 census clearly depict a pattern that has already been observed for the 1991 census. A unit increase in the age of an individual was associated with a 1.2 times increase in the odds of being in the married category; likewise, the odds of being in the previously married category increased 1.3 times for a unit increase in the age of the individual. Concerning the sex of the individuals, the findings show that the odds of being married increased more than three times (RRR = 3.386; $p = 0.000$) among females compared with males. Similarly, it the females had a higher likelihood of having been previously married (RRR = 10.124; $p = 0.000$).

Rural–urban differences were observed in the 2002 census results (Table 7.3) with regard to marriage patterns. As in the 1991 census findings, the 2002 census results show that residence in urban areas reduces both the odds of being married and invariably the odds of being previously married. The odds of being currently married in urban areas were 0.636 times compared with rural areas, the reference category; among the previously married the corresponding odds were 0.881.

Religious affiliation significantly influenced marital status, and the findings in Table 7.3 show a similar pattern earlier observed in the 1991 census. Christians and those belonging to other religions had lower odds of being in the married category compared with Muslims. Similarly, the Muslims had higher odds of being previously married compared with other religious groups, including Christians. The findings presented in Table 7.3 further show that the unemployed and the inactive were less likely to be currently married compared with those who were in employment. Finally, the findings in Table 7.3 suggest that there is an inverse relationship between education level attained and the likelihood of being married. Again these findings mirror what was found in the 1991 Uganda census findings, presented earlier in Table 7.3. The same pattern of relationships depicted for the currently married was also reflected in the previously married category, where those with a higher education had lower odds of being previously married compared with those individuals with no education. The corresponding findings for Tanzania 1988 and 2002 are presented in Table 7.4.

The findings presented in Table 7.4 only vary from the Ugandan findings presented in Table 7.3 in the sense that the IPUMS microdata set did not have the variable rural–urban residence for Tanzania in 1988; also Tanzania data do not reflect data on individual religion. However, for the rest of the variables analyzed, the results show a pattern clearly resembling that earlier seen with the Uganda findings. First, concerning the age of the individuals, if an individual's age were to increase by one year, the log-odds for being currently married relative to never married would be expected to

Table 7.4 Multinomial Logistic Regression Model Predicting the Odds of Being Currently and Previously Married in Tanzania in 1988 and 2002

Variable/Category	1988 Census		2002 Census	
	Currently Married	Previously Married	Currently Married	Previously Married
	Relative Risk Ratio (RRR)	Significance	Relative Risk Ratio (RRR)	Significance
Age (continuous)	***1.235	***1.302	***1.211	***1.276
Residence				
Rural (RC)	–	–	1.000	1.000
Urban	–	–	***0.706	***0.935
Sex				
Male (RC)	1.000	1.000	1.000	1.000
Female	***4.644	***12.634	***3.436	***11.107
Employment Status				
Employed (RC)	1.000	1.000	1.000	1.000
Unemployed	***0.187	***0.456	***0.390	***0.648
Inactive	***0.366	***0.416	***0.530	***0.475
Education level attainment				
None (RC)	1.000	1.000	1.000	1.000
Primary	***0.715	***0.617	***0.926	***0.790
Secondary +	***0.440	***0.294	***0.475	***0.293

increase 0.192 (RRR = 1.235) while holding other variables in the model constant. Similarly, the log-odds for being previously married relative to being single would increase by 0.264 (RRR = 1.302) if an individual's age were to increase by one year. As with previous findings for Uganda, the log-odds of being currently married relative to being single increased nearly five times (RRR = 4.644) among females compared with males, while the log-odds on being previously married relative to being single increased 12.6 times for females compared with males, holding all other variables in the model constant.

As with findings for Uganda earlier presented, the log-odds of being married relative to being single decreased if the individual was either unemployed or inactive compared with those who were employed. The log-odds of being currently married relative to being single were reduced by 1.678 units (RRR = 0.187) for individuals who were unemployed compared with those who were employed; among the inactive, the log-odds reduced to 0.366 times compared with the employed. This same pattern was reflected among those previously married relative to being single; again the unemployed and inactive exhibited lower log-odds of being previously married relative to being single.

Concerning educational level attainment, the findings in Table 7.4 show what is already reflected in the Ugandan analysis presented in Tables 7.3. The log-odds of being married relative to being single reduced with increases in education levels. Notably, there would be a reduction in the log-odds of being married 0.715 times if an individual had a primary level education compared with having no education. These odds would reduce further (RRR = 0.440) if an individual had a secondary and higher education level. For the category previously married, a similar pattern to that of the currently married was observed. The log-odds of being previously married relative to being single reduced with increases in education levels from primary to secondary education.

The results that follow (Table 7.4) are from the 2002 census data of Tanzania. Clearly they too mirror the Ugandan scenario and also the 1988 census data results for Tanzania as presented in Table 7.4. The results presented in Table 7.4 show that the log-odds of being married relative to being single increased 1.2 times for a unit increase in age, and likewise the log-odds of being previously married increased 1.3 times for a unit increase in the age of an individual. This finding is consistent with the rest of the findings presented earlier. The findings for Tanzania's 2002 census also suggest that the log-odds of being married increased 3.4 times among females compared with males. Concerning the previously married category, the log-odds of being previously married relative to being single increased eleven times among females compared with their male counterparts.

As in the findings already presented for Uganda and Tanzania, the log-odds of being currently married and previously married relative to being single reduced significantly among individuals who were unemployed and the inactive compared with those who were in employment (Table 7.4). Similarly, residence in urban areas of Tanzania in 2002 significantly reduced the odds of being married relative to being single (RRR = 0.706, p = 0.000). This same pattern was reflected for the previously married category relative to being single.

As expected, the findings with regard to employment status suggest that the log-odds of being married significantly reduced among individuals who were unemployed (RRR = 0.390) and those who were inactive (RRR = 0.530) compared with those who were employed. The log-odds of being previously married as opposed to being single reduced significantly (RRR = 0.648, p = 0.000) among those who were unemployed and reduced even further (RRR = 0.475) among the inactive compared with those who were employed. And, finally, the log-odds of being married relative to being single reduced as the education level of the individual increased. Similarly, the log-odds of being previously married in relation to being single reduced as education level increased. Individuals with a secondary and higher education had 0.293

times the odds of being previously married compared with those with no education, the reference category.

3.3 Limitations

The analyses presented in this chapter are not without limitations. Perhaps the most serious problem and constraint was the analytic sample size. Although a large sample size is preferred, criticisms related to high significance levels because of large sample sizes were apparent. Second, there was an intense localization of the nature of variables in the respective census data sets from the IPUMS microdata samples, such that a multicountry study is rendered extremely difficult and probably unsupportable by the existing information.

4 DISCUSSION AND CONCLUSION

Despite the constraints stated, the findings suggest that the timing of marriage in Africa is changing. SMAM estimates revealed that generally the mean age at marriage was increasing, as shown by the higher estimate for the more recent censuses of the countries included in the study. The study confirmed what is already known: that the mean age at marriage in South Africa is higher compared with other SSA countries. This latter result is supported by the work done by Palamuleni and Palamuleni (2011), who assert similar findings. The recent rise in women's age at first marriage could be explained as part of the wider change in social and family institutions, especially in intergenerational relationships, individualization, and women's empowerment. The latter is supported by a number of researchers, including those whose work has been on the marriage patterns in developing countries (Mair 1971; Lesthaeghe, Kaufmann, and Meekers 1989; Mason 1993; Hertrich and Locoh 1999; Thiriat 2000). In addition, the argument by Hertrich and Lesclingand (2012) that the weakening of family control over marriage and a greater involvement of young people in the choice of spouse could also have triggered this transition in nuptiality leading to increased age at marriage.

The analysis revealed that there are wide variations in mean age at marriage between males and females in some countries, especially in West Africa. In Guinea, Mali, and Senegal, the difference in SMAM for males and females was in the range of close to ten years compared with about two years in South Africa and about five years in East African countries. The study also showed that the proportion of males in the ever-married category was highest in Uganda, about 60 percent, compared with other countries included in this study. Perhaps this factor coupled with the low age at marriage could be contributing to the high fertility in the country. Any policy to address issues related to fertility in countries such as Uganda, therefore, should address male involvement in population issues.

The multinomial logistic regression results show a number of significant findings. First, concerning age, the findings from the four regression models estimated suggest that the log-odds of being married had a direct relationship to the age of the individual. This can be attributed to the centrality of marriage in an individual's life history; for this reason marriage tends to be universal and as individuals transition into the adulthood stage the aspiration to get married increases. The study further revealed that the unemployed and the inactive were less likely to get married. The latter finding points to the fact that marriage is an expensive venture and adequate resources are often needed to conduct the marriage ceremony and the associated familial obligations in the African marriage setting.

The logistic regression results also revealed that the odds of an individual being married were higher among females compared with males. This finding is consistent with literature elsewhere (Walker 2012) and is related to issues of gender inequality. Many women in the developing world and in Africa in particular are subjected to marriage at an early age. This curtails their continued participation in the formal school system and ultimately their labor force participation. Religious differences in the odds of being in the married category as reflected in the Ugandan findings are perhaps the result of differing norms and beliefs that may affect one's orientation toward marriage.

The findings with regard to residence status showed that the log-odds of being married were lower in the urban areas compared with the rural areas. As noted earlier, people living in urban areas are exposed to a more diverse lifestyle and subject to a weaker social control than those in rural areas. Rural areas, therefore, tend to have institutional and normative structures such as the kinship and extended family that promote early marriage and childbearing (Goode 1963; Dixon 1971; United Nations 1988, 1990). The higher odds of being currently married in the rural areas, therefore, can be explained by the variations in institutional and normative structures.

Finally, the education differentials showed an inverse relationship between the log-odds of being married relative to being single. This finding can be explained by the fact that education tends to remove girls from the domestic environment and offers literacy and exposure to new ideas and value systems that may compete with the traditional customs, values, and beliefs that promote early marriage (Westoff 1992; Caldwell, Reddy, and Caldwell 1983).

From the broader perspective, some findings in this chapter reiterate the already known theoretical issues related to marriage patterns in Africa; however, the analysis more importantly presents the possibility of using census data and statistical and demographic methods for population research. This research and analyses improve our understanding of marriage patterns and dynamics in Africa. Perhaps this study will provide insight into some of the simple empirical approaches of using available census data to inform research and policy environment.

ACKNOWLEDGMENTS

The author would like to thank the Minnesota Population Center for permission to access IPUMS–International database, and all the reviewers whose comments helped to improve the quality of this chapter.

REFERENCES

Antoine Philippe, 2006 : The Complexities of Nuptiality: From Early Female Union to Male Polygamy in Africa, in . Demography: Analysis and Synthesis, A Treatise in Population Studies, G. Caselli, J. Vallin and G. Wunsch (Editor), Vol 1, Elsevier, Academic Press, p. 355–371

Aryee, A.F. (1997) "The African Family and Changing Nuptiality Patterns." In *Family, Population and Development in Africa*, ed. Aderanti Adepoju, 78–96. London: Zed Books.

Bledsoe, C. (1990) "Transformations in Sub-Saharan African Marriage and Fertility." *ANNALS of the American Academy of Political and Social Science* 510:115–125.

Bledsoe, C., and G. Pison, eds. (1994) *Nuptiality in Sub-Saharan Africa: Contemporary Anthropological and Demographic Perspectives*. Oxford: Clarendon Press p 92–113.

Bongaarts, J., and G.W. Jones. (1982) "Fertility Determinants: Proximate Determinants." In *International Encyclopedia of Population*, ed. John Ross, 1:275–279. New York: Macmillan Publishing.

Caldwell, J.C. (2000) "Rethinking the African AIDS Epidemic." *Population and Development Review* 26 (1): 117–135.

Caldwell, J.C., P.H. Reddy, and P. Caldwell. (1983) "The Causes of Marriage Change in South India." *Population Studies* 37 (3): 343–361.

Dixon, R.B. (1971) "Explaining Cross-Cultural Variations in Age at Marriage and Proportions Never Marrying." *Population Studies* 25 (2): 215–234.

Dodoo, F. (1998) "Marriage Type and Reproductive Decisions: A Comparative Study in Sub-Saharan Africa." *Journal of Marriage and the Family* 60 (1): 232–242.

Goldman, N. (1993) "Marriage Selection and Mortality Patterns: Interferences and Fallacies." *Demography* 30 (2): 189–208.

Goode, William, J. (1963) *World Revolution and Family Patterns*. New York. Free Press of Glenoe.

Harwood-Lejeune A. (2001) "Rising Age at Marriage and Fertility in Southern and Eastern Africa." *European Journal of Population* 17 (3): 261–280.

Hertrich Véronique, and Marie Lesclingand. (2012) "Adolescent Migration and the 1990s Nuptiality Transition in Mali." *Population Studies: A Journal of Demography* 66 (2): 147–166.

Hertrich, Véronique, and Therese Locoh. (1999) *Rapports de genre, formation et dissolution des unions dans les pays en de´veloppement [Gender Relations, Union Formation and Dissolution in Developing Countries]*. Liege: IUSSP.

Isiugo-Abanihe, U.C. (1994) "Nuptiality Patterns, Sexual Activity and Fertility in Nigeria." DHS Working Paper No. 16, Macro Inc., Calverton, Maryland.

Isiugo-Abanihe, U.C., J. Ebigbola, and A. Adewuyi. (1993) "Urban Nuptiality Patterns and Marital Fertility in Nigeria." *Journal of Biosocial Science* 25 (4): 483–498.
Jensen, Robert, and Rebecca Thornton. (2003) "Early Female Marriage in the Developing World." In *Gender, Development and Marriage*, ed. Caroline Sweetman. Oxford: Oxfam: p 9–19
Kaufman, G.L., and D. Meekers. (1998) "The Impact of Women's Socioeconomic Position on Marriage Patterns in Sub-Saharan Africa." *Journal of Comparative Family Studies* 29 (1): 101–114.
Lesthaeghe, R., G. Kaufmann, and D. Meekers. (1989) "The Nuptiality Regimes in Sub-Saharan Africa, in Adolescent Migration and Nuptiality in Mali." In *Reproduction and Social Organization in Sub-Saharan Africa*, ed. R. Lesthaeghe, 238–337. Berkeley: University of California Press.
Mair, Lucy. (1971) *Marriage*. Harmondsworth: Penguin Books.
Mason, K.O. (1993) "The Impact of Women's Position on Demographic Change during the Course of Development." In *Women's Position and Demographic Change*, ed. N. Federici, K.O. Mason, and S. Sogner, 19–42. Oxford: Clarendon Press.
McCarthy, J. (1982) "Differentials in Age at First Marriage: Comparative Studies Cross National Summaries." Working Paper no. 19, World Fertility Survey and International Statistical Institute, London.
Minnesota Population Center. (2011) *Integrated Public Use Microdata Series International: Version 6.1 [Machine-Readable Database]*. Minneapolis: University of Minnesota.
Palamuleni, L.G., and M.E. Palamuleni. (2011) "Spatial Variation of Age at Marriage in South Africa." *Journal of Social Science* 29 (1): 39–46.
Pebley, A.R., and N. Rutenburg. (1986) "Marriage Patterns and Demographic Change in Sub-Saharan Africa." Paper prepared for presentation at the 1986 Annual Meeting of the Population Association of America, March.
Smith, D.P. (1980) "Age at First Marriage: Comparative Studies Cross National Summaries." Working Paper no. 7, World Fertility Survey and International Statistical Institute, London.
Smith, P.C. (1980) "Asian Marriage Patterns in Transition." *Journal of Family History* 5 (1): 58–96.
Thiriat, M.P. (2000) "Les pratiques matrimoniales, au principe des systèmes de genre [Matrimonial Practices, on the Principle of Gender Systems]." In *Rapports de genre et questions de population. II. Genre, population et développement [Gender Relations and Population Questions II. Gender, Population and Development]*, ed. M. Bozon and T. Locoh, 81–94. Paris: INED.
Udjo, E.O. (2001) "Marital Patterns and Fertility in South Africa: The Evidence from the 1996 Population Census." Poster presented at IUSSP XXIV International Population Conference, Salvador, Brazil, August 18–24.
United Nations. (1987) "Fertility Behaviour in the context of development: Evidence from the World Fertility Survey." *Population Studies* 100 p. 283–298.
United Nations. (1988) *First Marriage: Patterns and Determinants: ST/ESA/SER.R/76*. New York: United Nations.
United Nations. (1990) *Patterns of First Marriage: Timing and Prevalence*. New York: United Nations, Department of International Economic and Social Affairs.
Van de Walle, E. (1968) "Marriage in African Censuses and Inquiries." In *The Demography of Tropical Africa*, ed. W. Brass, A.J. Coale, P. Demeny, D.F. Heisel, F. Lorimer, A. Romaniuk, and E. Van de Walle, 183–238. Princeton, NJ: Princeton University Press.
Van de Walle, E., and D. Meekers. (1994) "Marriage Drinks and Kola Nuts." In *Nuptiality in Sub-Saharan Africa: Contemporary Anthropological and Demographic Perspectives*, ed. C. Bledsoe and G. Pison. Oxford: Clarendon Press, p. 57–73.

Walker, J.A. (2012) "Early Marriage in Africa—Trends, Harmful Effects and Interventions." *African Journal of Reproductive Health* 16 (2): 231–240.

Westoff, Charles F. (1992) *Age at Marriage, Age at First Birth and Fertility in Africa.* World Bank Technical Paper No. 169. Washington, DC: World Bank.

8 Population Distribution in Sub-Saharan Africa

Internal and International Migrations in Sub-Saharan Africa

Akanni Akinyemi and Sunday Omoyeni

1 INTRODUCTION

Migration data in Africa are very rare and mostly from fragmented sources. This is the unique opportunity provided by the ACAP-IPUMS project in providing African censuses from two waves of data sets. This analysis is focused on regional and interregional migration issues in Africa and its interlinkages with other demographic characteristics from censuses. The rate of rural–urban migration and urbanization in Africa since 1985 has been very high (UN 2003; Bouare 2006). Bouare (2006), in his analysis of thirty-two African countries, showed that the rate of urbanization peaked at 85 percent in Gabon, more than 50 percent in South Africa and Botswana. Whereas in the developed nations urbanization is in response to industrial growth, the experience in many African nations predates the limited industrialization.

International migration is largely construed as in part a reflection of peoples' reaction to prevailing internal factors within a country, attractive external opportunities in other countries, or a juxtaposition of both factors. Such views have been well articulated in significant literature on push and pull theories of migration (Ravenstein 1889; Lee 1966; Todaro 1969; Sassen 1988). These push factors include but are not limited to demographic, economic, political, security, and sociocultural and environmental factors in the places of origin. The pull factors comprise a plethora of attractions in receiving countries. These in part explain the migration trends and dynamics in most African countries. Historically, migration on the African continent can be traced back to early merchants and pastoralists in agricultural activities (Ratha and Shaw 2007; Adepoju 2010; Shimeles 2010) and tribal conflicts over resources (Bakewell and de Haas 2007). However, with changing social structures, migration in Africa assumes different typologies and is influenced by many challenging issues prevailing on the continent (Rayp and Ruyssen 2010). A quick reflection on some of these presents a clear case of a continent with spotlights of daunting critical challenges across the subregions. During the period 1969–1990, forty-three civil wars were fought in the world;

seventeen of those forty-three were in Africa. The continent accounts for about 9 percent of the global migrant population, constituting 17.1 million in 2005 (Spaan and van Moppes 2006; UN 2006) and an estimated 30 million in the year 2011 (World Bank 2011). The majority of African migrants remain in the region (Russel et al. 1990). Ratha et al. (2011) estimated that more than 60 percent of migrants from sub-Saharan Africa (SSA) migrate to other countries in the region while the bulk of migrants remain within their subregions (Black et al. 2004; Shaw and Williams 2007; Adepoju 2008, 2009; Shimeles 2010).

A major dynamic in African migration, as noted by Adepoju (2001), is the changing classification of countries from "sending countries" to "receiving countries" and vice versa. For instance, the DRC was one of the major receiving countries in Africa in the early 1990s, but in the late 1990s it developed into a sending country (Van Dijk, Foeken, and van Til 2001). Also, the volumes of female migrants in the region have significantly increased. The usual pattern where women migrate to join husbands is changing, and women constitute a large proportion of primary migrants. Previous analyses have been able to estimate intraregional migration in SSA, using projections from the World Bank's bilateral migration database (Rayp and Ruyssen 2010; Ratha et al. 2011; Shimeles 2010). Unlike previous works, the current analysis utilized census data from two time points.

2 THEORETICAL OVERVIEW

Regional and interregional migration explanations are indebted to deterministic theories developed by Ravenstein (1885) and Lee (1966) with the argument that distance is directly related to propensity to move. There are two major classic opposing viewpoints linking migration, regional boundaries, and development. One considered migration as a positive opportunity for individuals to escape some unpleasant situation related to unemployment, conflict, and war while providing macro benefits in terms of remittances to the state or countries (Todaro 1976; Goldring 2004; Levitt 1996). It also offsets labor shortages in the country of destination and creates wealth through migrant entrepreneurial activities (IOM 2006). In terms of the negative consequences, it is considered to hinder development in terms of a brain drain in the country of origin (Barclay 2010; Ammassari and Black 2001). Large volumes of migrant labor can undermine local wages and generate tension between host communities and migrants (African Union [AU] 2006). In a broader sense, regional or intraregional migration exerts some form of influence on labor force, either directly or indirectly, in either positive or negative ways. In providing explanations to this in relation to regional migration, scholars have tested some hypotheses in this regard (Muysken, de Neubourg, and van der Burg 1982; Gleave and Palmer 1980; Abraham 1983). DaVanzo (1981) introduced the concept of territorial restrictions of assets in terms of location-specific capital as a major impetus for regional/interregional movement. In Africa, professional certification of doctors in West Africa guarantees the possibility of practicing within the region without losing one's professional status. This may prove difficult in other regions as certification from West Africa may not be accepted. Also, many of the regional organizations have common educational control systems that ensure comparability in standards.

2.1 Determinants of Inter- and Intraregional Migration in Africa

Regional and interregional migration in Africa is entrenched in regional agreements by which citizens from a member state can move around without a special visa. Geographical contiguity and poor border management also influence migration decisions. This view was corroborated by Black et al. (2004) that migration within the Eastern Africa region was prevalent among countries with adjoining borders. Other major determinants of inter- and intraregional migration in Africa are voluntary or involuntary individual decisions to migrate (Barclay 2010). Many authors have linked migration patterns in SSA to the profound effect of colonialism ties (Bakewell and de Haas 2007; Barclay 2010; Shimeles 2010). Evidence of an increasing number of refugees and asylum seekers as well as labor migrants has also been documented by many scholars as factors sustaining the current tempo of migration within Africa (Adepoju 2005, 2008; Spaan and van Moppes 2006; USAID 1997; Robin 1997).

3 METHODOLOGY

The chapter utilized secondary data from African censuses archived by the University of Minnesota Population Center (2011). Analysis was limited to countries with at least two waves of census datasets. Eight countries were selected based on this, four in the east (Kenya, Rwanda, Uganda, and Tanzania), three in the west (Guinea, Mali, and Senegal), and only one in the south (South Africa). It is important to note that only 5 percent of the census data set was available, as such analysis was based on weighted proportions. Data from other sources were utilized to complement the analysis where data were not available in the census. Measurement of migration from the census data is limited to two definitions: country of birth and country of citizenship. These two concepts are limited in scope in identifying, for instance, place(s) of previous permanent residence and status of the migrant. A migrant in this analysis is defined in terms of country of citizenship. There are a few cases where this was alternated for country of birth if the required information for country of citizenship is lacking.

4 RESULTS

4.1 Urbanization and Rural–Urban Migration, 1985–2005

The 2003 United Nations data set was utilized to capture urbanization and rural–urban migration in selected African countries. Gabon had the highest level of urbanization at 85 percent, with the lowest in the Central African Republic (44 percent). In the Southern Africa region, Botswana and South Africa had an urbanization rate above 50 percent, while countries such as Malawi and Lesotho had rates of less than 20 percent. In the Eastern Africa region, Kenya had an urbanization rate of 42 percent, while Tanzania and Somalia had a rate of 38 percent and 36 percent, respectively. Four countries in West Africa had an urbanization rate of about 50 percent (Senegal, Nigeria, Ghana, and Benin). Whereas in many developed countries of the world, urbanization is a natural response to industrial growth and development, the African experience is largely attributable to rural–urban migration. According to Table 8.1, rural–urban migration in many African countries has shown a geometric upward surge. Between 1985 and 2005, the volume of rural–urban migrants almost tripled in Somalia and Malawi, and it doubled in Nigeria, Mali, Niger, Tanzania, and Mozambique.

Table 8.1 Volume of Rural–Urban Migration in African Regions, 1985–2005

	1985–1990	1990–1995	1995–2000	2000–2005
West Africa				
Ghana	553,897	661,033	745,255	529,722
Nigeria	3,758,881	4,512,958	5,361,112	5,567,517
Benin	175,306	216,848	245,892	277,560
Burkina Faso	195,602	167,430	189,862	258,482
Mali	257,952	321,935	399,348	488,569
Niger	143,666	192,748	262,214	354,767
Senegal	193,274	315,164	352,727	389,439
Togo	70,333	89,549	122,080	154,272
East Africa				
Uganda	221,044	102,564	98,228	118,718
Tanzania	1,081,869	1,621,348	1,879,589	2,024,057
Kenya	1,107,097	1,467,823	1,814,664	1,893,647
Somalia	97,221	128,596	197,130	297,642
Southern Africa				
South Africa	202,998	1,567,592	1,276,998	1,083,178
Swaziland	9,990	1,072	2,112	7,164

(continued)

Table 8.1 (continued)

	1985–1990	1990–1995	1995–2000	2000–2005
Zimbabwe	382,808	320,988	246,762	291,775
Angola	302,673	386,088	470,490	568,681
Mozambique	586,252	827,494	1,055,231	1,144,314
Botswana	186,962	84,353	44,469	42,564
Lesotho	11,778	2,706	4,514	10,796
Malawi	136,804	164,820	209,307	361,468
Central Africa				
Cameroon	551,781	606,402	650,898	663,376
Central African Republic	36,447	56,735	79,603	101,670
Congo	51,828	61,528	72,568	88,502
Gabon	86,227	88,169	70,889	52,012

Source: United Nations (2002, 2003) and Bouare (2006).

4.2 Trends in Regional Migration Estimates in Africa: 1990–2010

Between the years 1990 and 2010, the number of international migrants in Africa increased by more than 3.2 million, from almost seventeen million in 1990 to more than nineteen million in 2010. Over the two decades, Western and East African regions were host to more than two-thirds of the total number of migrants on the continent. According to United Nations (2009) estimates, the number of migrants in West Africa almost doubled between 1990 and 2010, while the number in East Africa showed a gradual decline from about six million in 1990 to about five million in 2010. Central Africa experienced an upward surge in the number of international migrants within the region, from 1.5 million in 1990 to 2.7 million in 1995, and a drop of almost half by year 2000 (see Table 8.2).

Table 8.2 Estimated Number of International Migrants in Africa by Region at Midyear Population

	West	East	Central	North	Southern	Total
1990	4,845,025	5,949,525	1,455,922	2,278,422	1,443,608	15,972,502
1995	6,440,729	5,347,098	2,651,377	2,185,783	1,296,358	17,921,345
2000	7,279,178	5,220,236	1,392,181	1,924,530	1,246,018	17,062,143
2005	7,703,228	5,124,070	1,566,684	1,836,287	1,505,331	17,735,600
2010	8,440,269	5,034,099	1,615,402	2,010,070	2,163,343	19,263,183

Source: Authors' computation from United Nations (2009).

A major indicator of the impact of volumes of international migrants on the local population is the percentage of total population represented by migrants. Although the number of international migrants residing in Africa increased significantly during the period 1990–2010, their share as percentage of midyear population in each of the region varies. In West Africa, the rate increased from 2.5 percent in 1990 to 3 percent in 1995 and maintained stability until year 2000, when it began to drop gradually to about 2.7 percent in 2010. The trend over the twenty-year period for West Africa showed an inverted U-shaped figure. In East Africa, the percentage of international migrants to the midyear population dropped from about 3.2 percent in 1990 to 2.3 percent in 1995 and dropped gradually over the year to about 1.5 percent in year 2010. The proportion of international migrants to midyear population in Central Africa soared from 2 percent in 1990 to about 3.2 percent in 1995 and took a very steep drop to about 1.4 percent in year 2000 all the way through to 2010. The North African region recorded the lowest proportion of international migration as a percentage of midyear population across the regions. The proportion peaked at 1.5 percent in 1990 and dropped gradually over the years to around 0.8 percent in 2010. It dropped from the 1990 percentage of 3.5 percent to 2.5 percent in 1995 and gradually increased from year 2000 to about 3.7 percent in 2010. These rates reflect the sociopolitical and economic situations in each region.

A major dynamic in African migration is the increasing volume and rate of female migration. There is evidence of increasing female autonomous migrants (Adepoju 2006, 2008). Although the UN data did not provide evidence on women as primary migrants, the proportion of female migrants to all international migrants can at best be a proxy to this.

4.3 Interregional Migration Matrix

Published evidence on the computation of migration matrix in Africa confirmed the volumes of interregional movements (World Bank 2011; Ratha et al. 2011; Shimeles 2010). The proportion of Southern African migrants captured in West Africa as a proportion of all migrants in the second round of censuses increased by 1.3 percent (from 0 percent to 1.3 percent); the rate for East African migrants decreased from 10.2 percent to 3 percent, while that of other Africans increased from 3.6 percent in the first round to 11.4 percent in the second round. The proportion of West African migrants as a total of all international migrants in Southern Africa increased from 0.8 percent in the first round of census to 2.8 percent in the second waves. Migrants from East Africa increased from 42.1 percent in the first round to 54 percent in the second round, while there was a slight decrease from 3.8 percent to 3.5 percent for other African migrants. In East Africa, the proportion of migrants from West Africa as a proportion of all international migrants declined from 0.4 percent to almost 0 percent; the proportion increased from 2.6 percent to 12.4 percent for Southern African migrants and decreased for other Africans from 80.3 percent to 70.3 percent. Only migrants from Southern Africa were captured in East Africa; they constituted 7 percent of all migrants (Ratha et al.

2011). A major discrepancy in the computation is attributed to the inclusion of intercountry movements within a region by World Bank, which was excluded in the current computation. The current analysis provided information on the movements within regions separately (see Table 8.3) and treated interregional migration as movements across regional boundaries (Figures 8.1 and 8.2).

Table 8.3 Interregional Migration Matrix in Sub-Saharan Africa 1983–2002 by Citizenship and Country of Birth

Citizen-ship	First Round of Censuses						Second Round of Censuses					
	West	South	East	Other Africans	Non-Africans	Number (in 000)	West	South	East	Other Africans	Non-Africans	Number (in 000)
West Africa	NA	—	10.2**	3.6	96.4	23	NA	1.3	3.0**	11.4	85.7	26
South Africa	0.8**	NA	42.1	3.8	54.1	279	2.8	NA	53.9	3.5	40.0	304
East Africa	0.4	2.6	NA	80.3	16.7	174	—	12.4	NA	70.3	17.3	100

**Data not available for country of citizenship but available for country of birth.

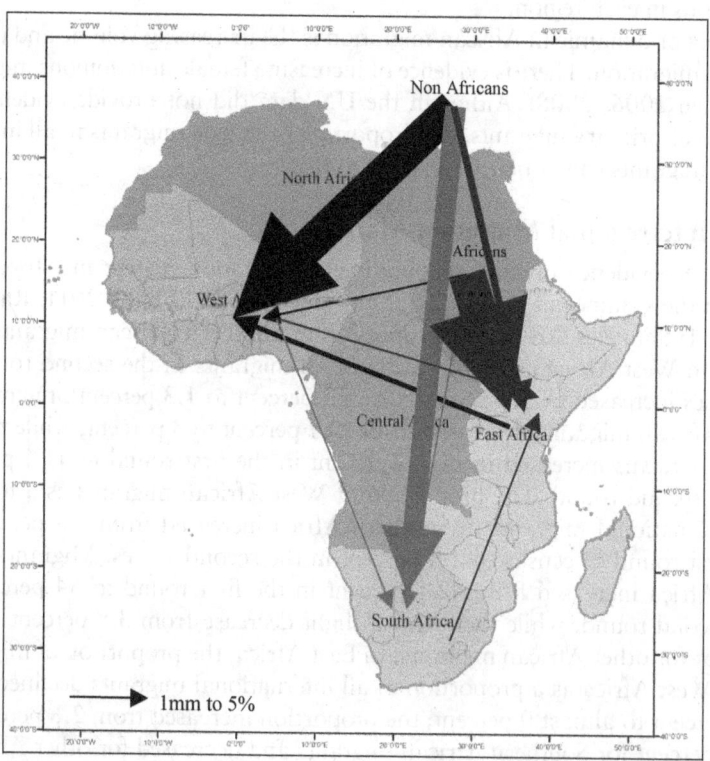

Figure 8.1 Map showing the flow of international migrants by source and destination from two waves of censuses.

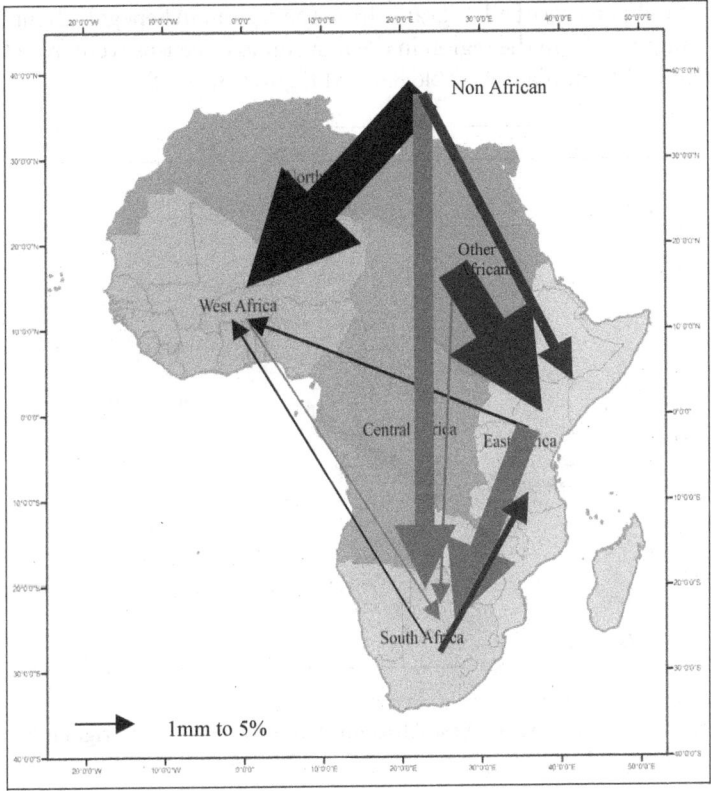

Figure 8.2 Map showing the flow of international migrants by source and destination from two waves of censuses.

4.4 Intercountry Migration Flow within Region

This section presents regional estimates of intercountry migration patterns.

4.4.1 West Africa Intercountry Migration Flow

The inflow from countries within the region of West Africa showed that more than 80 percent of migration to Guinea from the subregion in the first round of census was from Mali (40 percent), Sierra Leone (23 percent), and Senegal (18.2 percent). This configuration changed in the second round of census as migrants from Liberia (49 percent) and Sierra Leone constituted about 90 percent of all migrants to Guinea. This migration flow was directly connected to the civil war and disobedience that plagued Sierra Leone in the period 1991–2002 and the Liberian crisis of the 1990s. One obvious pattern from these two countries was migration to a contiguous country. In Mali, the first round of census captured migrants from Mauritania and Burkina Faso as constituting about 80 percent of total migrants from that region. By the second round of census, migrants from the Ivory Coast and Burkina Faso shared a larger proportion of migrants (64 percent) of all migrants from the region. In Senegal, about 72 percent of migrants from the region in the first round of census were from Guinea Bissau and Mauritania (see Table 8.4 and Figures 8.3–8.8).

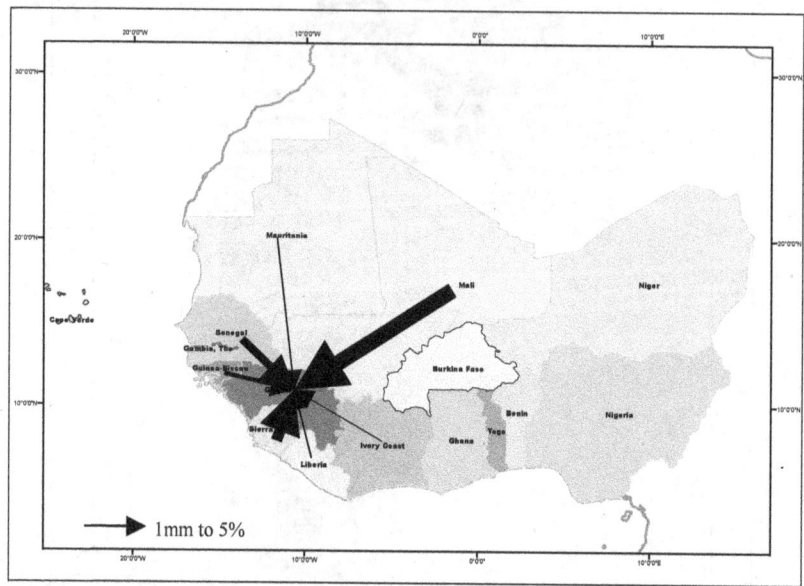

Figure 8.3 Map showing West Africa migrants by country of origin to Guinea, 1983 census.

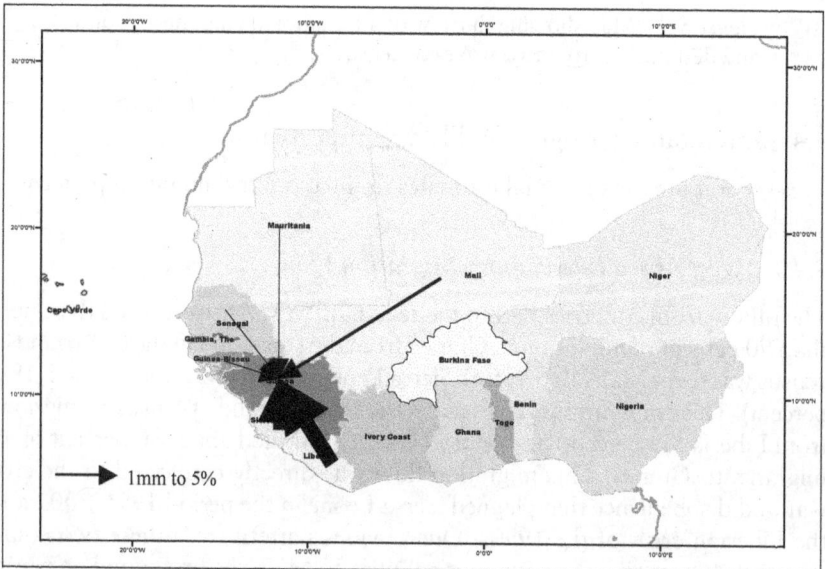

Figure 8.4 Map showing West Africa migrants by country of origin to Guinea, 1996 census.

Population Distribution in Sub-Saharan Africa 139

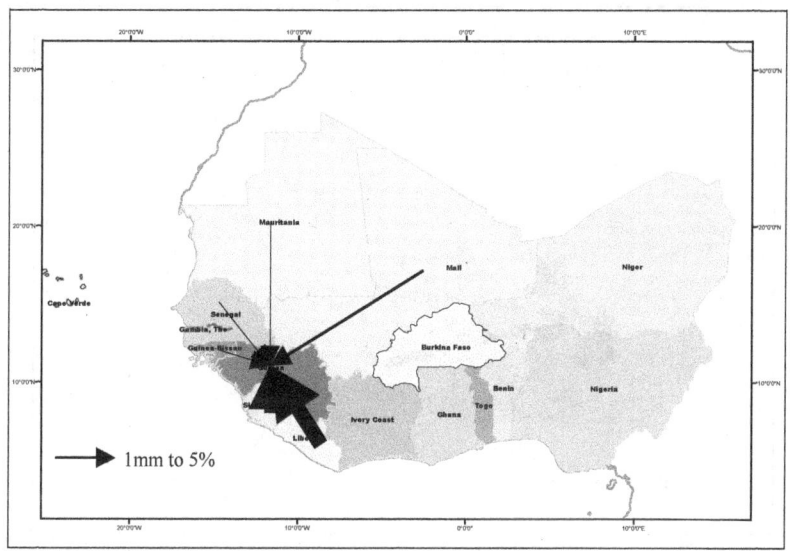

Figure 8.5 Map showing West Africa migrants by country of origin to Mali, 1987 census.

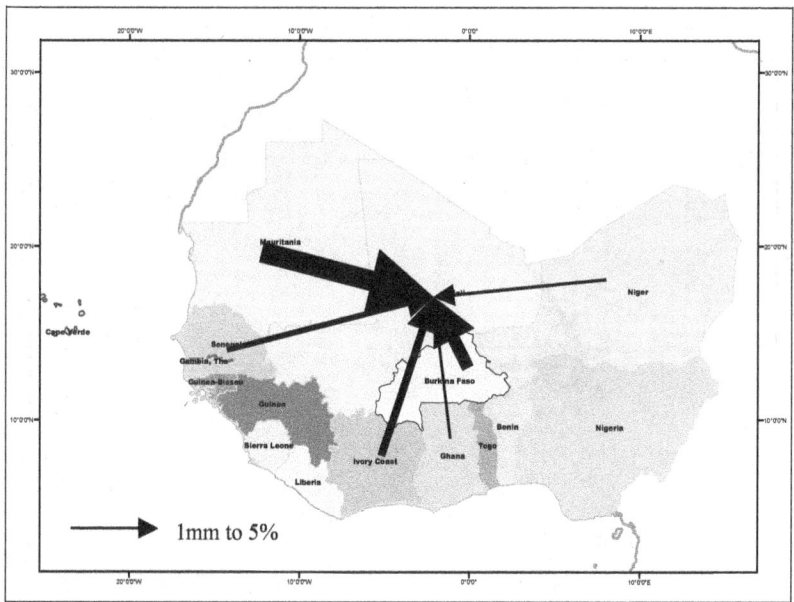

Figure 8.6 Map showing West Africa migrants by country of origin to Mali, 1998 census.

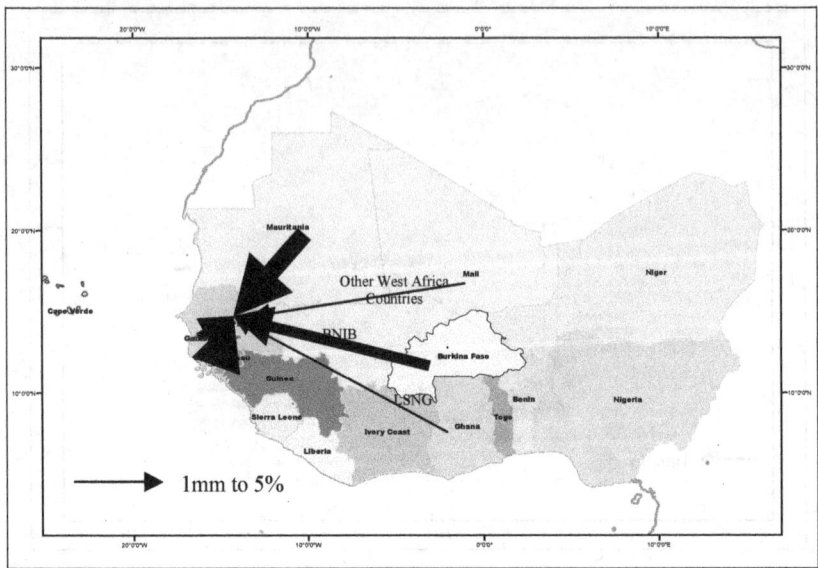

Figure 8.7 Map showing West Africa migrants by country of origin to Senegal, 1988 census.

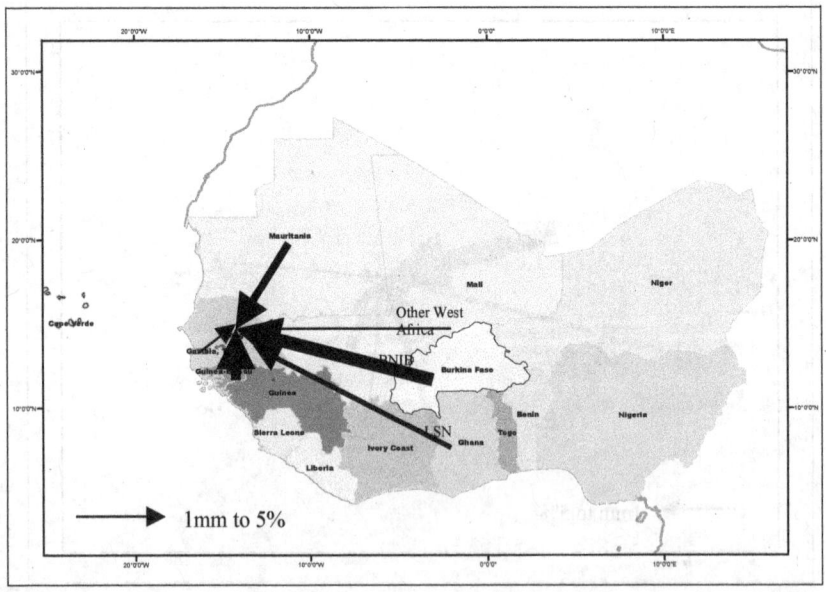

Figure 8.8 Map showing West Africa migrants by country of origin to Senegal, 2002 census.

4.4.2 Southern Africa

Migration flow to South Africa from the region is fairly the same in the two waves of census. The flow was dominated by three main countries within the subregion, Mozambique, Lesotho, and Zimbabwe. The only major noticeable change is the increase in percentages of those from Zimbabwe (10.5 percent in first round to 15 percent in the second) and a decrease in percentage of those from Lesotho (31 percent in first round and 2 percent in second round) from the first round of census to the second round. The percentage from Swaziland in the two rounds was fairly stable at 5 percent, for those from Botswana at 3 percent, the proportion of Malawians increased from 2 percent to 4 percent while Namibians decreased from 2 percent to 1.7 percent (Figures 8.9 and 8.10).

4.4.3 East Africa

As shown in Figure 8.11–8.18 and Table 8.2, the migration pattern within the region is more prevalent within contiguous countries. The first round of census in Kenya showed that about 86 percent of total migrants within the region were from Uganda (48 percent) and Tanzania (38 percent), while 8 percent, 4 percent, and 2 percent were from Ethiopia, Sudan, and Somalia, respectively. Major noticeable shifts in

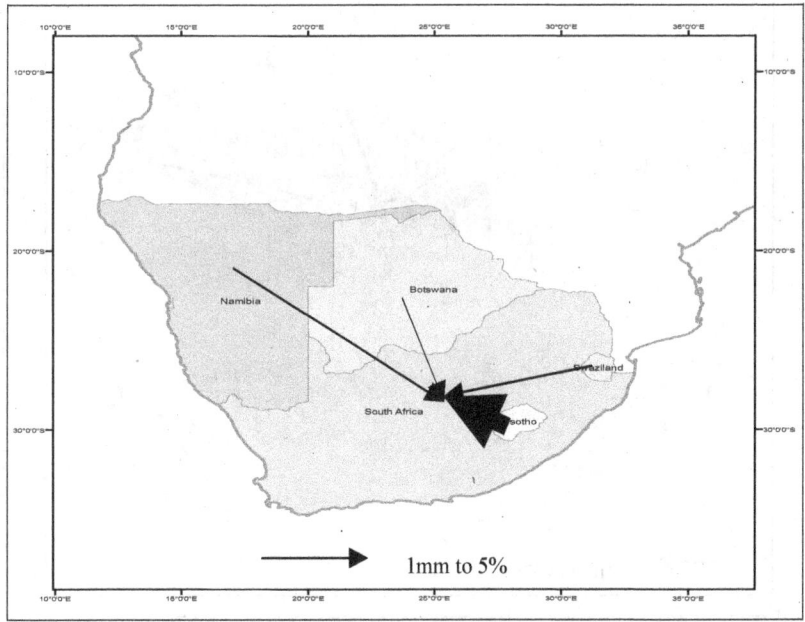

Figure 8.9 Map showing South African migrants by country of origin to South Africa, 1996 census.

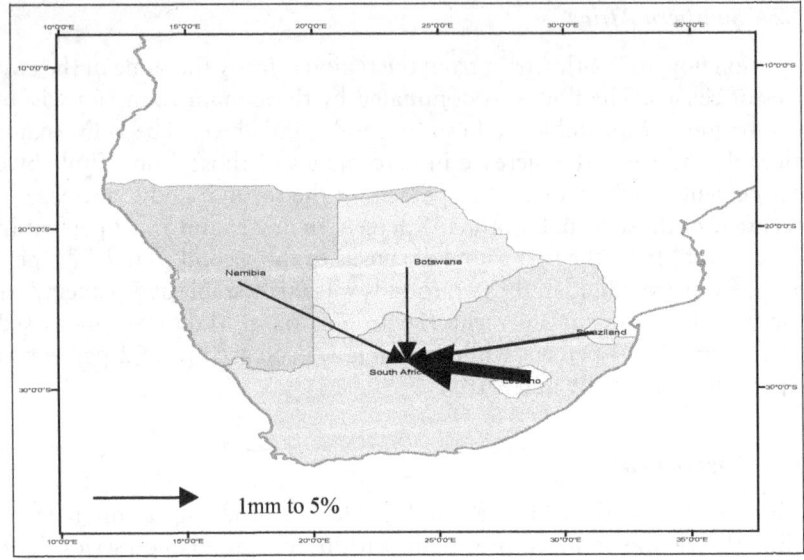

Figure 8.10 Map showing South African migrants by country of origin to South Africa, 2001 census.

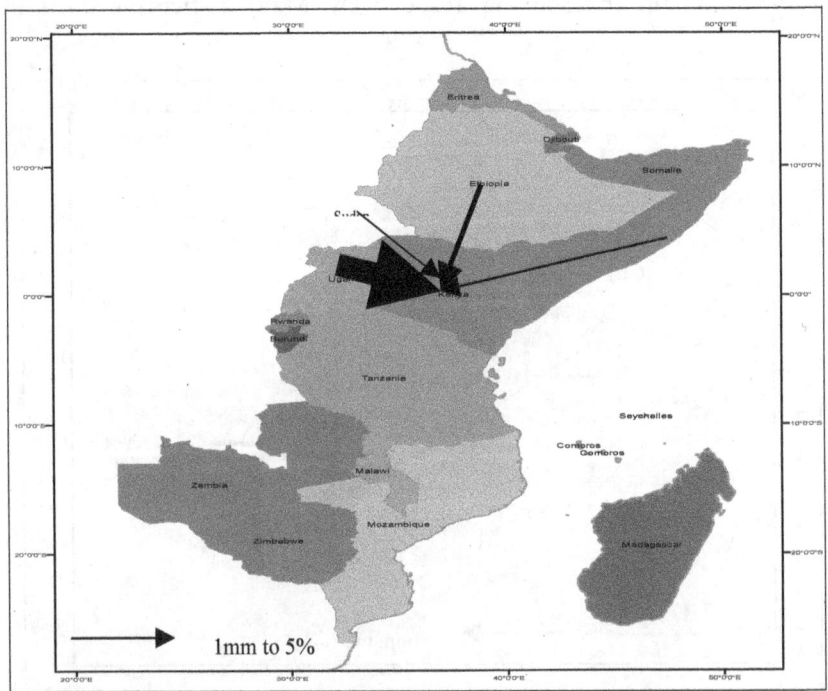

Figure 8.11 Map showing East Africa migrants by country of origin to Kenya, 1989 census.

the second round were the increase in the percentage of Ugandans (48 percent to 68 percent) and almost triple the percentage of Sudanese (3.8 percent to 9.3 percent) and Somalis (2.2 percent to 7.1 percent). In Rwanda, the first round of census showed that migrants from Burundi constituted about 85 percent of all migrants from the subregion, while the total migrants from Kenya, Uganda, and Tanzania represented 15 percent of all migrants from the subregion. The second wave of census showed a decrease in the percentage of migrants from Burundi (from 85 percent to 63 percent) and an upward surge in the proportion of migrants from Uganda, from 6 percent in the first round to 30 percent in the second round. In Uganda, the first wave of census was dominated by migrants from Rwanda (50 percent), while those from Burundi and Tanzania had 7 percent each; 8 percent each are Sudanese and Kenyans. The second round of census showed that 63 percent of all migrants from the region to Uganda were Sudanese (almost eight times more than in the previous census), 19 percent are Kenyans and 11 percent are from Tanzania. This signifies the movement of the people from crisis/conflict zones in Sudan to safer places in Uganda.

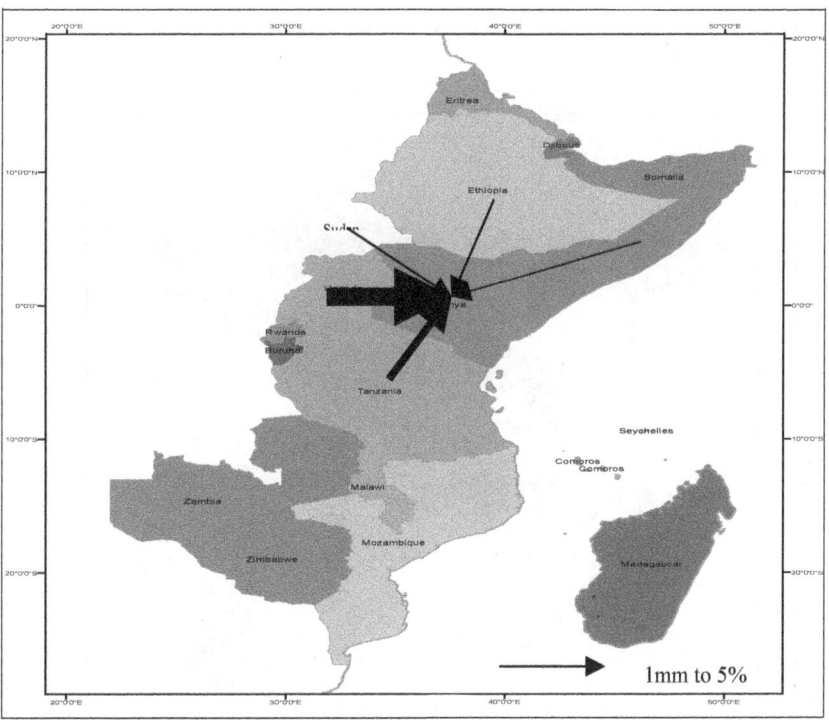

Figure 8.12 Map showing East Africa migrants by country of origin to Kenya, 1999 census.

144 *Akanni Akinyemi and Sunday Omoyeni*

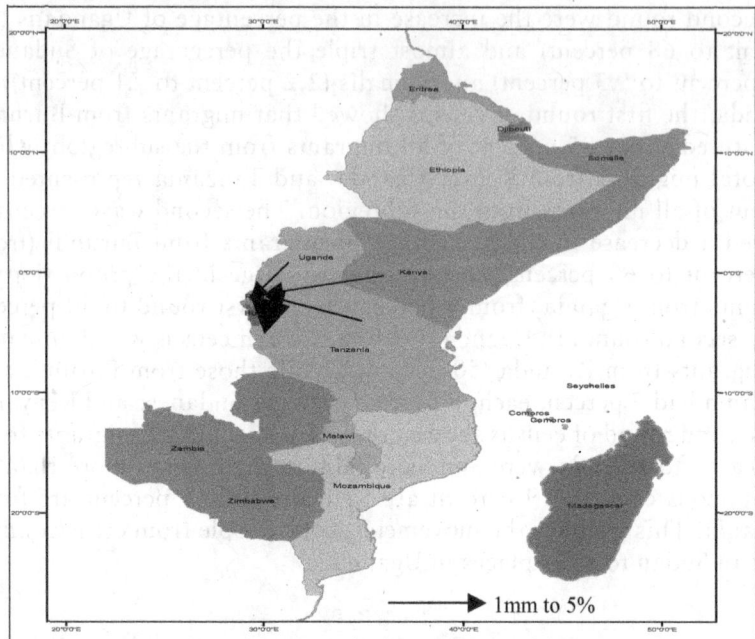

Figure 8.13 Map showing East Africa migrants by country of origin to Rwanda, 1991 census.

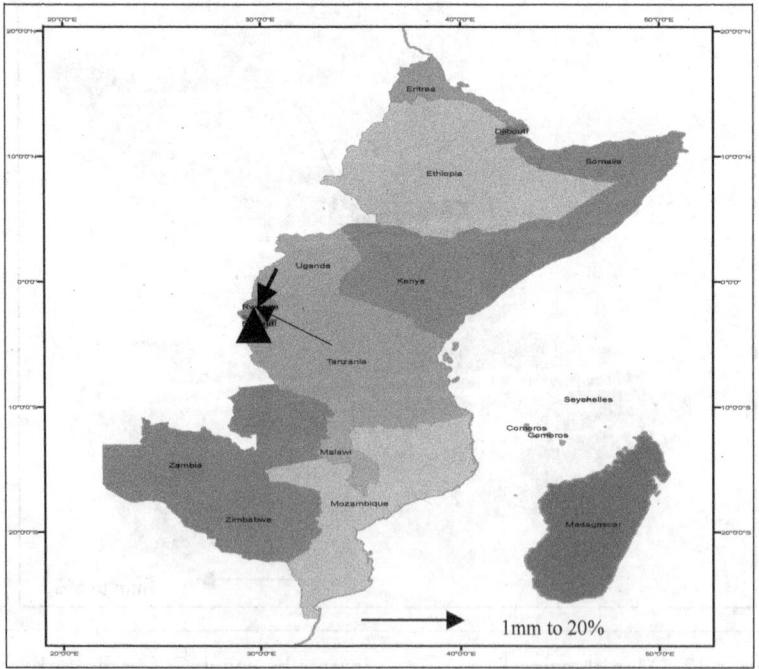

Figure 8.14 Map showing East Africa migrants by country of origin to Rwanda, 2002 census.

Population Distribution in Sub-Saharan Africa 145

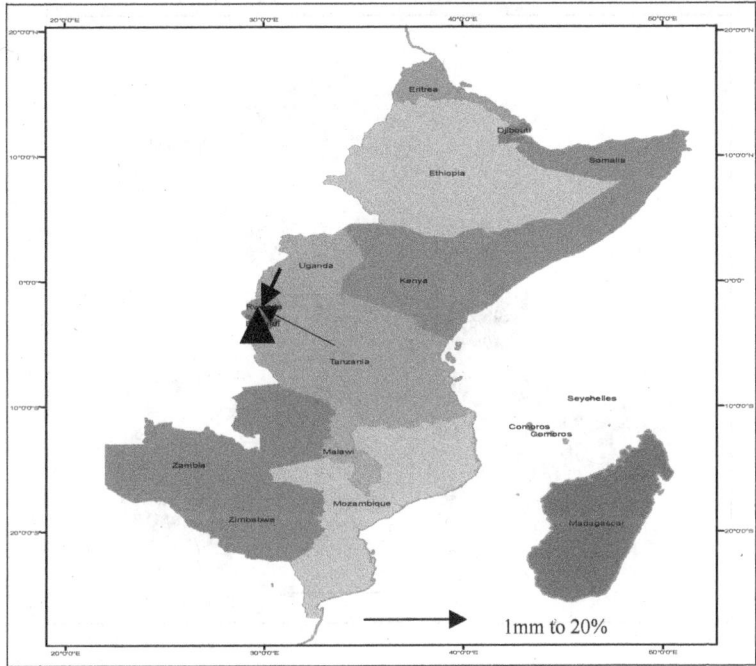

Figure 8.15 Map showing East Africa migrants by country of origin to Uganda, 1991 census.

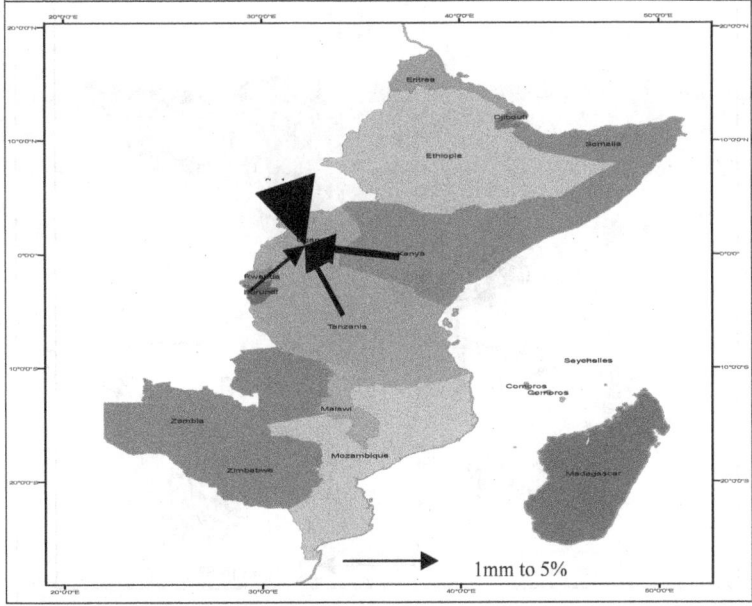

Figure 8.16 Map showing East Africa migrants by country of origin to Uganda, 2002 census.

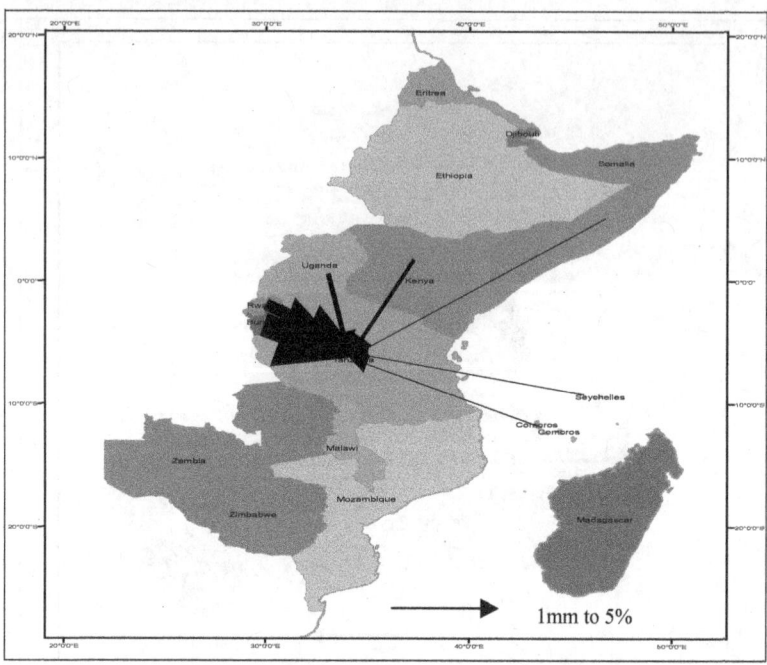

Figure 8.17 Map showing East Africa migrants by country of origin to Tanzania, 1998 census.

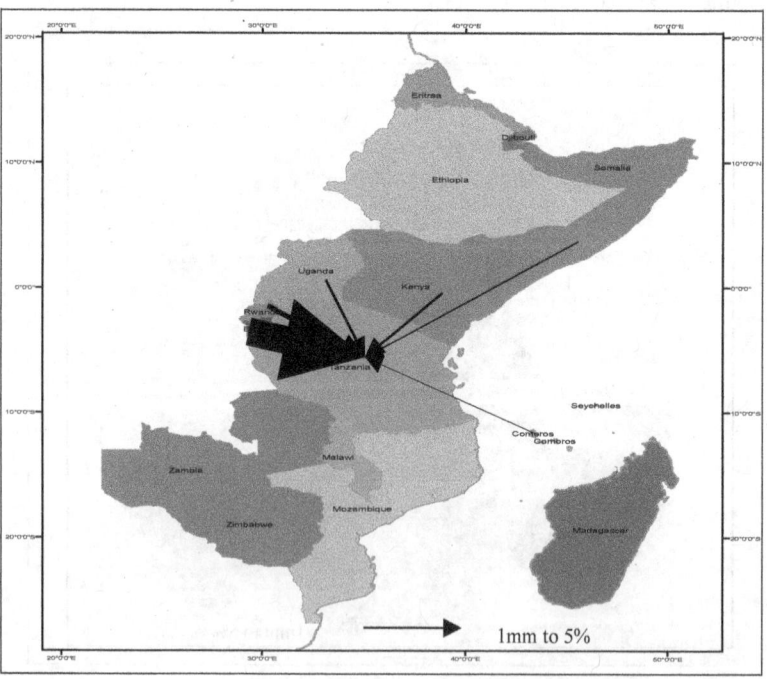

Figure 8.18 Map showing East Africa migrants by country of origin to Tanzania, census.

Table 8.4 Intercountry Migration Matrix for Countries with the Highest Migration Stock within the Three African Regions

West Africa

	Mali	Sierra Leone	Senegal	Guinea Bissau	Liberia	Mauritania	Ivory Coast
Guinea 1983 (n = 12,840)	40.2	22.7	18.2	9.7	3.3	3.3	2.5
Guinea 1996 (n = 255,020)	5.1	40.3	1.9	0.8	48.9	0.2	0.7

	Mauritania	Burkina Faso	Ivory Coast	Senegal	Niger	Ghana
Mali 1987 (40,400)	54.2	24.8	8.6	7.2	2.8	2.5
Mali 1998 (36,340)	12.1	29.0	34.3	10.0	6.5	1.9

	Mauritania	Guinea Bissau	Gambia	BNIB	LSNG	Other West Africa
Senegal 1988 (53,600)	38.5	33.7	10.3	12.9	1.6	3.0
Senegal 2002 (27,720)	16.6	20.4	3.1	26.0	8.8	1.4

South Africa

	Mozambique	Lesotho	Zimbabwe	Swaziland	Botswana	Malawi	Namibia
South Africa 1996 (n = 251,131)	43.2	31.4	10.5	5.4	3.0	2.2	2.0
South Africa 2001 (n = 319,113)	44.0	23.5	14.9	4.8	3.2	4.1	1.7

East Africa

	Uganda	Tanzania	Somalia	Ethiopia	Sudan
Kenya 1989 (n = 88,180)**	48.0	38.3	2.2	7.7	3.8
Kenya 1999 (n = 463,460)**	67.9	11.8	7.1	3.9	9.3

(continued)

Table 8.4 (continued)

	Burundi	Kenya	Uganda	Tanzania			
Rwanda 1991 (n = 36,180)	84.7	5.1	5.5	4.7			
Rwanda 2002 (n = 8,680)	63.1	—	30.4	6.5			
	Burundi	Kenya	Somalia	Sudan	Tanzania	Rwanda	Ethiopia
Uganda 1991 (n = 497,732)	17.6	8.2	0.4	7.9	16.1	49.8	0.04
Uganda 2002 (n = 233,120)**	7.3	18.6	—	63.1	10.9		
	Burundi	Kenya	Somalia	Comoros	Seychelles	Rwanda	Uganda
Tanzania 1998 (n = 191,729)	60.7	6.7	0.2	0.1	0.1	23.2	9.0
Tanzania 2002 (n = 290,184)	82.1	4.9	0.1	0.2		8.7	4.3

**Computation missing for country of citizenship but available for country of

4.5 Age-Sex Composition of Migrants by Source across Region

Disaggregated data on age and sex composition of migrants are important in understanding the dynamics of African migration. The proportion of young children and women is an indication or a proxy measure for forced migration, while the proportion of youth and prime age males is directly linked to economic migration. The general picture across the regions showed that the sex ratio in West and East Africa for the first round of census favored males, while the second census was in favor of females. The proportion of prime age males (15–64 years) dropped from the first census to the second for movements within region, while for females it dropped by almost 7 percent points; for West Africa, the proportion remained almost the same for other two regions (Table 8.5).

4.5.1 West Africa

In West Africa, the sex ratio for the first round of census was 1.27, while for the second round it was 0.97. The proportion of international migrants within the region aged less than 15 years increased from 26 percent to 40 percent for males, and from 33 percent to 40 percent for females, while the proportion of those in the prime ages (15–64 years) decreased from 68 percent to 56 percent for males and from 63 percent to 56 percent for females. The proportion of elderly males (65 years and above) dropped from 5.4 percent to 4 percent, while it slightly increased for elderly females from 3.9 percent to 4.2 percent. Considering migrants from other African regions, the sex ratio at both time points of the census was in favor of males (1.52 and 1.04), the proportion of people under age 15 years from other regions of Africa dropped from 30 percent to 24 percent for males and 38 percent to 21 percent for females. The proportion in the productive years (15–64 years) increased from 68.7 percent to 71.4 percent among males and 59.6 percent to 77 percent among females.

4.5.2 Southern Africa

The sex ratio for migrants irrespective of sources was generally in favor of males at 3.14 and 1.65 for movement originating from the region for the first and second census, respectively; 2.1 and 2.09 for migration from other African regions and 1.03 and 1.11 for migration from sources outside Africa. The proportion of those under age 15 captured in the South African censuses is lower than in other regions. For migrants from the Southern African region, the proportion of males under the age of 15 increased from about 4 percent to 9 percent, while females remained stable at about 13 percent. For those in the prime ages, the proportion dropped from 95 percent to 88 percent for males and also remained at 83 percent for females, with a slight increase in the proportion of the elderly for both male and female. A distinct feature of the South African distribution is that the bulk of migrants are in their prime ages, which explains to a large extent its economic implications in terms of labor force participation and the economic situation in the region.

4.5.3 East Africa

The sex ratio of migrants from the East African region was in favor of males (1.13) in the first round of census and in favor of females in the second round of census (0.98). This was also the case among migrants from other African regions (1.14 in the first and 0.88 in the second round). The sex ratio for migrants outside Africa was slightly more in favor of males for the two rounds of census (1.18). The proportions of young and elderly migrants under the age of 15 years and those of 65 years and above were highest in East Africa compared with other regions. The proportion of those in the prime working ages dropped slightly for males among migrants from the region (62 percent to 59 percent), and other regions (56 percent to 53 percent), and increased for those from outside Africa (63 percent to 71 percent). The percentage of females in the prime ages was almost equal for migrants within the region (61 percent), decreased slightly for those from other region (55 percent to 52 percent), and showed a slight increase for those from outside Africa (63 percent to 67 percent; see Table 8.5).

4.6 Education-Employment Status by Region across Sex

Migration in Africa is underscored by poverty and the quest for better economic opportunities. The employment variable in the census identified five categories: those not in the universe, the employed, the unemployed, the inactive, and those unknown. Controlling for age, we computed the proportion of those in employment by dividing the number of those in employment by those expected to be in the labor force. This excludes the inactive and those not in the universe. Table 8.6 presents the analyses of the share of those in employment categories by education. The emphasis is on those with secondary or tertiary education as a proportion of those unemployed. The overall employment situation among migrants showed that the employment rate increased from 54 percent to 56 percent among migrants from the region, dropped from 46 percent to 33 percent among migrants from other regions, and increased from 53 percent to 62 percent for migrants from outside Africa from the first to second round of census among all migrants. The distribution across West Africa showed that those with secondary school or more (high education) constituted about 8 percent and rose to 18 percent of the total unemployed among migrants from the region in the first and second census, respectively. Disaggregated by sex, the proportion of males with higher education among those unemployed for migrants from West Africa increased from

Table 8.5 Age-Sex Distribution of Migrants by Source, Round of Censuses across Three African Regions

	Migrants within Region				Other African Migrants				Non-African Migrants			
	1st Round		2nd Round		1st Round		2nd Round		1st Round		2nd Round	
	M	F	M	F	M	F	M	F	M	f	m	f
West Africa												
Age (n)	101,200	79,360	175,260	180,140	3,000	1,980	5,100	4,860	10,540	9,940	10,400	8,300
4 years or less	10.6	13.2	13.1	12.6	10.0	12.1	6.7	3.7	6.6	7.7	11.0	10.4
5–10 years	10.8	12.3	18.7	19.2	13.3	19.2	12.6	10.7	9.3	9.1	10.6	11.6
11–14 years	5.2	7.3	8.8	7.9	6.7	6.1	5.9	7.0	6.1	5.0	4.6	6.8
15–64 years	68.1	63.3	55.5	56.2	68.7	59.6	71.4	77	71.4	73.2	66.4	64.3
65 years +	5.4	3.9	4.0	4.2	1.3	3.0	3.5	1.7	6.6	5.0	7.5	7.0
Sex ratio	1.27:1		0.97:1		1.52:1		1.04:1		1.06:1		1.25:1	
South Africa												
Age (n)	101,725	32,412	103,137	62,559	9,501	4,521	19,803	9,466	64,266	62,034	63,757	57,326
4 years or less	1.1	4.4	3.3	5.3	2.2	8.2	4.1	6.3	1.9	2.3	1.2	1.6
5–10 years	1.3	4.9	3.3	5.0	5.0	12.4	4.3	8.9	3.4	3.4	2.6	2.9
11–14 years	1.3	3.8	2.8	3.0	2.7	7.4	2.6	6.8	2.4	2.6	2.2	2.4
15–64 years	94.8	83.8	88.2	83.1	87.0	64.8	87.1	74.2	72.2	68.7	68.3	66.5

(continued)

Table 8.5 (continued)

	Migrants within Region				Other African Migrants				Non-African Migrants			
	1st Round		2nd Round		1st Round		2nd Round		1st Round		2nd Round	
	M	F	M	F	M	F	M	F	M	f	m	f

South Africa (continued)

65 years +	1.6	3.1	2.5	3.6	3.0	7.3	1.7	3.9	20.1	23.0	25.6	26.6
Sex ratio	3.14:1		1.65:1		2.10:1		2.09:1		1.03:1		1.11	

East Africa

Age (n)	528,448	468,854	587,531	596,672	56,142	49,219	38,598	43,815	15,431	13,042	8,732	7,380
4 years or less	10.7	12.1	11.7	10.9	15.0	17.2	16.2	16.2	11.6	13.9	7.6	9.6
5–10 years	11.5	12.5	13.1	13.0	14.5	17.0	17.9	17.9	12.4	10.5	8.3	10.6
11–14 years	7.2	8.1	9.0	9.5	8.5	8.7	10.0	11.1	6.1	7.2	4.9	6.0
15–64 years	61.7	61.0	58.7	60.9	55.7	54.8	53.3	51.8	62.5	63.1	70.8	66.9
65 years +	8.9	6.4	7.5	5.8	6.3	2.4	2.6	3.1	7.5	5.4	8.4	7.0
Sex ratio	1.13		0.98:1		1.14:1		0.88:1		1.18:1		1.18:1	

5 percent to 21 percent, dropped from 50 percent to 46 percent for male migrants from other African regions, and increased from 30 percent to 57 percent for migrants from outside Africa. For women, the proportion was fairly stable across migrants' status for the two rounds of census and was estimated at 15 percent for migrants from the region and more than 60 percent for migrants from outside Africa.

The general employment situation among migrants in Southern Africa showed that the employment rate dropped from 81 percent to 58 percent among migrants from the zone and also fell from 62 percent to 51 percent for migrants from other African regions. It increased from 54 percent to 60 percent among migrants from outside Africa. In the Southern Africa region, the proportion of those highly educated among the unemployed rose from 10 percent to 13 percent for migrants from the region; it dropped from 77 percent to 63 percent among migrants from other regions of Africa and was constant at 72 percent for international migrants for the first and second round of census, respectively.

The employment situation among migrants in the East African region showed that the rate of employment dropped from 67 percent to 52 percent for migrants from within the zone, from 67 percent to 34 percent for migrants from other African regions, and increased from 58 percent to 61 percent for migrants from outside Africa. The proportion of educated people who were unemployed in East Africa dropped from 11 percent to 6 percent of the total unemployed migrants from East Africa region, and also from 6 percent to 4 percent of migrants from other African regions. It increased from 28 percent to 87 percent among migrants from outside Africa.

5 DISCUSSION AND CONCLUSION

The census definition of international migration is limited to questions concerning place of birth and country of citizenship. These concepts conceal other major parameters and issues that may be very relevant in migration discourses. Despite these challenges, the information in African censuses is sufficient for raising issues of a developmental agenda as it relates to the movements of people within the continent. The volume of migration within Africa is quite enormous, with great potential for development. With these potentials, there are also critical challenges. Rural–urban migration in Africa, as well as the resultant urbanization, is unprecedented. Most of the African countries witnessing rapid urbanization lack the basic social amenities and economic growth to sustain the rapid urbanization. The attendant consequences are deteriorating amenities and threats to lives, property, and social security. With the huge volume of migration within Africa, the concern is how best to translate this into developmental dividends. It is noteworthy that there is no singular formal method of money remittance within

Table 8.6 Education-Employment Status Distribution of Migrants by Source, Round of Censuses across Three African Regions

	Migrants within Region						Other African Migrants						Non-African Migrants					
	1st Round			2nd Round			1st Round			2nd Round			1st Round			2nd Round		
	i	U	E	i	u	e	I	U	E	I	u	E	i	u	e	i	u	e
West Africa																		
Education (n)	61,900	4,940	78,080	120,140	3,960	158,600	2,000	80	1,800	5,440	480	2,880	7,660	540	9,120	54,700	2,960	92,280
No/less pry	83.7	69.2	89.4	79.2	46.5	83.7	52.0	0.0	63.3	29.8	29.2	21.5	24.8	7.4	12.7	70.8	39.2	70.6
Primary	13.3	23.1	7.1	17.8	35.4	12.0	23.0	25.0	13.3	20.2	16.7	27.8	45.4	40.7	21.5	22.2	34.5	18.0
Secondary	2.7	4.5	2.6	2.3	16.7	-3.1	19.0	50.0	15.6	40.1	41.7	29.9	20.6	37.0	26.1	5.1	18.9	7.1
Tertiary	0.4	3.2	0.8	0.7	1.5	1.2	6.0	25.0	7.8	9.9	12.5	20.8	9.1	14.8	39.7	1.9	7.4	4.3
South Africa																		
Education (n)	8,713	9,968	80,279	29,097	31,920	83,667	1,964	679	4,331	7,146	4,762	12,608	37,005	2,447	46,516	32,157	4,440	54,833
No/less pry	23.6	26.5	43.3	13.6	22.9	29.5	9.2	16.9	7.8	6.1	9.2	6.1	8.7	10.6	4.2	3.0	5.4	2.0
Primary	46.9	63.2	48.2	44.3	64.6	50.6	32.7	6.5	19.7	27.8	28.3	12.8	24.6	17.8	11.6	24.7	22.5	12.9
Secondary	26.2	9.5	7.1	37.4	12.2	16.4	45.9	50.2	43.4	50.8	50.0	55.2	58.5	57.1	62.7	51.6	56.2	55.1
Tertiary	3.4	0.9	1.4	4.7	0.4	3.5	12.3	26.5	29.1	15.3	12.6	25.9	8.1	14.5	21.5	20.7	16.0	30.1
East Africa																		
Education (n)	197,173	12,339	435,083	456,318	50,140	540,843	21,258	345	44,473	31,977	9,945	21,556	7,249	179	10,051	4,949	247	8,120
No/less pry	78.3	53.7	76.6	71.9	48.8	57.3	85.9	37.1	81.3	79.5	77.8	57.5	45.0	38.6	21.6	44.8	4.8	8.1
Primary	19.1	35.8	19.8	24.3	45.7	36.2	13.0	57.2	17.2	16.6	18.2	29.9	30.7	33.4	24.0	20.3	7.6	10.2
Secondary	1.5	7.8	1.5	2.5	3.5	2.8	0.9	5.8	1.0	3.7	3.9	8.3	14.4	28.0	23.3	18.5	66.7	40.4
Tertiary	1.2	2.8	2.1	1.3	2.0	3.6	0.1	0.0	0.5	0.3	0.1	4.3	9.8	0.0	31.7	16.4	20.9	41.3

Africa. The major operations are covered by Western Union/MoneyGram. This is a huge opportunity for the African banking system. The African migration system also raises issues on the potential of skill transfers within the region. As reiterated in the Ninth Ordinary Session of the Executive Council of the African Union (AU 2006), there is a need to optimize the benefits of migration within Africa (AU 2006). In conclusion, migration may provide the drive toward economic development in Africa. To optimize the benefits of regional and interregional migration in Africa, there is a need for pragmatic research and policy development.

ACKNOWLEDGMENTS

The authors gratefully acknowledge the Minnesota Population Center for permission to access IPUMS–International database, and all the reviewers whose comments helped to improve the quality of this chapter.

REFERENCES

Abraham, Katharina G. (1983) "Structural/Frictional vs. Deficient Demand Unemployment: Some New Evidence." *American Economic Review* 73 (1983): 708–724.
Adepoju A. (2001) "Regional Organizations and Intra-Regional Migration in Sub-Saharan Africa: Challenges and Prospects." *International Migration* 39 (6): 44–57.
Adepoju, A. (2005) "Perspectives on Migration within and from Sub-Saharan Africa." Background paper for the Conference on Policy Coherence for Development: The African Experience, Paris, OECD, November 3–4.
Adepoju, A. (2006) "Leading Issues in International Migration in Sub-Saharan Africa." In *Views on Migration in Sub-Saharan Africa: Proceedings of an African Migration Alliance Workshop*, ed. C. Cross, D. Gelderblom, N. Roux, and J. Mafukidze. Cape Town: HSRC Press.
Adepoju, A. (2008) "Perspectives on International Migration and National Development in Sub-Saharan Africa." In *International Migration and National Development in sub-Saharan Africa: Viewpoints and Policy Initiatives in Countries of Origin*, ed. A. Adepoju, T. van Naerssen, and A. Zoomers. Leiden: Brill.
Adepoju A. (2009) "Migration Management in West Africa within the Context of the ECOWAS Protocol on Free Movement of Persons and the Common Approach on Migration: Challenges and Prospects." In ed. M. Trémolière.
Adepoju, A. (2010) *International Migration within, to and from Africa in a Globalised World*. Network of Migration Research in Africa, Sub-Sahara Publisher.
African Union. (2006) "Elements for an African Common Position on Migration and Development." Development, Working Paper Series (96. 04), Cambridge, MA, Harvard.
Ammassari, Savina, and Richard Black. (2001) "Harnessing the Potential of Migration and Return to Promote Development: Applying Concepts to West Africa." Migration Working Papers, Sussex, July.
Barclay, Anthony. (2010) "Regional Economic Commission and Intra-Regional Migration Potential in Africa: Taking Stock." In *International Migration within, to and from Africa in a Globalized World*, ed. Aderanti Adepoju.

Bakewell, O., and H. de Haas. (2007) "African Migrations: Continuities, Discontinuities and Recent Transformations." In *African Alternatives*, ed. L. de Haan, U. Engel, and P. Chabal. Leiden: Brill.

Black, Richard, Savina Ammassari, Shannon Mouillesseaux, and Radha Rajkotia. (2004) "Migration and Pro-Poor Policy in West Africa." Working Paper C8, DRC on Migration, Globalisation and Poverty, University of Sussex.

Bouare, O. (2006) "Levels of Urbanization in Anglophone, Lusophone and Francophone African Countries. Views on Migration in Sub-Saharan Africa." Proceedings of an African Migration Alliance Workshop.

Cohen, R. (1997) *Global Diasporas. An Introduction*. London: UCL Press.

DaVanzo, Julie. (1981) "Microeconomic Approaches to Studying Migration Decisions." In *Migration Decision Making: Multidisciplinary Approaches to Microlevel Studies in Developed and Developing Countries*, ed. R.W. Gardner. New York: Pergamon Press.

De Hass, H. (2007) "Turning the Tide? Why Development Will Not Stop Migration." *Development and Change* 38 (5): 819–840.

Gleave, David, and David Palmer. (1980) "Spatial Variations in Unemployment: A Typology." Papers of the RSA44, 57–71.

Goldring, L. (2004) "Family and Collective Remittances to Mexico: A Multi-Dimensional Typology." *Development and Change* 35 (4): 799–840.

Lee, E.S. (1966) "A Theory of Migration." *Demography* 3 (1): 47–57.

Levitt, P. (1996) "Social Remittances: A Conceptual Tool for Understanding Migration and Meeting on Migration and Development." Presented to the African Union, Algiers, April 3–5.

Minnesota Population Center. (2011) *Integrated Public Use Microdata Series International: Version 6.1 [Machine-Readable Database]*. Minneapolis: University of Minnesota.

Muysken, Joan, Chris de Neubourg, and Huib van der Burg. (1982) "Regional and Occupational Labour Market Imperfections. The Netherlands 1955–1980." R.U.G. Research Memorandum no. 105, Groningen.

Ratha, D., S. Mohapatra, C. Özden, S. Plaza, W. Shaw, and A. Shimeles. (2011) *Leveraging Migration for Africa: Remittances, Skills, and Investments*. Washington, DC: World Bank.

Ratha, Dilip, and William Shaw (2007) "South–South Migration and Remittances." World Bank Working Paper no. 102. http://siteresources.worldbank.org/intprospEcts/resources/334934-110315015165/southsouthmigrationandremittances.pdf.

Ravenstein, E.G. (1885) "The Laws of Migration." *Journal of the Royal Statistical Society* 48 (2): 167–277.

Ravenstein, E.G. (1889) "The Laws of Migration." *Journal of the Royal Statistical Society* 52:241–305.

Rayp, G., and I. Ruyssen. (2010) "Africa on the Move: An Extended Gravity Model of Intra- Regional Migration." http://doku.iab.de/veranstaltungen/2010/TOM_2010_Ruyssen_Rayp.pdf. Accessed July 23, 2012.

Robin, N. (1997) "Atlas des migrations ouest-africaines vers l'Europe—1985–1993." In *International Migration and Development in Sub-Saharan*, ed. Sharon S. Russell et al. Paris: Orstom éditions.

Sassen, Saskia. (1988) *The Mobility of Capital and Labour: A Study in International Investment Labour Flow*. Cambridge: Cambridge University Press.

Shimeles, A. (2010) "Financing Goal 1 of the MDGs in Africa: Evidence from Cross-Country Analysis." Memo, Development Research Department, African Development.

Spaan, E. and D. van Moppes. (2006) "African Exodus? Trends and Patterns of International Migration in Sub-Saharan Africa." Working Papers Migration and Development series, Report no. 4, Nijmegen.

Todaro, M.P. (1969) "A Model of Labor Migration and Urban Unemployment in Less Developed Countries." *American Economic Review* 59:138–148.

Todaro, M.P. (1976) *Internal Migration in Developing Countries: A Review of Theory, Evidence, Methodology and Research Priorities.* Geneva: International Labour Office.

UN General Assembly. (2006) *International Migration and Development, Report of the Secretary-General.* New York: United Nations.

United Nations. (2006) *International Migration and Development. Report of the Secretary-General.* New York: United Nations.

United Nations. (2003) *The World Urbanization Prospect: 2003 Revision.* New York: United Nations.

USAID. (1997) "DOS Bureau for Refugee Programs, USAID, FAO." http://www.info.usaid.gov/HORN/images/affpophr.gif.

Van Dijk, H., D. Foeken, and K. van Til. (2001) "Population Mobility in Africa: An Overview." In *Mobile Africa: Changing Patterns of Movement in Africa and Beyond*, ed. M. de Bruijn, R. van Dijk, and D. Foeken, Leiden: Brill.

World Bank. (2011) *Migration and Remittances Factbook, 2011.* 2nd ed. Washington, DC: World Bank.

9 Demography of Labor Force in Sub-Saharan African Censuses

Clifford O. Odimegwu

1 INTRODUCTION

Globally, the twenty-first century has witnessed tremendous progress in the application of demographic methods to the study of labor force dynamics. Changes in population structure have also led to changes in labor force trends, sizes, and compositions both in the African continent and in the other regions of the world. Ruzicka (1973) wrote that the growth in the labor force sizes, together with changes in labor force age-sex structure, is closely linked with the demographic characteristics of population in any country. Changing dynamics and patterns of labor force participation in Africa, including changing demographic structures, are a source of concern for the present and future sizes and structures of the labor force in the continent. Population characteristics such as age structure, age-sex composition, population's socioeconomic characteristics—educational attainments, population well-being, nutritional status, and so on—have enormous influence on labor force sizes, structures, and levels. Other important issues, such as changes relating to transition to prime age, quantum and proportion, female labor force, women as primary breadwinners, underage labor, elderly labor, and disruptions to prime ages (because of HIV/AIDS and migration), have great implications for the labor force sizes and structures.

On the one hand, migration attributable to globalization and market liberalization has greatly influenced the entrance of increasing numbers of people into the labor force in a location different from their usual places of residence, both within and outside their own countries. On the other hand, Wobst and Arndt (2004) stated that sufficient time has passed since the emergence of the HIV virus in Africa. As a result, the twenty-first century is expected to witness a good number of HIV-positive cases growing into full-blown AIDS. Currently, HIV prevalence is still low in some regions in the continent, but Southern and Eastern African regions have a high HIV prevalence rates, sufficiently high to cause concerns for the levels and structure of the labor force as well as the length of economically active life in the continent. Also, the global economic crisis to which the African continent is not immune has great implications for the sizes, structures, and compositions of labor force in the continent.

Further, between the mid-1970s and early 1980s many African countries attained the demographic transition stage of low mortality and high fertility, leading to a dramatic increase not only in the expectation of life at birth but also to a corresponding increase in the length of productive years or working life in many African countries. However, as earlier noted, from the mid-1980s and even to the present time, the emergence of the HIV/AIDS pandemic has had adverse effects both on the life expectancy of the whole population and on the length of working life of the labor force population. The hard-earned gain in terms of mortality reduction and increase in life expectancy is fast being eroded in many sub-Saharan African (SSA) countries because of the effects of the HIV/AIDS pandemic, which has adversely affected the whole working population.

In particular, able-bodied and energetic men and women who are the agents of socioeconomic development are at the greatest risk of contracting the deadly disease. These recent developments have had a tremendous effect on the size and pattern of age-sex structure as well as the length of working life of many countries in the continent (Wobst and Arndt 2004). Also, various political crises and civil unrest in many countries have affected the labor force population, sizes, and composition in many countries in the continent. Examples of countries in this category include Rwanda in 1994, Sudan for more than two decades, Liberia in the early 1990s, and recently Libya and some other Northern African countries. Certain other countries attracted a high proportion of youth at certain points—Nigeria hosted many Ghanaians in the late 1970s to early 1980s, while South Africa has also hosted high volumes of youth within the region.

In addition, trends toward a delayed entry into the labor market as well as a declining age of exit from the labor force have been observed in the developed nations (Brugiavini and Peracchi 2005). African countries are not immune to this situation of delayed entry into the labor force. Because of an extended period of education as a result of many years spent in school, men and women's entry into the labor force is delayed. Besides, as a result of high rates of unemployment arising from the economic crunch that came with the era of structural adjustments in many developing countries, entry into the labor force has become further delayed for more people. Also, there is an increasing trend toward late retirement, thereby exerting great influence on the length of working life, particularly among the workforce in the informal sector.

The average length of working life has been recognized as an important long-term social and economic indicator in any society (Fullerton and Byrne 1976). It permits the estimation of time lost from work as well as the replacement needs in occupations (Fullerton and Byrne 1976). Krishnan (1977) also noted that demographers' interest in the computation of working life tables lies in the fact that the socioeconomic development of any nation is partly dependent on the size of the workforce and its characteristics. The changes in the sizes and structures of labor force as well as patterns and length of working life stemming from the recent demographic and socioeconomic realities in Africa thus necessitate the need for a computation of the length of working life in the continent. Thus, this chapter examines the sizes and structures of labor force populations as well as the length of working life for selected African countries, using available census data.

As stated above, the central focus of this chapter is to examine the dynamics of the African labor force. Development activities are regarded as the most important aspects of any census. Population censuses also remain the main source of comprehensive data on a labor force, although countries such as South Africa and a few others have developed specialized labor force surveys as secondary and supplementary source of information. Krishnan (1977) earlier noted that censuses are the major source of information useful for the computation of economic activities in any nation. Often, in most censuses and labor force surveys, information that has been generated has been limited to computation and analysis of basic rates. This chapter therefore intends to extend the frontier of the use of African censuses in the analysis of African labor force by (a) providing analytical approaches to the structure of the labor force in selected African countries, (b) examining changes in the labor force structure of these countries, and (c) computing African tables of economically active life, or labor force life tables. The last objective becomes especially important within the context of the AIDS pandemic, as well as other demographic and socioeconomic realities in the continent.

1.1 Some Theoretical Perspectives

This chapter has its theoretical underpinning in the labor theory of value. We computed the length of working life because of the importance of the supply of labor for the socioeconomic development of any society. First postulated by Adam Smith, the labor theory of value claims that the value of a product is determined by the necessary labor time needed to produce or obtain the product (Cohen 1979). Murphy (2006) argues that the labor theory of value posits that the value or natural price of a commodity is determined by the labor required to produce it. Hence, this chapter examines the available labor time in terms of the length of working life available for the production of goods and services in the selected countries.

2 DATA SOURCES AND METHODS

The sources of data for these analyses include: South African 1996 and 2001 census data (to represent the Southern Africa region), Senegalese 1988 and 2002 census data (representing the West African region), and Rwandan 1991 and 2002 census data (to represent the East African region). The South Africa and Rwandan census data were utilized to track the effect of HIV/AIDS on the length of working life in the continent. The rationale for selecting these countries lies in the fact that the two countries have at least two census waves and the HIV prevalence rates for the two countries are higher compared with countries in the other regions (INDEPTH Network 2004), as is the case in many other Southern and Eastern African countries.

Undeniably, the populations of most of the countries in Africa are not stable, which is attributable to the effect of fluctuating fertility rates. In addition, the hard-earned gain in terms of mortality reduction in the continent is being eroded by the impact of the HIV/AIDS pandemic. As a result, life expectancy has plummeted in most African countries in the wake of the era of HIV/AIDS. Thus, the populations of many African countries are at best quasi-stable. In order to take care of this lack of perfect stability, the INDEPTH model life table is considered appropriate for these analyses.

The INDEPTH model life table utilizes empirical data from demographic surveillance sites across the region to identify the two prevailing model families for the computation of life table functions for the SSA countries (INDEPTH Network 2004). Two patterns of life table functions are available in the INDEPTH model life table. While pattern 1 is applicable in countries with a low prevalence of HIV/AIDS, pattern 2 reflects the mortality pattern in countries with a high HIV/AIDS prevalence rate. The former depicts the situation in Eastern and Southern Africa (having HIV prevalence typically above 10 percent), while the latter depicts the situation in central and West African sub-regions, which typically have a HIV prevalence of less than 10 percent. For this reason, survivorship functions of INDEPTH model life table are used for our analyses; and computations of working life tables are done by gender.

2.1 Methodological and Technical Issues

The United Nations' handbook on the principles and recommendations for the conduct of population and housing censuses provides adequate approaches to the measurement of labor force participation in various countries. A detailed report on census methodology and technical issues on economic activity and labor force participation is available elsewhere (United Nations 2008).

3 RESULTS

3.1 Size of African Labor Force

According to the UN guidelines, a country's labor force size is measured by the crude activity rate, defined as the percentage of the total population classified in the census as members of an economically active population (age 15–64).

3.2 Size of Rwandan Labor Force (1991–2002)

According to 1991 census data, the sizes of the male and female labor force populations were almost the same. The share of male labor force population aged 15–64 was 81 percent of the total male population, while that of their female counterparts was 82 percent. The proportions recorded in the 2002 census were 66 percent and 71 percent for males and females, respectively. A higher decrease in the size of the male labor force population relative to that of females could be ascribed to the effect of the country's genocide that claimed the lives of many able-bodied men during the protracted civil war.

3.3 Size of Senegalese Labor Force (1988–2002)

According to the 1988 Senegalese census, a predominantly higher proportion of males (78.4 percent) than females (23 percent) were found in the labor force population. During the intercensal period between 1988 and 2002, the proportion of the male population in the labor force slightly declined, from 78.4 percent in 1988 to 76.3 percent in 2002, while that of females had a remarkable increase, from 23 percent to 31 percent during the period under study. The increase in the share of female labor force population was the result of increased empowerment among women and an increased need for women to assist their spouses in providing for the households. Before the structural adjustment program (SAP) era, the majority of women were engaged in noneconomic activities, such as being a full-time housewives, but the introduction of the SAP in many African countries forced more women to become economically active.

3.4 Size of South African Labor Force (1996–2001)

The two South African censuses showed that the proportion of the working males as a percentage of total male population in the labor force increased from 59.1 percent in 1996 to 64.2 percent in 2001, while that of females increased from 44 percent to 52 percent during the same period. It is reasonable to assume that the increase in the proportion of male and female labor force population was the result of the increasing expansion of the country's economy, which now accommodates men and women who had previously been denied free participation in economic activities during the country's long apartheid regime.

3.5 Age-Sex Structure of African Labor Force

It is demographers' interest to calculate a country's specific activity rate. This is often calculated using the formula $AR = P_e/P_t$, where P_e is the number of economically active persons in a given category of the population and P_t is the total number of persons in the same category of the population. Activity rates can be calculated by specific population characteristics, such as the age-sex specific activity rate, activity rate specific for marital status, activity rate specific for educational attainment, and so forth.

A consideration of the 1990 round of censuses in the selected countries showed that, except for South Africa, activity rates in Africa among young men and women age 15–19 were high. For instance, while male and female activity rates were around 11 percent within age-group 15–19 in South Africa in 1996, the rates were around 30 percent in Rwanda and Senegal during the period under study. In addition, it is also noticeable that, generally, male and female activity rates peaked around age categories 30–34 and 35–39 for all the selected countries. This pattern is expected as more people are found in the economically active population in the prime of their years. It is also remarkable to note that except for Senegal in 1988, where male activity rates were more than double those of females, there was no remarkable difference between the male and female activity rates in Africa. This may be attributed to the fact that women who had traditionally remained at home while men moved around in search of paid jobs are now increasingly fulfilling their own economic needs as a result of increased education and empowerment among women.

According to the 2000 rounds of censuses, female activity rates slightly increased in Senegal during the 1988–2002 period. An increase of between 5 percent and 10 percent in male and female activity rates was observed in South Africa within the intercensal period of five years, (1996–2001). South Africa is a country in transition, and as the country's economy expands during the second decade of her democratization, many people who had previously been denied free participation in economic activities were now able to fulfill their economic needs. However, Rwandan data showed a totally different pattern, as there was a drastic decline in male and female activity rates during the period 1991–2002. This observed pattern in age-sex structure may be attributable to the fact that the country is yet to fully recover from the genocide of the 1990s. Indeed, the death of a large number of young people would have long-term implications on the age-sex structure of both the total population and that of the labor force.

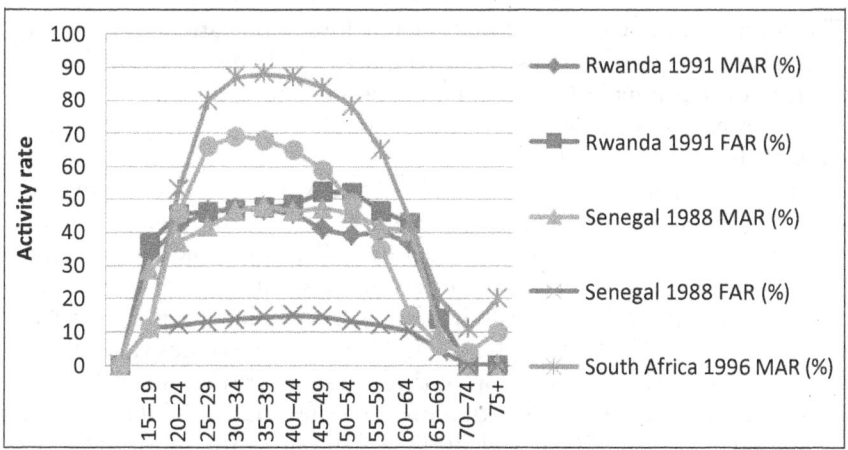

Figure 9.1 Age-sex activity rates of labor force by 1990 round of censuses.

Note: MAR = male activity rate, FAR = female activity rate.

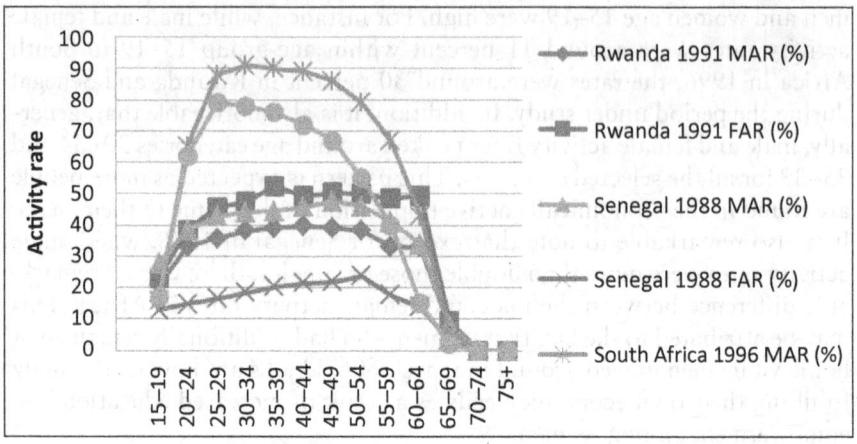

Figure 9.2 Age-sex activity rates of labor force by 2000 round of censuses.

3.6 Years of Economically Active Life in Africa

As pointed out earlier, the reality of the HIV/AIDS pandemic in Africa underscores the need for the computation of tables of economically active life in the continent. To account for the impact of the AIDS epidemic on the years of economically active life, survivorship functions of the INDEPTH life tables were used for the computation of life table estimates for each country. Specific life tables were computed for each country using the empirical data on the rates of infant ($_1q_0$) and under-five ($_5q_0$) mortality in each of the selected countries.

3.7 Years of Economically Active Life (Rwanda, 1991–2002)

The computed activity rates for the labor force population in age-group intervals of five years were used to extrapolate the hypothetical percentage of the working population working at the beginning of the age interval. This extrapolation is necessary because not all entrants to the labor force enter at the same age.

The years of economically active life for Rwanda were computed separately for males and females, using information from model life table and age-specific activity rates. As noted, Rwandan model life tables were computed based on the information on infant and under-five mortality for the period 1992–2005. Also, age-specific activity rates were computed using 1991 and 2002 data. There are no studies that utilized census data for the computation of the average working life in Rwanda.

The country's abridged working life tables for males and females were computed using the 1991 and 2002 Rwandan census data. The best working age-group among males and females indicates that the expectation of active life among females is slightly lower than that of males. This means that women lost more time to noneconomic activities than their male counterparts in their best working age-group. However, it is also remarkable to observe that women at older ages expended a higher percentage of their lifetime outside the economic sphere compared with their male counterparts. For instance, while older Rwandan men spent around half of their lives economically nonactive, their women counterparts in the older age-group spent up to 60 percent of their lives being economically inactive.

Comparing the results of the 1991 census data with data from the 2002 census, there is no remarkable difference in the country's expectation of active life. This is a reflection of stability in the country's mortality level during the period under study. According to the information on Rwandan 2005 Demographic and Health Survey (DHS), as indicated, the infant and under-five mortality rates (U5MRs) of 2005 had returned to the mortality levels of 1992. Results that show years of economically active life, according to the 2002 Rwandan census, display a form of stability in the country's length of working life for both males and females. Apparently, the country's mortality levels had returned to 1992 levels (Rwanda DHS) because the effect of genocide had eroded the gains that the country had recorded in terms of mortality decline. Although the mortality level has started to decline since the genocide, it may take many years before the decline reflects in the age-sex structure of the country's population.

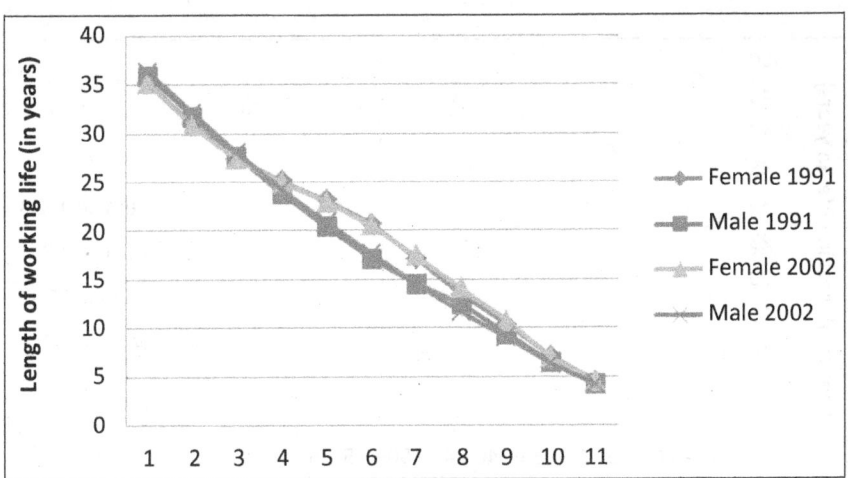

Figure 9.3 Rwandan length of working life, 1991–2002.

3.8 Years of Economically Active Life (Senegal, 1988–2002)

Senegal has a relatively high expectation of life at birth compared with other countries included in these analyses. The country's current life expectancy for both sexes stands at 63.1 years—65.1 for female and 61.0 for males. Also, the life expectancy based on our computation using the INDEPTH life table survivorship function puts the country's life expectancy at 64.6 years for females and 62.0 for males.

Information on the average work life span would be of interest to those engaged in matters related to labor force dynamics and planning in the country. Thus, according to 1988 census data, the percentage of lifetime lost to noneconomic activities for the best working age-group among Senegalese women was 22 percent, and it was 18 percent among their male counterparts. According to the country's 2002 census data, while there was a decline in the percentage of women's lifetime expended in noneconomic activities, there was a slight increase in the proportion of men's lifetime spent in activities that are considered economically inactive. This means that while there was increase in women's length of working life, there was a drop in the length of working life among the Senegalese men during the period under study.

3.9 Years of Economically Active Life (South Africa, 1996–2002)

The construction of the tables of economically active life is essentially based on the working population (Kpedekpo 1969). To compute the South African years of economically active life, we utilized the 1996 and 2001 census data to derive the age-specific activity rate (i.e., the proportion of working

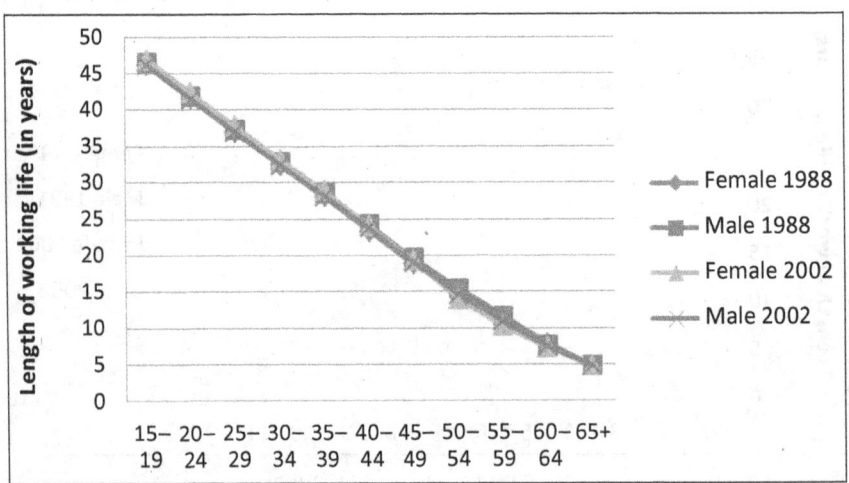

Figure 9.4 Length of working life Senegal, 1988–2002.

population to the total population in various five-year age categories). As previously shown, the computed activity rates for each age-group in five-year intervals were used to extrapolate the hypothetical percentage of the working population working at the beginning of the age interval.

The abridged table of economically active life, according to the 1996 census, indicates that the percentage of inactive lifetime among South African men rose gradually from age-group 15–19, later began to rise steeply around age 50–54, and peaked at age 65 plus. This pattern is expected. The percentage of inactive life is expected to rise with an increase in age. The data indicate that the South African men in their best working age-group would spend slightly more than a tenth of their lifetime economically inactive. Also, considering the economically active life for females, results show that about 20–60 percent of a South African woman's lifetime is expended, from a labor force point of view, in noneconomic activities. This may include the time spent doing household work, which mainly falls to the lot of women in most parts of SSA. Likewise, a higher proportion of lifetime spent by women outside the labor force may be the result of the HIV/AIDS pandemic that affects women more than their male counterparts.

A good use of the length of working life table is the computation of the losses from the economically active years as a result of death, disability, sickness, retirement, unemployment, or other reasons (Kpedekpo 1969). For a country such as South Africa, where HIV/AIDS prevalence is high, it is reasonable to expect that a substantial part of work life would be lost to death or permanent disability. The 2001 census data were utilized to estimate the changes (increase or decrease) in years of working life in South Africa. As a country in transition, the 2001 census and the previous one were conducted five years apart. Within the five-year period, South African men in their best working age-group would spend about one-seventh of

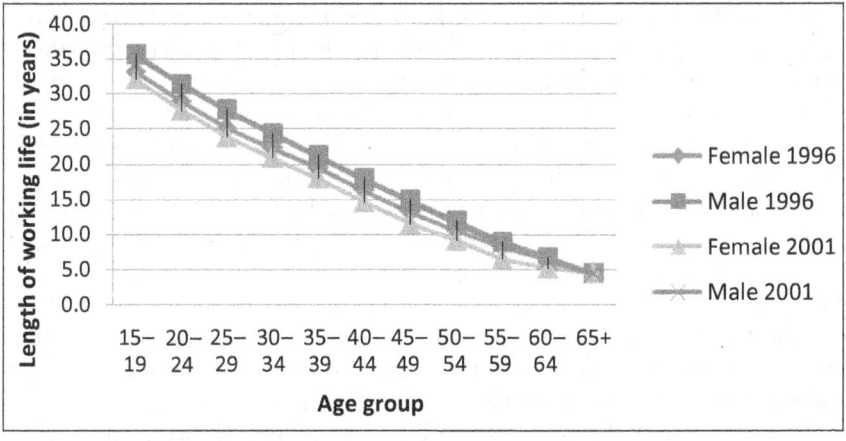

Figure 9.5 Length of working life South Africa, 1996–2001.

their lifetime outside the labor force. This shows some loss in the years of economically active life among the men. Also among women, instead of having some increase in years of economic active life because of the expansion in the country's economy, the observed trend indicates some loss in the length of working life during the period under study. Generally, losses in years of economically active life in South Africa could largely be attributed to the effect of the HIV/AIDS pandemic.

4 DISCUSSION AND CONCLUSION

Using census data, this chapter provides analytical approaches to studying the structure of the labor force and the changes in the labor force structure of the selected African countries Rwanda, Senegal, and South Africa. Also in this chapter, the African tables of economically active life were computed considering the recent socioeconomic realities and the effect of the HIV/AIDS pandemic on life expectancy in Africa. Although results showed that male and female activity rates mostly peaked around age categories 30–34 and 35–39 for all the selected countries, the results also indicate that the age structure of the labor force is becoming younger, with increased labor force participation at age 15–19 in the selected countries. Also, a higher decline in the proportion of male labor force population than that of females occurred between 1991 and 2002 in Rwanda. This pattern could be attributed to the effect of the country's genocide, which led to the death of many young and energetic men during the country's civil war. From a demographic standpoint, it is reasonable to assume that the death of a large number of young people would exert a long-term effect on the age-sex structure of the country's population; this will also invariably impact on the country's labor force population.

Also, the observed decline in the Senegalese male population in the labor force in 2002, in contrast to a remarkable increase in the female labor force population during the period, may be the result of increased empowerment of women as well as an increasing need for women to assist their spouses in providing for the economic needs of their households. This scenario has a beneficial implication for socioeconomic development as more women who were hitherto engaged in noneconomic activities move to participate in productive activities. This development is expected to lead to increased gross domestic product (GDP) and improved economic situation across the continent. Considering the South African data, it is reasonable to assume that the increase in the proportion of male and female labor force population was the result of the increasing expansion of the country's economy, which now accommodates men and women who had previously been denied free participation in economic activities during the apartheid era.

An examination of the age-sex specific activity rate showed that, except for South Africa, activity rates were high among young men and women aged 15–24 in the continent. Also, as earlier noted, for both sexes activity rates peaked around age categories 30–34 and 35–39 for all the selected countries. This pattern is similar to those found in the developed countries, as observed by Krishnan (1977). Such a pattern is expected as more people are found in the labor force population during the prime of their years. It is also remarkable that, except for Senegal in 1988, where male activity rates were more than double those of females, there was no remarkable difference between the male and female activity rates in Africa. In addition, and as earlier observed, more women are now found in the labor force because many women who had traditionally remained at home while men moved around in search of paid jobs are now sufficiently empowered to participate freely and fully in the labor force to fulfill their own economic needs.

Further, tables of economically active life provide useful information for socioeconomic planning relating to manpower and social security policies. The study of labor force trends, labor force sizes, and its age-sex structure provides useful information necessary for adequate manpower planning for any society (Wolfbein 1949). Considering the results of our analyses on the pattern and length of working life in the selected countries, some remarkable and interesting patterns were observed. Computation of the length of working life provides the basis to establish the losses incurred as a result of death, permanent disability, sickness, retirement, or other reasons. For a country such as South Africa, where HIV/AIDS prevalence is high, it is reasonable to expect that a substantial part of working life would be lost because of death or sickness. Our study showed that men in their best working age-group would spend around a tenth of their lifetime economically non-active, according to the 1996 census. But, according to the 2001 census, there was some sort of loss in the years of economically active life among the men. The 2001 data indicate that an average male worker who entered the labor force at age 15–19 would spend about one-seventh of his lifetime economically non-active. Also, the observed trend among women showed a similar pattern of loss in the years of working life during the period under study. This observed pattern in the loss of working life could be directly linked with the effect of HIV/AIDS on the country's total life expectancy.

During the period 1991–2002, the Rwandan working life tables indicate that the working lives tend to be shorter for men relative to women. This pattern is unexpected, but again it may be explained by the effect of the country's genocide, which led to the death of many able-bodied young men. As earlier stated, mortality levels may have started to decline since the genocide, but it would take several years before the decline in mortality rates reflect on the age-sex structure of the country's population. In addition, in Senegal, which has a higher life expectancy than other countries selected for this study, men unexpectedly spent a high proportion of their lifetime in economically inactive pursuits. While length of working life increased for women, working lives recorded some decline for men during the period under study.

Comparing the trends in length of working life for the three countries included in these analyses, overall, the Senegalese men and women in their best working age-groups would spend around one-fifth of their lives economically inactive. Although Senegalese life expectancy is higher than that of Rwanda (because of the effect of genocide) and South Africa (because of the effect of HIV/AIDS), working lives are found to be generally shorter for Senegal compared with South Africa and Rwanda. Additionally, it was observed that working lives tend to be shorter for women than men. This is expected and may include the time spent in doing household work, which mainly falls to the lot of women in various countries that have predominantly agrarian economies. We also attributed shorter working lives among women, which is attributable to the fact that HIV/AIDS affects women more than it affects their male counterparts.

Another usefulness of working life table is that it allows for comparisons between total life expectancy and working life expectancy, which could furnish useful information on the problem relating to old-age dependency (Wolfbein 1949). Our results indicate a widening gap between total life expectancies and working life expectancies in the selected countries. The results further indicate that the problem of old-age dependency is bulging in Africa. For instance, an average Senegalese male worker aged 15 has 57 years left as his life expectancy under 2002 conditions, but could only expect to remain in the labor force for another 46.1 years. If he survived to the older age-group, under this 2002 condition, he would have to make provisions for the average of 10.9 years that he would be out of the labor force. Thus it is remarkable to observe that the problem of old-age dependency seems more pronounced among women as a higher proportion of their old-age period is spent economically inactive.

The comparative picture of the labor force scenarios of the countries included in this study showed that the generally low level of life expectancy in SSA has had the effect of lowering the length of economically active life in the region. Perhaps the results of these analyses may also bear a close relationship to the importance of informal sectors in the economies of most of SSA countries.

Although males fare better than their female counterparts in labor force participation, there are generally increasing trends in female labor force participation in the selected countries during the period under study. The observed trend indicates that the gaps between male and female labor force participation would get smaller because female participation in the labor force is expected to increase and improve.

4.1 Limitations

Some limitations should be taken into consideration when interpreting the findings in this chapter. First, censuses are rarely conducted in Africa at regular intervals of ten years, hence Senegalese 1988 census, Rwandan

1991 census, and South African 1996 census data were used representing the 1990 round of censuses, and South Africa (2001), Rwanda (2002), and Senegalese (2002) censuses were used to represent the 2000 round of censuses. We utilized the available data because census data for the most recent times were not available. Nevertheless, findings in this chapter could still be regarded as a sound representation of the current situations in the selected countries. This is because the estimated life expectancies for the selected countries are not very different from the current life expectancies in the selected countries. Second, other countries, including North African countries, were not included in this chapter because of the non-availability of data; where they were available, only one data point was available. Third, the data utilized in this chapter were the 10 percent samples of the census data of the selected countries. However, these samples were chosen through multistage random probability sampling in order to ensure representativeness.

ACKNOWLEDGMENTS

The author gratefully acknowledges the Minnesota Population Center, for permission to access the IPUMS–International database, and all the reviewers whose comments contributed to refining the quality of this chapter.

NOTES

1. Access to Integrated Public Use Microdata Series (IPUMs) was provided by Minnesota Population Center, University of Minnesota, USA (2011).
2. INDEPTH is the acronym for the International Network for the Demographic Evaluation of Populations and Their Health in Developing Countries, and it is a global network of members that conduct longitudinal health and demographic evaluation of populations in low- and middle-income countries.
3. Children below age 15 and older people above age 65 were excluded from the analysis in order to allow for international comparisons across countries.
4. Specific life tables were computed for each country using the empirical data on the rates of infant ($_1q_0$) and under-five ($_5q_0$) mortality of the selected countries.
5. Activity rate is computed using P_e/P_t, where P_e is the number of economically active persons in a given category of the population and P_t is the total number of persons in the same category of the population.

REFERENCES

Brugiavini, Agar, and Franco Peracchi. (2005) "The Length of Working Lives in Europe." *Journal of the European Economic Association* 3 (2–3): 477–486.
Cohen, G.A. (1979) "The Labor Theory of Value and the Concept of Exploitation." *Philosophy and Public Affairs* 8 (4): 338–360.

Fullerton, Jr., Howard N., and James J. Byrne. (1976) "Length of Working Life for Men and Women, 1970." *Monthly Labour Review* 32:31–35.

INDEPTH Network. (2004) *INDEPTH Model Life Tables for Sub-Saharan Africa*. Ghana: Ashgate Publishing Company.

Kpedekpo, G.M.K. (1969) "Working Life Tables for Males in Ghana, 1960." *Journal of the American Statistical Association* 64 (325): 102–110.

Krishnan, P. (1977) "The Length of Working Life: India, 1971." *Journal of the Royal Statistical Society* 140 (3): 359–365.

Minnesota Population Center. (2011) *Integrated Public Use Microdata Series International: Version 6.1 [Machine-Readable Database]*. Minneapolis: University of Minnesota.

Murphy, Robert P. (2006) "The Labor Theory of Value: A Critique of Carson's Studies in Mutualist Political Economy." *Journal of Libertarian Studies* 20 (1): 17–33.

Ruzicka, L.T. (1973) "Length of Working Life for Australian Males: 1933–66." *Economic Record* vol. 2:280–289.

United Nations. (2008) *Principles and Recommendations for Population and Housing Censuses*.

Wobst, Peter, and Channing Arndt. (2004) "HIV/AIDS and Labor Force Upgrading in Tanzania." *World Development* 32 (11): 1831–1847. http://dx.doi.org/10.1016/j.worlddev.2004.06.012. Accessed on 25/6/2012

Wolfbein, Seymour L. (1949) "The Length of Working Life." *Population Studies* 3 (3): 286–294.

10 The Dynamics of Household Structure in Sub-Saharan Africa

Latifat D.G. Ibisomi and Nicole De Wet

1 INTRODUCTION

1.1 Definition and Types of Household Structure

The term *household* is not consistently defined. Many varying terms and criteria are used to define a household. For Bongaarts (2001), a household is defined as a group of persons (or one person) who make common provision for food, shelter, and other essentials for living. On the other hand, Dungumaro (2008) defines a household as the arrangement of persons according to their relationship to the head of household, whereas Goldstein and colleagues (2000) define a household as a person or group of persons related or not that usually live together in one or more dwellings, eat together, take care of their daily fundamental needs together, and are under the responsibility of a head whose authority is recognized by all members of the household. This definition was derived from the definitions in the various countries' census forms.

The composition of households is also not static; varied amalgamations of individuals make up households in Africa and elsewhere. For example, in recent times in Africa, two types of household structure have emerged. These are child- and grandparent-headed households. There is also a rapid growth of female-headed and single-parent households. The reasons contributing to the development of these households include HIV/AIDS and poverty. Rapid urbanization and slackened societal control also contribute to the growth of the latter group of households.

Household type is a constructed variable that describes the composition of households. It is constructed from the perspective of the household head (Minnesota Population Center 2011). From the IPUMS constructed categories, we reclassified the households into six as follows:

1. Single-person.
2. Nuclear: comprising the household head plus spouse or spouses with or without their children.
3. Single-parent household: household head with his or her children.

4. Extended: category 2 or 3 with other relatives. This also includes heads without a spouse or children but with other relatives.
5. Composite: category 2, 3, or 4 with nonrelatives (contains members of more than one biological family).
6. Other: this comprises nonfamily households and institutional or group quarters, as well as unclassifiable (largely because of quality of enumeration) households.

1.2 Characteristics of Households in Sub-Saharan Africa

The household size and composition and how the two vary over time are important elements to note when examining household structure. These two have consequences for the socioeconomic well-being as well as demographic outcomes within households. The size, sex, and age composition of members of households influence decisions regarding consumption, labor force participation, and savings. For instance, Bongaarts (2001) found that sub-Saharan Africa (SSA) has the highest average number of children and the lowest average number of adults per household. This is problematic from economic and social perspectives because of the high dependency on household resources in this type of situation.

In rural South Africa, trend data showed that average household size declined and female headship increased (Madhaven and Schatz 2007). At the national level in South Africa, the average household size in female-headed households (FHHs) was found to be higher than in male-headed households (MHHs) (Dungumaro 2008). One reason proposed for the larger household size in FHHs is that in African societies there is a tradition of leaving responsibilities to the females, including care for the sick and the elderly (Chant 2003). The study by Dungumaro (2008) further showed that 21.7 percent of FHHs in South Africa had at least one elderly person living there compared with 9.3 percent of MHHs. All these factors have implications for the generation of income, and its spending, as well as for the general welfare of people that constitute these households.

1.3 Female-Headed Households (FHHs)

The emergence and increasing growth of FHHs in Africa is of particular interest in emerging household typologies. The United Nations identifies female heads of households as "women (who) are financially responsible for their families and who are key decision makers and household managers or who are the main, economic contributors" (United Nations, cited in Sabra et al. 2006, 459). However, the presence of an adult male in the household, regardless of the adult female's financial contributions, has led to many regarding those as MHHs. This suggests that the proportion of FHHs may have been consistently underestimated because of widespread cultural practices that typically regard males as heads of households.

Bongaarts (2001) showed that there is a substantial proportion of FHHs in the forty-three countries that he studied. These ranged from 13 percent in the Near East/North Africa to 17 percent in Asia, and from 22 percent in SSA to 24 percent in Latin America. An important factor contributing to the increasing number of FHHs in SSA is HIV/AIDS (Peters, Walker, and Kambewa 2008; Bryceson 2006; Dorward, Mwale, and Tuseo 2006). Also, in cases of divorce and separation, children are more likely to live with their mothers (Iacovou and Skew 2011). Although small, the increasing trend in nonmarital childbearing, especially among older and relatively economically well-to-do women, also contributes to the growth of FHHs.

However, studies have shown FHHs to be disadvantaged, vulnerable to diseases, financially poor, and having limited access to resources compared with MHHs (Oppong 1997; Mbugua 1997). Many women become household heads after their economically active husbands die (Peters, Walker, and Kambewa 2008; Bryceson 2006; Dorward, Mwale, and Tuseo 2006). This loss of human capital creates a burden on women who are forced to provide for themselves and their children. The situation is often made worse if the female head is also sick. The economic difficulties of women have been tagged 'a triple burden,' which comprises (a) the disadvantage that women experience in terms of labor market participation and income, (b) the dual task of parenting and working, and (c) the higher dependency burden, because many of these women do not live in dual-income households (Dungumaro 2008). These burdens are, for instance, seen in Malawi, where up to 25 percent of households were headed by women of which 48 percent live below the poverty line (Takane 2009). Further, Moghadam (1997) showed that urban female heads of households in Zimbabwe were less likely to obtain income from employment and had fewer prospects of employment prospects than males.

1.4 Objectives of the Study

In this study, we (a) document the levels and pattern of the total number of households, average household size, and household types over time, across SSA, and (b) examine the dynamics of FHHs in the subregion. In discussing the results of the study, we relate the observed trends in household size and composition to trends in selected socioeconomic, demographic, and health indicators. This is because household size and composition have been associated with infant mortality and the number of children born as well as productivity and income within households (Adhikari and Sawangdee 2011; Mahfouz et al. 2009; White and Masset 2003; Charmarbagwala et al. 2004).

1.5 Rationale

The household is the basic family unit in most societies and is usually the nucleus of joint decisions regarding production, consumption, and savings. Thus, household size and composition and how the two vary over time have consequences for the socioeconomic well-being as well as demographic and health outcomes within households. Understanding the size and composition of households is therefore crucial to understanding the situation in which many Africans currently live. The recent growth of population amid urbanization, the HIV/AIDS pandemic, and slackened societal control has resulted in changes in household sizes and composition; most of these changes remain undocumented. The rapid growth in FHHs is of particular interest in this study as economic burdens that should ordinarily be shouldered by adult household members are often not shared but carried by only the female head in such households. For this reason, there is a need to establish the proportion and distributions of FHHs in SSA as well as the rate of change in the proportion, as these households are more vulnerable to economic crisis.

Further, household size, structure, and composition are varied and are constantly changing in contemporary African societies. The composition of households is no longer static, with wide community- and regional-level differences existing on the continent. These diverse patterns of household composition require further examination as consequences of the varying patterns may also be quite varied and could further aggravate the already existing health and socioeconomic inequality. Examining the total number of households—an often neglected area—is also of importance, as the combination of this factor with the average household size ultimately determines the total population.

Further, we have limited knowledge about the dynamics of household size and composition within the different types of households and how these are linked to aggregate socioeconomic indicators. Most studies on households have also been based on surveys and have rarely been done at national level. With the array of living arrangements in the subregion, there is a need for this detailed and comprehensive view of households using multicountry census data for a more complete picture of the similarities and or variability that exist within and among countries in the subregion.

2 METHODOLOGY

2.1 Data Source

The study used a 5 percent sample of Mali, Rwanda, Kenya, Tanzania, Uganda, Malawi, and South Africa integrated census data. These seven countries were chosen because they were the only sub-Saharan countries with at least two accessible data points from the IPUMS–International data bank from which we sourced the data sets (Minnesota Population Center 2011). The total fertility rates (TFR) and under-one mortality estimates were obtained from the StatCompiler of the measuredhs (from DHS data) website (see www.measuredhs.com), while some of the estimates for South Africa were obtained from CIA Factbook (2011). The human development index (HDI) and gender inequality index (GII) estimates were obtained from the UNDP (2011) 'Human Development Report.'

2.2 Data Analysis

Most of the analyses conducted used the household as the unit of analysis, but individuals were used in the computation of average household size and total population. It is important to note that group quarters were not utilized in the calculation of average household size. The samples were weighted (using record-specific weights supplied with the sample data) to give the overall population estimates in analyses. Analyses were restricted to households for which the records for the head are in the data set and whose heads were 10 years old and above. Our analyses are mostly descriptive and results presented largely using graphs and tables.

2.3 Limitations and Challenges

While harmonized data makes the data set usable in addition to making the countries as comparable as possible, it obscures certain details. For instance:

1. Relationship to head of households: all persons that were not a spouse/partner or child of heads of households were classified as other relatives, making it difficult to establish exact kinship relationships. It was also difficult to distinguish biological, adoptive, and stepparent–child relationships. This limited the analysis that we could do on extended household type.
2. The manner in which employment, marital status, and to some extent education were classified also limited the analysis that we could do using the harmonized data. Further, the definition varies across countries and even within countries over time.
3. The differential in household structure between urban and rural areas was not examined in this study because the variable was not available for all countries or the two census years in some countries.

2.4 Data Quality Assessment

Because the data have been cleaned by the national statistical offices and the IPUMS technical staff, they were considered clean on face value. We used age sparingly in the analysis and assumed that age misreporting and over- and undercount of the population were random. Although heads of household could have been culturally defined in some of these cases, we suspect that there could also be some data quality issues especially in cases where the heads of household were less than 10 years old. We thus excluded from analysis households headed by persons less than 10 years old. This is not expected to adversely affect the results as these cases were extremely small (< 0.005 percent in all cases).

3 RESULTS

3.1 Total Number of Households

As shown in Table 10.1, the total number of households increased in all the countries examined. The greatest percentage change in the number of households occurred in Tanzania, with a 58.5 percent increase, followed by Uganda with a 49.50 percent change. The countries with the lowest percentage change in number of households were Rwanda (16.5 percent) and Mali (19.0 percent).

Table 10.1 Trend in Total Number of Households ('000) and the Percentage Change in Number of Households between the Two Censuses by Type of Household

	Western Africa	Central Africa	Eastern Africa			Southern Africa	
	Mali	Rwanda	Kenya	Tanzania	Uganda	Malawi	South Africa
Total Number of Households ('000)							
Census 1	1,359	1,508	4,346	4,540	3,431	1,859	9,316
Census 2	1,617	1,757	6,301	7,196	5,129	2,272	11,522
Percentage Change in Number of Households							
Total	18.98	16.48	44.98	58.50	49.48	22.24	23.68
Single person	−12.26	−0.05	49.26	47.89	46.27	−3.02	20.30
Nuclear	26.50	−13.93	44.64	81.41	102.59	36.25	9.55
Single parent	13.11	71.32	31.42	100.25	43.90	4.95	16.57
Extended	−4.12	22.91	61.04	9.85	26.14	16.11	59.82
Composite	67.70	126.50	44.79	149.61	−27.19	14.79	−15.36
Other	121.70	18.72	−32.85	52.52	7.15	92.07	−10.82

3.1.1 Number of Households by Household Types

Although the number of households increased in all the countries at the aggregate level, there is variability in this trend by type of households. Table 10.1 shows the decline in the number of single-person households in Mali and Malawi; in the number of nuclear households in Rwanda; in the number of composite households in Uganda and South Africa; and in the number of other households in Kenya and South Africa. The notable decline in the number of nuclear households in Rwanda could be attributable to the disappearance of families and households as a result of the civil war. This perhaps accounts (in part) for the observed 126.5 percent increase in the number of composite households in Rwanda.

3.2 Average Household Size

Table 10.2 shows that average household size declined in four of the seven countries. A slight (about 1 percent) increase is observed in Uganda and Malawi and a notable increase in Mali (6 percent). Percentage changes in average household size in the four countries where average household size declined ranged from –9.6 percent in Kenya to –4.3 percent in Rwanda.

Table 10.2 Trend in Average Household Size and Percentage Change in Average Household Size between the Two Censuses by Type of Household

Type of Household	Western Africa	Central Africa	Eastern Africa			Southern Africa	
	Mali	Rwanda	Kenya	Tanzania	Uganda	Malawi	South Africa
Average Household Size							
Census 1	5.77	4.91	4.90	5.04	4.77	4.28	4.10
Census 2	6.12	4.70	4.43	4.64	4.82	4.34	3.84
Percentage Change in Average Household Size							
Total	6.07	–4.28	–9.59	–7.94	1.05	1.40	–6.34
Single person	0.00	0.00	0.00	0.00	0.00	0.00	0.00
Nuclear	0.98	–7.41	–11.17	–5.66	9.42	2.20	–3.69
Single parent	7.69	–17.48	–16.74	–0.26	3.17	1.40	–9.57
Extended	4.01	–6.31	–9.76	–11.09	0.84	–1.81	3.95
Composite	–0.32	–4.51	–9.56	–10.90	–1.19	–4.42	6.04
Other	2.22	–10.95	–36.72	–18.34	13.25	13.49	–0.68

Table 10.2 also shows the percentage change in average household size by household type in the countries examined. The observed increase in average household size in Mali is also exhibited by the various types of households in the country. Similarly, in Rwanda the decline in average household size at the national level is seen among all the household types.

The average household size declined among all household types in Kenya and Tanzania. The opposite is found in Uganda, where the average household size increased in all the types of household except in the composite type.

Changes in average household size in South Africa were exactly the reverse of the trend in Malawi, where average household size declined in nuclear and single-parent households and increased in extended and composite households.

3.3 Household Structure: Types of Households

Table 10.3 shows that nuclear and extended households are the dominant household types in all the countries studied, with extended households in the majority in the three East African countries. These are followed by composite and single-parent households. A single-person household is the least popular type, ranging from a low of about 1 percent in Mali to a high of about 5 percent in South Africa. Other types of household, which consist largely of unclassifiable households, comprise about 5 percent, except in census 2 in Mali and census 1 in South Africa.

The trend in percentage distribution of household types varies among the household types themselves and among the countries examined. The greatest positive change in distribution occurred in the growth of composite households in Rwanda and Tanzania; single-person households in Kenya; nuclear households in Uganda; extended households in South Africa and 'other' types of households in Mali and Malawi. The high percentage change in other types of households in Mali and Malawi could be attributable to the difficulty in categorizing households appropriately in the latter censuses. The decline in the percentage of nuclear households in Rwanda and the corresponding growth in single-parent, composite, and other household types could stem from household dissolution as a result of the civil war, which occurred between the two censuses examined. The situation in Uganda is somewhat different from this, as only the nuclear households grew in percentage change among the regular household types. This is in line with what is expected as young people transit into adulthood and form new households.

In Kenya, the increase in percentage of single-person and extended households might actually be related; young adults migrate especially to urban areas for employment, leaving their children with families

Table 10.3 Percentage and Change in Distribution of Types of Households

Type of Household	Western Africa			Central Africa			Eastern Africa								Southern Africa					
	Mali			Rwanda			Kenya			Tanzania			Uganda			Malawi			South Africa		
	1987	1998	% change	1991	2002	% change	1989	1999	% change	1988	2002	% change	1991	2002	% change	1987	1998	% change	1996	2001	% change
Single person	1.01	0.70	−30.69	1.54	1.30	−15.58	2.84	3.24	14.08	2.37	2.42	2.11	2.64	2.56	−3.03	2.50	1.96	−21.6	4.68	4.07	−13.03
Nuclear	42.33	44.48	5.08	53.27	37.43	−29.74	32.03	31.46	−1.78	26.89	31.71	17.92	29.34	43.08	46.83	39.33	44.18	12.33	28.9	27.04	−6.44
Single parent	3.80	3.67	−3.42	9.22	13.52	46.64	13.96	12.52	−10.32	8.26	11.44	38.50	8.57	8.44	−1.52	9.96	8.56	−14.06	9.86	9.37	−4.97
Extended	40.07	31.65	−21.01	20.88	21.21	1.58	37	41.05	10.95	45.54	30.69	−32.61	44.88	37.81	−15.75	38.51	35.41	−8.05	34.88	51.74	48.34
Composite	7.19	9.52	32.41	11.04	21	90.22	9.64	9.63	−0.10	14.35	22.01	53.38	11.68	5.56	−52.40	7.34	6.5	−11.44	4.28	3.43	−19.86
Other	5.6	9.98	78.21	4.06	5.54	36.45	4.52	2.11	−53.32	2.59	1.73	−33.20	2.89	2.54	−12.11	2.36	3.4	44.07	17.39	4.35	−74.99
Total Number (million)	7.85	9.92	26.37	7.43	8.43	13.46	21.24	28.15	32.53	23.11	33.44	44.70	16.57	24.99	50.81	8.00	9.92	24.00	40.49	44.74	10.50

***Number of people living in each type of household can be computed from the last row.

and relatives at their places of origin. The upsurge in the percentage of single-parent and composite households in Tanzania is worthy of note and could be a result of social changes that have impacted the living arrangements of the people. Percentage change in extended households in South Africa is high, at about 48 percent. It has been found that 18.3 percent of children in South Africa with both parents alive do not live with their biological parents (Dungumaro 2011). This perhaps explains the high growth recorded in extended households in the country. There was a general decline in single-person households in all the countries except Kenya and Tanzania. The nuclear households grew substantially in Uganda, by about 47 percent, and fell in Rwanda by about 30 percent—the latter probably because of the civil war as previously mentioned. Mali, Tanzania, and Malawi also recorded growth in the percentage change in nuclear households. The decline in 'other' household types in South Africa is more likely a result of better-quality data in relation to improved classification of households at census 2.

3.4 Focus on Female-Headed Households

Table 10.4 shows that the percentage of FHHs is quite substantial except in Mali. The proportion of FHHs grew substantially in Rwanda between the two censuses, which is likely attributable to the demise of the males during the civil war. The increase in Kenya, Tanzania, and South Africa could be a result of social changes, such as more empowered women, marital instability, and perhaps the loss of the male heads to HIV/AIDS.

Also from Table 10.4, the two top FHH types are single-parent and single-person. Female headship is also high in extended, composite, and other household types in East(ern) and South(ern) Africa. The percentage of female-headed nuclear households is also on the rise in the countries in the two regions, except in Uganda and Malawi. Further, at least four-fifths of single-parent households are female-headed.

3.5 Average Household Size by Sex of Head of Household

From Table 10.5, average household size is generally higher in MHHs than in the female-headed ones at the aggregate level and among the various types of households. The exception is South Africa, where the average household size is higher in FHHs compared with MHHs at the national level, as also found by Dungumaro (2008). Expectedly, average household size is higher in single-parent households headed by females than in single-parent households headed by males. Despite the higher average size in MHHs, the burden of the relatively lower average household size in FHHs on their heads of household could be substantially larger, given that there is often only one economically active person in such a household. At the national level, average household size in FHHs increased in Mali only.

Table 10.4 Percentage of Households Headed by Females by Type of Households

Type of Household	Western Africa			Central Africa			Eastern Africa									Southern Africa					
	Mali			Rwanda			Kenya			Tanzania			Uganda			Malawi			South Africa		
	1987	1998	% change	1991	2002	% change	1989	1999	% change	1988	2002	% change	1991	2002	% change	1987	1998	% change	1996	2001	% change
Single person	44.98	41.76	-7.16	28.96	37.69	30.15	31.97	33.32	4.22	33.48	36.57	9.23	31.77	29.54	-7.02	38.92	40.02	2.83	42.52	40.9	-3.81
Nuclear	0.35	0.31	-11.43	3.22	0.47	-85.40	3.7	6.53	76.49	5.48	6.18	12.77	1.18	0.85	-27.97	7.08	10.02	41.53	6.21	11.56	86.15
Single parent	85.62	81.23	-5.13	87.02	92.54	6.34	87.45	87.39	-0.07	83.29	86.35	3.67	81.16	79.47	-2.08	92.28	88.97	-3.59	87.76	87.34	-0.48
Extended	14.83	13.02	-12.20	43.77	47.92	9.48	40.88	44.48	8.81	36.43	38.67	6.15	34.43	30.58	-11.18	44.43	40.17	-9.59	50.51	54.84	8.57
Composite	10.66	10.33	-3.10	23.88	37.91	58.75	36.22	38.13	5.27	29.05	29.76	2.44	31.12	23.54	-24.36	35	27.7	-20.86	31.36	37.62	19.96
Other	14.92	15.08	1.07	22.05	37.17	68.57	30.51	27.66	-9.34	33.49	32.48	-3.02	30.11	30.01	-0.33	38.39	47.87	24.69	46.45	32.39	-30.27
Total	13.91	11.82	-15.03	24.75	35.01	41.45	35.02	36.85	5.23	31.51	32.92	4.47	28.45	23.12	-18.73	33.66	31.01	-7.87	37.77	41.89	10.91

Table 10.5 Average Household Size by Sex of Household Head and Type of Household

Type of Household	Western Africa		Central Africa		Eastern Africa						Southern Africa			
	Mali		Rwanda		Kenya		Tanzania		Uganda		Malawi		South Africa	
	1987	1998	1991	2002	1989	1999	1988	2002	1991	2002	1987	1998	1996	2001
Nuclear														
Male	5.1	5.4	5.3	4.9	5.3	4.7	4.8	4.5	4.7	5.1	4.1	4.2	3.8	3.7
Female	4.3	3.8	5.0	4.7	4.8	4.4	4.1	4.2	4.1	4.5	4.0	4.0	3.8	3.5
Single parent														
Male	3.3	3.9	3.7	3.7	3.8	3.4	3.5	3.6	3.4	3.6	3.2	3.5	3.2	3.0
Female	3.6	3.8	4.2	4.0	4.5	4.0	4.0	3.9	3.9	4.0	3.6	3.6	3.8	3.5
Extended														
Male	7.7	7.9	5.9	5.4	6.5	5.9	6.7	6.0	6.4	6.4	5.9	5.8	5.4	5.6
Female	4.9	5.1	4.3	4.3	5.6	5.1	5.3	4.9	5.1	5.1	5.1	4.9	5.2	5.5
Composite														
Male	9.6	9.6	6.8	6.7	7.5	6.8	8.2	7.2	7.9	7.8	7.5	7.1	5.4	5.8
Female	7.7	7.5	6.2	5.8	6.7	6.1	7.2	6.6	7.0	6.6	6.8	6.6	5.5	5.8
Total														
Male	6.1	6.4	5.1	5.0	5.0	4.5	5.3	4.8	5.0	5.0	4.4	4.5	4.0	3.7
Female	3.7	4.1	4.2	4.2	4.6	4.2	4.5	4.2	4.3	4.1	4.1	4.0	4.2	4.0

However, within categories of household types, increases were found in nuclear FHHs in Tanzania and Uganda, single-parent FHHs in Mali and Uganda, and extended FHHs in Mali and South Africa, as well as in composite FHHs in South Africa.

3.6 Socioeconomic Status of Heads of Household

The first panel of Table 10.6 shows that more male heads of households are employed compared with female heads of households, even in single-parent households that are predominantly headed by females. This finding further suggests the difficult conditions of living that the residents of FHHs might be in.

The second panel of Table 10.6 shows the educational disparity that exists between male and female household heads. At virtually all levels, the percentage of male heads with a secondary or higher level of education surpasses that of female heads. This also has implications for the access to resources enjoyed by the female heads and the eventual welfare of the residents of FHHs. For Rwanda, there are no data on level of education at census 1.

4 DISCUSSION

This study examined the levels and pattern of the total number of households, average household size, and household types over time, across SSA, with a special focus on FFHs. Results show that the average household size declined but with a greater proportional increase in the total number of households. The estimated average household sizes found in this study were generally similar to the estimates obtained from the countries' Demographic and Health Survey data sets except in Mali and to some extent Tanzania. Similar findings on average household size have been reported in the literature (see, for example, Pelser and Redelinghuys 2009; Dungumaro 2008; Madhaven and Schatz 2007; Bongaarts 2001). The decline in average household size has been ascribed, among other reasons, to social changes in living arrangements, aging of the population, rising divorce rates, and declining fertility rates (Pelser and Redelinghuys 2009).

The two top types of households were nuclear and extended. Also, single-parent households, about four-fifths of which were female-headed, were becoming prominent. Results further showed that the percentage of FHHs was high and increasing, even in the nuclear household type. Bongaarts (2001) reported a similar finding. However, the estimates obtained using the DHS data sets were generally lower than found in this study, especially in Tanzania; the reason for this is not apparent. The average household size in the FHHs was found to be almost as high as found in MHHs, but with female heads of households being less likely to have

Table 10.6 Percentage of Employed Heads of Household and Heads of Households with Secondary or Higher Level of Education

	Western Africa		Central Africa		Eastern Africa						Southern Africa			
	Mali		Rwanda		Kenya		Tanzania		Uganda		Malawi		South Africa	
Type of Household	1987	1998	1991	2002	1989	1999	1988	2002	1991	2002	1987	1998	1996	2001
					Employed									
Single person														
Male	85.71	85.11	91.80	88.45	91.59	90.12	93.92	87.80	88.88	74.70	91.14	91.28	62.09	50.83
Female	40.64	40.44	65.74	70.57	74.81	78.45	81.53	72.43	68.88	57.65	84.53	88.75	50.68	46.39
Nuclear														
Male	93.01	93.45	96.48	95.07	94.08	94.41	96.61	93.59	94.60	77.95	96.55	97.96	72.30	64.45
Female	40.71	42.86	97.19	93.42	71.52	70.01	82.70	71.02	75.49	64.92	84.90	87.98	38.43	35.33
Single parent														
Male	83.14	82.71	88.52	87.49	91.52	92.38	94.49	87.97	91.39	75.01	95.70	97.06	50.64	45.69
Female	51.50	46.25	94.49	94.12	81.46	81.58	91.31	83.27	82.33	65.26	92.14	93.38	35.10	34.22
Extended														
Male	91.49	91.53	84.98	87.21	90.20	89.82	94.01	88.20	90.90	75.53	93.00	94.78	51.35	42.90
Female	43.01	37.86	74.25	79.79	77.82	77.66	85.20	71.72	75.89	59.64	87.05	88.75	21.59	19.94
Composite														
Male	90.50	88.66	90.99	89.27	93.17	92.59	95.06	91.06	92.55	81.88	95.75	96.35	74.66	68.14
Female	42.19	41.92	84.69	85.41	81.59	80.06	87.13	73.95	76.52	65.55	87.46	88.22	42.14	41.25
Total														
Male	91.91	92.07	93.75	92.11	92.35	92.15	95.09	90.97	92.38	76.92	94.96	96.26	64.29	56.47
Female	46.10	42.86	84.00	86.36	78.84	78.80	86.45	76.19	77.00	61.54	88.20	89.64	32.32	30.86

The Dynamics of Household Structure 187

With Secondary or Higher Level of Education

Single person													
Male	5.19	6.28	—	4.07	4.2	8.22	9.68	1.45	8.78	3.27	8.95	22.63	26.48
Female	0.79	0.62		1.49	1.71	3.81	6.19	0.25	7.17	0.72	2.93	26.7	31.05
Nuclear													
Male	4.53	1.24	—	1.84	2.75	3.15	5.31	0.91	6.14	1.9	5.34	30.92	36.74
Female	0	0.79		0.83	0.89	1.16	3.81	0.59	4.01	0.15	1.15	19.09	29.52
Single parent													
Male	4.26	1.55	—	1.2	2.85	3.6	6.49	0.81	8.47	3.6	6.51	14.22	17.61
Female	0.52	0.38		0.17	0.56	0.92	2.32	0.1	2.9	0.17	1.21	12.71	18.73
Extended													
Male	4.17	2.73	—	3.18	4.14	4.73	8.11	1.43	10.75	4.34	11.35	16.68	20.08
Female	1.12	0.74		0.68	1.01	1.86	4.46	0.2	5.07	0.65	2.73	8.31	12.42
Composite													
Male	5.59	10.47	—	11.67	14.66	8.2	13.77	3	26.6	13.6	25.01	42.62	48.56
Female	8.75	4.04		2.8	5.03	4.97	9.47	0.36	16.67	15.49	11.47	23.8	32.48
Total													
Male	4.55	2.42	—	3.25	4.2	4.9	7.9	1.33	8.63	3.23	8.09	25.68	29.29
Female	1.11	0.87		0.77	1.24	12.1	4.63	0.2	5.13	0.72	2.48	14.73	19.95

secondary or higher levels of education or being employed. These findings certainly have implications for the well-being of persons that reside in FHHs. Other studies have also documented limited access to opportunities and resources by female heads (Takane 2009; Oppong 1997; Mbugua 1997; Moghadam 1997).

4.1 Link of Findings to Socioeconomic, Health, and Demographic Indicators

Between 1985 and 2005, a period that covers all the census time points examined in this work, infant mortality rate declined over time in all the countries except in South Africa and Kenya (see www.measuredhs.com). The declining trend suggests improving health care in the countries. Likewise, TFR declined in all the countries over the same period (see www.measuredhs.com), with a more rapid decline observed in Kenya and South Africa, suggesting that the various population control measures put in place in these countries were succeeding. The declining trend in TFR probably occasioned by the decline in IMR and other socioeconomic factors, such as improved female educational attainment, could be a contributory factor in the observed decline in average household size.

On the other hand, the HDI was low for almost all the countries examined, although it increased gradually over time (UNDP 2011).[1] The exceptions were found in Kenya and South Africa where the indexes remained at the same level. This could be a result of the increasing trend in infant and child mortality (an important input in the estimation of life expectancy) in these two countries. Further, all the countries were not performing well in the area of equality between the two sexes as assessed using the GII (UNDP 2011).[2] This is not surprising, given the disparities found in labor force participation and educational attainment by sex of heads of households in this study. The values of the HDIs and GIIs are certainly influenced by household size, composition, and the characteristics of members of the households. The gains in life expectancy in the countries where IMR declined and the general increase in the level of literacy in the region might have contributed to the small but gradual increase observed in the values of the HDI. Income, another component of the HDI, is also dependent on the composition of the households, and its effect could be positive or negative. For example, a large household with a large number of people working is likely to be better off. At the aggregate level, no definable pattern was seen in the trend of GDP in the countries, except in Mali and Tanzania, where there had been an upward trend over the last decade (see http://www.indexmundi.com/g/r.aspx?v=67).[3]

Overall, the trends in IMR, TFR, and the HDI in all the countries were generally in the expected directions, especially with recent reversals in IMR in Kenya and South Africa. However, the GII leaves much to be desired. All these indicators are affected by the size and composition of the household, as well as the characteristics of members of the household. It is thus important to be conscious of these relationships and pay more attention to the population at the household level.

4.2 Conclusions and Implications

Despite the declining trend in the number of children born per woman and average household size, the greater potential for continued growth in total number of people in the population suggested by the increase in total number of households and decline in under-one mortality should be noted and planned for, especially in Mali, Uganda, and Malawi, where average household sizes have even increased. This requires targeted plans for housing, social amenities, and infrastructure tailored to meet the needs of the teeming young people that will be transiting into adulthood and the types of households that will emerge as sweeping social changes continue to dictate and modify living arrangements. The various needs of the different cadres of the population should also be borne in mind and planned for. Further, the implication of the growth in the total number of households and the total number of people for the environment should be noted and control measures planned and put in place to prevent adverse consequences for the health and well-being of the populace. Needless to mention, efforts to control the bulging population should continue unabated.

The study has brought to the fore some social issues, in particular the high observed level and increasing percentage in FHHs, which is likely to continue to rise because of the various factors already highlighted. The existing gaps in socioeconomic opportunities between males and the females as shown by access to higher levels of education and employment, as well as by the GIIs, suggest that the sociocultural edge traditionally accorded to the males is still prevalent; the affirmative policy actions are yet to achieve the desired results. This calls for a reexamination of the effectiveness of the various measures taken by countries to promote the empowerment of women, especially in the areas of education, employment, and political leadership. Policy advocacy to promote the social relevance and economic empowerment of women should also be enhanced in order to broaden the measures to all sectors, while the promotion of girl-child education as obtains in most of the countries should be sustained to good effect.

ACKNOWLEDGMENTS

The authors gratefully acknowledge the Minnesota Population Center, for permission to access census data from IPUMS–International database, and all the reviewers whose comments helped to improve the quality of this chapter.

NOTES

1. The HDI is a measure of social and economic development. It combines indicators of life expectancy, educational attainment, and income.
2. The GII is a composite measure reflecting inequality in achievements between women and men in three dimensions: reproductive health, empowerment, and the labor market.
3. GDP per capita is GDP converted to international dollars using purchasing power parity rates.

REFERENCES

Adhikari, R. and Y. Sawangdee. (2011) "Influence of Women's Autonomy on Infant Mortality in Nepal." *Reproductive Health* 8 (7): 1–8.

Bongaarts, J. (2001) "Household Size and Composition in the Developing World in the 1990s." *Population Studies* 55 (3): 263–279.

Bryceson, D.F. (2006) "Ganyu Casual Labour, Famine and HIV/AIDS in Rural Malawi: Causality and Casualty." *Journal of Modern African Studies* 44 (2): 173–202.

Chant, S. (2003) "Female Household Headship and the Feminisation of Poverty: Facts, Fictions and Forward Strategies." LSE Gender Institute, New Working Paper Series, Issue 9, London School of Economics.

Charmarbagwala, R., M. Ranger, H. Waddington, and H. White. (2004) "The Determinants of Child Health and Nutrition: A Meta-Analysis." OED Working Paper, Washington, DC, World Bank.

CIA Factbook. (2011) geography.about.com/library/cia/blcsouthafrica.htm https://www.cia.gov/library/Publications/the-world-factbook/geos/sf.html. Accessed July 31, 2011.

Dorward, A.R., I. Mwale, and R. Tuseo. (2006) "Labour Market and Wage Impacts of HIV/AIDS in Rural Malawi." *Review of Agricultural Economics* 28 (3): 429–439.

Dungumaro, E.W. (2008) "Gender Differentials in Household Structure and Socioeconomic Characteristics in South Africa." *Journal of Comparative Family Studies* 39 (4): 429–451.

Dungumaro, E.W. (2011) "Trends, Patterns and Implications of Living Arrangement in Africa." Paper presented at the 58th World Statistics Congress of the International Statistics Institute, Dublin, August.

Goldstein, H., J. Rasbash, W. Browne, G. Woodhouse, and M. Poulain. (2000) "Multilevel Models in the Study of Dynamic Household Structures." *European Journal of Population* 16 (4): 373–387.

Iacovou, M., and A.J. Skew. (2011) "Household Composition across the New Europe: Where Do the New Member States Fit In?" *Demographic Research* 25 (14): 465–490.

Madhaven, S., and E.J. Schatz. (2007) "Coping with Change: Household Structure and Composition in Rural South Africa, 1992–2003." *Scandinavian Journal of Public Health Supplement* 69:85–93.

Mahfouz, M.S., A.A. Surur, D.A.A. Ajak, and E.A. Eldawi. (2009) "Level and Determinants of Infant and Child Mortality in Malakal Town—Southern Sudan." *Sudanese Journal of Public Health* 4 (2): 250–255.

Mbugua, W. (1997) "The African Family and the Status of Women's Health." In *Family, Population and Development in Africa*, ed. Aderanti Adepoju, 139–157. London: Zed Books.

Minnesota Population Center. (2011) *Integrated Public Use Microdata Series, International: Version 6.1 [Machine-Readable Database]*. Minneapolis: University of Minnesota.
Moghadam, V. (1997) "The Feminization of Poverty? Notes on a Concept and Trends." Occasional Paper OP2, Illinois State University Women's Studies.
Oppong, C. (1997) "The African Family and the Status of Women's Health." In *Family, Population and Development in Africa*, ed. Aderanti Adepoju, 158–182. London: Zed Books.
Pelser, A., and N. Redelinghuys. (2009) *Towards a 10-Year Review of the Population Policy Implementation in South Africa (1998–2008): Population, Environment and Development*. Johannesburg: Department of Social Development, Republic of South Africa.
Peters, P.E., P.A. Walker, and D. Kambewa. (2008) "Striving for Normality in a Time of AIDS in Malawi." *Journal of Modern African Studies* 46 (4): 659–687.
Sabra, A., S. Esim, L.H. Skalli, and S. Turkyilmaz. (2006) "Poverty." In *The Encyclopedia of Women and Islamic Cultures*, ed. S. Joseph, 459. Leiden: Brill.
Takane, T. (2009) "Disparities and Diversities among Female-Headed Households in Rural Malawi after 20 Years of Economic Liberalization." *Singapore Journal of Tropical Geography* 30:58–372.
UNDP. (2011) "Human Development Report." hdr.undp.org/en/statistics/ and hdrstats.undp.org/en/indicators/68606.html. Accessed May 15 2011
United Nations. (1996) *Women in a Changing Global Economy*. New York: Department for Policy Coordination and Sustainable Development.
White, H., and E. Masset. (2003) "The Importance of Household Size and Composition in Constructing Poverty Profiles: An Illustration from Vietnam." *Development and Change* 34 (1): 105–111.

11 Sub-Saharan African Children and Adolescents
Economic Gain or Burden?

Onipede Wusu and
Emmanuel Olagunju Amoo

1 INTRODUCTION

The current population of Africa is estimated at more than one billion with a rate of natural increase of 2.4 percent (Population Reference Bureau [PRB] 2011). Within the continent, the sub-Saharan region is playing a leading role in the prevailing rapid population growth rate in the world. This region comprises 84 percent of the population of Africa and is growing at 2.6 percent annually. The fastest-growing countries are all in the region. For example, Niger, Uganda, Burundi, and Burkina Faso each have a natural increase greater than 3 percent. In addition, Nigeria is at present the seventh most populous country and the only African country among the first ten most populous countries in the world (Bongaarts 1997; Bloom and Humair 2010; PRB 2011). The first ten, having between 45 percent and 50 percent under age 15, are all in sub-Saharan Africa (SSA). They include Niger, Uganda, Mali, Angola, Zambia, Burundi, Congo Democratic Republic, Mozambique, Chad, and Burkina Faso (PRB 2011). On average, in 2009, SSA had 43 percent of its population between age zero and 14 years, while the average for all low-income countries was 39 percent and the world average was 27 percent (Sippel et al. 2011; World Bank 2011).

The picture painted above demonstrates that SSA is the region in the world with the highest proportion of children. The situation is more pathetic if the proportion of adolescents is added. The United Nations International Convention Article 1 of the child right defines a child as anybody below age 18. It is also widely agreed that any person within the age-group 10–24 is an adolescent (Bahadur and Hindmarsh 2000; UNAIDS 2004; Federal Ministry of Health 2007; Bankole and Malarcher 2010). For the sake of clarity, in the context of the present study, children are conceptualized as persons within the age-group 0–9 while adolescents are considered as young people between ages 10 and 24 years. Therefore, SSA is certainly the world region with the highest concentration of children and adolescents. Forty-one percent of the population on the continent is below age 15. The proportion is 43 percent in SSA, 43 percent in the west, 44 percent in the east, 45 percent in middle Africa, and 31 percent in the south (PRB 2011; World Bank 2011). These figures suggest that about 50 percent of the population in the region comprises children and adolescents. The questions that are germane to this chapter are: what are the implications of these large proportions of children and adolescents in the region? Can they be considered as dividend or debt?

2 THEORETICAL FRAMEWORKS

A search for the answer to the questions raised above is attempted in this chapter within the age structure–economic framework and the other two supporting theories (economic theory of fertility and price of children theory).

2.1 Age Structure–Economic Framework

The age structure–economic framework stipulates the existence of a significant relationship between the population age structure of a country and its economic condition (Ashford, 2007; Bloom et al, 2007; Crespo-Cuaresma et al, 2007). Three main population age structures can be identified globally. The first consists of an age structure with a large proportion of children and adolescents under age 19 years, having a relatively small working age-group and very small number of the elderly. This age structure depicts a broad-based population pyramid. In the second type, the age structure is undergoing transition; there is a gradual reduction in the proportion of children and adolescents, a growing proportion of the productive age-group, and a growing cohort of the elderly. The pyramid of such populations manifests a shrinking base and burgeoning middle-age population. The third type of age structure depicts a small proportion of under-15 cohorts, a burgeoning working age-group, and a large proportion of the elderly. The type of age structure a population mirrors is a function of the stage of the demographic transition on course (Recher 2011).

Demographic transition theory is "a detailed description of change in mortality and fertility" that occurred in Europe and has been applied to other world regions, though with some limitations. Figure 11.1 depicts the phases of the demographic transition theory. The second phase represents the period of population explosion in a country where mortality has begun to decline but traditional reproductive health behavior sustaining high fertility still persists. This situation supports a real demographic problem with a very large proportion of young persons. The first age structure identified above is synonymous with the second phase of the classical demographic transition. The third and fourth phases represent the second and third age structures, respectively. Countries that are in the third phase of demographic transition exhibit the second age structure, in which fertility begins to decline. There is a significant reduction in the proportion of children and young persons, thereby promoting increase in the working age-group population. In this case the number under age 15 in the population begins to shrink. Reduction in dependants and subsequent increase in the working age-group presents the demographic bonus.

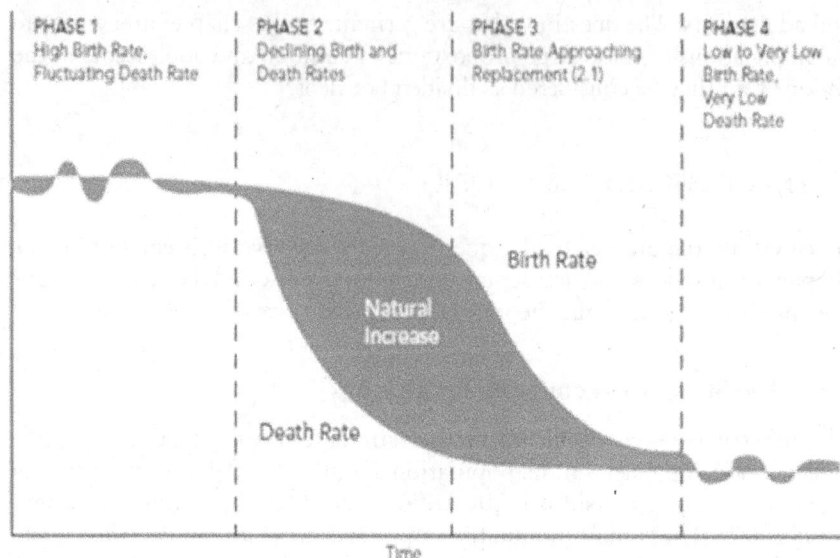

Figure 11.1 Classic phases of demographic transition.
Source: PRB (2011).

Countries that have completed their demographic transition are characterized by the features of the third type of age structure. Such countries benefited from the window of opportunity opened to them by their demographic change, in which they experienced a prolonged decline in fertility, leading to rapid increase in working age population, which promoted labor supply, savings, investment, and economic performance—referred to as demographic dividend (Bloom, Canning, and Sevilla 2003; Leete and Schoch 2003; Herrmann et al. 2011). In clear terms, the demographic dividend results from declining fertility and a growing workforce so that fewer resources are needed to cater for the dependants. More resources are then released for investment. A decline in birthrate can engender development opportunities that could profit succeeding generations in terms of access to education, health care services, employment opportunities, and increasing levels of productivity (Sippel et al. 2011). This brings about rapid economic growth and social welfare. However, this dividend is not an automatic process (Ross 2004; Bloom et al. 2007). According to Bloom and his colleagues, institutions such as the rule of law, transparency, efficient bureaucratic systems, freedom of political representativeness, freedom of speech, and so on, are very critical for any country to realize this dividend. Given the existence of the right institutional framework, countries in this category experienced rapid social and economic transformation during their demographic windows of opportunity. The dividend abated after some time and such countries now battle with a burgeoning population of the aged. Fortunately, the many years of development have enabled such societies to put in place social welfare policies that cater for the increasing proportion of the elderly that have resulted from a prolonged period of fertility decline. This age structure is typical of countries in Europe and North America, as well as Australia, Japan, and New Zealand (PRB 2011; World Bank 2011).

The second type of age structure is a reflection of societies that have reached an advanced stage in their demographic transition and are currently benefiting from their demographic window of opportunity. Such countries have been able to reduce their fertility and subsequently have a growing proportion of working age population. They are already realizing the demographic dividend. The existence of appropriate institutions is accelerating economic growth and development in such societies through increasing labor supply and savings. The experience of the Asian Tigers in the 1980s and 1990s best describes this category of age structure (Bloom and Williamson 1998; Wongboonsin, Guest, and Prachuabmoh 2005).

The first type of age structure is typical of countries where fertility is still very high and demographic transition is either very slow or has stalled. In this situation, the population age structure is dominated by children and adolescents; the population pyramid is generally with a broad base. The working age population is usually sparse and it is also characterized by a small proportion of the elderly. SSA countries and those of Southwest Asia are still at this stage of demographic transition, and it was projected that about 59 percent of world population growth between 1995 and 2025 would occur in these regions (Casterline 2001). North African countries have not fared too well, either. The whole of Africa still represents a high fertility region: demographic transition has been very slow or stalled in a few countries and in the majority it has not really taken off (Bongaarts 2008). Therefore, the age structure is largely a youthful one, with about 50 percent being children and adolescents. One important implication of this is that the working age population is likely to be limited. It is against this background that this chapter seeks to provide an answer to this question: what does this type of age structure portend for SSA?

2.2 Economic Theory of Fertility

The economic theory of fertility indicates that children are considered to be economic commodities, in which case couples evaluate the costs and benefits of children before the decision to procreate (Espenshade 1972; Lindert 1980; Becker 1973; Togunde and Newman 2005). The economic theory of fertility is related to children–parents wealth flow analysis especially as applicable to Africa. In this part of the world, children are often seen as a source of income, over and above any costs the parents might incur. Children in Africa are viewed as security for old age in terms of finance and care. They are considered to be helping hands on farms, for household chores, and in some cases work to augment the family income (Orubuloye

1987, 1991; Caldwell 1982; Caldwell, Caldwell, and Orubuloye 1992). However, with widespread civilization and the influence of globalization in the face of the absence of or the inadequacy of governmental welfare support, children are expected to go to school, be nurtured, sheltered, well fed, and protected, solely by their parents and guardians. This responsibility impacts heavily on parents' social and economic resources. Thus, rather than being dividends, children and adolescents are on the average, a burden.

2.3 Price of Children Theory

The price of children theory emphasizes the opportunity cost concept of children. It states the effects of cost of child rearing on parents' income and employment opportunities, and the relation between the quantity and quality of children (Lindert 1980; Becker and Barro 1988). The theory considers money expended on children in terms of expenses in bearing and raising them through parental expenditure on food, clothing, shelter, medical, education, and security, including other noneconomic costs (Espenshade 1972). Specifically, current economic realities demonstrate that the task of financing children's education and investing in their general development is enormous. For example, schooling has become more expensive in recent times. In addition, the current wealth flow indicates that more resources now flow from parents to children.

Although it is not currently clear how soon the preference for larger families in most SSA countries will abate, the increasing level of urbanization has considerably lessened the need for a large number of children. In addition, improvements in modern medicine and public health could culminate in improved life spans that could further result in an excessive supply of children and adolescents. There is no gainsaying the fact that the consequence of this situation, if left uncontrolled, would generate pressure on the available resources (Wolfgram 2005). It would create inadequacy that is most likely to aggravate poverty levels.

The age structure, economic theory, and the two supporting theories have demonstrated the economic implications of a large proportion of children and adolescents (especially under 15 years old). The rest of this chapter discusses an empirical analysis of the question of whether children and adolescents in SSA are a dividend or a debt. Section 3, data and methods, discusses how census data from purposively selected countries in SSA were used and the methods of analysis adopted. Section 4 presents the findings of the descriptive statistical and demographic analytical strategies employed in the analysis of census data of the selected countries. This section also includes the discussion of the findings. Section 5 attempts to explain the findings in the context of the age structure–economic performance framework, pointing out answers to the main question addressed in the study. In addition, salient conclusions are drawn and policy implications of major findings are highlighted.

3 DATA AND METHODS

This section presents a discussion on how this study was executed. To start with, one country each was selected to represent the eastern, western, and southern parts of SSA. The selection process was guided by the availability of at least two sets of census data.[1] In this regard, Kenya, Senegal, and South Africa were purposively selected. While Kenya and Senegal have two sets of census data each, South Africa has three sets. Three variables that are germane to this study are age, educational attainment, and employment status.

Individual population was classified into *children, adolescents, working*, and *old* populations using different age-groups in accordance with international standards. However, children and adolescents are the two population groups at the center of this study. Children were grouped as those in ages between 0 and 9 years, while those in age-group 10 to 24 were considered adolescents (UNICEF 2006; United Nations and UNICEF 2011). These age-groups were employed in highlighting children and adolescents in the construction of age pyramids to demonstrate the age distribution of the population for the selected countries. In a typical dependency ratio, the working population is classified as 15 to 64 years and those below age 15 and above 65 years of age are classified as dependants. However, as earlier indicated, since the study's target populations are children (age 0–9 years) and adolescents (10–24 years), in order to compute dependency ratio for children and adolescents (those who are not supposed to work), the age-groups were reclassified into 0–14 for dependants, 15–64 for the working age-group, and the old as 65 and above (elderly dependants), as shown in Table 11.2 This new age-group (0–14 years) includes children (0–9 years) and young adolescents between ages 10 and 14 years, who, by law, are not expected to be engaged in any economic activities.

The second main variable involved in the analysis undertaken is the educational status of children and adolescents. The measurement of this variable varied across the three countries. In Kenya and South Africa, education was measured in terms of educational status. Kenya's two censuses identified four categories of educational status, namely, none, standard 1–8, form 1–6, and tertiary. On the other hand, South Africa used three different but similar categorizations of educational status, which is consistent with the education policy in operation in the country. The measurement here was more of years of schooling. In 1996, six categories were used—none, year 0 (preschool), 1–3 years, 4–6 years, 7–9 years, and tertiary. In the 2001 census, the preschool category was excluded. The 2007 census measured educational status using similar categories but excluded no schooling. In the two censuses for Senegal, education attainment was classified into four categories (none, primary grade 1–5, secondary grade 6–12, and tertiary). In the analysis carried out using this variable, the emphasis was on the proportion of children and adolescents undergoing education and training in various countries. Although there is a great deal of variation in the classifications, it was easy to highlight the proportion not in school using a no education category. This cut across all the countries selected.

The employment status of the sampled populations was similar across the three countries. The study adopted employment status definitions that categorized responses to employed, unemployed, and not in the universe/missing/unknown. In order to achieve a simple presentation of the analysis with respect to the findings of this variable, the latter category was excluded.

Three main analytical strategies were applied. First, population pyramids were constructed for the selected countries to highlight the prevailing age-sex structure of various populations. This enabled us to capture graphically the age structure of the selected populations. The second level of analysis involved computing the dependency ratio vis-à-vis the general dependency ratio, percentage distribution of children and adolescents by educational attainment, and employment status. A projection was made in order to have an adequate perspective on the inherent burden of large number of dependants in transiting economies that are characterized by social and political inadequacies. Because of the limited formation available in the census data sets used, only ratio projection techniques moderated through sub-regional ratio projections could be used. This is also employed because it is census data dependent. Its procedures are not too stringent, coupled with the fact that it can also be used with or without age-sex details. This is, however, done using Population Analysis Spreadsheets for Excel (PASEX) as designed by the US Bureau of the Census, International Programs Center (US Census Bureau 2003; Kenya National Bureau of Statistics 2012).

All these were applied to highlight whether the groups of population under investigation are a dividend or a debt. The SPSS software for Windows Version 20.0 was used in all aspects of the analysis. Generally, a cross comparison among the three randomly selected countries was carried out to determine which of the countries share the highest burden or gain in terms of the age structure of the population.

4 RESULTS

This section presents a description of the findings. These are addressed under three main subsections.

4.1 Children and Adolescent Population Structure

Figure 11.2 shows the population pyramids of Kenya, Senegal, and South Africa. The three pyramids indicate that the age distribution of all the selected countries representing the eastern, western, and southern parts of Africa were largely youthful. Kenya's broad-based pyramid reflects that about 45 percent of the population are children and adolescents. Senegal's age distribution was similar to Kenya's. South Africa painted a relatively different picture, reflecting an apparent reduction in the proportion of the population below age 10, leading to a significant reduction in the proportion of children and adolescents. The situation exhibited in the pyramids indicates that although South Africa

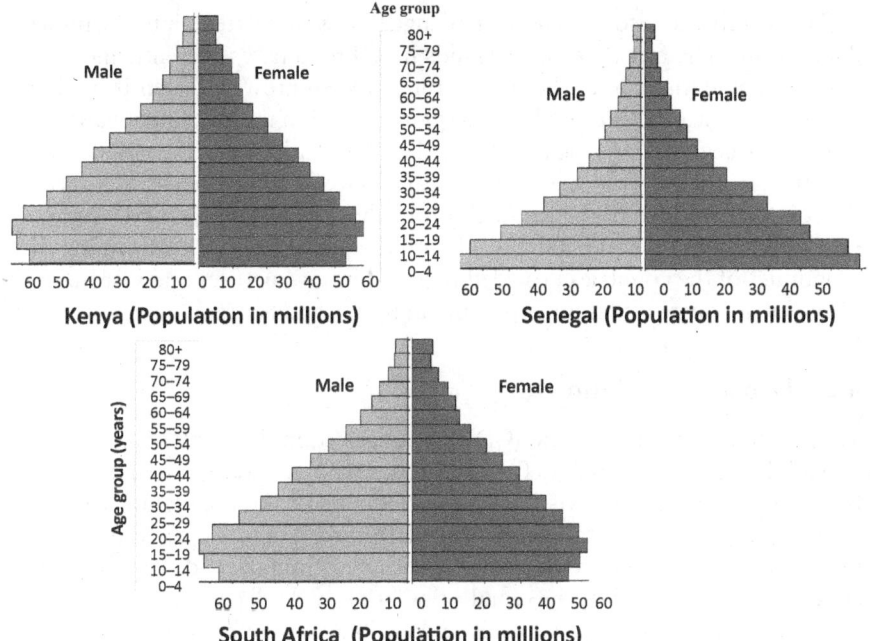

Figure 11.2 Population pyramid for Kenya, Senegal, and South Africa.
Source: Computed from available census data sets of Kenya, Senegal, and South Africa (1989–2007).

has begun to show a reduction in the proportion of young persons in her population, the populations of the three countries was still very young. The recent data released by the PRB (2011) indicate that 44 percent of Senegal's population, 42 percent of Kenya's, and 30 percent of South Africa's population were reported below 15 years of age, supporting the pyramid structure presented.

There is no doubt that the age distribution highlighted above may have some significant implications for the economies of the selected countries. In Kenya and Senegal, the proportion of the population that were children and adolescents suggests that the two countries had a large number of children and adolescents who were either in or outside schools. The population consisted largely of young people undergoing one form of training or another. Such population categories are generally dependants. Although the proportion of South Africa's population that was below age 10 was declining, the proportion is still capable of exerting a significant negative effect on both family and government resources. The proportion of children and adolescents in the three countries is likely to mount pressure on the purse of families (Wolfgram 2005) because their basic needs must be satisfied by their parents. The economic burden on families is exacerbated owing to the prevailing large number of biological and nonbiological children and adolescents. This is likely to exert a negative effect on their domestic saving ability, needed to improve family wealth status. Similarly, government finances in various countries are overstretched as a result of ever-increasing demands for social infrastructures, such as educational facilities, necessitated by the youth glut.

This youth glut also presents a challenge that would extend into the immediate future. The fact that the pyramids have broad bases currently indicates that the populations have the momentum to keep growing. Even if modern reproductive health attitudes begin to gain ground in these countries and fertility levels begin to fall, the possibility that the youth glut will continue for a long time is still high, especially in Senegal and Kenya. Thus, in the near future the economic burden of the youth glut is likely to be enormous. However, the youth glut could turn into a dividend with the possibility of transforming the economies of the countries provided required infrastructures and institutions are given adequate attention, especially in Kenya and Senegal.

4.2 Dependency Ratio

The children dependency ratio (CDR) is conceived in this context as children and adolescents between ages 0 and 14 years who are not required by law to be economically engaged vis-à-vis the proportion of the population who are expected to be economically active (aged 15–64). The basic objective of the use of this indicator was to illuminate the rate of child dependency in various countries compared with the usual population-wide dependency ratio. The total children dependency ratio was highest in Kenya (approximately 89 percent), followed by Senegal (85 percent), as shown in Table 11.1. South Africa exhibited the lowest, but is still relatively high if compared with what obtains in economically advanced countries of the world (Sippel et al. 2011). These high ratios indicate that out of every 100 in the working age population, there were 89, 85, and 53 children and adolescents depending on them in Kenya, Senegal, and South Africa, respectively, as shown in Table 11.1.

The demographic situation in the selected countries indicates a high prevalence of large proportions of children and adolescents constituting a heavy economic burden demonstrated in the high children and adolescent dependency ratio. The large proportions of children make tremendous contributions to the high prevailing total dependency ratio that have been undermining socioeconomic development of the region. This is reflected in the close gap between the two ratios. Out of the 95.1 percent total dependency ratio estimated for Kenya, children dependency was 88.5 percent. Senegal ranked second with 91.8 percent total dependency ratio, of which the children dependency ratio was 85 percent, while South Africa recorded a 62.4 percent total dependency ratio, of which children constituted 53.2 percent (Table 11.1). Apparently, the dependency burden in SSA is largely a function of the high proportion of children stemming from the persistence of high fertility and very low adoption of modern contraceptives (Cleland et al. 2006; United Nations 2011). These intertwined conditions continue to aggravate the poverty burden in the region (Merrick 2002; Phumaphi 2011). The high children dependency ratio implies large groups of dependants that must be cared for. This makes it difficult to increase domestic savings—individuals and governments are thus unable to adequately invest and contribute sufficiently to employment generation. This situation has sustained the vicious cycle of poverty over the years in SSA.

Table 11.1 Children and Adolescent Dependency Ratio versus Total Dependency Ratio by Selected Countries

Country	Year/Age-Group	0–14	15–64	65+	Total	Children Dependency Ratio	Total Dependency Ratio
South Africa	1996	1,223,929 (34%)	2,175,555 (60%)	221,680 (6%)	3,621,164 (100%)	56.3	66.4
	2001	1,209,795 (33%)	2,324,361 (62%)	191,499 (5%)	3,725,655 (100%)	52.0	60.3
	2007	313,980 (30%)	667,595 (64%)	66,082 (6%)	1,047,657 (100%)	47.0	56.9
	Total	2,747,704 (33%)	5,167,511 (62%)	479,261 (6%)	8,394,476 (100%)	53.2	62.4
Senegal	1988	327,850 (47%)	347,969 (50%)	24,380 (3%)	700,199 (100%)	94.2	101.2
	2002	423,411 (43%)	535,580 (54%)	35,571 (4%)	994,562 (100%)	79.1	85.7
	Total	751,261 (44%)	883,549 (52%)	59,951 (4%)	1,694,761 (100%)	85.0	91.8
Kenya	1989	514,312 (48%)	523,355 (49%)	36,431 (3%)	1,074,098 (100%)	98.3	105.2
	1999	612,043 (44%)	748,954 (53%)	46,550 (3%)	1,407,547 (100%)	81.7	87.9
	Total	1,126,355 (45%)	1,272,309 (51%)	82,981 (4%)	2,481,645 (100%)	88.5	95.1

However, it is worthy to note that the individual censuses indicate that, in the three countries, the ratio has been declining. South Africa manifested the highest level of decline in children and adolescents' dependency ratio. The ratio declined from 56.3 percent in 1996 to 47 percent in 2007. Although Kenya and Senegal experienced some decline in this ratio, it is actually insignificant. Thus the prospect for significant declines in children and adolescent dependency ratios in SSA is higher in South Africa than in the other two selected countries.

4.3 Literacy Level/Educational Attainment

Figure 11.3 shows that Senegal recorded proportion of illiterate population (those with no education) across all age-groups. The large proportion of illiterates (1998 = 63 percent; 2002 = 51 percent) among children aged 0–9 years may be a result of the fact that most of the children were likely not expected to be in school because of official minimum age requirements applicable in the countries. In contrast, the situation with adolescents where more than 50 percent had no education in both censuses represents

Figure 11.3 Education attainment by age-group across selected countries.

very serious problems. One in every five adolescents may not have been to any school in Senegal. Apparently, the decline in the proportion who were illiterate in the relevant population is quite insignificant.

The above situation suggests that the majority of adolescents in the country are not being prepared in skills acquisition in order for them to take advantage of employment opportunities in the formal sector. If such adolescents are equally not engaged in agricultural activities, they are likely to exacerbate the dependency burden in the country now; the problem will be more devastating in the future owing to the multiplier effect on the economy.

Kenyan and South African data performed better than Senegal's on this variable (children's and adolescents' educational status). In Kenya, the proportion of adolescents with no education declined from 12.3 percent in 1989 to 9.6 percent in 1999, while it fell from 7 percent in 1996 to 1.1 percent in 2007 in South Africa. The percentage of children who had no education followed a similar pattern. Generally, the data available for the two countries indicate that the educational status of children and adolescents in Kenya and South Africa has improved significantly. This implies that the populations are increasingly being equipped with basic skills, which is likely to position individuals to make quality contributions to the economies of their countries in the immediate future. Thus, they may currently be considered debts as a result of the high demand for educational facilities, but the probability is very high that they will become dividends sooner or later given that they were already acquiring necessary training.

However, it is noteworthy that the children and adolescents in the selected countries may not be regarded entirely as constituting economic burdens or debts, even currently. Ideally, anybody below age 15 is expected to be undergoing one form of training or another. With the exception of South Africa, in the selected countries, a significant proportion of children and adolescents under 15 years of age were reported as employed.

This is not surprising in a setting where child labor of different dimensions is prevalent. The International Labour Organization estimates that the greatest incidence of child labor in the world is present in SSA (28.4 percent of all 5–14 years old; it is just 14.8 percent for Asia and the Pacific and nine percent in Latin America) (see http://www.ilo.org/ipec/Regionsandcountries/Africa/lang—en/index.htm). The implications of this situation are both positive and negative. In the positive sense, the young people below 15 years of age contributed to the economy of their countries. On the other hand, the young population engaging in economic activities portends negative implications. They were supposed to be undergoing training that would position them for optimum economic contributions in the future when the demographic window is expected to open. Of course, growing up without such skills, such individuals would either become a burden to the society in the future or grossly underemployed.

4.4 Projected Dependency Levels for Children and Adolescents across the Selected Regions

The projection for dependency levels for children and adolescents was done on a subregional basis to ensure adequate comparison among the selected countries. The first two years' census data for each of the countries were used as the base. The dependants across the ages of 0–14 and 65 years and above were projected for the years 2012, 2020, and 2025 (Figure 11.4). It is also considered necessary to depict the likely trend of working population (15–64 years) who are to shoulder the responsibility of the dependants. This could be relevant in evaluating the dependency burden among the selected population.

It is observed from Figure 11.4 that dependants in age-group 0–14 years will be in keen competition with the working population across all projected years in Kenya and Senegal. The graph shows steady upward movement from 1989 in Kenya and continues until approximately 2025, after which there is seemingly a ray of decline. Owing to the high level of under-15 dependants coupled with the number of dependants among those that are 65 years old and above, it is not likely that the working group (15–64 years) would be sufficient to cater for them. Besides, the low-wage or low-income syndrome in developing nations (from where the sample countries were selected), the level of corruption, and government instability, to mention but a few problems, may work adversely against any support toward catering for these dependants. The emerging situation could possibly result in deprivation, squalor, disease, and sickness as well as other social menaces. Thus, rather than adding value (if any) to development in these countries, this group becomes an economic and social burden.

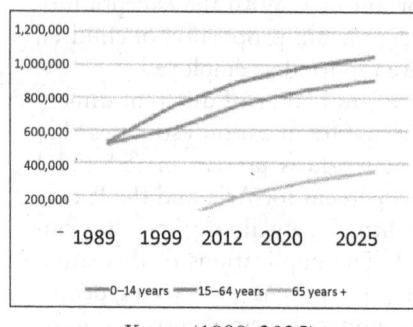

a. Kenya (1989–2025).

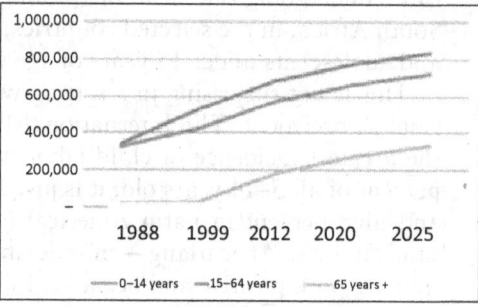

b. Senegal (1988–2025).

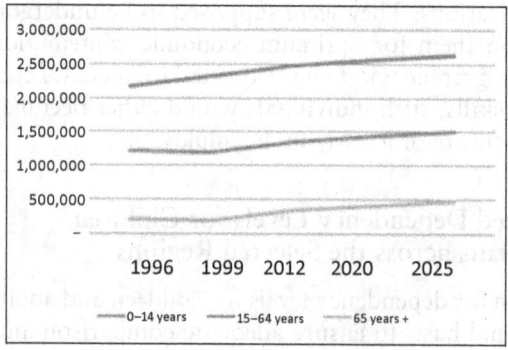

b. South Africa (1996–2025).

Figure 11.4 Projected dependency levels across the selected regions.

5 CONCLUSION

This study has examined the socioeconomic implications of SSA children and adolescents within the age structure and economic relationship framework. The census data analyzed show clearly that the region is still largely characterized by a soaring proportion of young people who are largely dependants. If urgent reductionate demographic policies are not sustainably implemented, the region has the potential for sustaining this momentum, probably for a long time. The analysis has demonstrated that the youthful population structure is the major contributor to the prevailing high dependency ratio in the region. Consistent with various age structures and economic relationship frameworks adopted for the study, the present proportions of children and adolescents are more of an economic burden at both micro (individual families) and macro (governments) levels. However, the census data analyzed revealed that a relatively significant proportion of children and adolescents below 15 years of age participated in the labor force in two of the three countries sampled (Kenya and Senegal). Be that as it may, the fact that a vast majority of the children and adolescents are still undergoing one form of training or another, which is expected to place pressure on resources at various levels, is most likely to aggravate the economic burden. Thus, currently the children and adolescents in the region are rather to be regarded as debts.

Nevertheless, if reductionate population policies are vigorously implemented now, and birthrates begin to decline in a sustainable way, the current large proportion of children and adolescents would graduate into the working age population in about a decade, while the dependency ratio would decline. If appropriate economic, social, and legal frameworks are put in place, this situation is most likely to propel rapid economic growth and social welfare. In the first place, a higher proportion of the population would be working owing to the graduation of the present children and adolescent into the working age-group. More resources will also be released to finance investment and employment as a result of the declining proportion of children and adolescents attributable to falling or low birthrates. Given that the dependency ratio would decline, both public and private savings are likely to increase. All things being equal, this situation should lead to a rise in investment and employment generation. Ultimately, economic progress should manifest in the region.

The challenge, however, is that most of the countries in the region do not have effective reductionate demographic strategies in place. With the exception of South Africa, where a fair process of demographic transition appears to be on course, the other two countries, representing the majority of the region, have manifested a stalling transition (Bongaarts 2008). This implies that the current broad-based population pyramids are most likely to persist for a longer time with an increasing dependency ratio stemming from a large proportion of children and adolescents. This situation will continue to exacerbate the pressure on resources in various countries for a much longer time, domestic savings will remain very low, and investment and employment generation will also continue to decline. Given the high level of private and public corruption and the prevalence of irresponsible governments in the region, SSA children and adolescents may remain more of a debt than a dividend (Mulinge and Lesetedi 2002; Hanson 2009).

Finally, African children and adolescents are the future of the continent, and have the potential to exert transformative impacts on economic and social spheres of the society. They are the parents and teachers of the next generation. The quantum of investment in them in the present time will determine the quality of the next wave of population. If they have access to education, decent working conditions, and sexual and reproductive health services, they will certainly become a strong force to drive economic development and positive social change in the region. However, if they are given only limited access to education, distortion in their sexual and reproductive health rights, and unemployment, they will ultimately become social and economic liabilities, and the hope of socioeconomic development in the region will continue to be compromised.

Table 11.2 Percentage Distribution of Children and Adolescents by Employment Status by Selected Countries

	0–9	10–14	15–64	65+	Total
Kenya 1989					
Employed	–	8.9	85.5	5.6	100.0
Unemployed	0.0	39.6	56.1	4.3	100.0
Total	0.0	20.4	74.5	5.1	100.0
Kenya 1999					
Employed	8.2	10.8	76.6	4.5	100.0
Unemployed	29.6	26.0	41.3	3.1	100.0
Total	16.5	16.7	62.9	3.9	100.0
Senegal 1988					
Employed	7.1	8.6	79.8	4.4	100.0
Unemployed	21.8	19.4	54.3	4.5	100.0
Total	16.1	15.1	64.3	4.5	100.0
Senegal 2002					
Employed	3.6	7.1	85.8	3.4	100.0
Unemployed	21.1	21.6	52.4	4.9	100.0
Total	27.1	15.9	65.5	4.3	100.0
South Africa 1996					
Employed	–	–	97.7	2.3	100.0
Unemployed	29.5	15.4	48.3	6.8	100.0
Total	22.6	11.8	59.8	5.8	100.0

(continued)

Table 11.2 (continued)

	0–9	10–14	15–64	65+	Total
South Africa 2001					
Employed	–	–	99.8	0.2	100.0
Unemployed	–	–	99.1	0.9	100.0
Total	–	–	99.3	0.7	100.0
South Africa 2007					
Employed	–	–	99.7	0.3	100.0
Unemployed	–	–	99.1	0.9	100.0
Total	–	–	99.4	0.6	100.0

ABBREVIATIONS

Sub-Saharan Africa (SSA)
Population Reference Bureau (PRB)
Joint United Nations Programme on HIV/AIDS (UNAIDS)
Population Analysis Spreadsheets for Excel (PASEX)
United Nations Children Fund (UNICEF)
Statistical Package for Social Sciences (SPSS)

ACKNOWLEDGMENTS

The authors gratefully acknowledge the Minnesota Population Center, for permission to access IPUMS–International database, and all the reviewers whose comments contributed to refining the quality of this chapter.

NOTES

1. Data for the selected countries were accessed from the IPUMS–International database archived by Minnesota Population Center (2011).

REFERENCES

Ashford, Lori S. (2007). Africa's Youthful Population: Risk or Opportunity? *Bridge*, June, 2007. Population Reference Bureau, USA. June, 2007. P1–4
Bahadur, G. & Hindmarsh, P. (2000). Age definitions, Childhood and Adolescent Cancers in relation to Reproductive Issues. *Human Reproduction*, Vol. 15, No. 1, 2000. pp227–230. DOI: 10.1093/humrep/15.1.227-230
Bankole, A. & Malanrcher, S. (2010). Removing Barriers to Adolescents' Access to Contraceptive Information and Services. *Studies in Family Planning*, Vol. 41, No. 2, pp117–124

Becker, Gary S. & Barro Robert J. (1988). A Reformulation of Economic Theory of Fertility. *Quarterly Journal of Economics*. Vol. 103, No 1, February, 1988. pp1–25. Oxford University Press.

Becker, G.S. (1973). A Theory of Marriage: Part I. *The Journal of Political Economy*, Vol. 81, No. 4 (July—August), 1973, pp813–846.

Bloom, D. & Williamson, J.G. (1998). Demographic Transition and Economic Miracles in Emerging Asia. *World Bank Economic Review*, Vol. 12, 1998. pp419–456.

Bloom, D. E. & Humair, S. (2010). Economic Development in Nigeria: A Demographic Perspective. Harvard Africa Seminar. April 3, 2010

Bloom, David E, Canning David, Fink Günther & Finlay Jocelyn (2007). Realizing the Demographic Dividend: Is Africa any different? Working Paper Series, No. 23, May 2007. Program on the Global Demography of Aging (PGDA), Harvard University, May 2007. http://www.hsph.harvard.edu/pgda/working.htm Accessed 2012-11-16.

Bloom, David, Canning David & Sevilla Jaypee (2003). Demographic Dividend: New Perspective on Economic Consequences Population Change. RAND Corporation, Santa Monica, California.

Bongaarts, J. (1997). *Future Population Growth and Policy Options*. Policy Research Division, The Population Council, New York December 1997.

Bongaarts, J. (2008). Fertility Transition in Developing Countries: Progress or Stagnation? *Studies in Family Planning*, Vol. 39, No. 2, 2008. pp 105–110

Caldwell, J.C. (1982). *Theory of Fertility Decline*. New York: Academic Press.

Caldwell, John C, Caldwell Pat & Orubuloye I.O (1992). The Family and Sexual Networking in Sub-Saharan Africa: Historical Regional Differences and Present-Day Implications. *Population Studies*, Vol. 46, No 3, 1992. P385–410

Casterline, J. B. (2001). The pace of Fertility Transition: National Patterns in second half of Twentieth Century. *Population and Development Review*. Population Council, Vol. 27 (Supplement), pp17–52.

Cleland, J' Bernstein, S; Ezeh, A.; Faundes, A.; Glasier, A. & Innis, J. (2006). Family Planning: The Unfinished Agenda. *The Lancet Sexual and Reproductive Health Series*, Vol. 368, No. 9549, 2006. Pp1810–1827

Crespo-Cuaresma, Jesus, Lindh Thomas, Malmberg Bo, Halvarsson Max, Prskawetz Alexia & Werner (2007). The Relationship between Demographic Change and Economic Growth in the EU. Research Report 32, July 2007. Vienna Institute of Demography, Wohllebengasse, July 2007.

Espenshade, T.J. (1972). The Price of Children and Socio-economic theories of Fertility. *Population Studies*. Vol. 26, No. 2, July 1972, pp207–221.

Federal Ministry of Health (FMOH), (2007). *Nature Strategic Framework on the Health and Development of Adolescents and Young People in Nigeria*. Federal Ministry of Health, Nigeria, Abuja. July, 2007.

Hanson, S. (2009). "Corruption in Sub-Saharan Africa". www.cfr.org/publication/19984. Accessed 25/01/2012.

Herrmann, M.; Guzman, J.M.; Juran, S. & Schensul, D. (2011). *Population Dynamics in the Least Developed Countries: Challenges and Opportunities for Development and Poverty Reduction*. United Nations Population Fund (UNFPA). New York, NY 10158 USA.

International Labour Organisation. http://www.ilo.org/ipec/Regionsandcountries/Africa/lang—en/index.htm. Accessed 25/01/2012.

Kenya National Bureau of Statistics (2012). Kenya National Seminar on Census Data Analysis.

Leete, R. & Schoch, M. (2003). Population and Poverty: Satisfying Unmet Need as the Route to Sustainable Development. In (eds.) Leete Richard, Royan Rabbi and Schoch Mickie, *Population and Poverty: Achieving Equity, Equality and Sustainability Series*. Population and Development Strategy Series, Number 8, 2003. United Nations Population Fund, New York. Pp9–38.

Lindert, P.H. (1980). Child Costs and Economic Development, In Richard A. Easterlin (ed.) *Population and Economic Change in Developing Countries*, pp3–80, University of Chicago Press. 1980. ISBN: 0-226-18027-1.

Merrick, T.W. (2002). Population and poverty: new views on an old controversy. *International Family Planning Perspectives*, Vol. 28, No. 1, pp41- 46.

Minnesota Population Centre (2011). Integrated Public Use Microdata Series International: Version 6.1 [Machine-readable database], Minneapolis: University of Minnesota, 2011.

Mulinge, M. M. & Lesetedi, G. N. (2002).Corruption in sub-Saharan Africa: Towards a More Holistic Approach. *African Journal of Political Science*, Vol. 7, No.1, 2002. pp 51–77.

Nairobi, Kenya. Kenya National Bureau of Statistics, March 19–22, 2012

Orubuloye, I. O. (1991).The Implications of the Demographic Transition Theory for Fertility Change in Nigeria. *International Journal of Sociology of the Family*, Vol. 21, pp161–174.

Orubuloye, I. Olatunji (1987). Some Socio-Cultural Factors Influencing the Determinants of Fertility: Selected Case Studies in Nigeria." In (eds.) Ebigbola, Joshua A. and Akin, J. and Van de Walle, Etienne. The Cultural Roots of African Fertility Regimes *The Proceedings of the Ife Conference on the Cultural Roots of African Fertility Regimes*. Department of Demography and Social Statistics, Obafemi Awolowo University, Ile-Ife and Population Studies Centre, University of Pennsylvania, USA. Pp331–345.

Phumaphi, J. (2011). *Family planning and economic growth*. Council on Foreign Relations Working Paper. New York: Council on Foreign Relations.

Population Reference Bureau (2011). 2011 World Population Data Sheet. Population Reference Bureau. Washington, DC. www.prb.org

Recher, D.S. (2011). Economic and Social Implications of the Demographic Transition. *Population and Development*. Vol. 37 (Supplement), ppP11–33

Ross, J. (2004). Understanding the Demographic Dividend. Policy Project. Washington: Fortunes Group.

Sippel, L; Kiziak, T., Woellert, F. & Klingholz, R (2011). Africa's Demographic Challenges: How a Young Population can Make Development Possible. Berlin: Berlin Institute for Population and Development.

Togunde, D. & Newman, S. (2005). Value of Children, Child Labour and Fertility Preferences in Urban Nigeria. *West Africa Review*, Issue 7. Africa Resource Center, Inc. 2005. ISSN: 1525-4488

U.S Census Bureau (2003). "Population Analysis Spreadsheets for Excel 97–2000 (PASEX)". International Programs Center, U.S. Census Bureau, Washington

UNAIDS (2004). ""HIV Testing of Specific Populations: Children and Adolescents". UNAIDS Global Reference Group on HIV/AIDS and Human Rights. Third Meeting, Geneva, 28–30 January 2004.

UNICEF (2006). Programming Experiences in Early Child Development. Early Child Development Unit, Programme Division, United Nations Children's Fund, New York, USA, November 2006.

United Nations, and UNICEF (2011). The State of the World's Children 2011: Adolescence: An Age of Opportunity. United Nations, UNICEF. New York, USA.

United Nations (2011).*World contraceptive use 2011*. New York: United Nations.

Wolfgram, F.A. (2005). *Population, resources and environment: A Survey of the Debate*. The Heritage Foundation, Population Research Institute, The Catholic Family and Human Rights Institute. The Catholic University of America.

Wongboonsin, K; Guest, P. & Prachuabmoh, V. (2005). Demographic Change and the Demographic Dividend in Thailand. *Asian Population Studies*, Vol. 1 No 2, 2005. pp 245–256.

World Bank (2011).*World Development Indicators*. World Bank Group, Washington DC.

12 Orphaned Children in Sub-Saharan Africa
What Can We Learn from Census Data?

Bruno Masquelier and
Abdramane B. Soura

1 INTRODUCTION

The fate of orphans in sub-Saharan Africa (SSA) has received increasing attention in recent years, mainly as a result of the HIV-TB epidemic. According to the latest estimates from UNICEF (2010), as many as 56 million children under the age of 18 had lost one or both parents in 2009; this represents 14 percent of the population aged 0–17 years in the region. About 26 percent of these orphans had lost one or both parents to AIDS (UNICEF 2010).

Research that document this "orphan crisis" are typically based on longitudinal case studies (Hosegood et al. 2007; Zaba et al. 2005) or data from sample surveys (see, among others, Bicego, Rutstein, and Johnson 2003; Monasch and Boerma 2004; Case, Paxson, and Ableidinger 2004; Beegle et al. 2010). Census data on orphanhood have been hardly exploited. This is unfortunate, because about 80 censuses conducted in SSA have included questions on parental survival. For many of them, basic tabulations of orphanhood status are available by age, regions, or place of residence in the published reports. In addition, a growing number of samples of census microdata are being distributed in the public domain, through the IPUMS–International database (Minnesota Population Center 2011). At the time of writing this chapter, this database contains seventeen samples of African censuses in which respondents were asked about their orphan status: Kenya (1989 and 1999, with 5 percent of persons recorded); Mali (1987 and 1998, 10 percent); Malawi (1998 and 2008, 10 percent); Uganda (1991 and 2002, 10 percent); Rwanda (1991 and 2002, 10 percent); Tanzania (1988 and 2002, 10 percent); Senegal (1988, 10 percent); Sierra Leone (2004, 10 percent); and South Africa (2 percent of persons recorded in 2007 and 10 percent of records of the 1996 and 2001 censuses).

Drawing on these IPUMS samples and on additional tabulations gathered mainly from published reports, this chapter provides three illustrations of the relevance of censuses to research on orphanhood. Firstly, we examine trends in orphanhood prevalence. We show that in some countries these trends differ substantially from those modeled by the Joint United Nations Program on HIV/AIDS (UNAIDS) and UNICEF. We argue that census estimates, along with those derived from household surveys, should be used to refine model-based estimates because some discrepancies cannot entirely be explained by misreporting of orphanhood status. Secondly, to stress the usefulness of censuses in providing statistics for small areas, we model and map the spatial distribution of orphans at the district or provincial level for five countries of the Great Lakes region (Kenya, Uganda, Rwanda, Tanzania, and Malawi). Lastly, we show that census data can complement what is learned about the vulnerability of orphans from household surveys, particularly as regards their school attendance, living arrangements, and participation in the labor market. Before presenting these illustrations, the ensuing section introduces how parental survival status is collected in African censuses. It also discusses some of the issues regarding the quality of data on orphanhood.

Orphans are usually defined as children under 18 years of age whose mother, father or both parents have died from any cause (UNICEF and UNAIDS 2004), but we will use various age ranges in the course of this chapter. In Section 3, we present orphanhood rates among 5- to 9-year-old children, because we supplement estimates derived from the IPUMS database with proportions computed from census reports, which are only available by five-year age-groups. In the last section, which deals with the vulnerability of orphans, we analyze individual-level data for 7- to 17-year-old children, because we focus on characteristics which refer to older children (such as school attainment, union formation, and labor force participation).

Unless otherwise stated, we use the UNAIDS categorization of orphans in this chapter, defining maternal/paternal orphans as children whose mother/father has died, irrespective of the survival status of the other parent (dual orphans are children who have lost both parents).

2 DATA COLLECTION AND QUALITY

In SSA, questions about parental survival first appeared in retrospective surveys in the late 1960s. Originally, they were aimed at allowing for the indirect estimation of adult mortality, taking advantage of the close relation that exists between the proportion of surviving parents and the probability of dying during the adult ages (Brass and Hill 1973; Timaeus 1992). In the 1990s, these questions were included in the household questionnaires of Demographic and Health Surveys (DHS) and UNICEF's Multiple Indicator Cluster Surveys (MICS). They were then restricted to children under 18, which indicates that the focus had shifted to the situation of orphans and vulnerable children (OVCs). To date, more than 135 large-scale surveys have collected information on the survival status of biological parents (Masquelier 2010).

Numerous census schedules have also included questions on orphanhood. Their primary purpose was also to allow for the estimation of adult mortality, but the HIV-TB epidemic has sparked a renewed interest in the situation of orphans. After reviewing questionnaires or reports from more than two hundred African censuses, we can point to seventy-nine censuses that include questions on parental loss (at least for mothers). Regrettably, some reports are never published and others do not systematically tabulate orphan prevalence by age. About six censuses out of ten in the 2000 round asked respondents about the survival of their parents. Some countries have collected orphanhood data at each round (e.g., Gambia since 1973, Kenya since 1969), whereas others have never done so until now (e.g., Guinea or Nigeria). Overall, questions on orphanhood are a little more frequent in Eastern Africa and Southern Africa; more sporadic in Central Africa (Masquelier 2010).

Censuses share some limitations with DHS-type surveys to study orphanhood. Firstly, the causes of death of parents are not recorded through verbal autopsies; therefore, it is not possible to distinguish between AIDS- and non-AIDS orphans, for instance. Secondly, neither the number of years that elapsed since the deaths of parents nor their ages at death are collected. Another limitation of census data, not present in surveys, is that it is seldom possible to identify vulnerable children who are not orphans, such as those living in households with an HIV-infected adult or with a chronically ill parent. In addition, censuses typically collect less information than household surveys on the characteristics of children (e.g., no information on nutritional status, immunizations, or parental residence). However, for some dimensions of child development, such as child labor, census schedules may contain questions that are not regularly asked in surveys. Another advantage of census microdata is that the sample sizes are large enough to allow for the comparison of subcategories of orphans and to obtain estimates for small areas.

In censuses and surveys, there is a general consensus that the orphanhood status is poorly reported, chiefly because of the adoption effect. This term refers to misreports of foster parents as biological parents, resulting in underestimates of proportions of orphaned children. Young orphans are particularly at risk of being reported as nonorphans. According to Blacker (1984, 85), in the presence of adults noted as parents in questions about the relationship to the household head, "enumerators rarely bother to probe whether the children are the true offspring of these so-called parents and automatically record the fathers and mothers as being alive without asking the questions." Foster parents may also deliberately or inadvertently claim adopted orphans as their own offspring. In addition, many children in SSA do not cohabit with their parents but are fostered in the extended family (Renata 2009). This practice may be detrimental to the quality of data on orphanhood status. The adoption effect is less pronounced in reports relative to older children, partly because at older ages both biological and foster parents are more likely to be deceased.

Robertson et al. (2008) evaluated the extent of the adoption effect in a cohort study conducted in Manicaland (Zimbabwe). They found that, of 198 children reported as maternal orphans in the first round of the study and followed up to the third round, as many as one-third were reported as nonorphans at least once in the next two rounds. Interestingly, the reports on parental survival were more consistent, because only 13 percent of paternal orphans were later reported as having a living father. As suggested later in this chapter, the higher consistency of reports on paternal orphanhood status could be explained by a higher likelihood of paternal orphans to live with their surviving mother (as compared with maternal orphans with their surviving father); surviving partners will provide more accurate information than more distant relatives. Likewise, higher remarriage rates among widowers can play a role here. It is, however, difficult to assess the extent of the biases in the orphanhood prevalence, as there might be compensating errors; a certain percentage of nonorphans could also be misreported as orphans (and nonorphans are much more numerous).

In addition to the adoption effect, proportions of orphans are usually biased by the absence of data. For this chapter, we discarded data with missing values and 'don't know,' with the assumption that ignorance of parental survival is unrelated to the likelihood of being orphan. Ages reported in censuses are also characterized by inaccuracies and the attraction of round digits (i.e., age heaping). Age exaggeration will result in a downward bias, because orphan rates rise with age (Ewbank 1981).

3 ASSESSING TRENDS IN ORPHANHOOD RATES WITH CENSUS DATA

The right-hand panel of Figure 12.1 presents, for twenty-five countries in SSA, proportions of maternal orphans among 5- to 9-year-olds for both sexes, as observed in fifty-three censuses conducted between 1966 and 2009, for which we had access to tabulations by age. These proportions range from 1.4 percent (Kenya 1989) to 8.7 percent (Lesotho 2006). The left-hand panel displays proportions of paternal orphans, ranging from 3 percent (Niger 2001) to 23 percent (Rwanda 2002). More children are reported as fatherless because fathers are in general older than mothers and males experience higher mortality rates. Some declines are apparent in the 1970s and 1980s (e.g., in Gambia and Sierra Leone) but the most notable change is the upsurge in the proportions of orphaned children in recent decades. Only a handful of countries have experienced declines in these proportions during the 1990s and 2000s (Mali, Niger). The highest proportions of orphans are observed in Eastern and Southern Africa, the two regions that have been hardest hit by the HIV/AIDS epidemic. Proportions of maternal orphans among 5- to 9-year-olds exceeded 5 percent in several censuses; apart from Sierra Leone in 1974 and Rwanda

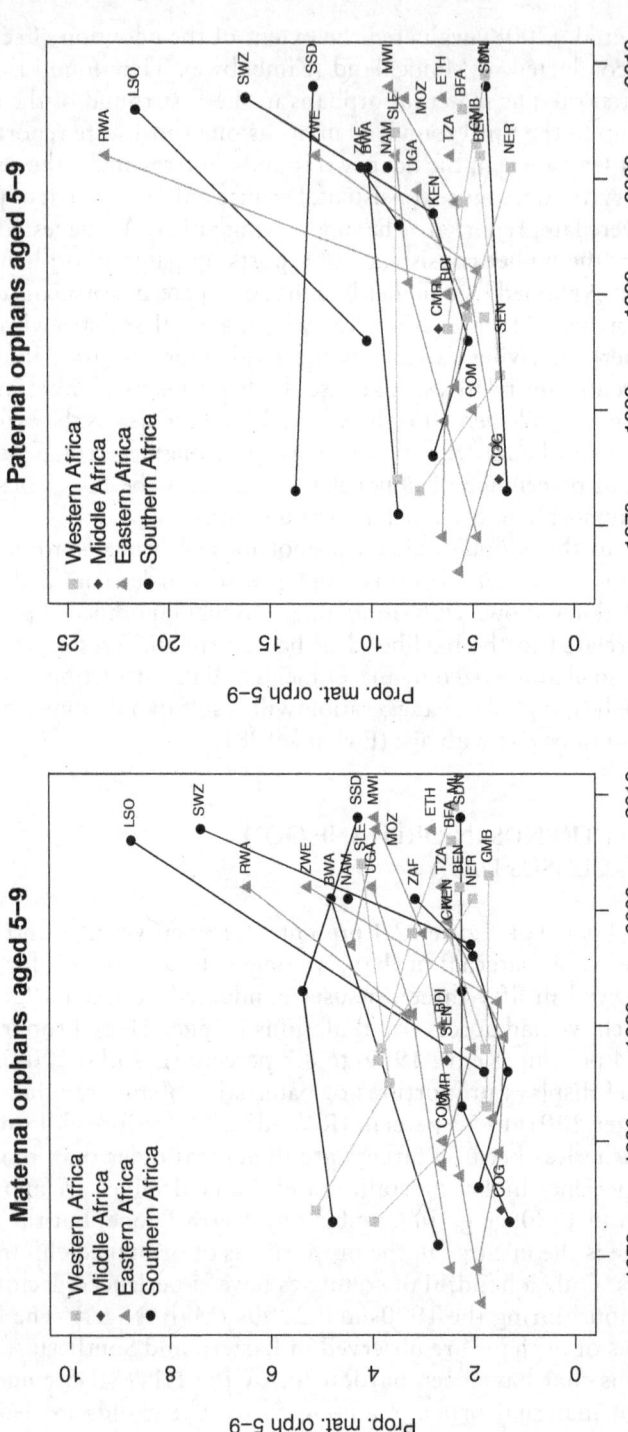

Figure 12.1 Percentage of children aged 5–9 who have lost their mother or father; West, Middle, East and Southern Africa, 1970–2010.

in 2002, all were conducted after 2000 on the southern tip of the continent. More than one out of ten children aged 5–9 had lost their father in Botswana (2001), Lesotho (1986 and 2006), South Africa (2001 and 2007), Zimbabwe (2002), Swaziland (2007), and Rwanda (2002). Also salient is the considerable variation between countries since 2000. Even in Western Africa, where the prevalence of orphanhood has been the lowest in recent years, the proportion of motherless children aged 5 to 9 in recent years has varied from 1.7 percent in Gambia (2003) to 4.2 percent in Sierra Leone (2004).

As mentioned earlier, census and survey data are deemed to underestimate the orphanhood prevalence. In addition, they do not provide the time series needed to reconstruct past trends over long periods (consider, for instance, the only two point estimates for Botswana, indicated as BWA in Figure 12.1). For these two reasons, UNICEF and UNAIDS estimate the number of orphans from mathematical models relying on fertility and mortality rates. The estimation method, developed by Grassly and Timaeus (2005), starts with the distribution of adult deaths by age and calendar year, and consists in estimating how many children were born to those adults, and whether these children are still alive at the time of interest. To calculate the number of maternal orphans attributable to AIDS, the method accounts for the vertical transmission of the virus, the lower fertility of infected mothers, and the additional risks of dying faced by orphans (Zaba et al. 2005). The estimation of paternal orphans is further complicated by the need to account for the effect on child survival of HIV transmission between parents, as well as the reduced fertility of partners of infected men.

To date, neither surveys nor census data have been used to calibrate model-based estimates of orphan numbers. However, there are striking discrepancies between the two types of estimates. For this analysis, we extracted the trends in the proportions of maternal and paternal orphans among 5- to 9-year-olds from the latest version of Spectrum (2011), the software used by UNICEF and UNAIDS (Stover et al. 2010). Ideally, these estimates should be either in agreement with proportions observed in the censuses, or higher in cases of a pervasive adoption effect. However, Figure 12.2 shows that this is not as clear-cut.

The agreement between estimates varies by sex and by subregion. With the exception of the Namibian census of 2001, census-based estimates of the fraction of maternal orphans are consistently lower than Spectrum outputs. The correlation coefficient between both series of proportions is 0.88. This is consistent with similar comparisons made by Grassly et al. (2004) with survey estimates. They concluded that the background adult mortality of the United Nations, which is underpinning model-based proportions of orphans, could be too high, although part of the discrepancies can be ascribed to the adoption effect. However, Grassly et al. (2004) also noted that paternal orphanhood prevalence was more

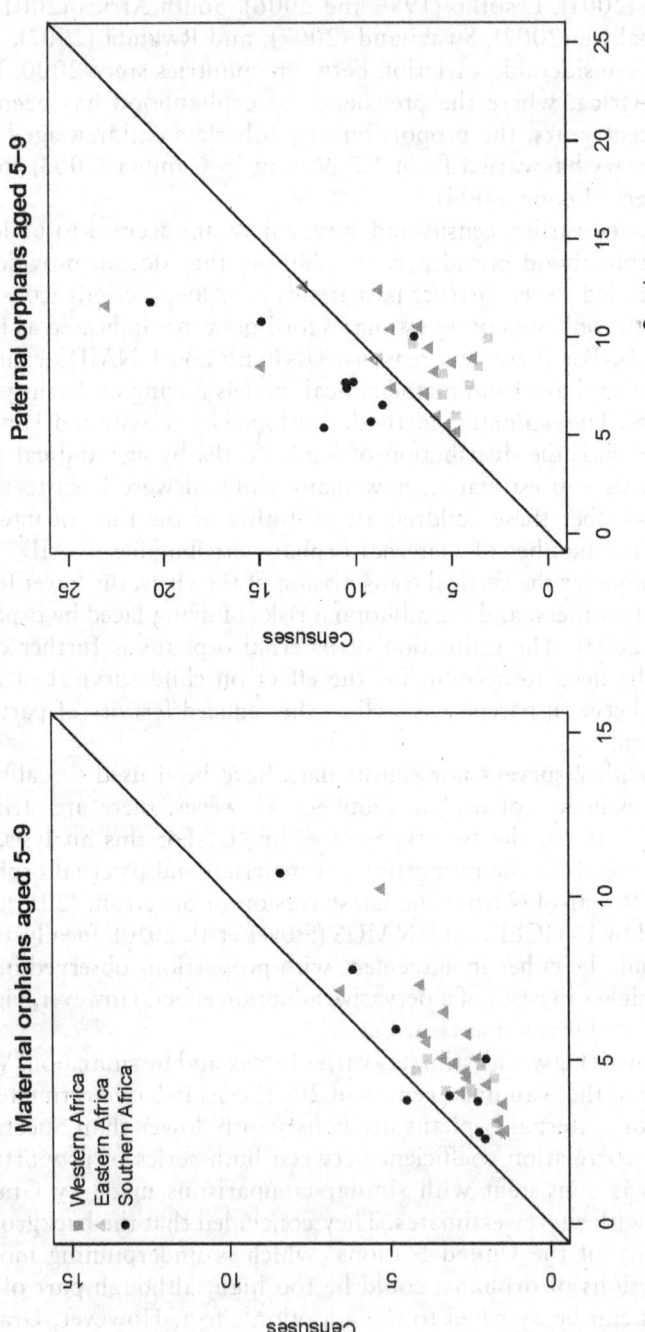

Figure 12.2 Comparison of the percentage of children aged 5–9 who have lost their mother or father, as estimated by Spectrum and reported in censuses.

in agreement with model outputs, with a closer congruence in countries with a high HIV prevalence. This is not what we observe here. Many estimates lie above the equivalence straight line, especially in Eastern and Southern Africa. In Lesotho (1996 and 2006), Mozambique (2007), Namibia (2001), and Rwanda (2002), census-based estimates are more than 50 percent higher than estimates obtained from Spectrum. Pinning down the reasons behind such discrepancies is beyond the scope of this chapter and requires further analysis. However, this comparison suggests that, combined with survey estimates, census data could help refine model outputs.

4 MAPPING THE GEOGRAPHIC VARIATION OF ORPHAN PREVALENCE

Household surveys can, at best, yield acceptable estimates for broad regions. Consequently, little is known about the within-country distribution of orphans at smaller geographical scales. This distribution is mainly shaped by geographical inequalities in adult mortality, but the latter are themselves poorly documented in sub-Saharan Africa, even at the basic level of disaggregation by type of residence.

In the late 1970s and 1980s, according to estimates assembled by Timaeus (1993), adult mortality was lower in urban areas than in rural areas, and the differential was larger in countries with a low life expectancy, suggesting that the survival advantage of urban areas could decrease as mortality rates decline. This trend has undoubtedly been disrupted by the advent of HIV-AIDS, as HIV prevalence is considerably higher in urban areas (Mishra et al. 2009). Consequently, it is difficult to hypothesize whether the orphanhood rates will be higher or lower in rural areas. Empirical research on this issue remains scarce and equivocal (Monasch and Boerma 2004). In addition, the within-country distribution of orphans is not reducible to the distribution of adult deaths. It is also altered by the migration of orphans and widows, who are typically highly mobile (Ford and Hosegood 2005). Orphans are sometimes cared for by members of their extended family residing far away, necessitating traveling long distances across the country (Ansell and Young 2004). Adult deaths also result in the dissolution and reformation of new households elsewhere (Urassa et al. 2001). Even before the death, children can move with their terminally ill parents to seek a better support in their communities of origin, resulting in "returning home to die" migrations, mostly to rural areas (Clark et al. 2007). Conversely, rural-to-urban migrations can be prompted by the need to find employment for orphans and widows (Foster and Williamson 2000).

Urban–rural differentials can be studied with household surveys, but census data are needed to work at smaller geographical scales. As an illustrative exercise, we model and map the orphanhood prevalence in subnational divisions from five censuses: Malawi 1998, Kenya 1999, Rwanda 2002, Uganda 2002, and Tanzania 2002. We retain these censuses because they refer to contiguous countries in the Great Lakes region and provide a snapshot of the orphanhood prevalence around the year 2000. The scale of geographical breakdown available in the IPUMS database varies from counties (in Uganda) to provinces (in Rwanda), and districts are identified in Malawi, Kenya, and Tanzania. Because changes in administrative boundaries have occurred over time, the units identified here do not necessarily represent the most up-to-date geographical divisions. Administrative boundaries were obtained from the GADM database (www.gadm.org).

We use a mixed-effects Poisson regression model, controlling only for age (and age squared), with a varying intercept by district, county, or province. The advantage of this model is that it shrinks the estimates toward the overall mean when the number of children is sparse. We assume that the age pattern of orphanhood is similar across administrative divisions within each country, and include only children up to age 17 in the model.

We present here predicted proportions of maternal orphans at age 7, in order to control for differences in the age distribution of children (Figure 12.3). Within this subregion of the Great Lakes, maternal orphanhood prevalence is the highest in all provinces in Rwanda, as well as around the borders of Lake Victoria, both on its western shore in Uganda (Masaka, Kampala), and on its eastern shore in Tanzania (Kagera) and Kenya (Nyanza). Other pockets of high maternal orphanhood are apparent in the north central region of Uganda, around the northern tip of Lake Malawi, in the Iringa region in Tanzania, as well as in the southern region of Malawi. By contrast, an area stretching from the Rift Valley Province of Kenya to the northeastern districts of Tanzania had a small burden of orphans around 2000.

Although some areas with high orphan burden are also those with the highest HIV prevalence (such as the Nyanza province in Kenya or Kagera and Iringa in Tanzania), this map is not exactly a reflection of the spatial variation of HIV prevalence. For instance, using the geographical coordinates of the communities sampled in the DHS conducted in Kenya in 2003, Montana, Neuman, and Mishra (2007) modeled the HIV prevalence and they did not observe the gradient from west to east that is apparent in Kenya for maternal orphans (Nyanza stands out as an exception). However, this pattern should be considered with caution as the northeastern province and the northern part of the eastern province in Kenya are the most sparsely populated (hence a higher degree of shrinkage toward the overall mean).

There is room for improvement in the modeling of orphanhood prevalence, but this first exploratory analysis shows that census data can generate valuable insights into the subnational variations of orphanhood.

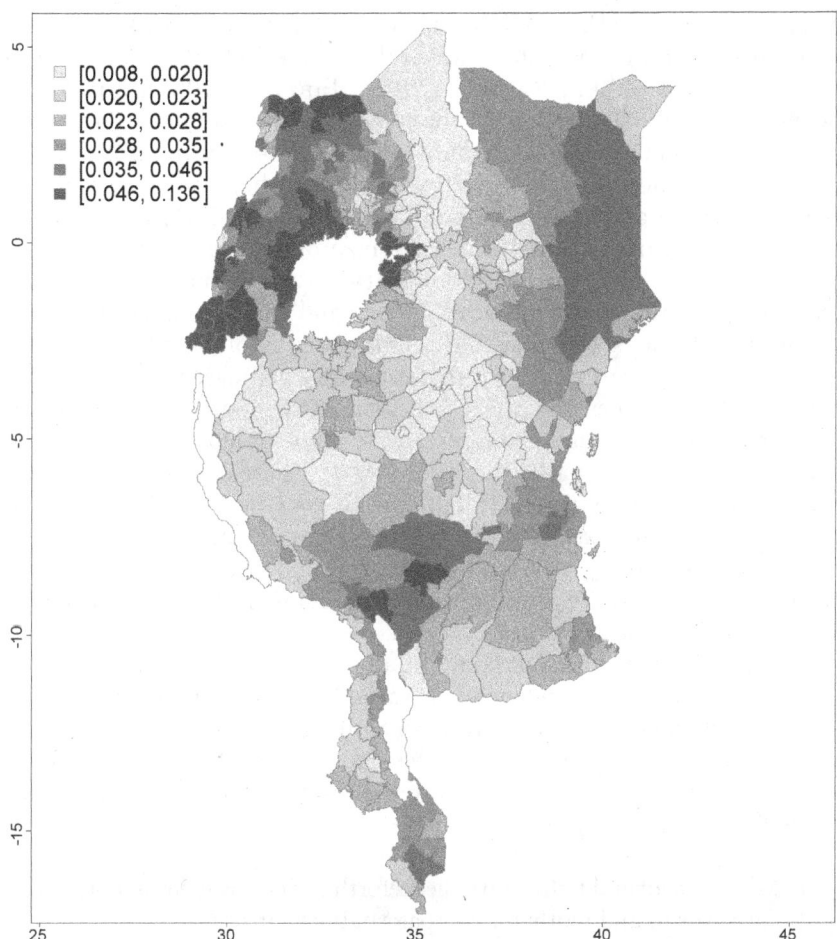

Figure 12.3 Proportions of maternal orphans at age 7 estimated from mixed-effects Poisson regression models from IPUMS data (Kenya 1999, Uganda 2002, Tanzania 2002, Rwanda 2002, and Malawi 1998).

5 ANALYZING THE VULNERABILITY OF ORPHANED CHILDREN

An extensive literature has been devoted to the educational outcomes of orphans, their living arrangements, and their health, including their sexual and reproductive behaviors or nutritional status (Palermo and Peterman 2009; Beegle et al. 2010). To date, this literature has made almost no use of census data (Marcoux, Noumbissi, and Zuberi 2010). In this section, we seek to determine whether census data provide results that are consistent with sample surveys, and we insist on the value added by censuses. We use the latest censuses available in the IPUMS database with information on parental loss: Malawi (2008), Mali (1998), Kenya (1999), Uganda (2002), Rwanda (2002), Tanzania (2002), and Sierra Leone (2004). We did not retain the census conducted in Niger in 1988, because the data is somewhat outdated. We also discarded the large-scale survey conducted in 2007 in South Africa because the social and economic development of this country and its large-scale social grants system render cross-national comparisons problematic.

We first examine the orphanhood status of children according to the relationship to the household head, his sex and educational level, as well as the wealth index of households. This index is obtained by combining the flooring, wall, and roof materials of dwellings. Households are considered poor when they have a beaten earth floor (or similar types of flooring such as stones or bricks), walls made of mud bricks (or clay), and roof in thatch (or cane, wood, or straw). These characteristics were retained because they were available in all censuses and easily comparable across countries. Secondly, we analyze the school attendance of orphans aged 7 to 17 years and the educational attainment of children aged 15 to 17 years. We also focus on the employment status of orphans and on the types of work they perform.

Logistic regression models combine all children and include the parental survival status as an independent variable. Then, separate models are run for each category of orphans, controlling for age, sex, living standards, relationship with household heads, and their educational attainment. Unlike in previous sections, children are now classified in four mutually exclusive categories:

1. Mother dead and father alive (henceforth defined as maternal orphans)
2. Father dead and mother alive (paternal orphans)
3. Both dead (dual orphans)
4. Both alive

5.1 Living Arrangements

Based on censuses, the living arrangements of orphans can often be analyzed solely from their relationship to the household head. In some cases (e.g., Malawi 2008), questions about parental survival are supplemented by questions about parental residence, but this is not true in most censuses. Table 12.1 presents row percentages of children by parental survival status according to the relationship to household heads (for children aged 7 to 17). These percentages confirm that single orphans, especially paternal orphans, mostly co-reside with the surviving biological parent (Monasch and Boerma 2004). Between 39 percent and 76.4 percent of fatherless children are reported as children of the household head, probably their mother (or her new partner) in most cases. However, some

Table 12.1 Relationship to the Household Head by Parental Survival Status (7- to 17-Year-Olds, Row Percentages)

Country	Type	Head	Sibling	Spouse/Partner	Child	Grandchild	Other Relative	Non-relative	Unknown
Mali 1998	Both alive	0.2	1.1	2.7	83.2		9.7	2.9	0.2
	Mother dead	0.6	3.0	5.7	68.4		17.8	4.4	0.1
	Father dead	0.7	17.5	6.4	39.2		30.3	5.8	0.1
	Both dead	2.5	15.7	9.1	26.9		38.6	7.1	0.1
Kenya 1999	Both alive	0.6	2.2	0.5	76.2		17.3	3.2	0.0
	Mother dead	1.6	6.9	1.4	40.9		43.1	6.1	0.0
	Father dead	1.2	4.9	1.0	62.8		25.2	4.8	
	Both dead	2.5	13.5	1.8	9.3		63.6	9.4	
Rwanda 2002	Both alive	0.2	0.8	0.3	88.8	4.9	2.1	2.0	0.9
	Mother dead	1.9	11.4	0.7	55.9	11.4	10.7	5.9	2.1
	Father dead	0.3	1.4	0.4	76.4	9.7	7.1	3.8	0.9
	Both dead	3.9	27.2	0.5	5.5	25.3	26.7	9.7	1.2
Uganda 2002	Both alive	0.4	2.8	0.9	81.1		12.9	1.0	0.9
	Mother dead	1.2	8.2	2.3	47.3		36.6	2.9	1.5
	Father dead	1.1	6.4	1.8	58.2		29.1	2.1	1.3
	Both dead	2.3	14.9	2.2	14.0		60.4	4.3	1.9

(continued)

Table 12.1 (continued)

Country	Type	Head	Sibling	Spouse/Partner	Child	Grandchild	Other Relative	Non-relative	Unknown
UR Tanzania 2002	Both alive	0.7		0.7	74.3	9.0	9.6	5.7	
	Mother dead	1.5		1.5	39.3	19.9	25.8	12.0	
	Father dead	1.3		1.4	52.0	13.0	21.3	11.0	
	Both dead	3.2		2.1		29.5	46.1	19.1	
Sierra Leone 2004	Both alive	0.4	3.9	0.7	64.8	10.8	17.0	2.4	
	Mother dead	0.6	8.2	1.8	44.4	12.7	28.7	3.6	
	Father dead	0.6	9.6	1.8	40.3	12.9	31.4	3.4	
	Both dead	0.6	18.9	3.1	22.1	13.2	37.2	4.9	
Malawi 2008	Both alive	0.2		1.0	82.4		15.4	1.0	
	Mother dead	0.6		1.8	33.2		62.1	2.3	
	Father dead	0.5		1.6	63.7		32.5	1.7	
	Both dead	1.0		1.9	14.4		79.4	3.3	

of them could also be children fostered or adopted by the household head and not residing with their mother. Apart from Mali (1998) and Sierra Leone (2004), proportions of maternal orphans reported as children of the household head are much lower; below 50 percent in Tanzania, Kenya, Malawi, and Uganda. The exceptions of Mali and Sierra Leone (where maternal orphans are more likely to live with their surviving father) could reflect a more systematic enforcement of rules related to the patrilocal residence.

Maternal orphans reported as children of the household head are most often observed in blended families, because the household heads are (re)married in a majority of cases. Conversely, paternal orphans reported as children of the household head are more frequently observed in single-parent families, because these household heads are more often widowed or separated.

The proportion of orphans who are household heads, albeit marginal (less than 4 percent), indicates a certain vulnerability, because most of them are required to enter the job market earlier. An early entry into union may also be a consequence of parental loss, as evidenced by the proportions of orphans who are a spouse or partner of the household head. In Mali (1998), as many as 9 percent of dual orphans were either a spouse or partner of the household head. They were girls in more than 85 percent of cases. In the Malian census, 36 percent of girls aged 17 who had lost both parents were already in a union, as against 20 percent for nonorphans (Table 12.2). This pattern is apparent in every census, but it could be less pronounced after controlling for individual- and household-level characteristics (Palermo and Peterman 2009). Finally, a third category of potentially vulnerable children represents orphans living in sibling-headed households. This situation concerns a large percentage of dual orphans, from 13.5 percent in Kenya (1999) to 27.2 percent in Rwanda (2002).

In censuses conducted in Tanzania, Sierra Leone, and Rwanda, children living with a grandparent are explicitly identified. Although the proportions of children in this configuration do not vary much with parental survival status in Sierra Leone (between 11 and 13 percent), in Rwanda and Tanzania orphans are disproportionately found in such households, especially motherless children and dual orphans (up to 30 percent of dual orphans in Tanzania).

As observed from DHS (Monasch and Boerma 2004; Bicego, Rutstein, and Johnson 2003), orphans are also more likely to be found in female-headed households (FHHs), as well as in households whose head has not completed primary education (Table 12.2). By contrast, when considering the standards of living, there are no obvious differences between households with orphans and other households. In some cases (Uganda 2002, Tanzania 2002), the percentage of nonorphans living in poor households is even higher than the corresponding percentage for

Table 12.2 Percentage of Girls in Union at Age 17 According to Parental Survival Status, and Percentage of Children (Aged 7–17) According to Parental Survival Status and Selected Characteristics of Households

	Percentage of Girls in Union at age 17			
	Mother Dead	Father Dead	Both Dead	Both Alive
Mali 1998	27	28	36	20
Kenya 1999	13	11	19	8
Rwanda 2002	4	2	3	2
Uganda 2002	19	17	16	14
Tanzania 2002	14	12	14	10
Sierra Leone 2004	23	22	25	15
Malawi 2008	15	13	14	12

	Percentage of Children Living in Female-Headed Households (7–17)			
	Mother Dead	Father Dead	Both Dead	Both Alive
Mali 1998	6	36	12	6
Kenya 1999	36	81	50	35
Rwanda 2002	24	84	50	20
Uganda 2002	27	67	41	15
Tanzania 2002	26	71	43	31
Sierra Leone 2004	25	46	30	24
Malawi 2008	33	67	42	21

	Percentage of Children Living with a Household Head Who Has Not Completed Primary Education (7–17)			
	Mother Dead	Father Dead	Both Dead	Both Alive
Mali 1998	91	90	92	89
Kenya 1999	56	61	56	45
Rwanda 2002	75	81	70	72
Uganda 2002	55	64	56	51
Tanzania 2002	50	56	51	44
Sierra Leone 2004	76	79	79	75
Malawi 2008	68	75	68	66

(continued)

Table 12.2 (continued)

	Percentage of Children Living in Poor Households (7- to 17-Year-Olds)			
	Mother Dead	Father Dead	Both Dead	Both Alive
Mali 1998	66	63	66	64
Kenya 1999	35	35	28	34
Rwanda 2002	10	11	7	10
Uganda 2002	33	40	29	42
Tanzania 2002	38	43	32	44
Sierra Leone 2004	29	29	31	29
Malawi 2008	43	51	42	52

orphans. This is not unexpected. Data from DHS and other in-depth surveys indicate that orphans are not necessarily found in the most economically disadvantaged households (Bicego, Rutstein, and Johnson 2003; Mishra and Bignami-Van Assche 2008). Households caring for orphans could be positively selected for certain characteristics correlated with household wealth. It is also possible that our indicator of standard of living is too crude. A composite index based on more household assets would be more appropriate.

5.1.1 School Attendance and Educational Attainment

Table 12.3 indicates that among all countries that were considered, Mali has the lowest school attendance rates. These rates are lower than 35 percent irrespective of the survival status of parents. This under-enrollment is well documented in the Sahelian region, with a more conspicuous disadvantage for young girls (Marcoux, Noumbissi, and Zuberi 2010).

Orphans tend to attend school less frequently than children whose parents survive, except in Malawi. In other censuses, differences in school attendance rates range from 7 to 20 percentage points between nonorphans and dual orphans. Single orphans occupy an intermediate position in almost all censuses considered. Differentials are also observed in terms of school attainment, assessed here as the proportion of children aged 15 to 17 who had already completed primary school. Orphaned children are worse off than nonorphans, except for Malawi, as well as Rwanda and Uganda in the case of dual orphans.

Table 12.3 School Attendance of 7- to 17-Year-Olds, School Attainment of 15- to 17-Year-Olds, and Percentage of Children (7- to 17-Year-Olds) in Employment, by Parental Survival Status

	Percentage of Children Attending School (7–17 y)			
	Mother Dead	Father Dead	Both Dead	Both Alive
Mali 1998	23	25	16	31
Kenya 1999	68	71	67	79
Rwanda 2002	52	60	57	64
Uganda 2002	77	78	75	83
Tanzania 2002	62	63	60	68
Sierra Leone 2004	61	62	50	70
Malawi 2008	61	60	61	54

	Percentage of Children Who Achieved Primary School (15–17 y)			
	Mother Dead	Father Dead	Both Dead	Both Alive
Mali 1998	9	10	6	12
Kenya 1999	50	53	52	58
Rwanda 2002	19	21	26	25
Uganda 2002	53	54	55	53
Tanzania 2002	63	64	63	67
Sierra Leone 2004	28	28	23	34
Malawi 2008	32	33	36	30

	Percentage of Children in Employment by Parental Survival Status (7- to 17-Year-Olds)			
	Mother Dead	Father Dead	Both Dead	Both Alive
Mali 1998	45.6	44.5	47.2	39.4
Kenya 1999	6.1	5.4	6.7	3.8
Rwanda 2002	22.1	16.8	21.1	13
Uganda 2002	11.7	10.9	12.4	7.3
Tanzania 2002	21.4	21.6	23.9	16.2
Sierra Leone 2004	30.7	30.2	37.7	22.4
Malawi 2008	14.3	13.4	14.6	13.2

Broad comparisons of school attendance by parental survival status tend to underestimate the disadvantages of orphans, because orphans are on average older than nonorphans, and school attendance is generally slightly higher after age 10. Therefore, we estimated odds ratios for current school attendance from a regression model controlling for sex, age, relationship to the household head and his educational attainment, wealth index, and parental survival. Compared with nonorphans, the odds for single orphans of being currently in school are significantly lower than 1 in every census except for Malawi in 2008. The loss of a mother is particularly detrimental (Bicego, Rutstein, and Johnson 2003). The unexpected result in Malawi has already been observed and it has been ascribed to a pattern of fostering in which orphans are relocated to reside with relatives that are more able to take care of them (Government of Malawi and UNICEF 2007). But it is unclear why this is only the case in Malawi. Another counterintuitive observation concerns a higher attendance of dual orphans in Rwanda, compared with nonorphans. Again, this has been observed in survey data (World Bank 2003). This result could reflect a targeting of dual orphans by NGOs, as well as the effect of the tax-funded Genocide Fund (FARG).

Similar models were run for each orphanhood status, to assess if the effects on school attendance of the various covariates differ depending on this status. Again, the coefficients are not presented here for the sake of conciseness; we only summarize the main conclusions.

Firstly, census data tend to support the conclusions of Case, Paxson, and Ableidinger (2004), who found that children living with distant relatives or unrelated caregivers are less likely to attend school. Compared with orphans *reported as child of the household head* (either a biological child or fostered child), the odds of attending schools for maternal or paternal orphans are significantly lower than 1 for almost all other types of relationships to the household head. They are particularly low for orphans who have no relationship to the household head. Unsurprisingly, when children are heads of household or partners, the chances to attend school are also very low.

The positive association between the educational attainment of the household head and the school attendance of children holds true, irrespective of the parental survival status. Compared with those living with a household head who has not completed primary school, the odds ratio are much larger than 1 for other children.

Also evident is the fact that poor families have difficulties sending their children to school. Both orphans and nonorphans are indeed less likely to go to school when they live in poor housing conditions. With regard to the sex of children, with the exceptions of Rwanda and Malawi, census data highlight the disadvantage of girls, regardless of the parental survival status. However, these broad patterns observed among orphans are also observed among nonorphans. The lower school attendance of orphans is therefore mostly explained by their tendency to live with caregivers that are more distantly related, and in families with poorer educational outcomes.

5.2 Work Involvement

With the death of a primary caregiver, the household budget can plummet because of reduced income and increases in dependency ratios. Before the death, a substantial fraction of the family budget can also be allocated to health care. To compensate, children may have to take a more active role in household chores, caring for siblings, or income-generating activities. Measuring the effect of orphanhood on the work involvement of children is tricky, partly because of the lack of standard operational definition of child labor. A variety of measures and terms are used and understood differently. That may bias cross-national comparisons based on census data. In addition, the same category of activities can fall into different codes in different censuses, especially activities performed in family agricultural holdings.

With these caveats in mind, we focus here on children's employment, as defined by the ILO (2010). This concerns children performing economic activities, for pay or profit, or performing domestic work outside the child's own household for an employer. This term is more restrictive than other definitions of child labor that include nonmarket household activities. For instance, using DHS and MICS data, Monasch and Boerma (2004) compared the proportion of orphans and nonorphans aged 10–14 years who worked more than twenty and forty hours per week (including household chores), and found no significant difference between the two groups. Because censuses contain no information on the time spent on housework, it is not possible to identify unpaid family workers who work for excessive hours. Therefore we focus here only on paid employment and self-employment among children aged 7 to 17 (see the bottom panel of Table 12.3).

Descriptive statistics indicate that the census carried out in Mali in 1998 is the one in which child employment was by far the most common: about four nonorphans out of ten, and nearly five out of ten orphans were working. This is simply the counterpart of their low school attendance. The lowest rates are observed in Kenya. However, care should be exercised when interpreting these results, because the reference period for the questions about employment status varies across censuses.

The disadvantage of orphans in terms of work involvement is apparent in almost every census, the census conducted in Malawi in 2008 again being a noticeable exception. This penalty persists when controlling for the same household characteristics we used previously for school attendance. In several countries (Uganda, Rwanda, Sierra Leone), motherless children are more likely to participate in the job market than fatherless children, although we anticipated that the loss of a father would force more children to search for alternative sources of earnings. Quite surprisingly, according to the regression outputs, dual orphans in Kenya and Rwanda appear to have an advantage over nonorphans, and once again we hypothesize that this results from assistance from NGOs or government structures. If this assistance aims to increase the school enrollment of dual orphans (as observed in Rwanda), it will also limit their participation in the labor market.

Orphans in employment are mostly agricultural and fishery workers, especially in Mali (90 percent of the orphans aged 7 to 17). In Sierra Leone, the elementary occupations (street sales, cleaners, etc.) also concern a significant share of orphans (40 percent of the orphans aged 7 to 17). About two out of ten orphans are employed in such activities in Rwanda and Tanzania, and one out of ten orphans in Uganda.

As expected, age is positively associated with participation in the labor market, irrespective of the parental survival status and the country. Girls are also less involved in the labor market, except in Rwanda and Sierra Leone. As regards the relationship to the household head, regression results show that children who are themselves household heads (and their wives) participate much more frequently in the labor market, other things being equal. Spouses in Mali are the only exception to this rule; this probably results from the dominance of Islam in this country.

As was the case for school attendance, children who are unrelated to the household head, both among orphans and nonorphans, are more likely to be in employment. Also noticeable is the inverse relationship between the employment of children and educational attainment of their household heads in all countries but Kenya. This Kenyan exception is observed in terms of living standards too. It is possible that some of these children are domestic workers working and residing in richer and more educated households, but why this is observed only in Kenya remains unclear.

6 CONCLUSION

In the last fifty years, many African countries have collected data on orphanhood through their censuses. Given their increasing availability, thanks to databases such as IPUMS, it is surprising that such data remain scarcely exploited. To demonstrate their usefulness, we presented three illustrations in this chapter.

Firstly, we showed that censuses can help estimate the numbers of orphans more precisely. These numbers are regularly produced by UNAIDS and UNICEF to track progress in the fight against HIV/AIDS, and estimate the funding required to meet the needs of OVCs. However, orphanhood rates derived from census data sometimes differ from estimates obtained by demographic modeling, and these discrepancies cannot entirely be explained by misreportings attributable to the adoption effect. Ideally, censuses should therefore be used to calibrate model-based estimates of orphanhood rates in combination with DHS and MICS surveys, even if only to obtain lower bounds.

Secondly, censuses constitute the only source of information allowing researchers to document spatial inequalities in orphanhood on small geographical scales. Identifying areas receiving numerous OVCs is crucial to properly allocating funds and designing policies. To date, at least fifteen African governments have developed and implemented national plans of action for OVCs to strengthen families and communities caring for OVCs and improve access to services, policy and legislation (Engle 2008). Numerous nongovernmental organizations are also involved in developing community outreach, peer support, financial assistance, and access to health or childhood development activities. The identification of priority areas where orphans are clustered may greatly increase the effectiveness of these actions.

Thirdly, census data can complement the analysis of the vulnerability of orphans. To a large extent, results from our exploratory analysis are consistent with previous research based on surveys and longitudinal case studies, even when they are apparently counterintuitive (as is the case in Rwanda and Malawi). Further analysis could take better advantage of the potential of censuses by focusing on specific categories of orphans that are poorly understood with survey data because of small sample sizes (such as sibling-headed and child-headed households).

In sum, all African countries should strive to collect data on orphanhood more systematically. In their recommendations for the content of population censuses, the United Nations (2008, p.143) state that the questions on orphanhood are to be given lower priority. It is timely to raise this priority level.

ACKNOWLEDGMENTS

We wish to thank the staff behind the IPUMS database at the Minnesota Population Center and the statistical offices in Kenya, Mali, Malawi, Uganda, Rwanda, Tanzania, Senegal, Sierra Leone, and South Africa. We are also grateful to Patrick Gerland for providing several census tabulations of orphanhood status by age and all the reviewers whose comments contributed to improving the quality of this chapter.

REFERENCES

Ansell, N., and L. Young. (2004) "Enabling Households to Support Successful Migration of AIDS Orphans in Southern Africa." *AIDS Care* 16 (1): 3–10.

Beegle, K., D. Filmer, A. Stokes, and L. Tiererova. (2010) "Orphanhood and the Living Arrangements of Children in Sub-Saharan Africa." *World Development* 38 (12): 1727–1746.

Bicego, G., S. Rutstein, and K. Johnson. (2003) "Dimensions of the Emerging Orphan Crisis in Sub-Saharan Africa." *Social Science and Medicine* 56 (6):1235–1247.

Blacker, J. (1984) "Experience in the Use of Special Mortality Questions in Multi-Purpose Surveys: The Single-Round Approach" In *Databases for Mortality Measurement*, ed. United Nations, 79–89. New York: United Nations.

Brass, W., and K. Hill. (1973) "Estimating Adult Mortality from Orphanhood." *Proceedings of the International Population Conference: Liège* 3: 111–123.

Case, A., C. Paxson, and J. Ableidinger. (2004) "Orphans in Africa: Parental Death, Poverty, and School Enrollment." *Demography* 41 (3): 483–508.

Clark, S., M. Collinson, K. Kahn, K. Drullinger, and S. Tollman. (2007) "Returning Home to Die: Circular Labour Migration and Mortality in South Africa." *Scandinavian Journal of Public Health* 35 (3): S35–S44.

Engle, P. (2008) "National Plans of Action for Orphans and Vulnerable Children in Sub-Saharan Africa: Where Are the Youngest Children?" Working Paper no. 50, Bernard van Leer Foundation, The Hague, the Netherlands.

Ewbank, D. (1981) "Age Misreporting and Age-Selective Underenumeration: Sources, Patterns and Consequences for Demographic Analysis." Committee on Population and Demography, Report no. 4.

Ford, K., and V. Hosegood. (2005) "AIDS Mortality and the Mobility of Children in Kwazulu Natal, South Africa." *Demography* 42 (4): 757–768.

Foster, G., and J. Williamson. (2000) "A Review of Current Literature of the Impact of HIV/AIDS on Children in Sub-Saharan Africa." *AIDS* 14: S275–S284.

Government of Malawi and UNICEF. (2007) *Orphanhood in Malawi 2004–2006*. Lilongwe, Malawi: Government of Malawi and UNICEF.

Grassly, N., J. Lewis, M. Mahy, N. Walker, and I. Timaeus. (2004) "Comparison of Household-Survey Estimates with Projections of Mortality and Orphan Numbers in Sub-Saharan Africa in the Era of HIV/AIDS." *Population Studies* 58 (2): 207–217.

Grassly, N., and I. Timaeus. (2005) "Methods to Estimate the Number of Orphans as a Result of AIDS and Other Causes in Sub-Saharan Africa." *JAIDS Journal of Acquired Immune Deficiency Syndromes* 39:635–675.

Hosegood, V., S. Floyd, M. Marston, C. Hill, N. McGrath, R. Isingo, A. Crampin, and B. Zaba. (2007) "The Effects of High HIV Prevalence on Orphanhood and Living Arrangements of Children in Malawi, Tanzania, and South Africa." *Population Studies* 61 (3): 327–336.

International Labour Organization. (2010) *Accelerating Action against Child Labour: Global Report under the Follow-Up to the ILO Declaration on Fundamental Principles and Rights at Work*. Geneva, Switzerland: International Labour Office.

Marcoux, R., A. Noumbissi, and T. Zuberi. (2010) "Orphans in Three Sahelian Countries: Exploratory Analyses from Census Data." *Canadian Studies in Population* 375 (1–2): 245–267.

Masquelier, B. (2010) *Estimation de la mortalité adulte en Afrique subsaharienne à partir de la survie des proches. Apports de la microsimulation.* PhD dissertation, Presses Universitaires de Louvain.
Minnesota Population Center. (2011) *Integrated Public Use Microdata Series, International: Version 6.1 [Machine-Readable Database].* Minneapolis: University of Minnesota.
Mishra, V., and S. Bignami-Van Assche. (2008) *Orphans and Vulnerable Children in High HIV Prevalence Countries in Sub-Saharan Africa.* Claverton: Macro International.
Mishra, V., A. Medley, R. Hong, Y. Gu, and B. Robey. (2009) "Levels and Spread of HIV Seroprevalence and Associated Factors: Evidence from National Household Surveys." DHS Comparative Reports no. 22, Claverton: Macro International.
Monasch, R., and J. Boerma. (2004) "Orphanhood and Childcare Patterns in Sub-Saharan Africa: An Analysis of National Surveys from 40 Countries." *AIDS* 18 (2): 55–65.
Montana, L., M. Neuman, and V. Mishra. (2007) "Spatial Modelling of HIV Prevalence in Kenya." DHS Working Paper no. 27, Claverton: Macro International.
Palermo, T., and A. Peterman. (2009) "Are Female Orphans at Risk for Early Marriage, Early Sexual Debut, and Teen Pregnancy? Evidence from Sub-Saharan Africa." *Studies in Family Planning* 40 (2): 101–112.
Renata, S. (2009) "Child Fostering in Africa: When Labor and Schooling Motives May Coexist." *Journal of Development Economics* 88 (1): 157–170.
Robertson, L., S. Gregson, C. Madanhire, N. Walker, P. Mushati, G. Garnett, and C. Nyamukapa. (2008) "Discrepancies between UN Models and DHS Survey Estimates of Maternal Orphan Prevalence: Insights from Analyses of Survey Data from Zimbabwe." *Sexually Transmitted Infections* 84 (1): S57–S62.
Stover, J., P. Johnson, T. Hallett, M. Marston, R. Becquet, and I. Timaeus. (2010) "The Spectrum Projection Package: Improvements in Estimating Incidence by Age and Sex, Mother-to-Child Transmission, HIV Progression in Children and Double Orphans." *Sexually Transmitted Infections* 86 (2): S16–S21.
Timaeus, I. (1992) "Estimation of Adult Mortality from Paternal Orphanhood: A Reassessment and a New Approach." *Population Bulletin of the United Nations* 33:47–63.
Timaeus, I. (1993) "Adult Mortality." In *Demographic Change in Sub-Saharan Africa, Panel on the Population Dynamics of Sub-Saharan Africa, Committee on Population, Commission on Behavioral and Social Sciences and Education, National Research Council*, ed. K. Foote, K. Hill, and L. Martin, 218–255. Washington, DC: The National Academies Press.
UNICEF. (2010) *Children and AIDS: Fifth Stocktaking Report.* New York, USA: UNICEF.
UNICEF and UNAIDS. (2004) "The Framework for the Protection, Care and Support of Orphans and Vulnerable Children Living in a World with HIV and AIDS". http://www.unicef.org/aids/files/Framework_English.pdf. Accessed November 22, 2013.
United Nations. (2008) *Principles and Recommendations for Population and Housing Censuses.* New York: Department of International Economic and Social Affairs, United Nations.
Urassa, M., J. Boerma, R. Isingo, J. Ngalula, J. Ng'weshemi, G. Mwaluko, and B. Zaba. (2001) "The Impact of HIV/AIDS on Mortality and Household Mobility in Rural Tanzania." *AIDS* 15 (15): 2017–2023.

World Bank. (2003) *Education in Rwanda: Rebalancing Resources to Accelerate Post-Conflict Development and Poverty Reduction.* Washington, DC: World Bank.

Zaba, B., J. Whitworth, M. Marston, J. Nakiyingi, A. Ruberantwari, M. Urassa, R. Issingo, G. Mwaluko, S. Floyd, A. Nyondo, and A. Crampin. (2005) "HIV and Mortality of Mothers and Children: Evidence from Cohort Studies in Uganda, Tanzania, and Malawi." *Epidemiology* 16 (3): 275–280.

13 Profiling the Elderly
Understanding Recent Trends in Acceleration of Sub-Saharan African Population Aging

Henry Victor Doctor

1 INTRODUCTION

Recently, the world's population has experienced a remarkable transition, from a stage of high birth rates and death rates to one characterized by low death rates (Shrestha 2000). The core of this transition has been the growth in the number and proportion of older persons (Bloom, Canning, and Fink 2008; Olshansky and Carnes 2007; Smith and Mensah 2003). In the history of civilization, the unprecedented growth in the elderly population has been remarkable and calls for urgent attention to the needs of the elderly. The recent dynamics of aging in less developed countries (LDCs) implies that LDCs will have less time to cope with the effects of population aging than more developed countries (Makoni 2008; Tucker and Buranapin 2001). Since aging involves social, behavioral, and biological processes, studies that range from genetic contributions to chronic disease susceptibility (e.g., Olshansky et al. 2005) to the effects of economic growth on the elderly's living arrangements (e.g., McGarry and Schoeni 2000) are inevitable. Aging involves many multifaceted processes that have implications at the micro level for the analysis of individual lives and at the macro level for the analysis of population and historical changes (Schafer and Ferraro 2009).

The unprecedented international demographic change has resulted in some striking imbalances. For example, the United Nations (2009a) reports that one in five Europeans, compared with one in twenty Africans, is 60 years or older. Considering the rapid pace of aging in Africa over the last few years, we take advantage of the African census archival data to assess the recent paths of population aging and report on future levels of indicators of aging and the speed at which they change. We will show how these depend on whether changes in longevity are taken into account.

There are many merits in adopting a comparative approach to studying population aging in Africa. Briefly, this approach entails a more specific examination of whether processes or structures differ between nations. For example, structural or policy characteristics of one country may influence its inhabitants' aging experiences in ways that differ from another country. Africa has gone through (and continues to experience) very different socioeconomic environments that have implications for the elderly. For example, the United Nations Economic Commission for Africa (UNECA) (2009) reported that between 2006 and 2008, the gains in the continent's per capita income had been modest and recent estimates also showed that the poverty rate in sub-Saharan countries in 2005 was the same as the rate of 50 percent in 1981. Ravallion and Chen (2008) reported that the number of poor people during the same period had actually doubled. Globally, oil-importing and oil-exporting countries experienced significant increases in inflation rates in 2008. High inflation rates compromise growth and macroeconomic stability leading to, *inter alia,* low savings and investments rates in many African countries.

Nevertheless, by 2008, economic performance varied across subregions. For example, growth in the gross domestic product (GDP) decelerated in three of the five subregions of Africa. West and Central Africa grew at 5.4 percent and 4.9 percent in 2008, compared with 5.2 percent and 3.9 percent in 2007, respectively. In 2008, GDP growth rates decreased in North Africa based on 2006 values (5.8 percent to 5.4 percent), East Africa (6.2 percent to 5.7 percent), and Southern Africa (6.1 percent to 4.2 percent) (for details, see UNECA 2009). Although we do not attempt to discuss details of cross-country variations or long-term historical trends in economic performance in this chapter, it is important to note that during the same period (i.e., 2006–2008), some countries led GDP growth on the continent whereas others experienced plummeting growth. For example, Ethiopia led East Africa with an 8.0 percent real GDP growth, Egypt in North Africa at 6.2 percent, Liberia in West Africa at 8.0 percent, Equatorial Guinea in Central Africa at 9.0 percent, and Angola in Southern Africa at 12.9 percent (UNECA 2009). In some countries, slow growth in GDP was associated with largely postelection violence (e.g., Kenya at 3.5 percent), poor rainfall (e.g., Eritrea at 1.0 percent), food and oil costs, weaker European Union demand for exports (e.g., Tunisia at 4.8 percent), political upheavals (e.g., Guinea at 2.0 percent), and high interest rates and weaker global economic activity (e.g., South Africa at 3.1 percent).

Socioeconomic dynamics and processes across Africa and elsewhere are building blocks for understanding the demographic transition theory (DTT). According to the DTT, the shift toward low mortality and fertility rates occurs when there is a process of overall modernization resulting from industrialization, urbanization, education, empowerment of women, and substantial overall socioeconomic development (Kirk 1996; Caldwell 1976). Despite undergoing several criticisms, the DTT has remained a useful framework for discussing the dynamics of fertility and mortality change in the world. Recent literature demonstrates that Africa continues to experience high levels of fertility, especially in sub-Saharan Africa (SSA), which is largely influenced by a blend of cultural and socioeconomic factors that affect the attitudes and behavior of people toward childbearing (Caldwell and Caldwell 1990). The high incidence of fertility in other countries such as Mali and Niger reflects that reproduction and first marriages generally occur very early. Further, contraceptives are rarely used and not widespread (Kaggwa, Diop, and Storey 2008).

Many countries in Africa have experienced substantial mortality declines, which have been sustained for over half a century. The mortality decline caused by economic and social progress is also related to advances in medicine, improvements in hygiene, and the reduction of infant mortality (Adetunji and Bos 2006). In general, the synergy between Africa's recent socioeconomic performance and the elements of DTT suggests that, overall, human and social development remains low in Africa and achievements are diverse; select groups such as the aged and the youth are still more affected than others (Kimokoti and Hamer 2008; Tucker and Buranapin 2001). This calls for evidence-based information on past and projected trends in longevity to ensure mainstreaming of the special needs of these groups into policy-making and implementation frameworks. This study is an attempt to contribute to the existing literature on the dynamics of the growing elderly population. To sum up, the study aims at (a) assessing recent paths of population aging, (b) reporting on future levels of indicators of aging and the speed at which they change, and (c) documenting how these depend on whether changes in longevity are taken into account.

2 METHODOLOGY

2.1 Data Source

This chapter uses census data from selected African countries from the 1980s to the most recent round of censuses to document past and estimate future trends in the pace and acceleration of population aging.[1] The data came from the archives of the Integrated Public Use Microdata Series (IPUMS) International, based at the University of Minnesota Population Center (2011; see also https://international.ipums.org/international/), and the United Nations 2008 Revision of World Population Projections.[2] The IPUMS database, the main source of the data used here, only includes data from countries that have released their census data for public use. At the time of the study, most African censuses had not provided their data for archiving and public use. As a result, availability of data was not universal across Africa.

2.2 Methods

After identifying and addressing data quality issues such as those related to age reporting and smoothing of age distributions,[3] the study uses conventional measures of aging that are based on chronological age. These measures assume that a 70-year-old person in 2000 was just as old as a 70-year-old person in 2010 because each had lived the same number of years. The issue is whether it is reasonable to say that the two had aged at the same rate. After all, the 70-year-old in 2010 would, on average, have many more remaining years of life. This underscores the fact that population aging is not only about the presence of more old people but also about people living long lives.

To assess the recent trends and estimate future trends in the course of aging, the study employs indicators that explicitly take changes in the remaining life expectancy into account. Compared with the traditional age that matters for institutional arrangements, such as pension systems, the measures employed provide more information on the changing human condition in which more people can plan for a longer and healthier life with consequences for their behavior (Lutz, Sanderson, and Scherbov 2008).

The conventional measures are the proportion of the population aged 60+ (Prop. 60+), the median age (MA) of the population and its average age (aver. age). The alternative indicators to measure the proportion of elderly people do not depend on a fixed age boundary but on a fixed remaining life expectancy. The Prop. RLE 15–is the proportion of the population in age-groups that have a remaining life expectancy of 15 years or less. If longevity increases, the minimum age included in Prop. RLE 15–increases. The adjusted version of the MA is called standardized or prospective median age (PMA). It is the age of a person in the year under consideration (e.g., an individual in Guinea in 2000) who had the same remaining life expectancy as a person at the MA in the year under consideration (e.g., 2009). The change in the PMA over a defined period is roughly the change in the MA minus the change in life expectancy at the MA (Lutz, Sanderson, and Scherbov 2008).

Projections were made for periods beyond the available recent censuses.[4] In all census years, country specific life tables associated with the census were used. In some cases, indirect methods (e.g., Brass, Coale, and Demeny 1968) were used to generate life tables. Where necessary, the WHO series of life tables for Africa, the United Nations life tables and the INDEPTH model life tables (MLTs) were also used in the analyses.[5] We assessed the future levels of aging up to 2050, a period beyond the deadline for meeting the Millennium Development Goals (2015).

In general, the two types of MLTs that are usually used in population projections, that is, Coale-Demeny (C-D) Regional and the UN MLTs for developing countries were not used for projections beyond 1995 for two key reasons. First, these MLTs did not take into account the African experience except for the UN MLTs that used data from Tunisia. Second, they were developed before the onset of the HIV epidemic. Specifically, the C-D tables were based on European mortality experience in the period 1871–1953 whereas the UN tables used mortality data (1920–1976) from Central Africa, temperate and tropical South America, East Asia, South Asia, Southwestern Asia, and Tunisia (Coale and Demeny 1983; United Nations 1982). As others (e.g., Udjo 2008a, 2008b) have argued, the mortality schedules illustrated by these MLTs do not depict the characteristic 'hump' in the mortality curve for the young adult ages, a result of increased AIDS-related deaths in these age-groups. Considering that the first HIV cases in Africa were diagnosed around the early 1980s, and the 9–10 year incubation period, it is reasonable to use MLTs that incorporate HIV/AIDS on the assumption that the impact of HIV/AIDS probably became substantial after 1995 in populations with a generalized epidemic (for details, see Udjo 2008b). To our advantage, the UN World Population Projections (2008 revision) provide life tables estimates, which incorporate the impact of HIV/AIDS.

3 RESULTS

The demographic and socioeconomic profiles of the ten countries included in the analysis are presented in Table 13.1. As of 2011, Egypt had the highest population, estimated at 82.6 million, followed by South Africa at 50.5 million, Tanzania at 46.2 million, Kenya at 41.6 million, and Uganda at 34.5 million. The population of Rwanda, Guinea, Senegal, and Mali ranged between 10.4 and 15.4 million. The country with the lowest annual population growth rate was South Africa (0.5 percent), with the highest recorded in Uganda at 3.4 percent. In terms of gross national income (GNI) per capita, the highest was South Africa and Egypt at $10,050 and $5,680, respectively. The lowest GNI per capita was recorded in Malawi at $940. Life expectancy at birth (both sexes) was low at 52 years in Mali compared with a high of 73 years in Egypt. The highest HIV prevalence among adults aged 15–49 years was recorded in South Africa at 17.8 percent and the lowest (< 0.1 percent) in Egypt.

Table 13.1 Brief Demographic and Socioeconomic Profile of Selected Countries as at Mid-2011

Country	Population in Millions	Population Growth (Annual %)	GNI PPP per Capita ($)	Life Expectancy at Birth	HIV Prevalence % (15–49 years)
Egypt	82.6	2.0	5,680	73	<0.1
Guinea	10.2	2.7	940	54	1.3
Kenya	41.6	2.7	1,570	57	6.3
Malawi	15.9	2.7	780	54	11.0
Mali	15.4	3.1	1,190	52	1.0
Rwanda	10.9	2.1	1,130	55	2.9
Senegal	12.8	2.8	1,810	59	0.9
South Africa	50.5	0.5	10,050	53	17.8
Uganda	34.5	3.4	1,190	54	6.5
Tanzania	46.2	2.9	1,360	57	5.6

Source: 2011 World Population Data Sheet from the Population Reference Bureau, www.prb.org (accessed October 8, 2011).

Table 13.2 presents the basic description of selected African census data from the IPUMS–International database. Most of the censuses were either de facto, de jure or both and data used in this study were either 5 percent or 10 percent samples of all the main data sets, a standard public release agreement between IPUMS and most of the African governments. The results in this chapter are based on data from the 1990s since most of the associated data (e.g., life tables or distribution of deaths by age-group) from the 1980s or much earlier are not readily available as inputs into the projections. The earliest census year reported in

Table 13.2 Basic Description of Selected African Census Raw Data

Country	Year	Sample Size	De Jure / De Facto	Missing/ Nonstated ages Percent (n)
Egypt	1996	5,902,246	De facto	0.01 (404)
Egypt	2006	7,282,434	De facto	0.00 (0)
Guinea	1983	457,837	Both	0.01 (59)
Guinea	1996	729,071	Both	0.25 (1,825)
Kenya	1989	1,074,098	De facto	0.12 (1,321)
Kenya	1999	1,407,547	De facto	0.00 (0)
Malawi	1998	991,393	De facto	0.00 (0)
Malawi	2008	1,341,977	Both	0.07 (931)
Mali	1987	785,384	Both	1.52 (11,977)
Mali	1998	991,330	Both	0.45 (4,508)
Rwanda	1991	742,918	Both	0.00 (0)
Rwanda	2002	843,392	Both	0.00 (0)
Senegal	1988	700,199	Both	0.03 (218)
Senegal	2002	994,562	Both	0.00 (0)
South Africa	1996	3,621,164	De facto	1.19 (43,145)
South Africa	2001	3,725,655	De facto	0.00 (0)
South Africa	2007	1,047,657	Both	0.00 (0)
Uganda	1991	1,548,460	De facto	0.06 (856)
Uganda	2002	2,497,449	Both	0.00 (0)
Tanzania	1988	2,310,424	De facto	0.00 (0)
Tanzania	2002	3,732,735	De facto	0.00 (0)
Total		42,727,932		

Notes: Because censuses in many African countries are not conducted exactly ten years apart, according to the United Nations recommendation, the census years are classified as 1990s, 2000s, and 2010s to denote census years close to these periods.
Source: IPUMS–International.

Table 13.2 is 1983 for Guinea, with 2008 as the most recent for Malawi. The most recent data for South Africa, that is, 2007, come from a large community survey involving about 286,000 households. Guinea's 1983 census had the lowest proportion of missing or nonstated ages at 0.01 percent, with the highest (1.52 percent) being observed in the Mali 1987 census. An important observation for the majority of the countries is the decline in the proportion of people with missing or nonstated ages between censuses, an indicator of improved reporting or methods of collecting data on age. For example, Kenya's 1989 census had 0.12 percent of individuals with nonstated ages and none in 1999. Mali's population with nonstated ages declined from 1.52 percent in 1987 to 0.45 percent in 1998. Uganda had 0.06 percent of nonstated ages in 1991 and none in 2002.

All five measures of aging are listed in Tables 13.3 and 13.4 for selected African countries and dates. Despite minor fluctuations, all of them indicate that aging will continue until 2050. In Guinea, the average age is expected to increase from 22.3 years in the 1990s to 26.6 years in 2050, with the proportion aged 60-plus years steadily increasing from 5 percent in 2000 to 10 percent in 2050. The median age for Guinea leaps from 17.0 years in the 1990s to 19.6 years in 2020 before rising to 27.4 years in 2050. The Prop. RLE 15– is relatively stable at roughly 0.04 across the years under consideration. The reference period for the PMA is 1990. As a result, the value of the MA in the 1990s is the same as that of the PMA in the same year, since 1990 is the reference year. In Guinea, results show that the PMA declined from 16.5 years in the 2000s to 9.0 years in the 2010s, 7.5 years in 2020 increasing to 11.3 in 2050. This implies that, for example, in the 2010s the age of a Guinean in the year 1990 who had the same remaining life expectancy as a person at the median age in 2010 was 9.0 years old. In simple terms, the individual in 1990 had the same remaining life expectancy at a very young age as the individual in 2010. To illustrate this further, let's assume that the life expectancy at age 9.0 years in 1990 was 20 years. This means that the expected age at death (everything being constant) at that age was 29 years (i.e., 20 + 9). With improved survival in 2010, the expected age at death was 38.5 years (i.e., 20 + 18.5). The interpretation of the measures for the other countries is similar to the one provided for Guinea.

Generally, all countries considered in Tables 13.3 and 13.4 with the exception of Egypt, Kenya, Malawi, and South Africa show increased gains in life expectancy between the 1990s and 2050. For example, South Africa has lost the gains in life expectancy achieved earlier. This is evidenced by the values of PMA, which are greater than those of MA for all the dates considered. All the indicators show increased proportions of the elderly population over the decades up to 2050.

For Africa as a whole, the proportion of the elderly increased from 5 percent in the 1990s to 11 percent in 2050. The MA is expected to

Table 13.3 Indicators of Aging for Selected African Countries for Both Sexes

Country (Census Years)	Indicator	1990s	2000s	2010s	2020	2030	2040	2050
Egypt (1996, 2006)	Aver. Age	24.2	25.9	27.6	29.3	31.0	32.7	34.4
	Prop. 60+	0.03	0.04	0.08	0.10	0.13	0.15	0.20
	MA	20.0	22.0	24.4	27.5	30.5	33.6	36.9
	Prop. RLE 15–	0.04	0.04	0.05	0.04	0.03	0.03	0.05
	PMA	20.0	27.9	30.8	35.6	39.9	44.0	47.6
Guinea (1983, 1996)	Aver. Age	22.3	23.0	23.7	24.4	25.1	25.9	26.6
	Prop. 60+	0.07	0.05	0.05	0.06	0.06	0.08	0.10
	MA	17.0	17.8	18.5	19.6	21.7	24.4	27.4
	Prop. RLE 15–	0.04	0.03	0.03	0.04	0.04	0.03	0.04
	PMA	17.0	16.5	9.0	7.5	7.4	8.6	11.3
Kenya (1989, 1999)	Aver. Age	20.4	21.5	22.6	23.7	24.8	25.9	27.0
	Prop. 60+	0.04	0.04	0.04	0.05	0.05	0.07	0.09
	MA	15.0	17.0	18.5	19.2	20.8	22.8	24.6
	Prop. RLE 15–	0.03	0.03	0.03	0.03	0.04	0.04	0.06
	PMA	15.0	13.1	19.5	22.1	30.2	33.9	36.7
Malawi (1998, 2008)	Aver. Age	21.9	21.3	22.0	22.7	23.4	24.1	24.8
	Prop. 60+	0.05	0.05	0.05	0.05	0.04	0.04	0.05
	MA	17.0	17.0	16.9	16.6	17.2	18.4	19.6
	Prop. RLE 15–	0.02	0.02	0.02	0.02	0.02	0.02	0.03
	PMA	17.0	22.0	18.2	22.5	24.9	27.8	30.0
Mali (1987, 1998)	Aver. Age	21.6	22.1	22.5	23.0	23.5	24.0	24.5
	Prop. 60+	0.06	0.04	0.04	0.04	0.04	0.06	0.07
	MA	16.0	17.0	17.6	18.5	20.4	22.9	25.5
	Prop. RLE 15–	0.05	0.04	0.04	0.04	0.03	0.02	0.02
	PMA	16.0	17.1	15.3	13.7	13.1	13.3	14.8
Rwanda (1991, 2002)	Aver. Age	20.8	21.0	21.2	21.4	21.6	21.8	22.0
	Prop. 60+	0.05	0.04	0.04	0.05	0.05	0.06	0.10
	MA	16.0	17.0	18.7	19.0	21.4	24.3	27.0
	Prop. RLE 15–	0.03	0.02	0.02	0.01	0.02	0.02	0.03
	PMA	16.0	19.7	16.3	13.9	14.0	15.0	16.8

Notes: Some of the time periods for the indicators are based on the census year for a specific country. For example, the "1990s" period for Guinea refers to Guinea's 1996 census; non-stated or missing cases have been excluded (see Table 13.2 for magnitude); highlighted values were calculated based on a number of assumptions attributable to lack of census data (see Table 13.5 on some notes on measures of aging); reference year for PMA is 1990; "—" not available at the time of the study.

increase by 11 years from 17.5 years in the 1990s to 2050. Whereas the Prop. RLE 15- is expected to fluctuate between 3 percent in the 1990s to a low of 2 percent in 2010 before rising to 5 percent in 2040, it will end up at 4 percent in 2050. However, the adjusted version of the MA shows that Africa will benefit from gains in life expectancy.

Table 13.4 Indicators of Aging for Selected African Countries for Both Sexes (Continuation of Table 13.3)

Country (Census Years)	Indicator	1990s	2000s	2010s	2020	2030	2040	2050
Senegal (1988, 2002)	Aver. Age	21.6	22.1	22.5	23.0	23.5	24.0	24.5
	Prop. 60+	0.04	0.05	0.04	0.04	0.05	0.07	0.09
	MA	16.5	18.0	18.0	19.6	22.4	25.4	28.4
	Prop. RLE 15-	0.02	0.02	0.02	0.02	0.01	0.02	0.03
	PMA	16.5	19.1	17.6	17.2	17.7	18.5	20.8
South Africa (1996, 2001)*	Aver. Age	26.1	26.8	27.3	27.9	28.4	29.0	29.6
	Prop. 60+	0.07	0.08	0.07	0.10	0.11	0.12	0.14
	MA	22.0	23.0	24.9	26.5	28.1	29.8	31.9
	Prop. RLE 15-	0.02	0.02	0.03	0.04	0.05	0.06	0.04
	PMA	22.0	32.8	37.6	36.8	36.1	34.4	35.5
Uganda (1991, 2002)	Aver. Age	20.5	20.2	20.4	20.6	20.8	21.0	21.2
	Prop. 60+	0.05	0.05	0.04	0.04	0.04	0.05	0.07
	MA	16.0	15.0	15.6	16.6	18.5	21.2	24.2
	Prop. RLE 15-	0.03	0.03	0.03	0.02	0.02	0.03	0.04
	PMA	16.0	16.2	9.9	7.6	7.1	8.0	10.4
Tanzania (1988, 2002)	Aver. Age	22.0	22.1	22.2	22.3	22.4	22.5	22.5
	Prop. 60+	0.04	0.06	0.05	0.05	0.05	0.06	0.08
	MA	17.2	17.0	17.5	18.0	19.7	22.2	24.8
	Prop. RLE 15-	0.03	0.03	0.03	0.03	0.04	0.04	0.05
	PMA	17.2	19.0	14.4	13.2	13.2	13.8	15.4
Africa Region	Aver. Age	—	—	—	—	—	—	—
	Prop. 60+	0.05	0.05	0.05	0.06	0.07	0.08	0.11
	MA	17.5	18.5	19.7	21.2	23.4	25.9	28.5
	Prop. RLE 15-	0.03	0.03	0.02	0.04	0.05	0.05	0.04
	PMA	17.5	17.6	16.7	16.2	16.5	17.1	18.8

Notes: Same as in Table 13.3; *South Africa 2007 large Community Survey results were: aver. age = 28.4, prop. 60+ = 0.09, MA = 24.0.

Figure 13.1 shows four of these measures (based on Tables 13.3 and 13.4) of aging as they evolve over time for the selected African population. Similar illustrations for the other countries (detailed results not presented in this chapter) show that aging will continue throughout to 2050.

Figure 13.2 displays the changing speed of increase in selected indicators of aging for Africa. This is calculated as the increases per decade in the level of the indicator divided by the maximum increase projected over the period under consideration. Results show that the PMA and Prop. RLE 15–decelerates between 1990 and 2010 and then accelerates thereafter. The Prop. RLE 15–decelerates again from the 2010–2020 period to the end of the projection period, despite a relative stabilization occurring between 2020–2030 and 2030–2040. Generally, from the 2000–2010 period to the end of the projection period, three indicators (MA, PMA, and Prop. 60+) have an accelerating speed, reaching the highest rate of increase during the 2040–2050 period. These results show that, even under widely varying demographic and socioeconomic conditions, Africa is expected to experience a significant acceleration in the speed of population aging over the coming years.

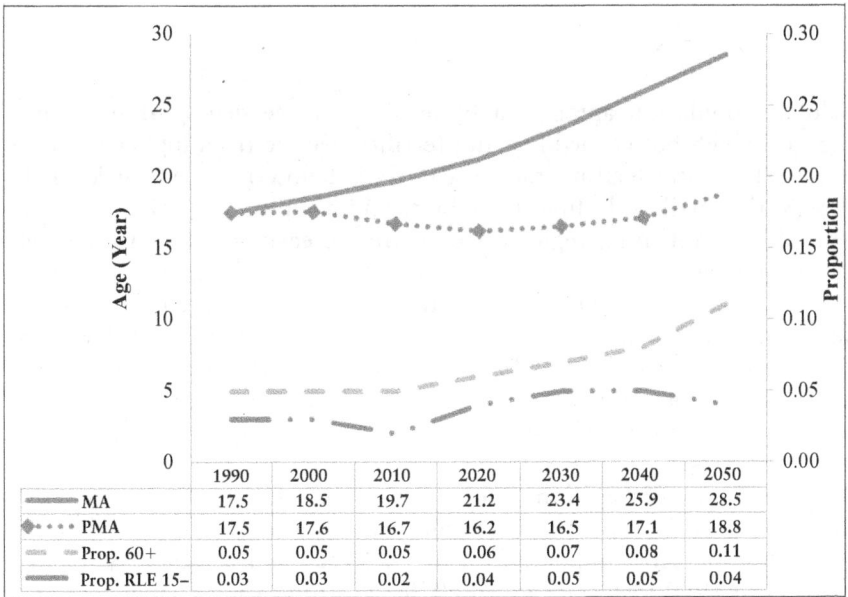

Figure 13.1 Projected changes in the levels of aging for Africa for four indicators of aging.

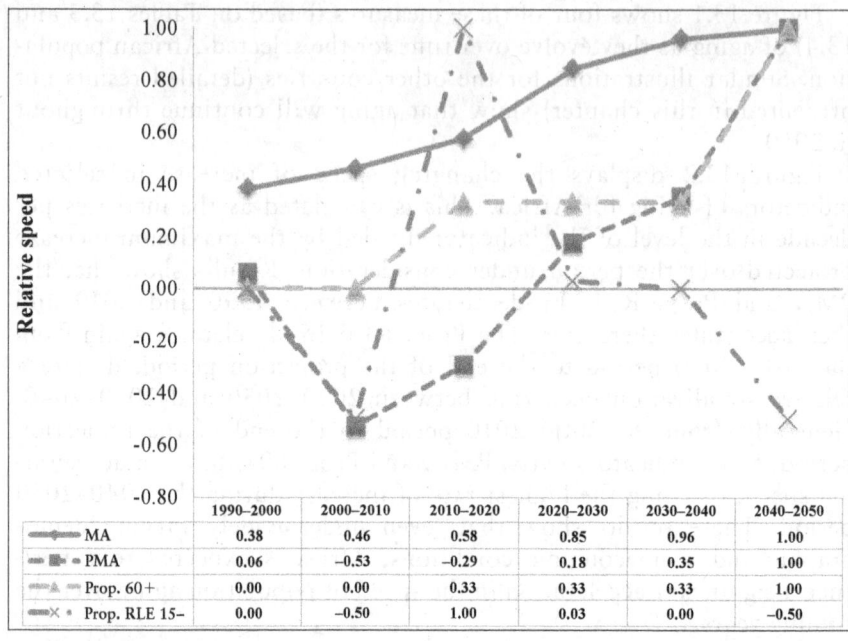

Figure 13.2 The changing decadal speed of increase in Africa's selected indicators of aging.

4 DISCUSSION

Global population aging is a by-product of the demographic transition in which both mortality and fertility decline from higher to lower levels. The total fertility rate in MDCs is below replacement level. In LDCs, the fertility decline started late and has proceeded faster than in the MDCs. Yet in all regions people are increasingly likely to increase their longevity (United Nations 2009b). Results on the assessment of the recent paths of population aging and the speed at which they change show that in Egypt, Guinea, Kenya, Malawi, Mali, Senegal, Rwanda, South Africa, Uganda, and Tanzania, as well as Africa as a whole, generally all the measurements indicate that aging will continue in the next four decades, albeit at a slow pace. The two swiftly increasing indicators (the proportion of individuals aged 60 years and over and MA) are based on the traditional definition of age, suggesting the need for institutional adjustment to cope with the expected increases. The proportion of the African population 60-plus years old will increase from 5 percent in 1990 to 11 percent in 2050. This increase is tremendous in a region characterized by poverty as well as life-threatening diseases such as HIV/AIDS.

Except for Egypt, Kenya, Malawi, and South Africa, where the PMA has consistently exceeded the MA, the two measures adjusted for longevity change show a slower pace of change. For example, in South Africa, the gains in life reduced between 2000 and 2010 compared with the early 1990s, probably attributable to HIV/AIDS. The lost years will be regained from 2050 (and hopefully beyond) when the gap between PMA and MA starts to narrow. That HIV/AIDS has impacted life expectancy in South Africa has been documented elsewhere (e.g., Groenewald et al. 2005; Hosegood, Vanneste, and Timaeus 2004). Countries such as Egypt, Kenya, and Malawi show little or virtually no sign of regaining the lost years beyond 2050. This may be related to profound socioeconomic problems (e.g., in Egypt; see Lofgren 1993) that severely impact the living standards of people in these countries as well as the negative impact of HIV/AIDS on longevity in countries such as Kenya and Malawi, despite the recent declines in HIV prevalence. The Prop. RLE 15–does not vary much for Africa and the selected countries, from 2 percent in 1990 to 5 percent in 2050. The stability of the RLE 15–suggests that how people age remains stable despite the increases in MA. In addition, the results have shown that Egypt has the highest MA among the selected cases, and is likely to keep this position until 2050, with its MA likely to increase to above 36 years, followed by South Africa (31.9 years), Senegal (28.4 years), and Rwanda (27.0 years).

The chance of Prop. 60+ for Africa being more than a third of the population is close to zero, even by the end of the century (Lutz, Sanderson, and Scherbov 2008). However, population aging (irrespective of the magnitude) has critical implications on individuals and societies. In addition to changes in its level, the speed of aging in Africa is a policy concern because of the difficulties of adaptation to demographic change. Africa as a whole and the selected countries in particular, face the challenge of an accelerating speed of aging over the coming decades. These results call for African governments to brace themselves to take care of an aging population.

5 CONCLUSION

African governments should respond appropriately to the growing elderly populations by ensuring that policies are developed or reviewed to enable individuals to adjust their behavior in the face of population aging. One of the common policies is to alter retirement incentives so that people can have the opportunity to opt for longer working years in expectation of greater longevity. Old-age pension systems need to be flexible to allow individuals to reap their retirement packages and at the same time work in their old age. Governments should also institute laws against age discrimination by employers. It is apparent that the changing economy in many countries is generating demands for skills that may not be possessed by the old. Opportunities should be made available for the old to acquire skills that would make them as competitive as the young. However, there is a need to balance resources that will address the needs of the elderly against those aimed at addressing Africa's high unemployment, especially among the youth.

Although it is a policy option to see many elderly people working, only those who are healthy will do so. This calls for investments in the health infrastructure to cater for the health needs of those aged 60 years and above. These efforts should cover the entire population, since those who are likely to lead healthy lives in their young years are more likely to survive to older ages. More important, African governments should start recognizing the challenges of the increased elderly population and start calling for discussions of appropriate responses to the needs of the elderly based on the socioeconomic environment and dynamics of each country.

5.1 Limitations

The results reported here have a number of limitations. First, projections into the distant future are uncertain and the results may be slightly different when evaluated ex post. Second, African census data are marred by age misreporting. Although the analysis excluded individuals with missing or nonstated ages, the proportion of people misstating their ages may affect the results. That is a result of digit preference, a common phenomenon in African census data. Third, life tables used to calculate the longevity measures are often based on incomplete and defective data. Fourth, since the cross-sectional nature of censuses to a certain extent limits their ability to provide long-term assessment of aging dynamics, data from Health and Demographic Surveillance System (HDSS) sites such as those spearheaded by the INDEPTH Network (www.indepth-network.org) could play an important role in monitoring trends in aging in localized settings. Not only are the majority of HDSS sites collecting longitudinal data from rural and disadvantaged areas in selected low-income countries; they provide a core set of components of population change—births, deaths, and migrations—as well as data on marriage. Data collection intervals vary by sites, from one to four times annually with regular updates of the educational status of individuals and other socioeconomic characteristics (Bangha et al. 2010). Although data from INDEPTH member sites provide more detailed information than those collected from censuses or surveys, they are often located at the district level and some of their results may not be generalized. However, the availability of multiple HDSS locations in some countries may provide more coverage. Since no single data set can provide information across various dimensions, researchers should triangulate the available data sets in order to understand nuances associated with aging over time at the national and subnational level. And, lastly, some of the input data are not available by sex, thereby restricting the results to both sexes. Despite these limitations, the results provide an understanding of how aging is expected to evolve. The results should be interpreted with caution, in line with the limitations highlighted here.

Table 13.5 Some Notes on Measures of Aging for Selected African Countries

Country	Year	Measure(s)	Comments
Kenya	2000–2050	MA; Prop. 60+	World Population Projections (WPP) 2008 medium variant.
Guinea	1970 and 1980	Prop. RLE 15–	Used figure for 1983 as 1980; and from the UN for 1970.
	1996	Prop. RLE 15–	WWP 2008 for 1995–2000 population and life tables for the same period. For population from 1996, used WPP, i.e., 2000s.=.2000, 2010s.=.2010.
	2000–2050	Prop. 60+; MA	WPP PD; medium variant as at March 15, 2011.
	1970s (= 1970)	Prop. 60+; MA	WPP PD for 1970; medium variant as at March 15, 2011.
	2000–2050	Aver. age	Annual increase of 1.03%; aver. age in 1970 reduced by 1.03%.
Mali	2000–2050	Prop. 60+; MA	WPP PD; medium variant as at March 15, 2011.
	2000–2050	Aver age	Annual increase of 1.02%; aver. age in 1970 reduced by 1.02%.
	1970s (= 1970)	Prop. 60+; MA	WPP PD for 1970; medium variant accessed March 15, 2011.
Rwanda	2010–2050	Prop. 60+;	WPP PD; medium variant as at March 15, 2011.
	2010–2050	Aver. age	Annual increase of 1.01%; aver. age in 1970s and 1980s reduced by 1.01%.
	1970s–1980s	Prop. 60+; MA	WPP PD for 1970 and 1980; medium variant as at March 15, 2011.
	2010–2020	MA	Rwanda population projections based on 2002 census.
	2020–2050	MA	WPP PD; medium variant; accessed March 15 2011.
Senegal	1970s (= 1970)	Prop. 60+; MA	WPP PD for 1970; medium variant; accessed March 15, 2011.
	2010–2050	Aver. age	Annual increase of 1.02%; aver. age in 1970 reduced by 1.02%.
	2010–2050	Prop. 60+; MA	WPP PD; medium variant; accessed March 15, 2011.
	1990s (= 1995)	Prop. 60+; MA	WPP PD for 1995; medium variant; accessed March 15, 2011.
South Africa	2010–2050	Prop. 60+; MA	WPP PD; medium variant; accessed March 15, 2011.
	2010–2050	Aver. age	Annual increase of 1.03%; aver. age in 1970 and 1980 reduced by 1.03%.

(continued)

Table 13.5 Some Notes on Measures of Aging for Selected African Countries

Country	Year	Measure(s)	Comments
Uganda	2010–2050	Prop. 60+; MA	WPP PD; medium variant; accessed March 15, 2011.
	1970s; 1980s; 2010–2050	Aver. age	Decline by 1.01% for 1970s and 1980s; for 2010–2050 it will increase by 1.01%.
	1980s (= 1980)	Prop. 60+; MA	WPP PD for 1980; medium variant; accessed March 15, 2011.
	1970s (= 1970)	Prop. 60+; MA	WPP PD for 1970; medium variant; accessed March 15, 2011.
Tanzania	1990s (= 1995)	Prop. 60+; MA	WPP PD for 1995; medium variant; accessed March 15, 2011.
	1970s	Aver. age	Increase by 1.004% for 1970s and for 2010s and beyond increases by the same rate.
	1970s (= 1970)	Prop. 60+; MA	WPP PD for 1970; medium variant; accessed March 15, 2011.
	2010–2050	Prop. 60+; MA	WPP PD; medium variant; accessed March 15, 2011.

Notes:
- WPP PD refers to World Population Projections Population Database.
- Data prior to 1990 not reported because of incompleteness. The period 1990 onward had reliable data.
- Guinea, no country level projections from official figures at time of study (from 1996 onward).
- Life tables for 2010s: used WHO life tables for 2008 if country-specific not available.
- PMA computed based on year 2000 as reference since by then most countries had censuses available or 1990s.
- Conservative Prop. RLE 15– estimates for 1970s and 1980s until prior projections are available.

ACKNOWLEDGMENTS

The author acknowledges the financial and technical support received from Statistics South Africa, the African Development Bank, IPUMS–International at the Minnesota Population Center, and colleagues working on the project.

NOTES

1. The number of countries included in the analysis was based on the availability of census data to enable projection of future trends. Countries with at least two recent census data points were selected.
2. Available from the United Nations, Department of Economic and Social Affairs (http://esa.un.org/wpp/). Note that at the time of finalizing this chapter, the 2010 revision had just been released.

3. Reported and smoothed age distributions were examined; their impact on the results was insignificant.
4. The medium variant assumptions of projections were assumed, that is, medium fertility and mortality decline.
5. The use and applicability of life tables varied depending on the available data and demographic trends in the selected country. The absence of reliable life tables for some African countries posed a challenge in the analysis of future demographic scenarios. These and other related issues were taken into consideration in order to come up with reasonable results.

REFERENCES

Adetunji, J., and E.R. Bos. (2006) "Levels and Trends in Mortality in Sub-Saharan Africa: An Overview." In *Disease and Mortality in Sub-Saharan Africa*, 2nd ed., ed. D.T. Jamison, R.G. Feachem, M.W. Makgoba, E.R. Bos, F.K. Baingana, K.J. Hofman, and K.O. Rogo, 11–14. Washington, DC: World Bank.

Bangha, M., A. Diagne, A. Bawah, and O. Sankoh. (2010) "Monitoring the Millennium Development Goals: The Potential Role of the INDEPTH Network." *Global Health Action* 23:5517.

Bloom, D.E., D. Canning, and G. Fink. (2008) *Population Ageing and Economic Growth*. Washington, DC: International Bank for the Reconstruction and Development/World Bank.

Brass, W., A.J. Coale, and P. Demeny. (1968) *The Demography of Tropical Africa*. Princeton, NJ: Princeton University Press.

Caldwell, J.C. (1976) "Toward a Restatement of Demographic Transition Theory." *Population and Development Review* 2 (3–4): 321–366.

Caldwell, J.C., and P. Caldwell. (1990) "High Fertility in Sub-Saharan Africa." *Scientific American* 262 (5): 118–125.

Coale, A.J., and P. Demeny. (1983) *Regional Model Life Tables and Stable Populations*. New York: Academic Press.

Groenewald, P., N. Nannan, D. Bourne, R. Laubscher, and D. Bradshaw. (2005) "Identifying Deaths from AIDS in South Africa." *AIDS* 19 (3): 193–201.

Hosegood, V., A. Vanneste, and I.M. Timaeus. (2004) "Levels and Causes of Adult Mortality in Rural South Africa: The Impact of AIDS." *AIDS* 18 (4): 663–671.

Kaggwa, E.B., N. Diop, and J.D. Storey. (2008) "The Role of Individual and Community Normative Factors: A Multilevel Analysis of Contraceptive Use among Women in Union in Mali." *International Family Planning Perspectives* 34 (2): 79–88.

Kimokoti, R.W., and D.H. Hamer. (2008) "Nutrition, Health, and Aging in Sub-Saharan Africa." *Nutrition Reviews* 66 (11): 611–623.

Kirk, D. (1996) "Demographic Transition Theory." *Population Studies* 50 (3): 361–387.

Lofgren, H. (1993) "Economic Policy in Egypt: A Breakdown in Reform Resistance." *International Journal of Middle East Studies* 25 (3): 407–421.

Lutz, W., W. Sanderson, and S. Scherbov. (2008) "The Coming Acceleration of Population Ageing." *Nature* 451:716–719.

Makoni, S. (2008) "Aging in Africa: A Critical Review." *Journal of Cross Cultural Gerontology* 23:199–209.

McGarry, K., and R.F. Schoeni. (2000) "Social Security, Economic Growth and the Rise in Elderly Widow's Independence in the Twentieth Century." *Demography* 37:221–236.

Minnesota Population Center. (2011) *Integrated Public Use Microdata Series International: Version 6.1 [Machine-Readable Database]*. Minneapolis: University of Minnesota.

Olshansky, S.J., and B.A. Carnes. (2007) "A Realistic View of Aging, Mortality, and Future Longevity." *Population and Development Review* 33 (2): 367–381.

Olshansky, S.J., M. Grant, J. Brody, and B.A. Carnes. (2005) "Biodemographic Perspectives for Epidemiologists." *Emerging Themes in Epidemiology* 2:10 http://www.ete-online.com/content/2/1/10. Accessed March 25, 2014.

Ravallion, M., and S. Chen. (2008) *The Developing World Is Poorer Than We Thought, but No Less Successful in the Fight against Poverty*. Washington, DC: World Bank.

Schafer, M.H., and K.F. Ferraro. (2009) "Data Sources for Studying Aging." In *International Handbook of Population Aging*, ed. P. Uhlenberg, 19–36. Dordrecht, Netherlands: Springer.

Shrestha, L.B. (2000) "Population Aging in Developing Countries." *Health Affairs* 19 (3): 204–212.

Smith, S.M., and G.A. Mensah. (2003) "Population Aging and Implications for Epidemic Cardiovascular Disease in Sub-Saharan Africa." *Ethnicity and Disease* 13 (2): S77–S80.

Tucker, K.L., and Buranapin, S. (2001) "Nutrition and Aging in Developing Countries." *Journal of Nutrition* 131 (9): 2417S–2423S.

Udjo, E.O. (2008a) "Demographic Projections of Africa's Population for the Period 2000–2050 Taking Account of HIV/AIDS and Its Implications for Development." *Southern African Business Review* 12 (3): 76–101.

Udjo, E.O. (2008b) "A Re-Look at Recent Statistics on Mortality in the Context of HIV/AIDS with Particular Reference to South Africa." *Current HIV Research* 6:143–151.

United Nations. (1982) *Model Life Tables for Developing Countries*. New York: United Nations.

United Nations. (2009a) "The Ageing of the World's Population. Population Division, Department of Economic and Social Affairs, United Nations Secretariat." http://www.un.org/esa/socdev/aging/popaging.html. Accessed November 7, 2009.

United Nations. (2009b) *World Population Ageing 2009. Population Division, Department of Economic and Social Affairs, United Nations Secretariat*. New York: United Nations.

United Nations Economic Commission for Africa. (2009) *Economic Report on Africa 2009: Developing African Ventures through Regional Value Chains*. Addis Ababa, Ethiopia: United Nations Economic Commission for Africa.

14 Sex Profile in Education and Educational Attainment in Sub-Saharan Africa

Serai Daniel Rakgoasi

1 INTRODUCTION

There is little doubt that human development, through education, is a key to sustaining social and economic development. One of the outcomes of the 1994 International Conference on Population and Development was the adoption by member countries of a Program of Action (PoA), which identified a set of specific practical actions to be taken at national and international level to implement the ICPD recommendations. Among the specific demands to governments were that they bring women into the mainstream of development, promoting their health, education, and economic contributions, promote education for all, and close the gender gap in education.

The UN's millennium declaration of 2000 shows that education is not only a fundamental constitutional right but is also a key priority essential for social and economic progress, human development, and advancement in all countries. Consequently, 189 UN member states of the United Nations have made a commitment to attain the goals of the seven Millennium Development Goals (MDGs). Two such MDGs focus on education and gender equality. MDG 2 seeks to achieve universal access to primary education, while MDG 3 focuses on the promotion and attainment of gender equality and elimination of the gender disparity at all levels of education by 2015.

While the attainment of the seven MDGs by 2015 has been a target priority for many developing countries, it is clear than many countries, especially sub-Saharan countries, are nowhere near meeting virtually all of these targets. The failure of most sub-Saharan African (SSA) countries to reach the targets of the MDGs is not only a function of economic challenges faced by many such countries but it is also a function of the way the MDGs were conceptualized. Easterly (2008) argues that because MDGs were poorly and arbitrarily designed to measure relative progress against poverty and deprivation, their design not only makes Africa look worse than it really is but also causes some African successes to be portrayed as failures. However, despite the criticism leveled against MDGs, they provide a road map against which many countries can measure their efforts. This chapter uses census data from selected SSA countries to examine access to formal education and educational attainments, and to determine factors that influence both access and educational attainment in selected African countries.[1]

1.1 Access to Education in Africa

Achieving Education for All (EFA) and the MDGs requires expanded access to both primary and secondary education. Consequently, expanded access to a basic education, including lower secondary, and economic growth strategies that require human resources with knowledge are the policy focus of many sub-Saharan governments. Between 1950 and 1985, many developing countries experienced increases in educational attainment and a narrowing of the gender gap in education (Schultz 1993). Access to education and educational attainment has increased significantly in Africa and the developing world. The number of years of formal education in the developing world has increased from 2.1 to 7.1 between 1950 and 2010 (Barro and Lee 2011). Returns to formal education have also increased substantially over time. According to Barro and Lee (2011), the rates of return for an additional year of schooling range from 5 to 12 percent globally, while for SSA this rate stands at is 6.6 percent.

While available evidence suggests that there has been improved access to education; increased educational attainment and the narrowing of the gender gap (Schultz 1993), there are obstacles to the attainment of gender equality in education (UNESCO 2010) and the gender gap has increased, even in countries where such gaps had declined previously (Schultz 2004). In most societies, deep-seated inequalities result in unequal access to education. Too many girls and women still remain excluded from learning, with twenty-eight countries having not achieved gender parity in primary education (UNESCO 2010). In Africa and much of the developing world, entrenched social and cultural norms and beliefs have historically differentiated access to education according to gender, creating obstacles for female access to education compared with males. In five Southeast Asian countries, women are less likely to have secondary or tertiary education than their male counterparts (Cameron, Dowling, and Worswick 2001).

1.2 The Need for Census Data to Monitor Access to Education

Despite the irrefutable progress in improved access to education in Africa, such improvements are neither uniform nor irreversible. In many contexts, structural factors such as poverty and low economic growth, political instability and the ensuing social disruption have the potential to either stall or even reverse some of the gains made in improved access and equity in education. This brings into focus the need for cost-effective means to monitor access to formal education generally and gender equity in access to formal education in particular. While in many contexts custom designed surveys can fill this gap, in poorer contexts the cost of regular surveys may be prohibitive, thus leaving countries with no effective mechanisms for monitoring. In turn, the absence of effective monitoring of policy and programs makes it difficult to spot and address the gaps in the implementation of policies and programs.

Censuses, which are a constitutional requirement in many countries, represent a potentially cost-effective means for monitoring effects of policies and programs on access to education and equity. Censuses are very costly to conduct and analyze, yet beyond the basic analysis required for production of country census reports, most census data remain largely poorly analyzed and therefore underutilized, especially for monitoring and assessing policy and program initiatives.

1.3 Availability and Use of Census Data

The 2010 World Program on Population and Housing Censuses was approved by the Statistical Commission at its thirty-sixth session and adopted by the United Nations Economic and Social Council in resolution A/2005/13. It recognized population and housing censuses as one of the main sources of data for effective development planning and objective decision making, monitoring population trends and programs and policy evaluation. One of the outcomes of the 2010 World Program on Population and Housing Censuses was the Marrakech Action Plan, which identified the implementation of the 2010 World Program on Population and Housing Census as a key area of action for improvements in national and international statistical capacity. Under the Marrakech Action Plan, countries are expected to plan and conduct a census during the 2010 census round, with the United Nations providing guidance for the collection of official statistics, including the coordination of international standards for outputs and support for countries undertaking censuses. The outcome of such initiatives is the improvement in availability and quality of census data that can not only be used to study and appreciate demographic trends in several key areas, such as population growth, mortality, urbanization, migration, and education, but can also be used locally in administrative and policy-relevant applications.

Given the monetary, human capital, and technical skills that are expended in collecting census data, such data remain grossly underutilized since most are not analyzed much beyond the usual census reports. The result is that the improved availability of census data and the costs of collecting census data remain poorly reflected in administrative and policy-relevant applications. Census data are increasingly becoming available and accessible, which represents a cost-effective means of monitoring access to formal education and educational attainment in Africa, as well as evaluating the results of other policy initiatives. Such monitoring is especially important in contexts such as Africa, where a combination of factors may impede improvement in access to education and equity. These include entrenched sociocultural values and gender norms that promote inequality between men and women, declining socioeconomic conditions and poverty. Thus, census data, if carefully crafted, can yield useful indicators and time series data on the size of the gap in access to formal education and educational attainment between males and females and how this gap changes over time, as well as factors that influence access and attainment. The realization of the utility of census data for policy monitoring and assessment means that, increasingly, questions in successive censuses can then be crafted to maximize their utility in this role.

1.4 Theoretical Orientation

The link between human capital and development was first postulated by Theodore Schultz in the early 1960s, and gave birth to Schultz's Human Capital Theory, the premise of which is that individuals acquire skills and knowledge to increase their value in the labor market, and that education makes people productive and healthy for long (Schultz 1961). While Schultz's theory has been criticized for serving the needs of those in power and placing the onus on the individual for becoming 'educated,' it has nevertheless dominated thinking in international development in the 1980s, and motivated investments in vocational and technical education (Hollis and Srinivasan 1988). Previously, demographic thinking was dominated by a focus on population size and composition and its impact on economic growth and development. For example, in the late twentieth century, demographers' focus was on relating economic growth and societal well-being to the changing relative sizes of age-groups, also known as the demographic dividend paradigm. By the twenty-first century, there was a growing body of research pointing to the link between socio-economic development and improved human capital through improved education, (Lloyd, Kaufman, and Hewlett 2000; Lucas 1991; Garenne et al. 2004).

Thus the middle to late twentieth century ushered in a paradigm shift away from models that are focused on the age-sex structure, as has been traditionally the case, models that incorporate a 'quality dimension' to the age-sex structure through the explicit incorporation of education (Saxton 2000; Lutz, 2010). According to Saxton (2000), increased human capital formation resulting from increased levels of education was shown to have extensive benefits not only to the national economy but for individuals and societies, as well. Evidence that showed that investments in human capital through increased access to secondary education were a key driver of economic development in many countries, especially Asian countries (Lutz, 2008) helped to bolster this position within population and development cycles.

2 DATA SOURCES AND METHODS

Data used in this chapter are drawn from a 10 percent sample of the 1990s and 2000s round of censuses for seven sub-Saharan countries, obtained from the IPUMS–International archives (Minnesota Population Center 2011). The countries are Guinea, Kenya, Senegal, South Africa, Tanzania, Uganda, and Mozambique. These countries were chosen using a combination of criteria. The primary criterion for inclusion in the analysis was availability of at least two census data points and geographic representation of SSA (i.e., Southern, Central, East Africa, and West Africa). Each country selected would have at least two census data points, one of which had to be recent, preferably in the 2000 round of censuses. Second, some countries, such as Kenya, Tanzania, and South Africa, have in the past implemented models of free and universal education in an effort to expand access to basic education. These countries were included in order to check if they fared any better relative to other countries where such models were never implemented. Other countries, such as Mozambique and Uganda, have just emerged from periods of protracted civil strife and social disruption. These countries were included in order to gauge how their experience might have affected access to basic education.

In addition, compared with other countries included in the analysis, Guinea and Senegal are relatively poorer and represent contexts where there are scarce resources invested in not only education but also for monitoring and assessing policy and program effects of expanded access to education. In all, the countries selected for inclusion in the analysis are geographically widely dispersed, covering Southern, Central, East, and West Africa, with different experiences and sociodemographic, economic, and political realities.

2.1 Methods

2.1.1 Access to Education

Access to education is measured using gross enrollment ratios (GERs), calculated as the proportion of school-going-age population that is enrolled in each of the three levels of formal education, namely, primary, secondary, and tertiary levels. The GERs are used to measure the access to formal education in the respective countries, and selected background variables are also used to determine their influence on the access to formal education.

Next, gender parity indexes (GPIs) for each level of education are calculated using age-specific gross enrollment rates for males and females. GPI are computed as the quotient of the value of indicator for females divided by the value of indicators for males at each level of formal education, multiplied by a constant, in this case 100.

2.1.2 Educational Attainment

Educational attainment is measured as the percentage of each country's adult population that has attained a given level of formal education, namely, primary, secondary, and tertiary education. Educational attainment GPIs for primary, secondary and tertiary are calculated. GPIs for primary, secondary, and tertiary education are computed as the quotient of the value of indicator for females divided by the value of indicator for males at each level of formal education, multiplied by a constant, in this case 100. Thus GPIs more than 100 indicate a predominance of females while an index less than 100 points to a predominance of males.

Binary logistic regression is used to estimate the likelihood of enrollment in or attainment of a certain level of education. The form of the logistic equation fitted to the data is as follows:

$$\ln\left(\frac{p}{1-p}\right) = \beta_0 + \beta_1 X$$

Where p is the probability that an individual is enrolled for a certain level of education or has attained a specified level of education and 1–p is the probability that an individual is not enrolled or has not attained a certain level of formal education. β_0 and $\beta_1 X$ are components of the regression equation; the βs represent regression coefficients and Xs represent a set of independent variables. The key independent variables used are age, sex, and year of census.

3 FINDINGS

3.1 Access to Primary Education

Table 14.1 shows primary school GERs for males and females for the two census data points, as well as the corresponding GPIs. All countries experienced improvements in the enrollment rates for primary-age population during the period between the two censuses. However, despite the improved enrollment rates, for all countries except South Africa and Tanzania, enrollment rates are higher for males than females. All countries except South Africa and Tanzania had gender parity indexes less than 100 percent, indicating a predominance of boys over girls in enrollment at primary education level. Guinea and Senegal, which had GPIs of 67 and 68 percent respectively, experienced the biggest improvements during their intercensal periods, reaching parity levels of 75 and 92 percent respectively. South Africa and Tanzania, which had parity indexes of 102 and 109 percent respectively, experienced a slight decline during their intercensal period, reaching 101 and 103 percent, respectively, while the GPI for Kenya remained almost unchanged, at 99 percent.

Table 14.1 Primary Education Gross Enrollment Rates and Gender Parity Index (Population 7–13 Years) in Selected Sub-Saharan African Countries

Country	Period	Males	Females	Total	GPI_1
Guinea	1983	36.1	24.2	30.5	67.0
	1996	60.5	45.4	53.6	75.0
Kenya	1989	84.5	83.6	84.1	98.9
	1999	82.1	81.6	81.9	99.4
Senegal	1988	52.4	36.0	44.1	68.7
	2002	55.4	50.7	53.0	91.5
S. Africa	1996	87.3	89.0	88.2	101.9
	2001	93.5	94.2	93.8	100.7
Tanzania	1988	46.4	50.7	48.5	109.3
	2002	68.3	70.0	69.1	102.5
Uganda	1991	67.4	61.9	64.7	91.8
	2002	87.1	86.4	86.8	99.2
Mozambique	1997	50.3	43.2	46.8	85.9
	2007	73.1	70.7	71.9	96.7

Table 14.2 shows the GERs derived from this analysis as well as the 2004 net enrollment ratios from the UNICEF's 2004 *State of the World's Children* report. While the two ratios may not be comparable because they are defined slightly differently and also refer to different time periods, they nevertheless show a certain pattern and consistency, in that countries with low gross enrollment rates also have low net enrollment rates and vice versa.

Table 14.2 Gross Enrollment Ratios and Comparison with UN Estimates

Country	Year	GER	NER (UNICEF) 2004
Guinea	1996	53.6	47
Kenya	1999	81.9	69
Senegal	2002	53.0	63
S. Africa	2001	93.8	89
Tanzania	2002	69.1	47
Uganda	2002	86.8	87
Mozambique	1997	46.8	54

Results of the logistic regression model (Table 14.6) show that South Africa and Tanzania were the only two countries where, at primary level, girls were more likely to be enrolled than boys. In both countries, girls were 1.15 times more likely to be enrolled, controlling for age and year of census. Compared with the population aged 7–9 years, those aged 10–13 were significantly more likely to be enrolled, except in Mozambique. For all countries except Kenya, primary enrollment increased significantly between the two data periods. For example, in Uganda, Guinea, and Tanzania, 7–13 years olds were 3.7, 2.6, and 2.7 times more likely to be enrolled in primary education compared with ten years previously, and the corresponding figures for South Africa and Senegal are 2.1 and 1.4, respectively.

3.2 Access to Secondary Education

Table 14.3 shows gross enrollment rates for secondary age population (14–18 years) by country and sex, as well as the corresponding GPIs. Without exception, enrollment rates for secondary education are relatively lower than those for primary education. All countries with the exception of Guinea experienced increases in secondary school enrollment GPI. The GPI for secondary enrollment declined from 54 to 42 percent in Guinea between 1983 and 1996, while that of Senegal increased from 46 percent in 1988 to 68 percent in 2002. Uganda and Mozambique experienced the

Table 14.3 Secondary Education Gross Enrollment Rates and Gender Parity Index (Population 14–18 Years) in Selected Sub-Saharan African Countries

Country	Period	Males	Females	Total	GPI_P
Guinea	1983	35.8	19.2	27.5	53.6
	1996	44.6	18.8	31.5	42.2
Kenya	1989	77.6	67.1	72.3	86.5
	1999	65.2	59.2	62.2	90.8
Senegal	1988	36.1	16.7	25.8	46.3
	2002	36.6	25.0	30.5	68.3
S. Africa	1996	88.5	86.9	87.7	98.2
	2001	86.0	84.0	85.0	97.7
Tanzania	1988	45.2	37.8	41.4	83.6
	2002	52.5	43.4	47.9	82.7
Uganda	1991	56.0	34.6	45.0	61.8
	2002	70.7	60.2	65.4	85.1
Mozambique	1997	41.9	24.2	32.9	57.8
	2007	68.4	50.6	59.4	74.0

greatest improvement in gender parity index among secondary school-age population. For Uganda, this index increased from 62 to 85 percent between 1991 and 2002, while that of Mozambique increased from 58 to 74 percent between 1997 and 2007.

For all countries, the GPI among secondary-school-age population (14–18 years) is less than 100 percent, indicating enrollment rates in favor of boys. For both census periods, Kenya and South Africa had the highest GPIs. This index increased from 87 to 91 percent in Kenya between 1989 and 1999, while the same index remained relatively unchanged for South Africa between 1996 and 2009, at 98 percent among 14–18 year olds enrolled in formal education.

Logistic regression results (Table 14.6) show that with the exception of Kenya and South Africa, the likelihood of secondary enrollment was significantly greater during each country's subsequent census. In all countries studied, girls aged 14–18 were significantly less likely to be enrolled in secondary education than boys of the same age. In South Africa women were 0.86 times more likely than males to be enrolled in secondary education, while in Tanzania and Kenya they were 0.7 times more likely than men to be enrolled. In Guinea, Senegal Uganda, and Mozambique, women were between 0.3 and 0.5 more likely than their male counterparts to be enrolled in secondary education. For most of these countries, with the exception of Kenya and South Africa, the likelihood of enrollment in secondary education was significantly higher during the later census compared with the first one, possibly suggesting an improvement in access to formal education among this age-group during the intercensal period. South Africa and Kenya, which already have high enrollment and almost equitable GPIs at the primary level, experienced slight reductions in the likelihood of enrollment at secondary level.

3.3 Access to Tertiary Education

Table 14.4 shows the percentage of population aged 19–23 years enrolled in tertiary education by sex and the corresponding GPIs. Tanzania, Uganda, and Mozambique recorded increases in enrollment rates in the tertiary age population during their respective intercensal periods, while Senegal experienced a slight decline in male enrollment rates and a modest increase in female enrollment rates. On the other hand, Kenya and South Africa experienced declines in enrollment rates at ages 19–23 for both males and females.

Guinea, Tanzania, Uganda and Mozambique have low GPIs, in favor of males. While the GPIs for tertiary education enrollment in Senegal, Uganda, and Mozambique improved during each country's intercensal period, these indexes remain below 50 percent. Guinea and Kenya experienced declines in gender parity index at tertiary education level, while the tertiary enrollment GPI for Tanzania remained almost constant, with very marginal improvement.

Table 14.4 Tertiary Education Gross Enrollment Rates and Gender Parity Index (Population 19–23 Years) in Selected Sub-Saharan African Countries

Country	Period	Males	Females	Total	GPI_1
Guinea	1983	28.3	9.9	17.7	35.0
	1996	26.4	7.6	16.1	28.8
Kenya	1989	29.4	19.1	21.8	65.0
	1999	18.7	11.0	14.6	58.8
Senegal	1988	18.1	6.8	12.1	37.6
	2002	17.1	10.3	13.6	60.2
S. Africa	1996	48.6	45.3	46.8	93.2
	2001	40.0	35.8	37.8	89.5
Tanzania	1988	5.5	2.2	3.6	40.0
	2002	9.0	3.7	6.0	41.1
Uganda	1991	19.4	5.9	12.0	30.4
	2002	29.4	14.2	21.1	48.3
Mozambique	1997	10.2	3.8	6.6	37.3
	2007	30.7	16.4	22.7	53.4

Overall, logistic regression results suggest that women's likelihood of enrollment in formal education compared with men declines with increasing levels of education attainment. While the women are almost as likely as men to be enrolled at age 7–13 years, at 14–19 years they are considerably less likely to be enrolled compared with males. At the tertiary level, the difference in likelihood of enrollment between men and women is most marked. Except for South Africa and Tanzania, where the likelihood of enrollment has remained the same for ages 13–18 and 19–24 years (0.86 and 0.46, respectively), virtually all the countries had significantly lower chances of enrollment for older youths (19–24 years) compared with younger ones (13–18 years). This may not be surprising, because in contexts where there are limited opportunities for education, a large portion of older youths may join the labor market and thus be lost to the formal education system.

3.4 Educational Attainment

Table 14.5 shows the level of educational attainment of the adult population in the seven sub-Saharan countries, and the corresponding GPIs for educational attainment. The percentage of the population with tertiary education is generally very low in all countries. Among all the countries, Senegal has the highest percentage of population with tertiary education (slightly more than 10 percent), while other countries have considerably

Table 14.5 Educational Attainment and Gender Parity in Educational Attainment (Population 25+ Years) in Selected Sub-Saharan Countries

Level of Educational Attainment among Population 25 years and over in Africa

Country	Period	Primary				Secondary				Tertiary			
		Males	Females	Total	GPI_1	Males	Females	Total	GPI_2	Males	Females	Total	GPI_3
Guinea	1983	23.2	22.0	22.8	94.8	38.7	47.5	22.8	122.7	—	—	—	—
	1996	26.0	31.9	27.6	122.7	50.3	53.8	27.6	107.0	5.9	7.0	6.2	118.6
Kenya	1989	62.9	70.3	65.8	111.8	35.1	28.6	32.5	81.5	2.0	1.1	1.7	55.0
	1999	58.7	67.5	62.8	115.0	38.5	31.1	35.1	80.8	2.8	1.3	2.1	46.4
Senegal	1996	46.3	56.6	49.9	122.2	40.4	36.9	39.2	91.3	13.3	6.5	11.0	48.9
	2001	44.6	56.0	49.2	125.6	40.0	35.5	38.2	88.8	15.5	8.5	12.7	54.8
S. Africa	1988	31.7	32.9	32.4	103.8	55.9	57.7	56.9	103.2	8.7	6.8	7.7	78.2
	2002	29.2	29.9	29.6	102.4	58.8	58.4	58.6	99.3	7.3	8.1	7.7	111.0
Tanzania	1991	90.6	94.4	92.0	104.2	8.6	5.5	7.5	64.0	0.8	0.2	0.6	25.0
	2002	86.8	90.1	88.3	103.8	11.6	8.7	10.3	75.0	1.6	1.2	1.4	75.0
Uganda	1997	75.5	83.1	78.4	110.1	23.3	16.5	20.7	70.8	—	—	—	—
	2007	67.7	77.3	71.7	114.2	21.9	16.0	19.5	73.1	7.9	5.4	6.9	68.4
Mozambique	1997	85.9	90.8	87.5	105.7	13.1	8.5	11.6	64.9	1.0	0.7	0.9	70.0
	2007	82.8	87.2	84.8	105.3	16.0	12.0	14.2	1.1	0.8	1.0	72.7	

lower percentages of population with tertiary education. The results show that Tanzania, Uganda, and Mozambique have the highest percentages of population whose highest level of education is primary. In these countries, between 70 and 90 percent of the population had attained primary education, compared with South Africa, where about a third of the population had primary education. Kenya and Senegal have the highest percentages of population with primary education after Tanzania, Uganda, and Mozambique. The percentage of population with primary education in Kenya is slightly more than 60 percent, while that of Senegal is close to 40 percent. Countries with a large percentage of population whose highest level of education is primary also tend to have the lowest levels of secondary and tertiary education attainment.

In all countries under study, the level of penetration of secondary education is significantly less compared with primary education. Guinea, Kenya, Senegal, and South Africa have the highest proportions of population with secondary education. In South Africa, close to six out of every ten people over the age of 25 years have secondary education. For most countries, gender parity in primary educational attainment among population over 25 years of age favors women, while at the secondary level, with the exception of Guinea and South Africa, the index tends to favor men. At the tertiary level, with the exception of Guinea in 1996 and South Africa in 2002, the GPI is in favor of men. Thus, while the level of penetration of tertiary education is low in most of the countries under study, the few who make it to tertiary education are likely to be disproportionately male.

Table 14.6 Binary Logistic Regression Coefficients of the Likelihood of Being Enrolled in Formal Education

Logistic Regression Log Odds of the Likelihood of Enrollment in Primary Education							
	Guinea	*Kenya*	*Senegal*	*S. Africa*	*Tanzania*	*Uganda*	*Mozambique*
Sex							
Male	1.000	1.000	1.000	1.000	1.000	1.000	1.000
Female	0.553	0.954	0.686	1.148	1.149	0.856	0.963
Age							
7–9	1.000	1.000	1.000	1.000	1.000	1.000	1.000
10–13	1.242	1.489	1.112	2.142	4.630	1.857	0.646
Census							
Census 1	1.000	1.000	1.000	1.000	1.000	1.000	1.000
Census 2	2.652	0.853	1.425	2.057	2.681	3.678	***

(continued)

Table 14.6 (continued)

Logistic Regression Log Odds of the Likelihood of Enrollment in Secondary Education							
	Guinea	Kenya	Senegal	S. Africa	Tanzania	Uganda	Mozambique
Sex							
Male	1.000	1.000	1.000	1.000	1.000	1.000	1.000
Female	0.337	0.696	0.489	0.863	0.692	0.521	0.526
Age							
14–15	1.000	1.000	1.000	1.000	1.000	1.000	1.000
16–18	0.525	0.351	0.543	0.306	0.212	0.313	0.283
Census							
Census 1	1.000	1.000	1.000	1.000	1.000	1.000	1.000
Census 2	1.246	0.626	1.304	0.808	1.340	2.442	***

Logistic Regression Log Odds of the Likelihood of Enrollment in Tertiary Education							
	Guinea	Kenya	Senegal	S. Africa	Tanzania	Uganda	Mozambique
Sex							
Male	1.000	1.000	1.000	1.000	1.000	1.000	1.000
Female	0.246	0.471	0.460	0.860	0.385	0.342	0.608
Age							
19–21	1.000	1.000	1.000	1.000	1.000	1.000	1.000
22–24	0.523	0.289	0.606	0.340	0.317	0.417	0.506
Census							
Census 1	1.000	1.000	1.000	1.000	1.000	1.000	1.000
Census 2	1.000	0.599	1.203	0.665	1.737	2.010	***

4 DISCUSSION

Research shows that formal education leverages many variables that are related to demographic change, as well as social and economic development, such as health, mortality, and productivity (Schultz 1993, 2004), earnings (Barro and Lee 2010), and fertility (Ainsworth, Beegle, and Nyamete 1996; Lloyd, Kaufman, and Hewlett 2000), and that educational attainment influences human health, economic growth, and the functioning of democracies through the entry of better education cohorts into the decisive age-groups (Lutz, 2010). This makes access to education and improved educational attainment important priorities for many countries' social and economic development.

This analysis has shown that despite challenges relating to gender equality in access to formal education, especially at secondary and tertiary levels, there has been significant improvement in access to education and educational attainment during each country's ten-year intercensal period. The fact that most countries' enrollment rates were more likely to have increased for both primary and secondary education during the ten-year intercensal period is an encouraging sign of investments in improved access to education in these countries. For many countries, not only have both the primary and secondary enrollment rates improved over time. There has also been an improvement in gender balance at primary level. For example, while boys were more likely to be enrolled in primary education in most (except two) countries, the likelihood of enrollment in primary education for girls improved significantly during the intercensal period. In Kenya, Lucas and Mbiti (2012) found that while Kenya's free primary education initiative improved (primary school completion rates and increased access to primary education), the policy widened the gender gap by creating an imbalance in primary completion rates and access in favor of males.

A 1999 assessment of the Guinea primary education system found that while progress had been made along most indicators such as gross and net enrollment rates and funding, there were a number of challenges in sustaining this momentum, which included poverty, inefficiency, inadequate funding, policy failure, and implementation challenges. For example, the assessment found that three-quarters of the space and capacity of the entire system was taken up by students destined to drop out and remain functionally illiterate and that it took, on average, four additional years to produce a primary school graduate (American Institute for Research 1999). For example, while in 2009 Guinea's net enrollment ratio in primary education was estimated at 79 percent for boys and 69 percent among girls (UNICEF 2009), in 2010, lack of investment in education in Guinea had precipitated a decline in primary school enrollment rates, which had previously been on the rise (UNICEF 2010).

For all countries studied, secondary education is relatively less accessible than primary education and access to tertiary education is even more restricted; the corresponding GPI for tertiary education is heavily slanted toward males. However, despite the relatively restricted access to secondary education, there were improvements in gross secondary education enrollment rates in most countries studied. These improvements in gross secondary enrollment rates, while being relatively modest compared with improvements in primary enrollment rates, were significant in some countries, indicating improvement in access to education beyond primary school. Access to secondary and tertiary education, however, favors males compared with females. The analysis of educational attainment among the adult population in these countries shows that females are more likely than males to have attained primary education, whereas males are more likely to have attained secondary and tertiary education.

Research shows that improved access to secondary education was an important factor in the rapid economic and social development experienced by some Asian economies (Lutz, 2008). Thus, for many sub-Saharan countries, investment in improved access to basic formal education beyond primary level is an important development imperative. For these countries, improved access to secondary education should necessarily involve addressing the sometimes pervasive social, cultural, and other norms and beliefs that impede girls' access to formal education. Gender equality in education beyond primary level is important given many developing countries' experience with failed development projects and experimentation with different development models. Returns to education are higher for females than males (Flabbi 1999; Aslam 2006; Boothby and Rowe 2002); thus gender equality in education is an affordable investment with high-yielding returns, and one that many developing African countries can ill afford to forgo. When girls are educated, livelihoods, civic responsibility, and education are enhanced (UNESCO 2010). As such, sustainable poverty reduction approaches cannot ignore the role of education and its implications for employment, earnings, and social development (Sackey 2007).

Despite the limitations inherent in census data, these data provide a cost effective means for periodically monitoring some key indicators. Access to formal education and educational attainment are among the issues that can easily be monitored through in-depth analysis of existing census data.

Thus, if used appropriately, census data can provide a baseline for specialized surveys, and can also be useful for discerning trends in access to education and educational attainment over time. The persistence, in Africa and much of the developing world, of certain social, cultural, and other norms and beliefs that may impede access to formal education for certain sectors of society makes the monitoring of access to education and educational attainment all the more important. In many parts of Africa, economic challenges have resulted in declining economies and reduced social expenditure in education, which may limit access to formal education and negatively affect gender equity in access to education.

Censuses are limited in the sense that despite their enormous cost, very few questions can be included in the census questionnaire, and the data are available only after long intervals. However, if the full utility of the census (beyond producing the census reports and understanding demographic trends) is realized, especially their potential in monitoring and assessment of policy and program effects, this will create a need to reevaluate the utility of questions that are currently included in census in favor of ones that will make the greatest impact on the utility of census as a monitoring and assessment tool.

4.1 Limitations

There are a number of limitations inherent in using census data, the most obvious being the long intercensal interval, which is ten years for most countries. This means that it takes a long time for new census statistics to become available. The other challenge is the limited number of questions that are usually contained in the census, which doesn't facilitate in-depth analysis of many issues. A third limitation is the quality of census data, especially the age-sex data. Many censuses contain errors related to age reporting, which requires correcting.

ACKNOWLEDGMENTS

The author gratefully acknowledges the Minnesota Population Center, for permission to access the IPUMS–International database, and all the reviewers whose comments contributed to improving the quality of this chapter.

NOTES

1. Data for the selected countries were accessed from the IPUMS–International database archived by Minnesota Population Center (2011).

REFERENCES

American Institutes for Research (1999) Primary Education in Guinea: Limited Sector Assessment Final Report (November 1999), www.ieq.org/pdf/Primary_Education-Guinea.pdf, accessed September, 2011.
Ainsworth, M Beegle, K and Nyamete, A. (1996) "Impact of Women's Schooling on Fertility and Contraceptive Use: A Study of Fourteen Sub-Saharan Countries", *World Bank Economic Review*, 10 (1): 85–122.
Aslam, M. (2006) *"Rates of Return to Education by Gender in Pakistan", Economic and Social Research Council Global Poverty Research Group*, Oxford University.
Barro, R., and J-W. Lee. (2010) "A New Data Set of Educational Attainment in the World, 1950–2010." *NBER Working Paper* 15902.
Barro, R, and J-W Lee (Revised 2011) "A new data set of educational attainment in the world, 1950–2010": NBER Working Paper No. 15902. The National Bureau of Economic Research; http://www.nber.org/papers/w15902 accessed March 15th 2012.
Boothby, D., and G. Rowe. (2002) *Rate of Return on Education: A Distribution Analysis Using the LifePaths Model*. Human Resources Development Canada, Quebec, CANADA
Cameron, L., M. Dowling, and C. Worswick. (2001) "Education and Labor Market Participation of Women in Asia: Evidence from Five Countries." *Economic Development and Cultural Change* 49: 459–477.
Easterly, W. (2008) "How the Millennium Development Goals are Unfair to Africa." *World Development* 37 (1): 26–35.
Flabbi, L. (1999) "Returns to Schooling in Italy: OLS, IV and Gender Differences." Universita Bocconi Working Papers.
Garenne, M., S.M. Tollman, M.A. Collinson, and K. Khan. (2006) *Fertility Trends and Net Reproduction in Agincourt, Rural South Africa 1992–2004*. Popline, Bethesda Maryland, USA.

Hollis, C., and T.N. Srinivasan. (1988) *Handbook of Development Economics.* Elsevier, Amsterdam, Netherlands.

Lloyd, C., C.E. Kaufman, and Hewlett, P (2000) "The Spread of Primary Schooling in Sub-Saharan Africa: Implications for Fertility Change." *Population and Development Review* 26 (3): 483–515.

Lucas, A.M., and I.M. Mbiti. (2012) "Does Free Primary Education Narrow Gender Differences in Schooling? Evidence from Kenya." *Journal of African Economies* 21 (5): 691–722.

Lucas, D. (1991) *Mass Education and Fertility decline: Implications for Southern Africa.* Paper presented at the International Union for the Scientific Study of Population [IUSSP] Committee on Comparative Analysis of Fertility and University of Zimbabwe Seminar on the Course of Fertility Transition in Sub-Saharan Africa, Harare, Zimbabwe, 19–22 November 1991. p. 35.

Lutz, W (2008) "Data Sheet: Asian Demographic and Human Capital" International Institute for Applied Systems Analysis, Austrian Academy of Sciences Press, www.populationasia.org/Publications/.../VID_asianDataSheet08, accessed 12th November 2012.

Lutz, W (2010) "Education will be at the heart of 21st Century Demography." *Vienna Yearbook of Population Research*, International Institute for Applied Systems Analysis, Austrian Academy of Sciences Press, http://www.jstor.org/stable/23025506, accessed 3rd January 3rd, 2013.

Minnesota Population Center. (2011) *Integrated Public Use Microdata Series International: Version 6.1 [Machine-Readable Database].* Minneapolis: University of Minnesota.

Sackey, H.A. (2007) "Determinants of School Attendance and Attainment in Ghana—A Gender Perspective." *African Economic Research Consortium Research Paper 173.*

Saxton, J. (2000) *Investment in Education: Private and Public Returns.* US Congress Joint Economic Committee, Washington, DC 20515.

Schultz. T. (1961) "Investment in Human Capital." In *Human Capital*, ed. Gary Becker, 1–17. New York: National Bureau of Economic Research.

Schultz, T. (1993) "Investments in the Schooling and Health of Women and Men: Quantities and Returns." *Journal of Human Resources,* 28 (4): 694–734.

Schultz, T. (2004) "Evidence of Returns to Schooling in Africa from Household Surveys: Monitoring and Restructuring the Market for Education." *Journal of African Economies,* 13(2): 95–148.

UNESCO. (2010) *Gender Equality in Education.* United Nations Educational, Scientific and Cultural Organization, place de Fontenoy, Paris, France.

UNICEF. (2009) *State of the World's Children Report.* United Nations, NY, New York, USA.

UNICEF. (2010) *State of the World's Children Report.* United Nations, NY, New York, USA.

15 Living Arrangements of Children in Sub-Saharan Africa and Their Implications on Schooling

Esther W. Dungumaro

1 INTRODUCTION

This chapter examines living arrangements of children in Africa and assesses their implications on schooling. A vast majority of literature points to changing living arrangements in Africa (Bongaarts 2001; Noumbissi and Zuberi 2001; Zulu and Sibanda 2005; Dungumaro et al. 2006; Dungumaro 2008). While changes in living arrangements in Western societies occurred during the agricultural and industrial revolutions, changes in Africa took place in the absence of such revolutions (Goody 1989), leading to various impacts on different population segments.

AIDS-related adult mortality is still high in Africa and continues to have a significant influence on children's living arrangements. In 2010, about 68 percent of all people living with HIV resided in sub-Saharan Africa (SSA) (UNAIDS 2011). A high AIDS-related mortality rate has led to increasing numbers of orphans and more fostering (Yamano, Shimamura, and Sserunkuuma 2005). However, regardless of parental survival status, child fostering has been an important aspect of African family systems (McDaniel and Zulu 1996). This practice notwithstanding, the ever-increasing number of children orphaned by HIV/AIDS has raised concerns about the long-term investment in education for orphans (UNAIDS/UNICEF/USAID 2004; Ainsworth and Filmer 2006; Case, Paxson, and Ableidinger 2004).

Since child fostering also occurs on a voluntary basis (Madhavan 2004) because of economic or social reasons (Ainsworth 1996), orphans are not the only children whose living arrangements have continued to change. Social reasons leading to child fostering include mutual help among family members, socialization, education, and strengthening of family ties (Pilon 2003). Cohabitation and increasing divorce, parents' migration, and modernization also contribute to changing living arrangements (Montemayor and Leigh 1982). Demographic changes, such as a decrease in fertility and mortality and an increasing rate of urbanization, also affect living arrangements (Jenkins and Wilkinson 2002). In sum, children's living arrangements are responsive to various social, economic, and cultural changes.

The decreasing resilience of extended families has contributed to the increasing number of children living in difficult conditions (Beegle et al. 2009). This claim is to some extent supported by the increasing number of children residing with grandparents (Beegle et al. 2009). As opposed to experiences in the past, where grandchildren paid only short visits to grandparents, today more than ever before grandparents are residing with their grandchildren and assume parental roles. Bicego, Rutstein, and Johnson (2003) document an increase in orphans cared for by grandparents in Tanzania and Zimbabwe in the 1990s, and a shift in care giving from relatives to grandparents is observed by Monasch and Boerma (2004) in Tanzania, Namibia, and Zimbabwe. In the light of HIV/AIDS, it is of paramount importance that grandparents are there for their grandchildren who have lived in troubled situations (Hoff 2007). However, given their advanced age and lack of stable income, grandparents are unable to adequately support children under their care.

While studies on living arrangements of children in Africa have received widespread attention (McDaniel and Zulu 1996; Sibanda 2011; Marcoux, Noumbissi, and Zuberi 2010), little is known about the trends and patterns across the region as well as their implications on children's schooling. For instance, while changes in living arrangements of children and their influence on access to educational opportunities are widely acknowledged, little is demonstrated in the literature. A number of scholars have examined investments in education for orphans only (Ainsworth and Filmer 2006; Case, Paxson, and Ableidinger 2002; Bicego, Rutstein, and Johnson 2003). Furthermore, relationships between living arrangements and children's schooling have been inconsistent. Doctor (2004) sees no significant difference in school enrollment between orphans and nonorphans. Lloyd and Blanc (1996) observe that the loss of a parent makes little difference in children's schooling. Yet, other scholars maintain that some nonorphans live in poorer households than do orphans (Urassa et al. 1997). Ainsworth and Filmer (2006) argue that differences in enrollment between poor and nonpoor children make generalization difficult.

Against the above backdrop, this chapter aims to: establish trends and patterns of children's living arrangements; identify factors that predict children's living arrangements; assess implications of living arrangements on children's schooling; and identify factors that predict children's schooling.

2 THEORIES, DATA, AND ANALYTICAL METHODS

The impact of living arrangements on children's education and health remains highly debatable. While various theories dominate the debate, family composition and family processes are most prominent. Subscribers of the family composition theory argue that two-parent families are the best living arrangements for children. The argument is that children not residing in two-parent intact families are bound to experience lower levels of well-being (Coleman 1988). Adults who are not biological parents to the children they reside with lack the financial responsibility for the children. In addition, children with a father or mother only in the households lose close connection to the nonresidential parent. In this context, the nonresident parent loses the sense of financial responsibility. Opponents of this theory argue that substitute parents can replace biological parents and adequately invest in children's well- being (Acock and Demo 1994).

Theorists favoring the family process idea argue that the nature of the relationship between parents is more important for children's well-being than family structures. They argue that good parental relationships, regardless of whether or not they live together, enhance children's well-being. They emphasize that emotional ties are more important than the physical presence (Wenk et al. 1994). This chapter applies the family composition perspective given that the model involves social and demographic variables that are found in census data. On the other hand, the family process model centers on psychological factors that cannot be obtained from census data. Five percent of census data archived by the Integrated Public Use Microdata Series (IPUMS) project of the University of Minnesota (Minnesota Population Center 2011) is used to examine trends and patterns of living arrangements of children in Africa and their implications on schooling. The countries involved are located in three regions of Africa as shown:

- East Africa: Kenya, Tanzania, Uganda, and Rwanda
- West Africa: Senegal
- Southern Africa: South Africa and Malawi

These countries have at least two data points that allow for the examination of trends of children's living arrangements.

2.1 Limitations

Census data are chosen in preference to Demographic and Health Survey (DHS) because it provides an opportunity to examine children aged 0–17 years, which is the focus in this chapter. DHS collects information on children aged 0–14 years; therefore not appropriate for the the study. However, census data have their own limitations. For instance, they do not collect information on children living in institutions. This can result in underestimations of the proportion of children. Another limitation relates to errors bound to occur as a result of widespread fostering practice in Africa (Lloyd and Blanc 1996). In most African countries, adopted or fostered children are nieces, cousins, or children from any close relative, and, hence, referring to them as adopted is uncommon. This could result in overestimation of children in the study.

2.2 Definition of Terms and Variables

2.2.1 Child

Convention on the Right of the Child, Article 1, defines a child as any human being below the age of 18 (Hodgkin and Newell 2007). This UN-accepted definition takes care of differences in age definitions between countries. Furthermore, in most cases individuals below 18 are still at school.

2.2.2 Orphan

An orphan is a child below the age of 18 years with one or both parents being dead. The death of a parent results in changing living arrangements for the child (Marcoux, Noumbissi, and Zuberi 2010). Responses on the survival status of father and mother are used to present direct estimates of the survival status of parents.

2.2.3 Living Arrangements

Living arrangements refer to whether a person lives alone or with other persons, and whether or not they are related. This variable is derived from responses to questions about the relationships among people who live in a household, since census and surveys do not have a question on living arrangements.

2.2.4 Household

Different countries define households differently. A household is defined as "a group of persons (or one person) that makes common provision for food, shelter and other essentials for living" (Bongaarts 2001). Others define it as "the residential and livelihood arrangements in which family and non-family members coexist" (Zulu and Sibanda 2005, 218). The UN definition of household states:

> The concept of household is based on the arrangements made by persons, individually or in groups, for providing themselves with food or other essentials for living. A household may be either: a one-person household, that is to say a person who makes provision for his or her food or other essentials for living without combining with any other person to form part of a multi-person household; or a multi-person household, that is to say, a group of two or more persons living together who make common provision for food or other essentials for living (United Nations Statistics Division 2004, 20).

This is the operational definition in this chapter.

2.2.5 Analytical Methods

Descriptive analysis is used to estimate the percentage of children over time and establish with whom they live. Multinomial logistic regression is used to estimate living arrangements of children since the dependent variable consists of three categories, namely, (a) living in a nuclear household, (b) living in an extended household, and (c) living in a nonrelated household.

3 RESULTS

3.1 Proportion of Children across Time and Countries

While an increasing proportion of younger children (0–4) is observed in Malawi, the rest of the countries registered a declining trend, except for Tanzania, whose proportion remained almost the same (32 percent). In these countries, children make up about 34 to 65 percent of all household members. All countries except South Africa have demonstrated an increasing trend. A plausible explanation for this is South Africa's low fertility rate as compared with other countries.

3.2 Trends and Patterns of Children's Living Arrangements

3.2.1 Distribution of Children by Parental Survival Status

Table 15.1 presents the proportion of children aged 0–17 years by the survival status of parents. A positive increase in paternal orphans is observed in South Africa, Rwanda, Malawi, and Kenya. Rwanda has more than doubled its intercensal paternal orphans (6.8 and 19.2 in 1991 and 2002, respectively). The Rwandan case suggests the impact of the genocide in the 1990s. Uganda is the only country that registered a negative change. Successes in HIV/AIDS campaigns and interventions in Uganda could account for the observations.

Table 15.1 Trends in Percentage of Children by Survival Status of Parents

	Kenya		Malawi		Rwanda		Senegal	South Africa		Tanzania	Uganda	
	1989	1999	1998	2008	1991	2002	1988	1996	2001	2002	1991	2002
Both parents alive	92.6	89.9	91.2	87.7	89.7	72.0	92.5	88.8	85.7	90.1	88.3	86.9
Father only dead	5.8	7.9	5.2	7.5	6.8	19.2	4.6	8.8	10.6	6.0	8.0	7.9
Mother only dead	1.2	1.9	2.3	2.0	2.8	4.3	2.3	1.4	2.3	2.3	2.6	2.6
Both parents dead	0.4	1.3	1.3	2.9	0.7	4.5	0.6	1.0	1.4	1.2	1.1	2.6

Source: Computed from Population and Housing Census microdata, MPC.

The proportion of maternal orphans is lower than the prevalence of paternal orphans across the countries. These results are consistent with those observed elsewhere (Marcoux, Noumbissi, and Zuberi 2010; Doctor 2004; Bicego, Rutstein, and Johnson 2003). Differentials in maternal and paternal orphanhood are attributable to the fact that women outlive men, and men tend to marry much later and marry younger women (Marcoux, Noumbissi, and Zuberi 2010). The proportion of double orphans is less than that of maternal and paternal orphans for all the countries except Malawi (2008 census, where double orphans are more than maternal orphans) and Rwanda (2002 census, also the proportion of double orphans is higher than that of maternal orphans). A similar observation is made by Bicego, Rutstein, and Johnson (2003). Generally, we observe a consistent increase in all types of orphans across the countries except Malawi, which registered a decline in maternal orphanhood, and Uganda with a decline in paternal orphanhood.

3.2.2 Living Arrangements of Children by the Survival Status of Parents

Tanzania, South Africa, Rwanda, and Uganda are considered for analysis given uniformity in the variables. In Rwanda a small proportion of double orphans is fostered, while others live with nonrelatives and the majority reside with grandparents, siblings, and other relatives. The majority of the nonorphans in Tanzania live with their parents. The majority of double orphans are enumerated as 'grandchild,' 'other relative,' and 'nonrelatives.'

The pattern of children's living arrangements by the survival status of parents observed in Uganda is similar to that of Rwanda and Tanzania. In South Africa, the majority of double orphans live with grandparents, siblings, and other relatives. Observations for nonorphans are similar to those presented for other countries in this section.

Results suggest that the loss of both parents is related to residing with grandparents, siblings, and other relatives or nonrelatives. South Africa shows a substantial proportion of double orphans enumerated as 'adopted child.' This indicates that child adoption is common in this country. A change is observed in the trend of children enumerated as 'child' of the head of household, as one moves from those with both parents alive to those without surviving parents. The majority of orphans reside with relatives as opposed to nonrelatives. This observation demonstrates the importance of family networks that absorb orphans in Africa (Goody 1982; McDaniel and Zulu 1996; Foster 2002).

Compared with older children (10–14 and 15–17), younger children (0–4) co-reside with both parents. Marked differences exist across countries, with South Africa recording the lowest score of younger children residing with both parents (27 percent in 1996 and 26 percent in 2001). The proportion of children living in the household with a mother only is significantly higher than those with a father only. Results confirm the perception by both researchers and policy makers that fathers' involvement in the care and support of children in Africa remains limited (Richter 2006). This observation is informed and shaped by both political and socioeconomic systems. In South Africa, for instance, literature indicates that about 55 percent of Black African children live in households with fathers 'absent' (Posel and Devey 2006). This observation is highly influenced by the political history of the country.

A profound outcome in this analysis is the significant proportion (ranging from 15 percent in Malawi, 1998, to 25 percent in South Africa, 2001) of younger children (0–4) who live with neither parent in the household. This observation could be linked to a decline in marriages. South Africa, for instance, is known for a well-established decline in marriage (Udjo 2001; Budlender, Chobokoane, and Simelane 2005).

3.3 Determinants of Children's Living Arrangements

3.3.1 Household Structure and Living Arrangements of Children

A question on the relationship of household members to the head of the household is used to categorize types of households into three groups:

1. Nuclear household: consists of couple and biological children only.
2. Extended household: consists of nuclear plus other relatives.
3. Nonrelated: consists of nonrelated members.

Analysis shows that more than 60 percent of the children with both parents alive reside in nuclear households. South Africa scored lowest (62.1 percent), the reason being its low levels of marriage and a high proportion of spouses living apart from each other (Zulu and Sibanda 2005). A significant proportion (more than 10 percent in all countries except Rwanda) of nonorphans reside in extended households. This observation accentuates the importance of child fostering in Africa, as noted by Goody (1973) and McDaniel and Zulu (1996).

An increase in the proportion of nonorphans living in extended households is observed in Kenya (16.9 in 1989 and 18.8 in 1999), South Africa (29.8 in 1996 to 36.7 in 2001), and Rwanda (from 7.4 in 1991 to 22.1 in 2002), while a decrease is registered in Malawi (18.9 in 1998 to 13.6 in 2008). While considerable differences exist, child fostering remains a critical living arrangement for children in Africa.

3.3.2 Determinants of Children's Living Arrangements

Data for Uganda 2002 and Rwanda 2002 with similar important variables for analysis are used to estimate living arrangements of children. Multinomial logistic regression is used to predict three possible outcomes for children's living arrangements: nuclear, extended, and nonrelated person households. The reference category is nuclear household; regression is run for children aged 5 to 17 years.

Table 15.2 presents the results of a multinomial logistic regression model of predictors of living arrangements of children in Uganda. The first set shows the likelihood that a child resides in an extended household as opposed to a nuclear household. The second set of results shows the likelihood that a child is living in a nonrelated person's household versus living in a nuclear household. Results show that the survival status of parents is a strong predictor of children's living arrangements. This observation is made given that the odds that a child will live in an extended household as opposed to a nuclear household differ significantly according to the survival status of the parent. The first set of coefficients shows that a child with either surviving parents or who has lost one parent is significantly less likely to live in an extended household relative to double orphans residing in nuclear households. Compared with a double orphan, a child with both parents alive is 85 percent less likely (OR = 0.15) to live in an extended household than a nuclear household; a paternal orphan is 78 percent less likely (OR = 0.22) to live in an extended household than in a nuclear household, whereas a maternal orphan is 95 percent less likely (OR = 0.05) to live in an extended household than in a nuclear household.

Table 15.2 Multinomial Logistic Regression Model of Predictors of Living Arrangements of Children Aged 5–17 Years in Uganda in 2002

Variable	Living in Extended Household vs. Nuclear Household		Living in Nonrelated Persons Household vs. Nuclear Household	
	Odds Ratio (OR)	95% Confidence Interval (CI)	Odds Ratio (OR)	95% Confidence Interval (CI)
Survival status of parents				
Both parents dead (ref)	1.00		1.00	
Both parents alive	0.15***	0.14–0.15	0.18***	0.16–0.19
Father only dead	0.22***	0.21–0.23	0.28***	0.25–0.31
Mother only dead	0.05***	0.04–0.05	0.09***	0.08–0.10
Children age-groups				
5–9	0.85***	0.83–0.87	0.25***	0.2–0.27
10–1	1.00	0.97–1.02	0.66***	0.63–0.69
15–17 (ref)	1.00		1.00	
Marital status of head of household				
Widowed (ref)	1.00		1.00	
Single/never married	0.93	0.75–1.15	2.47*	1.22–5.01
Married/in union	0.51**	0.41–0.64	0.98	0.48–2.00
Separated/divorced/ spouse absent	1.00	0.73–1.38	2.12	0.93–4.83

*P < 0.05; ***P < 0.001 (n = 458,276)

Results for age show that, compared with older children (15–17 years), younger children (aged 5–9 years) are about 15 percent less likely (OR = 0.77) to live in extended households than in nuclear households. There is no significant difference between children aged 10–14 and 15–17. Compared with households headed by widows, a child living in a household headed by a married person is 49 percent less likely (OR = 0.51) to live in an extended household than in a nuclear household.

When the analysis is replicated for the nonrelated versus nuclear households, the same trend is observed. Results show that compared with a double orphan, a child with both parents alive is 82 percent less likely (OR = 0.18) to live in a nonrelated household than in a nuclear household; a paternal orphan is 72 percent less likely (OR = 0.28) to live in a nonrelated household than in a nuclear household, whereas a maternal orphan is 91 percent less likely (OR = 0.09) to live in a nonrelated household than in a nuclear household.

Results based on the age of the child show that compared with older children (15–17 years), younger children (aged 5–9 years) are about 75 percent less likely to live in nonrelated households than in nuclear households (OR = 0.25). Children aged 10–14 are 34 percent (OR = 0.66) less likely to live in a nonrelated household than a nuclear household. Results based on the marital status of the head of household show that compared with households headed by widows, living in a household headed by single or never married individuals increases the odds of living in a nonrelated household by 2.47 times.

Table 15.3 presents multinomial logistic regression results for Rwanda, 2002. Except for the magnitude, results are consistent with those observed for Uganda in the 2002 census. To this end, the two equations in two countries used to demonstrate multinomial logistic regression to predict children's living arrangements show a similar pattern. We can fairly argue that parents' survival status, age of the child, and, to a lesser extent, the marital status of a parent are predictors of children's living arrangements.

3.4 Implications of Children's Living Arrangements on Schooling

3.4.1 School Attendance

Various scholars hold contending views on the capabilities of extended families to take care of children, notably orphans. While some argue that these families are capable (e.g., Hunter 1990), others maintain that extended families' capabilities have been stretched to the limit (e.g., Foster 2000). Analysis of school attendance by living arrangements of children shows that proportion of children in nuclear households attending school is higher than those who never attended. Figures range from 75 percent in Kenya to 42 percent in Malawi. The percentage of those who

Table 15.3 Multinomial Logistic Regression Model of Predictors of Living Arrangements of Children Ages 5–17 Years in Rwanda in 2002

Variable	Living in Extended Household vs. Nuclear Household		Living in Nonrelated Persons Household vs. Nuclear Household	
	Odds Ratio (OR)	95% Confidence Interval (CI)	Odds Ratio (OR)	95% Confidence Interval (CI)
Survival status of parents				
Both parents dead (ref)	1.000		1.000	
Both parents alive	0.005***	0.004–0.005	0.011***	0.010–0.013
Father only dead	0.014***	0.012–0.015	0.021***	0.018–0.024
Mother only dead	0.035***	0.031–0.039	0.041***	0.035–0.047
Children age-groups				
5–9	1.476***	1.401–1.554	0.486***	0.446–0.530
10–14	1.308***	1.245–1.374	0.878***	0.819–0.940
15–17 (ref)	1.000		1.000	
Marital status of head of household				
Widowed (ref)	1.00		1.000	
Single/never married	0.588	0.282–1.226	0.718	0.240–2.153
Married/ in union	0.111***	0.049–0.253	0.091***	0.027–0.308
Separated/divorced/ spouse absent	1.518	0.452–5.100		

*$P < 0.05$; ***$P < 0.001$, n = 110,229.
Source: Computed from Population and Housing Census microdata, MPC.

attended in the past in extended households is higher than those attending in similar living arrangements. Results suggest that children living in extended and unrelated person households are less likely to attend school than their counterparts in nuclear households. The percentage of children who are no longer attending school (i.e., they did so in the past) is higher for extended than for nuclear households. This observation suggests that because of changing living arrangements or inadequate resources and lack of opportunity, children are forced to drop out of school. Furthermore, results are consistent with Hamilton's rule, which states that closeness of biological ties governs altruistic behavior (Hamilton, 1964). Hamilton hypothesizes that altruistic behavior between any two individuals is an increasing function of the degree of genetic relatedness between them (Daly and Wilson 1987). In other words, one's own children would be favored over close and distant relatives.

A model for school attendance is estimated in order to examine determinants of children's schooling. Most studies on children use co-residence with biological parents as a predictor variable for children's welfare, including health and education. However, if children do not reside with their own biological parents, which is the case for a significant proportion of children as demonstrated in this chapter, there is a need to consider broader ranges of co-residence.

Table 15.4 presents results on multivariate logistic regression of predictors of school attendance. Results indicate that wealth is a strong predictor of children's schooling. Children in poor and middle-class households in Rwanda are significantly less likely to be attending school than those from rich households. Children in middle-income households in Rwanda are 29 percent (OR = 0.71) and children in poor households are 49 percent (OR = 0.51) less likely to attend school than children in rich households. However, in Uganda there is no statistically significant difference in school attendance between children in rich and middle-income households. The only difference is observed between the rich and the poor, where the latter are 48 percent (OR = 0.52) less likely to attend school than the former.

The survival status of parents shows inconsistent results, suggesting that this variable is not always a strong predictor of children's schooling. Results for Rwanda show that there is no statistical difference in children school attendance between double orphans and paternal orphans. The only difference is observed in maternal orphans who, compared with double orphans, are 25 percent (OR = 0.75) less likely to attend school than double orphans. Results for Uganda show that compared with double orphans, non-orphans and paternal orphans are 21 percent more likely (OR = 1.21) to attend school. Maternal orphans are also slightly more likely (OR = 1.06) to attend school than double orphans.

3.4.2 Type of Household

The type of household is a strong predictor of children's school attendance. Results for both countries show that children in non-related households are less likely to attend school than those in nuclear and extended households. In Rwanda, a child living in a nuclear household is 3.53 times more likely to attend school than a child living in a non-related household. A child residing in an extended household is 3.22 times more likely to attend school than a child in a nonrelated household. Uganda shows the same pattern with a different magnitude. A child living in a nuclear household is 2.80 times more likely to attend school than a child living in a nonrelated household. A child living in an extended household is 2.76 times more likely to attend school than a child living in a nonrelated household.

3.4.3 Age of the Child

Younger children (5–9 years) in Rwanda are about two times more likely to attend school than older children (OR = 2.04). Those aged 10–14 are about four times more likely to attend school than older children (OR=4.40). A similar pattern is observed in Uganda. Younger children (5–9) are slightly more likely than older children to attend school (OR = 0.98). Children aged 10–14 are about three times more likely (OR = 3.05) to attend school than older children (15–17). In sum, the study finds wealth index, age of the child, and type of household to be important predictors of children's schooling. The survival status of a parent is to a lesser extent a predictor of children's schooling.

Table 15.4 Multivariate Logistic Regression of Predictors of School Attendance in Rwanda and Uganda, 2002

Variable	Rwanda (n = 110,229) Odds Ratio (OR)	95% Confidence Interval (CI)	Uganda (n = 458,276) Odds Ratio (OR)	95% Confidence Interval (CI)
Wealth quintile				
Rich (ref)	1.00		1.00	
Middle	0.71***	0.69–0.74	0.99	0.97–1.01
Poor	0.51***	0.50–0.53	0.52***	0.51–0.52
Parent survival status				
Both parents dead (ref)	1.00		1.00	
Both parents alive	1.01	0.95–1.08	1.21***	1.17–1.26
Father only dead	0.94	0.89–1.00	1.21***	1.16–1.27
Mother only dead	0.75***	0.69–0.81	1.06*	1.00–1.11
Type of household				
Nonrelated (ref)	1.00		1.00	
Nuclear	3.53***	3.30–3.77	2.80***	2.67–2.92
Extended	3.22***	3.00–3.45	2.76***	2.64–2.89
Age of child				
5–9	2.04***	1.98–2.11	0.98*	0.96–100
10–14	4.40***	4.26–4.54	3.05***	2.99–3.12
15–17 (ref)	1.00		1.00	

*Borderline significance, P-value slightly < 0.05; **P < 0.005; ***P < 0.001.
Source: Computed from Population and Housing Census microdata, MPC.

4 CONCLUSION AND POLICY RECOMMENDATIONS

The chapter has established trends and patterns of children's living arrangements; identified factors that predict children's living arrangements; assessed the implications of living arrangements on children's schooling; and, finally, identified factors that predict children's schooling. A change in children's living arrangements is observed. The study examined the level of orphanhood across and within countries over time. It has been established that orphanhood is common in the seven countries. Again, change is observed in orphanhood, with some countries experiencing an increasing trend while a decrease is registered in others. The proportion of orphanhood increased in all countries except Uganda, which is known for its effective interventions to fight HIV/AIDS. As expected, the proportion of children reporting the father dead is higher than those who reported the mother dead. The fact that men tend to marry later and marry younger women could partly explain the difference between maternal and paternal orphanhood. A notable observation is made among regions. East and Southern Africa have a relatively higher proportion of orphans than West Africa.

Results show that younger children are more likely than older children to live with both parents. Higher scores of children residing in nonrelated households are observed among older children (15–17). The proportion of children living in households with a mother only is significantly higher than those with a father only in the household. The observed results perhaps confirm the perception that fathers' involvement in the care and support of children in Africa remains limited. Children who are enumerated as heads of households substantiate the prevalence of child-headed households. Yet others are enumerated as spouses to the head of household. These two living arrangements are common among double orphans, implying that the loss of both parents is associated with assuming adulthood responsibility at a young age. The proportion of children enumerated as siblings to the head of household implies that the children's heads of household take care of their siblings.

A considerable proportion of children reside with grandparents. The profound challenge to this living arrangement is the fact that most sub-Saharan countries do not have support for older persons. Taking care of grandchildren is therefore a formidable challenge to them, not only because of their advanced age but also financial constraints. Another striking observation is that considerable proportions of nonorphans do not reside with their biological parents. The highest score in this category is observed in South Africa. The political history of South Africa and the established decline in marriage are plausible explanations behind this observation. A more substantial proportion of orphans residing in extended (as opposed to nonrelated) households underscores the importance of child fostering in African societies.

Multinomial logistic regression shows that the survival status of a parent, the age of a child, and, to a lesser extent, marital status are plausible predictors of children's living arrangements. Results from multivariate logistic regression are consistent with descriptive analysis, showing that the types of households, wealth index, and age of the child are important predictors of children's schooling. The survival status of a parent is to a lesser extent a predictor of children's schooling. This observation fits better in the family composition model than in the family process model.

Based on these findings, the study recommends that the research on changes in the living arrangements of children should not focus on orphans only, but also on nonorphans. Policy efforts may be effective if designed to expand social and economic security for poor families to enable them invest in children's education. Concerns about the future of the children are based on the high fertility in the region as well as the youthful structure that warrants rapid increase. Children's welfare, especially in education, should therefore be at the center of policy efforts.

ACKNOWLEDGMENTS

The author would like to gratefully acknowledge the Minnesota Population Center, for permission to access the IPUMS-International database, and all the reviewers whose comments contributed to refining the quality of this chapter.

REFERENCES

Acock, A., and D. Demo. (1994) *Family Diversity and Well-Being*. Thousand Oaks, CA: Sage Publications.

Ainsworth, M.K. (1996) "Economic Aspects of Child Fostering in Cote d'Ivoire." *Research in Population Economics* 8:25–62.

Ainsworth, M., and D. Filmer. (2006) "Inequalities in Children's Schooling: AIDS, Orphanhood, Poverty, and Gender." *World Development* 34 (6): 1099–1128.

Beegle, K., D. Filmer, A. Stokes, and L. Tiererova. (2009) "Orphanhood and the Living Arrangements of Children in Sub-Saharan Africa." Policy Research Working Paper 4889, the World Bank Development Research Group, Poverty Team and Human Development and Public Services Team.

Bicego, G., S. Rutstein, and K. Johnson. (2003) "Dimensions of the Emerging Orphan Crisis in Sub-Saharan Africa." *Social Science and Medicine* 56:1235–1247.

Bongaarts, J. (2001) "Household Size and Composition in the Developing World in the 1990s." *Population Studies* 55:263–279.

Budlender, D., N. Chobokoane, and S. Simelane. (2005) "Marriage Patterns in South Africa: Methodological and Substantive Issues." *Southern African Journal of Demography* 9 (1): 1–25.

Case, A., C. Paxson, and J. Ableidinger. (2002) Orphans in Africa." Working Paper 9213, National Bureau of Economic Research, Massachusetts.

Case, A., C. Paxson, and J. Ableidinger. (2004) "Orphans in Africa: Parental Death, Poverty and School Enrollment." *Demography* 41 (3): 483–508.

Coleman, J. (1988) "Social Capital and the Creation of Human and Family Cohesion." *American Journal of Sociology* 94:95–120.

Daly, M., and M. Wilson. (1987) "The Darwinian Psychology of Discriminative Parental Solicitude." *Nebraska Symposium on Motivation* 35:91–144.

Doctor, V.H. (2004) "Parental Survival, Living Arrangements and School Enrolment of Children in Malawi in the Era of HIV/AIDS." *Journal of Social Development in Africa* 19:31–53.

Dungumaro, E.W. (2008) "Gender Differentials in Household Structure and Socioeconomic Characteristics in South Africa." *Journal of Comparative Family Studies* 39 (4): 329–351.

Dungumaro, E.W., A.J. Mturi, N. Nzimande, and D. Sekokotla. (2006) "Household Structures in Contemporary South Africa." *LOYOLA Journal of Social Sciences* 20 (1): 19–41.

Foster, G. (2000) "The Capacity of the Extended Family Safety Net for Orphans in Africa." *Psychology, Health and Medicine* 5 (1): 55–62.

Foster, G. (2002) *Understanding Community Responses to the Situation of Children Affected by AIDS—Lessons for External Agencies. In HIV and Development.* Geneva: United Nations Research in Social Development.

Goody, E. (1982) *Parenthood and Social Reproduction: Fostering and Occupational Roles in West Africa.* New York: Cambridge University Press.

Goody, J. (1973) "Inheritance, Property, and Marriage in Africa and Eurasia." *Sociology* 3 (1): 55–76.

Goody, J. (1989) "Future of the Family in Rural Africa." *Population and Development Review* 15:119–144.

Hamilton, W.D. (1964) "The Genetical Evolution of Social Biology." *Journal of Theoretical Biology* 7:1–16.

Hoff, A. (2007) "Patterns of Intergenerational Support in Grandparent–Grandchild and Parent–Child Relationships in Germany." *Ageing and Society* 27 (5): 643–665.

Hodgkin, R., and P. Newell. (2007) *Implementation Handbook for the Convention on the Rights of the Child.* UNICEF. Regional Office for Europe Geneva, Switzerland.

Hunter, S.S. (1990) "Orphans as a Window on the AIDS Epidemic in Sub-Saharan Africa: Initial Results and Implications of a Study in Uganda." *Social Science and Medicine* 31 (6): 681–690.

Jenkins, P., and P. Wilkinson. (2002) "Assessing the Growing Impact of the Global Economy on Urban Development in Southern African Cities: Case Studies in Maputo and Cape Town." *Cities* 19 (1): 33–47.

Lloyd, C.B. ,and A.K. Blanc. (1996) "Children's Schooling in Sub-Saharan Africa: The Role of Fathers, Mothers, and Others." *Population and Development Review* 22:265–298.

Madhavan, S. (2004) "Fosterage Patterns in the Age of AIDS." *Continuity and Change. Social Science and Medicine* 58:1443–1454.

Marcoux, R., A. Noumbissi, and T. Zuberi. (2010) "Orphans in Three Sahelian Countries: Exploratory Analyses from Census Data." *Canadian Studies in Population,* 37 (1–2): 245–267.

McDaniel, A., and E. Zulu. (1996) "Mothers, Fathers and Children: Regional Patterns in Child–Parent Residence in Sub-Saharan Africa." *African Population Studies* 11:1–18.

Minnesota Population Center. (2011) *Integrated Public Use Microdata Series International: Version 6.1 [Machine-Readable Database].* Minneapolis: University of Minnesota.

Monasch, R., and J. Ties Boerma. (2004) "Orphanhood and Child Age Patterns in Sub-Saharan Africa: An Analysis Of National Surveys from 40 Countries." *AIDS* 18 (2): S55–S65.

Montemayor, R., and G.K. Leigh. (1982) "Parent–Absent Children: Demographic Analysis of Children." *Family Relations* 31:567–573.

Noumbissi, A., and T. Zuberi. (2001) "Household Structure and Aging in South Africa: A Research Note." Prepared for the Virtual Conference on African Households: An Exploration of Census Data, organized by the African Census Analysis Project, Population Studies, Philadelphia.

Pilon, M. (2003) "Foster Care and Schooling in West Africa: The State of Knowledge." http://portal.unesco.org/education/en/file. Accessed July 20, 2012.

Posel, D., and R. Devey. (2006) "The Demographic of Fatherhood in South Africa: An Analysis of Survey Data, 1993–2002." In *Baba Men and Fatherhood in South Africa*, ed. R. Morell and L. Ritcher, 38–52. Cape Town: HSRC Press.

Richter, L. (2006) *The Role of Health Sector in Strengthening Systems to Support Children's Healthy Development in Communities Affected by HIV/AIDS: A Review*. Geneva: World Health Organization. http://www.hsrc.ac.za. Accessed September 17, 2012.

Sibanda, A. (2011) "Ethnic Difference in the Living Arrangements of Children in South Africa." *Journal of Comparative Family Studies* 42 (4): 479–508.

Urassa, Mark, J. Ties Boerma, Japheth Z.L. Ng'weshemi, Raphael Isingo, Dick Schapink, and Y. Kumogola. (1997) "Orphanhood, Child Fostering and the AIDS Epidemic in Tanzania." *Health Transition Review Supplement* 27:141–153.

Udjo, E. (2001) "Marital Patterns and Fertility in South Africa: The Evidence from the 1996 Population Census." Presented at the IUSSP Salvador, Brazil, August 18–24.

UNAIDS. (2011) "World AIDS Report." www.unaids.org. Accessed January 15, 2012.

UNAIDS/UNICEF/USAID. (2004) "Children on the Brink 2004. A Joint Report of New Orphan Estimates and a Framework for Action, July 2004." http://data.unaids.org/publications. Accessed January 15, 2012.

United Nations Statistics Division. (2004) *Demographic Yearbook Review National Reporting of Household Characteristics, Living Arrangements and Homeless Households: Implications for International Recommendations*. Department of Economic and Social Affairs Statistics Division. New York: United Nations.

Wenk, D., C.L. Hardesty, C. Morgan, and L.S. Blair. (1994) "The Influence of Parental Involvement on the Wellbeing of Sons and Daughters." *Journal of Marriage and the Family* 56:229–234.

Yamano, T., Y. Shimamura, and D. Sserunkuuma. (2005) "Living Arrangements and Schooling of Orphaned Children and Adolescents in Uganda." *American Journal of Agricultural Economics* 87 (2): 91–119.

Zulu, E.M., and A. Sibanda. (2005) "Racial Differences in Household Structure." In *The Demography of South Africa*, ed. T. Zuberi, A. Sibanda, and E. Udjo, 218–252. New York: M.E. Sharpe.

16 Armed Conflict and Demographic Outcomes in Mozambique and Rwanda
What Can Censuses Tell Us?

Carlos Arnaldo

1 INTRODUCTION

Conflict and civil war are part of African history. First there was the resistance to colonization and the armed struggles that led to the independence of many African countries in the 1950s, 1960s, and 1970s. Second, after gaining independence, many African countries have been involved in civil wars, mainly rooted in ideological and political contradictions and ethno-regional frictions. Recent data show that Africa is still home to some of the most violent conflicts in the world, with at least one-third of the 131 active armed conflicts recorded by the Uppsala Conflict Data Program from 1989 to 2009 (Harbom and Wallensteen 2010).

Beside their economic, political, and social consequences, these conflicts also cause immediate and long-term changes in the structure and dynamics of the population. Randall (2005) identifies three stages in which demographic behavior can be influenced by many voluntary and involuntary forces during or after conflict: *disorder*, at the beginning of the conflict when the responses are to the different environment created by the fighting; *limbo*, when the conflict is established and people have learnt how to cope with it despite the uncertainty of the future; and the *new order*, the reconstruction of economic life and the reestablishment of the social and political order. According to Randall (2005), past exposure and preconflict relationships with other populations are determinant factors for the way in which the conflict population will respond to the conflict.

The demographic consequences of conflict may include excess mortality; population displacement because of mass migration and refugee flows; and fertility decline (Avogo and Agadjanian 2008; Blayo and Bergouignan 2003; Guha-Sapir and Gijsbert 2004; Lindstrom and Berhanu 1999; O'Hare and Southall 2007; Silva and Ball 2008). For mortality, the effect of conflict can be either direct through the death of combatants and civilians, or indirect through the: (a) waste of huge amount of resources and destruction of public and private property; (b) damage to health facilities and infrastructures; (c) crowding out of health-related government expenditures because of the need to increase the spending on military equipment and personnel; (d) effect of military violence on social cohesion; and (e) traumatic experience and psychological distress related to the military violence (Li and Wen 2005). Li and Wen (2005) analyzed a sample of seventy-six countries from 1961 to 1999, and found that the exposure to armed conflict was significantly associated with an increase of between 6 and 10 percent in the adult mortality rate of both males and females in the long-term and short-term respectively. Urdinola (2003) suggested that the slower pace of infant mortality reduction in Colombia in comparison with other Latin American countries was related to armed conflict.

Fertility may drop during wartime and rebound in the postwar period as a result of delayed marriage, spousal separation, and intentional postponement of births during the war (Agadjanian and Prata 2001, 2002). According to Woldemicael (2008), there are different pathways through which armed conflict may affect fertility: (a) unintentional limiting of births because of social and economic disruption that stems from the conflict itself; (b) the displacement of people and separation of couples; (c) reduction in the number of live births because of a deterioration of health systems and compromised nutritional status of pregnant women, leading to an increase in the number of still births, spontaneous and voluntary abortions; (d) reduction in fecundity and the frequency of intercourse because of traumatic experience and psychological stress associated with a decline in reproductive health status; and (e) conscious adjustment in fertility behavior because of couples opting to avoid births during war.

Despite the sustained interest of demographers in the demographic consequences of violent conflicts, the study of the impact of conflict on demographic outcomes faces some methodological challenges; violent conflicts often hinder data collection or lead to the destruction of the data needed to estimate their consequences. To date, most studies on the effect of conflict on demographic outcomes have mainly used survey data with information on birth histories that allows one to see whether a particular demographic event occurred during the period of conflict. However, the small number of cases that characterize most surveys do not allow for subnational analyses. This analysis uses a series of censuses, which allows for a rural–urban breakdown as well as covering a longer period. This chapter draws on existing pre- and postconflict census data, to trace demographic changes that may be related to conflict in two postconflict African countries, Mozambique and Rwanda, selected on the bases of the availability of data. The focus is on how age and sex structure, fertility, and under-five mortality changed during the conflict period in comparison to pre- and postconflict periods.

2 DATA SOURCE AND METHODS

The analysis is based on 10 percent samples of the 1980, 1997, and 2007 Mozambique's census and the 1991 and 2002 censuses of Rwanda. The data for Mozambique were obtained from the National Institute of Statistics (INE), while the data for Rwanda were downloaded from the IPUMS–International website (Minnesota Population Center 2011). The analytical approach used comprises two parts: first, an analysis of changes in age and sex structures is performed based on the age-sex distributions from successive census data of each country. Although the specific shape of a population pyramid reflects the contribution of more than one factor (Hobbs 2008), a review of the history of each of the study countries, particularly the period of civil war and its intensity, allows one to draw some conclusions regarding its potential impact on the demographic outcome.

Second, using standard demographic and indirect techniques, under-five mortality rates (U5MRs) and total fertility rates (TFRs) are derived on annual or period bases and a trend analysis is performed to assess the timing of mortality and fertility change (if any) in relation to the conflict period. If a change in either mortality or fertility is conflict-led, we expect the conflict period to show high mortality and low fertility patterns when compared with the periods before and after the conflict. The U5MR is estimated from the census child survivorship data using the Trussell variant of the Brass children ever born/children surviving method using West model life tables. This method uses age pattern of fertility and the proportions of children dead among children ever born to women of different ages and estimates life table probabilities of dying between birth and exact age x (q(x)) using the following equation:

$$q(x) = k(i)D(i)$$

Where the multiplier $k(i)$ is meant to adjust nonmortality factors determining the value of $D(i)$, the proportion of children deceased by age of the mother.

Brass (1975) developed a set of multipliers by using a third-degree polynomial of fixed shape but variable age location to represent fertility. Brass applied a logit system generated by the general standard to provide the mortality element, and a growth rate of 2 percent per annum to generate a stable age distribution for females (for more details, see United Nations 1983, 73–96). Sullivan (1972) estimated another set of multipliers by using least-squares regression to fit Brass's equation to data generated from observed fertility schedules and the Coale-Demeny life tables; Trussell (1975) estimated a third set of multipliers by the same means but using data from the fertility schedules model developed by Coale and Trussell (1974). Trussell's multipliers are preferred because they are based on a wider range of model situations than those developed by either Sullivan or Brass (Singh et al. 2005).

For the Brass method to produce reliable estimates, mortality and fertility must have remained constant in the recent past. If fertility has been changing, the ratios of average parities used in the calculation of the multipliers will not accurately represent the experience of any cohort of women, and will also not provide a good index for the distribution of the timing of births to women in each age-group (Singh et al. 2005). In Mozambique and Rwanda, fertility has not declined significantly in such a way that this assumption is violated (Shapiro and Gebreselassie 2009). The assumption on constant mortality may not hold because under-five mortality has been declining in the study countries although the conflict and the HIV/AIDS epidemic may have been slowing the pace of the decline. However, the constant mortality assumption was eased by Feeney's (1980) development of a method for estimating a time reference period; with estimates of specific five-year age-groups of mothers pertaining to a different number of years before the census.

The risk of a child dying is assumed to be a function of a child's age only and not of other factors, such as the age of the mother or the birth order of the child. However, the estimates are vulnerable to reporting errors, including the underreporting of deceased children, the inclusion of stillbirths in the number of deceased children, underreporting of children ever born, and age misreporting (Ewbank 1982; Feeney 1980; Palloni 1980). Given the evidence that these and other errors are more severe for the very young and for older women, mortality estimates were based on women aged 20 to 39 years. The United Nations Population Division Program, QFive, was used in the estimation.

The Own-Children method was applied to the four (except Mozambique 1980) sets of census data to generate estimates of fertility for the fifteen years before each census. The Own-Children method is a reverse survival method that allows the estimation of age-specific fertility rates for up to fifteen years preceding a census or survey from information on the enumerated number of children classified by single year of age and by single year of age of the mother (Cho, Retherford, and Choe 1986; Retherford et al. 1979; Rindfuss 1977). The enumerated children under 15 years old are first matched to their mothers within households on the basis of answers to questions on age, sex, marital status, number of living children, and relationship to the head of household. The matched children classified by their own age and the mother's age are then reverse-survived to estimate the number of births by age of the mother in previous years. Women are also reverse-survived to estimate their number by age in previous years. A major limitation of this method is that it can only use the reports of living children, and the estimates produced can be seriously distorted by age misreporting (Brass 1996). Most of the reporting errors cannot be corrected, but an assessment of the age data was made (results not shown) to identify the pattern of errors in order to obtain a better interpretation of the resulting estimates.

In this analysis, children were matched to their mothers based on age, sex, and relationship to the head of household, because the information on the number of living children was not collected for women above 50 years of age. The information on marital status was also not used in the matching procedure because in the study countries childbearing is not restricted to married women (Arnaldo 2007; INSR and ORC Macro 2006). On average, 21 percent of the enumerated children below 15 years of age could not be matched to their mothers and were allocated to women by assuming that their age distribution for each age of mother was the same as the age distribution of matched children. If this assumption does not hold, the resulting estimates may be affected but the magnitude of the effect cannot be determined although it is believed to be small given the percentage of the unmatched children.

Life table survival ratios for both children and women were obtained from the West Family of the Coale and Demeny Regional Model Life Tables (Coale and Demeny 1983), believed to represent the most general mortality pattern as it is derived from the largest number and broadest variety of cases (United Nations 1983, 13) selected on the basis of the $_5q_0$ values estimated from each census. Mortality was assumed to be constant over each of the estimation periods. The assumption of unchanging mortality seems reasonable because, as a result of the conflict and the HIV/AIDS epidemic, the two countries did not experience a huge improvement in mortality in the estimation periods (Arnaldo et al. 2011; Hong et al. 2009). Indeed, own-children estimates are not very sensitive to errors in the level and pattern of mortality (Retherford et al. 1979; Cho, Retherford, and Choe 1986). The estimate of an age-specific fertility rate is the product of an age-specific child–woman ratio and a quotient of two reverse-survival ratios, one for children and the other for women. As each of these two reverse-survival ratios tends to be close to one, and the quotient of the two tends to be even closer to one, the range of variability in this quotient across different levels of mortality is small (Cho, Retherford, and Choe 1986, 46).

3 THE STUDY CONTEXT

3.1 Mozambique

Mozambique is a southeast African country with 23.0 million inhabitants in 2011 (INE 2010). Its recent history was marked by violent conflicts. First there was a ten-year (1964–1974) struggle by the Frente de Libertação de Moçambique (FRELIMO) that led to independence from Portugal in 1975. Although the transition from the Portuguese administration was reasonably smooth, some Portuguese solders and FRELIMO dissidents regrouped in Rhodesia (Zimbabwe). Starting in 1976 and with support from both Rhodesia and South Africa, they waged a devastating war against the post-independence government (Newitt 1995; Young 1991). In 1977, the RENAMO (National Resistance Movement) opposition movement was formed, initially with its base in Rhodesia and later in South Africa, and intensified the war, targeting health and education infrastructures, cutting off railway lines and main roads, and making the movement of goods difficult, except by air and sea (Kanji 1990).

In the 1980s, Mozambique's government started negotiations to end the war, first with the South African apartheid government, aiming to end its support of RENAMO, and later directly with the RENAMO movement that culminated with the General Peace Agreements on October 4, 1992 (Newitt

1995; Young 1991). By the end of the sixteen-year (1976–1992) conflict, more than seven hundred of the country's sixteen hundred health posts were destroyed or closed, and rural health personnel were scarce, either because they had fled to urban centers or had been kidnapped (Cossa et al. 1994, 117). About 58 percent of the total schools (3,530) in 1983 had been destroyed or closed, affecting more than 1.5 million pupils (Ministério da Educação 1994, 8). More than one million Mozambicans are estimated to have lost their lives (Baden 1997, 9), 1.7 million became refugees in neighboring countries, and three million were internally displaced (Gaspar 2002).

3.2 Rwanda

Rwanda is a central African country with 10.7 million people as of 2011 (National Institute of Statistics of Rwanda 2009). Like most African countries, Rwanda was a colony first of Germany and later administered by Belgium. The history of conflict in Rwanda goes back to the precolonial era, when the Rwandese were divided along ethnic lines, according to three ethnic groups; the Hutu, Tutsi, and Twa (Bula 2006). The ethnic Tutsi were the privileged group and dominated politically and economically until the 1950s, when in response to their claim to an independent Rwanda, Belgium provided military and political aid to the Hutu to overturn the privileged position of the ruling Tutsi.

According to Schindler and Brück (2011), political power changed after the Hutu staged a successful coup and became independent from Belgium in 1962, with Grégoire Kabyibanda as the first president. In the following years, ethnically motivated violence and political campaigns against the Tutsi resulted in waves of Tutsi fleeing Rwanda to neighboring countries and later forming the rebel group that attacked the Kigali regime in 1990 (Bula 2006; Longman 1998; Verwimp 2004). This was the beginning of the civil war that brought several political and economic upheavals that exacerbated the ethnic tensions culminating with Rwanda's President Juvénal Habyarimana's airplane crash on April 6, 1994, killing the president and all others on board (Verwimp 2004). This was a start of the genocide by the Hutu against the Tutsi, which ended in July1994 after more than eight hundred thousand people had been killed, the equivalent of 10 percent of the general population and approximately 75 percent of the Tutsi ethnic minority. Thousands of Tutsi women were individually raped or gang-raped, held in sexual slavery, or sexually mutilated by Hutu militiamen and soldiers (Bula 2006; Longman 1998; Peterson 2000; Prunier 1998; Verwimp 2004).

4 CONFLICT AND CHANGES IN AGE-SEX STRUCTURE

Although the age distribution of a population reflects the contribution of more than one factor (Hobbs 2008), conflict-related population displacement and increased mortality of males across the military ages may produce changes in the age distribution. However, to the extent that the civilian population is directly involved in or affected by the conflict, the impact of conflict on mortality may be evenly distributed with no noticeable change on the age-sex structure.

4.1 Mozambique

In Mozambique, the history of census undertaking dates back to 1930, with a decennial series that was only interrupted by the civil war in 1980. However, reliable data are only available from 1940 for the total population, and from 1980 for the age distribution (Arnaldo 2007). Mozambique's population grew from 6.4 million in 1950 to 20.6 million in 2007, at an average annual growth rate of 2 percent (Arnaldo et al. 2011). The analysis of the intercensal growth rates from 1940 to 2007 shows an increasing pattern interrupted only in the 1980–1997 period (Table 16.1), with a 32 percent decrease in the annual growth rate, compared with the previous period. This decrease may be attributable to a war-related increase of mortality and population displacement (Arnaldo et al. 2011). During this period the infant mortality rate declined by only 7 percent (as against 19 percent in the previous period) and the life expectancy decreased by 3 percent (against a 9 percent increase in the previous period) (Arnaldo and Muanamoha 2011). Five percent (eight hundred thousand) of the enumerated population in the 1997 census was in neighboring countries in 1992, months before the end of the war, suggesting that these were refugees who had fled the war.

To assess changes in the age distribution, the population pyramids from the 1980 and 1997 censuses are compared. Although the civil war started in 1976, by 1980 it had not been felt in most of the country; hence, its demographic impact is assumed to be negligible. The overlap of the two pyramids and the sex ratios by age-group (Figure 16.1) do not show any clear evidence of a war-related change from 1980 to 1997. However, there

Table 16.1 Population Growth Rate, Mozambique, 1940–2007

Period	Growth Rate (%)	% Change
1940–1950	1.2	—
1950–1960	1.6	33.3
1960–1970	2.1	31.3
1970–1980	2.5	19.0
1980–1997	1.7	−32.0
1997–2007	2.7	58.8

Source: Arnaldo et al. (2011, table 1).

is a shortage of adult males aged 20–39 in 1980 compared with 1997 that may probably reflect losses attributable to the liberation war (1964–1974), the historical male labor migration to South Africa, and/or differential coverage and reporting between the censuses.

The magnitude of the difference between the age distributions can be summarized by calculating the index of dissimilarity, an index based on the differences between the percentages for each age-group, and the differences for corresponding age-groups of the two populations that are first summed without regard to sign, and one-half of the sum is taken (Hobbs 2008). The resulting index represents the percentage of the people who would have to change age-groups in order for the two percentage distributions to be the same. This index, however, can only compare two populations at a time and its magnitude is affected by the number of age classes in the distribution as well as the size of the differences (Hobbs 2008; McKibben and Faust 2008). For Mozambique, three comparisons of age distributions are made: 1980 versus 1997; 1997 versus 2007; and 1980 versus 2007. The results (not shown) show that the three age distributions are very similar, but the 1997 age distribution is slightly more dissimilar to the age distribution in 1980 than to that in 2007. The absence of pronounced differences between the two pre- and postconflict (1980 and 1997) age-sex distributions may also reflect the fact that the war affected not only the male population of military age but also the entire civilian population. In fact, the analysis of the age-sex distribution of the population that was in neighboring countries just before the end of the war in 1992 recorded in 1997 (results not shown) suggests that war-related emigration was not selective: whole families fled to take refuge in neighboring countries.

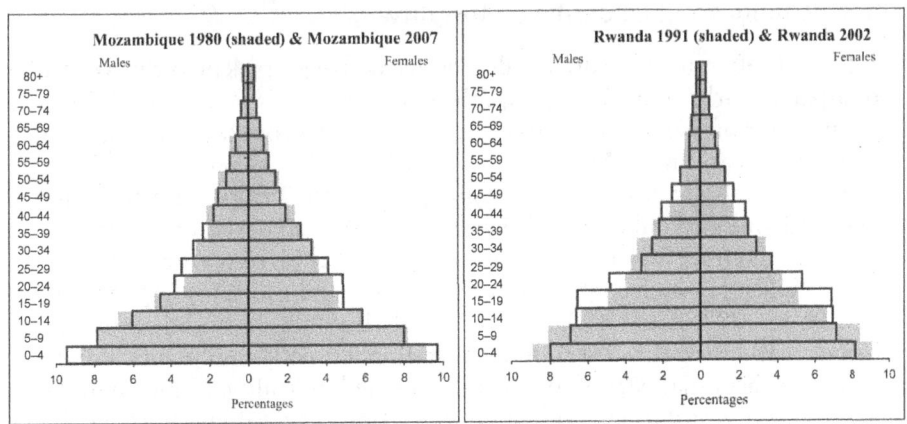

Figure 16.1 Age-sex distributions, Mozambique, 1980 and 1997, and Rwanda, 1991 and 2002.
Source: 1980 and 1997 censuses, INE Database for Mozambique; 1991 and 2002 censuses, IPUMS Database for Rwanda.

4.2 Rwanda

Three censuses were conducted in post independence Rwanda, in 1978, 1991, and 2002, with the population almost doubling from 4.8 million in 1978 to 8.2 millions in 2002 (National Census Service Rwanda 2003). The population growth rate was 3.0 percent in the period 1978–1991 and 1.2 percent in the period 1991–2002, with the drop in growth rate being attributed to the disruptive effects of the war and genocide in 1994 that killed thousands of Rwandese (Bula 2006).

The computation of the dissimilarity index between the 1991 and 2002 censuses shows that the two age distributions are 7.7 percent different, with the differences being slightly higher among males (8.2 percent) than females (7.2 percent). The overlap of the two population pyramids (Figure 16.1) shows a shortage of children aged 0–9 for both sexes, men aged 25 to 39 years and women aged 30 to 34 years in the 2002 census compared with the 1991 census, and an excess of population aged 10 to 24 years and 40 to 49 years. While some of the differences may be a result of differential coverage and reporting between the two censuses, the shortage of adult males, which is also reflected by lower sex ratios among the adult population (results not shown), is consistent with an excess mortality during the war-genocide period. The analyses of the house-to-house survey of genocide victims in western Rwanda (Verwimp 2004) and of the Rwandan 2000 DHS (de Walque and Verwimp 2009) show that adult males were most likely to die during the genocide. The drop in the proportion of children below 10 from 1991 to 2002 is an indication of a decline in fertility, some of which may be related to the conflict.

4.3 Conflict and Under-Five Mortality

The mortality rate of children under the age of five years depicts the welfare of a particularly vulnerable group, the children, and is widely accepted as an indicator of social welfare and overall health of a country. Although in a war children are among civilian victims, they are also vulnerable to indirect effects, as well. By destroying economic, social, and health infrastructures and undermining public health systems, in particular the immunization program, conflict has a negative effect on the health and nutritional status of children, which contributes to high under-five mortality (Agadjanian and Prata 2003; Kinfu 1999a). Silva and Ball (2008) have shown in East Timor that during times of conflict mortality indirectly resulting from conflict is a substantial part of total conflict-related mortality. In Burundi, the exposure to war during childhood significantly affected children's health outcomes (health status, early childhood malnutrition, and stunting), with longer exposure being related to a much larger impact (Bundervoet, Verwimp, and Akresh 2008).

In this section, the trend in the U5MR is analyzed from the preconflict era through the postconflict era for each country. Figures 16.2 and 16.3 present results of the under-five mortality estimates for Mozambique and Rwanda, respectively. The estimates were graphed together with DHS estimates taken from the respective DHS reports for consistency checking. For Mozambique (Figure 16.2), under-five mortality remained high and almost unchanged from the late 1960s to the mid-1970s, experienced a slight decline from the late 1970s to the early 1980s, from where it rose and peaked at about 250–260 deaths per 1,000 live births in the early 1990s, and thereafter declined to about 160–170 deaths per 1,000 births in 2002.

During the 1950s and 1960s there was a high prevalence of diseases such as malaria, and the health services provided by the Portuguese administration were concentrated in urban areas and intended largely for the nonindigenous population (United Nations 1981). The slight decline in the late 1970s may reflect the "heath revolution" brought by the postindependence government, where health services became free and mass vaccination campaigns were established for primary and preventive care, primarily in rural areas (Macassa et al. 2003; Potts and Marks 2001; Segall 1977). The increase in under-five mortality from the mid-1980s may reflect the effect of civil war and related economic hardship. During that period the fighting intensified all over the country and the economy collapsed, leading to the introduction of the World Bank and International Monetary Fund economic rescue package, structural adjustment program in 1987. Furthermore, the country also suffered from a severe drought and natural disasters that also affected the economy in the early 1980s (Macassa et al. 2003). Separate analyses for urban and rural areas show the same pattern (results not shown).

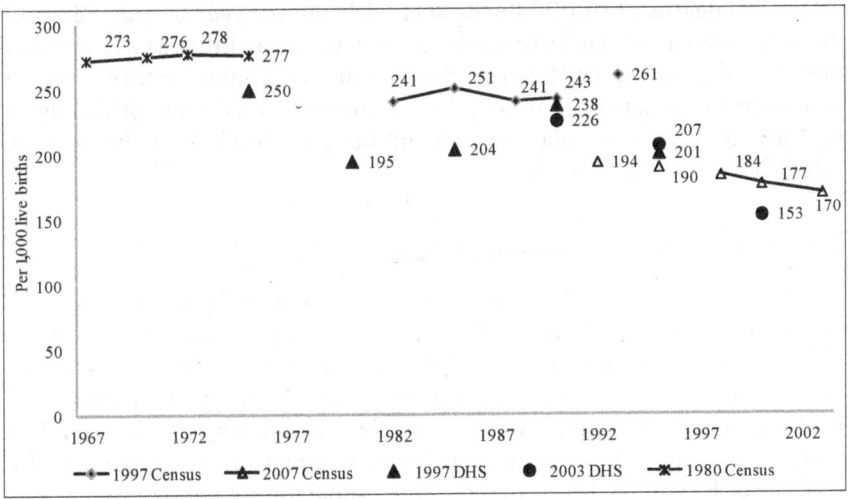

Figure 16.2 Under-five mortality over time, Mozambique.
Source: 1980, 1997, and 2007 censuses, INE Database; INE and MISAU (1998, 2005).

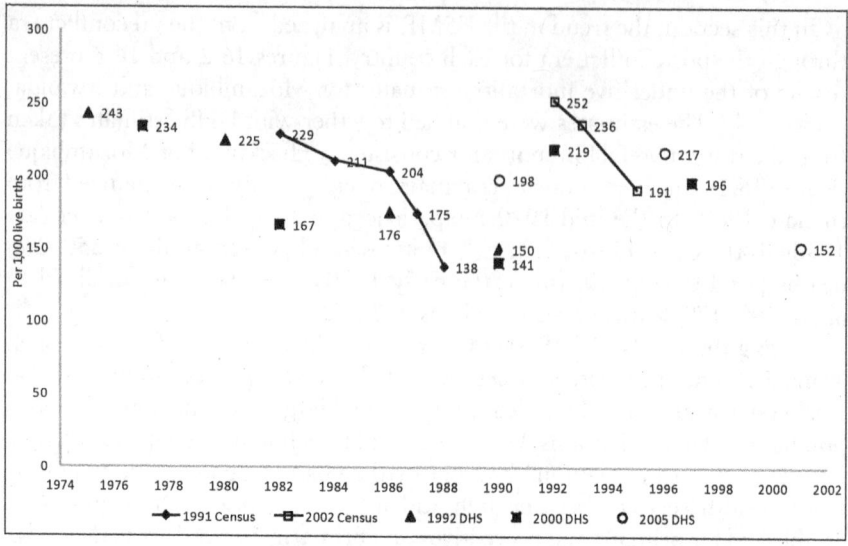

Figure 16.3 Under-five mortality over time, Rwanda.
Source: 1991 and 2002 censuses, IPUMS database; ONAPO (2006, 1994); ONAPO and ORC Macro (2001).

Because of the concentrated nature of the conflict, the impact of conflict on under-five mortality is much clearer in Rwanda than in Mozambique. Figure 16.2 shows that under-five mortality declined from slightly less than 250 deaths per 1,000 live births in the mid-1970s to its lowest value of 138 per 1,000 births around 1990, and rose rapidly to peak at about 250 deaths per 1,000 births around 1994, the year of genocide, and declined thereafter. Unfortunately, an urban–rural breakdown was not possible because the 1991 census data set did not contain information on urban–rural residence. However, these results are consistent with analyses performed by other scholars (e.g., Schindler and Brück 2011; Hong et al. 2009) based on survey data.

4.4 Conflict and Total Fertility Rate

Fertility may respond in different ways to war or political instability. According to Lindstrom and Berhanu (1999), assuming conscious fertility control, it is expected that women or couples will delay births in response to sudden declines in income or increased uncertainty. Thus, the uncertainty and confusion resulting from the outbreak of conflict or change in the prevailing social order may sometimes be enough to discourage births temporarily. An analysis of Ethiopian data found that the probability of conception in years of heavy military activities was low compared with other years (Lindstrom and Berhanu 1999). This led the authors to suggest that spousal separation because of conscription was an important mechanism by which the intensity of military conflict affected fertility in that country. Likewise, Woldemicael (2008) found evidence that conflict contributed to fertility decline in Eritrea. On the other hand, the Tuareg of Mali maintained their fertility pattern and age at marriage unchanged as an important feature of cultural identity during a time of inter-ethnic conflict (Randall 2005). In order to establish if fertility responded to conflict in Mozambique and Rwanda, this section examines the trends of TFR estimates from the Own-Children method.

Figure 16.4 shows annual TFRs for the period 1983–2007 in Mozambique for national as well as for urban and rural women. The estimates are three-year moving averages to lessen the distortion attributable to age misreporting. The total and rural curves show that fertility increased from 1983 to reach its peak at values above 7 children per woman between 1991 and 1994; declined to about 5 children per woman between 1996 and 1997; and rose again to around 6.5 children per woman in the 2001–2003 period. On the other hand, urban fertility declined from above 7 in 1983 to just below 6 in the period 1995–1996 and increased to values above 6.5 children between 1998 and 1999. These patterns appear to be more influenced by age misreporting and migration of young adults than by a conflict-led fertility change (Arnaldo 2007). The low values of TFR for total population and rural areas shown between 1983 and 1988 are probably a result of migration of children of secondary school age from rural to urban areas in order to continue their studies because secondary schools were only available in urban areas (Arnaldo 2007). The fact that urban fertility is much higher than national and rural fertility supports this explanation.

The high levels of fertility between 1991 and 1994 may be an artifact of age misreporting (Arnaldo 2007). There were two major historical events in that period, the end of the civil war in 1992 and the first democratic elections in 1994, which may have been used in the estimation of the age of those who did not know their age, resulting in an overestimation of children born during that period. This hypothesis is strengthened by the fact that this pattern is not evident in urban areas, where age reporting is better.

The rise in fertility after 1994 may be genuine and a response to political stability achieved after the end of the war and after the country had successfully held its first general elections in 1994. Crisis-induced fertility declines are usually followed by a rebound as the severity of the conditions leading to the decline lessens and couples tend to compensate for lost reproductive time (Lindstrom and Berhanu 1999). This pattern has been observed in previous studies from other countries. For instance, in Ethiopia (Kinfu 1999b) and Iran (Abbasi-Shavazi 2000) fertility rose after the respective revolutions in 1974 and 1979, respectively. In Angola, women living in conflict-affected areas had lower fertility during the conflict period followed by a rebound after the end of the conflict (Agadjanian and Prata 2002).

Annual total fertility rates for Rwanda were estimated for the period 1977–2002 for the whole country, while for rural and urban areas, estimates are only provided from 1988 to 2002 (Figure 16.5). Fertility remained above 7 children per woman until 1990 when it suddenly dropped to a

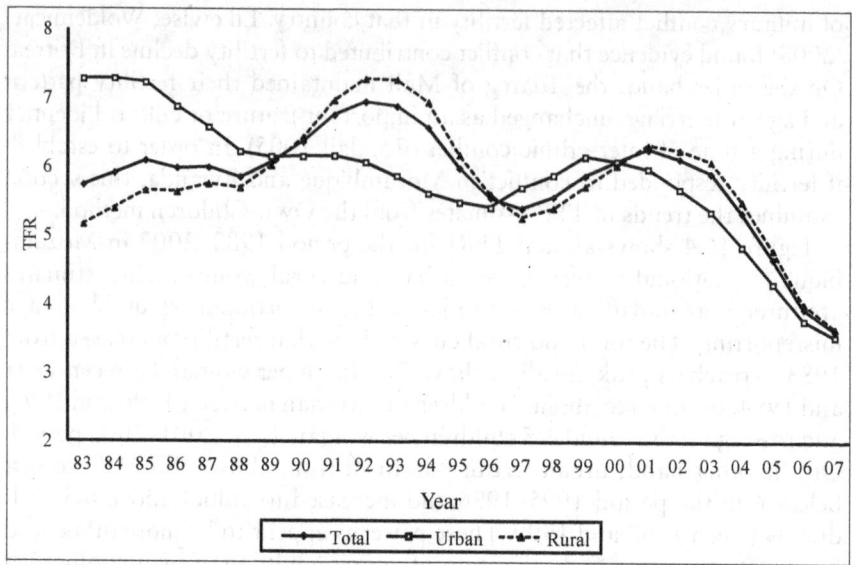

Figure 16.4 Trends in total fertility rate, Mozambique, 1983–2007.
Source: 1997 and 2007 censuses, INE database.

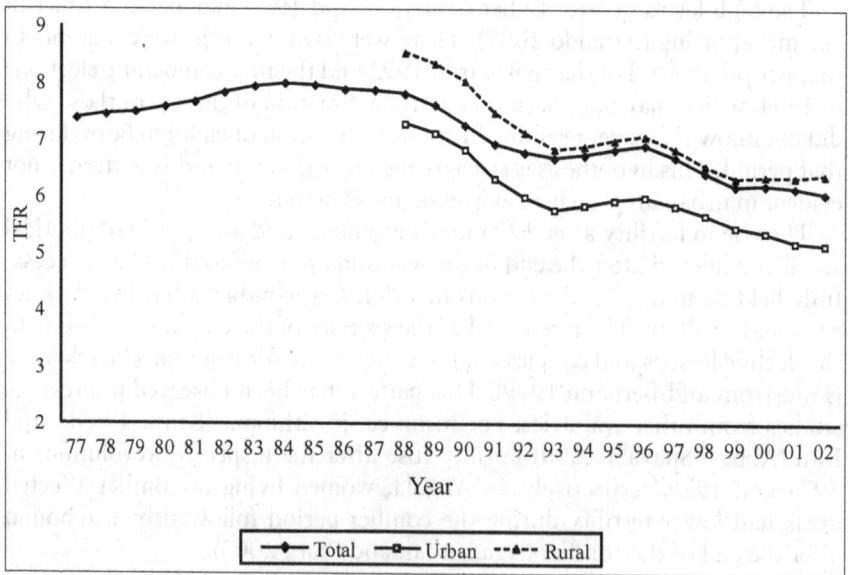

Figure 16.5 Trends in total fertility rate, Rwanda, 1977–2002.
Source: 1991 and 2002 censuses, IPUMS database.

value of about 6.5 children in the period 1993 to 1994, and rose to about 7 in 1996, declining thereafter. The sudden fall in fertility coincides with the conflict period, suggesting a conflict-driven decline. In fact, this pattern has been reported by other studies that used survey data. For instance, Schindler and Brück (2011), found a "clear and robust" effect of conflict on fertility through the replacement effect, when women choose to have children in the postconflict period to compensate for child loss during the conflict period and exposure to sibling mortality.

5 CONCLUSION

In both Mozambique and Rwanda, the population growth rate declined in the conflict period compared with the periods before and after the conflict, suggesting an impact of conflict on at least one component of the population growth. The analysis of age-sex distributions and sex ratios by age-group shows that in Rwanda there was a shortage of adult males in 2002 compared with 1991. In Mozambique, however, no noticeable differences are observed in the age distribution. The nature, duration, and characteristics of the conflict may be important factors. The conflict in Rwanda was short and killed more adult males than any other group (Verwimp 2004), while in Mozambique the conflict was long (sixteen years) and civilians of all ages were equally affected either as conflict casualties or as refugees in neighboring countries. In Randall's (2005) classification, Rwanda's demographic effect was during the *disorder* stage when people adjust to instability created by the pre-genocide and genocide period, and there was no *limbo* stage as the conflict ended rapidly. In Mozambique, on the other hand, the conflict remained for a longer period in the *limbo* stage, and people learned to cope with war conditions resulting in a lesser impact on the demographic outcome.

Findings from the trend analysis of under-five mortality show a close correspondence between the years of conflict or of high military intensity with high under-five mortality. This pattern is much clearer for Rwanda than for Mozambique. In Rwanda under-five mortality had been declining since the early 1980s, before the outbreak of conflict, but increased rapidly from early 1990 and peaked in 1993–1994, a pattern similar to that found in the analysis of DHS data (Hong et al. 2009; Schindler and Brück 2011).

In Mozambique the decline in under-five mortality was not clearly established before the beginning of the civil war, partly because the civil war started almost a year after the end of the liberation war and mortality was very high in the colonial era. Only 7 percent of the population could read or write at independence and the coverage of the health system was very poor (Arnaldo 2007). During the first years of independence, mass education and health programs were put in place, which may have been responsible for the slow decline starting from the late 1970s. This decline was interrupted in the mid-1980s when, probably because of the intensification of the hostilities and the collapse of the economy, under-five mortality started to rise, reaching the peak levels in the early 1990s, at the end of the civil war. This is consistent with Macassa et al.'s (2003) analysis of the 1997 DHS data. However, Garenne, Cominx, and Dupuy (1997) showed that in central Mozambique child mortality rose sharply between 1975 and 1986 and declined between 1986 and 1990. This differs from the present study with regard to the later period. The fact that Garenne, Cominx, and Dupuy's (1997) study was done in an area heavily affected by the war may partly explain its differences from our findings (Macassa et al. 2003). In addition, in the late 1980s the intensity of the conflict had decreased in central Mozambique. Countries coming out of a conflict usually experience mortality decline in the postwar period as the process of reconstruction take place. This appears to have been the case for both Rwanda and Mozambique, as under-five mortality fell after the end of the genocide and at the end of civil war, respectively.

The analysis of the trends in total fertility rate suggests that in both Rwanda and Mozambique fertility may have fallen during the conflict periods and rebounded after the conflict had ended. For Rwanda, the findings are consistent with findings of other studies conducted in the country (Schindler and Brück 2011). For Mozambique, apart from our own earlier analysis (Arnaldo 2004), few studies have addressed this issue. At the same time, the assessment of Mozambique age data (results not shown) found a pattern of age misreporting, particularly the age misreporting of children under 15 years, which may have affected the estimates.

The analysis of age ratios from the 1997 census shows that the age ratios centered on age 3 are higher compared with the adjacent ages, suggesting that the election year was used as a reference for the estimation of age. However, given the evidence of fertility rebounding following a conflict (e.g., Agadjanian and Prata 2002), it is possible that at least some of the fertility increase observed in the early 1990s in Mozambique was genuine.

Finally, despite the limitations of not being able to place the events on the dates in which they occurred (as it is usually possible with survey data) and of age misreporting, census data can provide a good complement to our understanding of the consequences of conflict for demographic outcomes. However, given that fertility may either increase or decline as a result of conflict, the effects of the two trends may cancel each other out and result in an underestimation of the impact of conflict on the demographic outcome.

ACKNOWLEDGMENTS

The author gratefully acknowledges the National Institute of Statistics of Mozambique and University of Minnesota Population Center for providing the data used for this analysis; Victor Agadjanian, Sandra Gonçalves,

Bonaventura Cau, and anonymous reviewers for their useful comments; and Hélio Maúngue for research assistantship.

REFERENCES

Abbasi-Shavazi, M. Jalal. (2000) "Effects of Marital Fertility and Nuptiality on Fertility Transition in the Islamic Republic of Iran, 1976–1996." Working Papers in Demography No.84, Demography Program, Canberra, Australian National University.

Agadjanian, Victor, and Ndola Prata. (2001) "War and Reproduction: Angola's Fertility in Comparative Perspective." *Journal of Southern African Studies* 27 (2): 329–330.

Agadjanian, Victor, and Ndola Prata. (2002) "War, Peace, and Fertility in Angola." *Demography* 39 (2): 215–231.

Agadjanian, Victor, and Ndola Prata. (2003) "Civil War and Child Health: Regional and Ethnic Dimensions of Child Immunization and Malnutrition in Angola." *Social Science and Medicine* 56 (12): 2515–2527.

Arnaldo, Carlos. (2004) "Regional Fertility Trends in Mozambique." *Journal of Population Research* 21 (2): 177–197.

Arnaldo, Carlos. (2007) *Fecundidade e seus Determinantes Próximos em Moçambique: uma análise dos níveis, tendências, diferenciais e variação regional.* Maputo: Texto Editores.

Arnaldo, Carlos, and Ramos Cardoso Muanamoha. (2011) "Comportamento Demográfico e desafios de Desenvolvimento sócio-económico em Moçambique." *Revista de Estudos Demográficos* 49:40–52.

Arnaldo, Carlos, Ramos Cardoso Muanamoha, Inês Raimundo, Rogers Justo Hansine, and Freide Albino César. (2011) *Crescimento Populacional e Desenvolvimento sócio-económico em Moçambique.* Maputo: Centro de Análise de Políticas e Centro de Estudos Africanos, Universidade Eduardo Mondlane.

Avogo, Winfred, and Victor Agadjanian. (2008) "Childbearing in Crisis: War, Migration and Fertility in Angola." *Journal of Biosocial Sciences* 40 (5): 725–742.

Baden, Sally. (1997) *Post-Conflict Mozambique: Women's Special Situation, Population Issues and Gender Perspectives to be Integrated into Skills Training and Employment Promotion.* Geneva: Training Policies and Systems Branch, International Labour Office.

Blayo, Chantal, and Christophe Bergouignan. (2003) "Measuring the Demographic Consequences of Conflict (from Methodological Principles to Specific Results): Presentation of two Experiences." Presented at the IUSSP Seminar on the Demography of Conflict and Violence, Oslo, Norway, November 8–11.

Brass, William. (1975) *Methods for Estimating Fertility and Mortality from Limited and Defective Data. Vol. An Occasional Publication, Laboratories for Population Statistics.* Chapel Hill: Carolina Population Center.

Brass, William. (1996) "Demographic Data Analysis in Less Developed Countries: 1946–1996." *Population Studies* 50:451–467.

Bula, Clement. (2006) *Fertility in Rwanda: Impact of Genocide. Analysis of Fertility before, during and after the 1994 Genocide.* Unpublished Masters Dissertation, Department of Statistics, University of Western Cape, Cape Town.

Bundervoet, Tom, Philip Verwimp, and Richard Akresh. (2008) "Health and Civil War in Rural Burundi. A Micro Level Analysis of Violent Conflict." Research Working Paper 5, Institute of Development Studies, Brighton, University of Sussex.

Cho, L., R.D. Retherford, and M.K. Choe. (1986) *The Own-Children Method of Fertility Estimation.* Honolulu: East-West Center Population Institute.

Coale, Ansley J., and P. Demeny. (1983) *Regional Model Life Tables and Stable Populations.* New York: Academic Press.

Coale, Ansley J., and T. James Trussell. (1974) "Model Fertility Schedules: Variations in the Age Structure of Childbearing in Human Populations." *Population Index* 40 (2): 185–258.

Cossa, H.A., S. Gloyd, R.G. Vaz, E. Folgosa, E. Simbine, M. Diniz, and J.K. Kreiss. (1994) "Syphilis and HIV Infection among Displaced Pregnant Women in Rural Mozambique." *International Journal of STD and AIDS* 5 (2): 117–123.

de Walque, Damien, and Philip Verwimp. (2009) "The Demographic and Socio-Economic Distribution of Excess Mortality during the 1994 Genocide in Rwanda." Policy Research Working Paper no. 4850, Development Research Group, Human Development and Public Services Team, The World Bank.

Ewbank, D.C. (1982) "The Sources of Error in Brass's Method for Estimating Child Survival: The Case of Bangladesh." *Population Studies* 36 (3): 459–474.

Feeney, Griffith. (1980) "Estimating Infant Mortality Trends from Child Survivorship Data." *Population Studies* 34 (1): 109–128.

Garenne, M.L., R. Cominx, and C. Dupuy. (1997) "Effects of the Civil War in Central Mozambique and Evaluation of the Intervention of the International Committee of the Red Cross." *Journal of Tropical Pediatrics* 43:318–323.

Gaspar, Manuel da Costa. (2002) "Population Size, Distribution, and Mortality in Mozambique, 1960–1997." In *Population-Development-Environment in Mozambique: Background Readings*, ed. A. Wils,5–34. Luxemburg: International Institute for Applied Systems Analysis.

Guha-Sapir, Debarati, and Willem Gijsbert. (2004) "Conflict-Related Mortality: An Analysis of 37 Datasets." *Disasters* 28 (4): 418–428.

Harbom, Lotta, and Peter Wallensteen. (2010) "Armed Conflicts, 1946–2009." *Journal of Peace Research* 47 (4): 501–509.

Hobbs, Frank. (2008) "Age and Sex Composition." In *The Methods and Materials of Demography*, ed. J.S. Siegel and D.A. Swanson, 125–174. Bingley: Emerald Group Publishing Limited.

Hong, Rathavuth, Mohamed Ayad, Shea Ruststein, and Ruilin Ren. (2009) *Childhood Mortality in Rwanda: Levels, Trends, and Differentials. Further Analysis of the Rwanda Demographic and Health Surveys 1992–2007/08. Vol. DHS Further Analysis Reports No. 66*, DHS Further Analysis Reports No. 66. Calverton, MD: ICF Macro.

INE. (2010) *Projecções Anuais da População Total, Rural e Urbana, 2007–2040.* Maputo: Intituto Nacional de Estatistica.

INE and MISAU. (1998) *Moçambique: Inquérito Demográfico e de Saúde—1997.* Maputo: Instituto Nacional de Estatística.

INE and MISAU. (2005) *Moçambique: Inquérito Demográfico e de Saúde—2003.* Maputo: Instituto Nacional de Estatística.

INSR and ORC Macro. (2006) *Rwanda Demographic and Health Survey 2005.* Calverton, MD: INSR and ORC Macro.

Kanji, Nazneen. (1990) "War and Children in Mozambique: Is International Aid Strengthening or Eroding Community-Based Policies?" *Community Development Journal* 25 (2): 102–112.

Kinfu, A. Yohannes. (1999a) "Child Undernutrition in War-Torn Society: The Ethiopian Experience." *Journal of Biosocial Sciences* 31:403–418.

Kinfu, A. Yohannes. (1999b) "Revolution within a Revolution: An Essay on the Demographic Consequences of Ethiopia's 1974 Revolution." Paper presented at the International Conference on New African Perspectives, Perth, Australia, November 26–28.

Li, Quan, and Ming Wen. (2005) "Effect of Armed Conflict on Adult Mortality: A Time Series Cross-National Analysis." *Journal of Peace Research* 42 (4): 471–492.

Lindstrom, David P., and Betermariam Berhanu. (1999) "The Impact of War, Famine, and Economic Declined on Marital Fertility in Ethiopia." *Demography* 36 (2): 247–261.
Longman, Timothy. (1998) "State, Civil Society, and Genocide in Rwanda." In *State, Conflict, and Democracy in Africa*, ed. R. Joseph, 339–358. London: Lunne Rienner Publishers.
Macassa, G., G. Ghilagaber, E. Bernhardt, and B. Burstrom. (2003) "Trends in Infant and Child Mortality in Mozambique during and after a Period of Conflict." *Public Health* 117: 221–227.
McKibben, Jerome N., and Kimberly A. Faust. (2008) "Population Distribution." In *The Methods and Materials of Demography*, ed. J.S. Siegel and D.A. Swanson, 105–124. Bingley: Emerald Group.
Ministério da Educação. (1994) *Impacto da Guerra na Educação, 1983–1992*. Maputo: Direcção de Planificação, Projecto de Emergência.
Minnesota Population Center (2011) *Integrated Public Use Microdata Series International: Version 6.1 [Machine-Readable Database]*. Minneapolis: University of Minnesota.
National Census Service Rwanda. (2003) *The General Census of Population and Housing Rwanda 2002. Report on the Preliminary Results*. Kigali: National Census Commission.
National Institute of Statistics of Rwanda. (2009) *National Population Projection 2007–2022*. Kigali: National Institute of Statistics of Rwanda.
Newitt, Malyn. (1995) *A History of Mozambique*. London: Hurst and Company.
Office National de la Population Rwanda. (1994) *Enquête Démographique et de Santé 1992*. Kigali: Office National de la Population.
Office National de la Population Rwanda and ORC Macro. (2001) *Enquête Démographique et de Santé, Rwanda 2000*. Kigali: Office National de la Population and ORC Macro.
O'Hare, Bernadette A.M., and David P. Southall. (2007) "First Do No Harm: The Impact of Recent Armed Conflict on Maternal and Child Health in Sub-Saharan Africa." *Journal of the Royal Society of Medicine* 100: 564–570.
Palloni, A. (1980) "Estimating Infant and Childhood Mortality under Conditions of Changing Mortality." *Population Studies* 34 (1): 129–142.
Peterson, Scott. (2000) *Me against my Brother: At War in Somalia, Sudan, and Rwanda*. London: Routledge.
Potts, Deborah, and Shula Marks. (2001) "Fertility in Southern Africa: the quiet revolution. *Journal of Southern African Studies* 27 (2): 189–205.
Prunier, Gérard. (1998) "The Rwandan Patriotic Front." In *African Guerrillas*, ed. C. Clapham, 119–133. Oxford: James Currey.
Randall, Sara. (2005) "The Demographic Consequences of Conflict, Exile and Repatriation: A Case Study of Malian Kel Tamasheq." *European Journal of Population* 21: 291–320.
Retherford, Robert D., C. Pejaranonda, L. Cho, A. Chamratrithirong, and F. Arnold. (1979) *Own-Children Estimates of Fertility for Thailand Based on the 1970 Census, Papers of the East-West Population Institute No. 63*. Honolulu: East-West Center.
Rindfuss, R.R. (1977) *Methodological Difficulties Encountered in Using Own-Children data: Illustrations from the United States, Papers of the East-West Population Institute, No. 42*. Honolulu: East-West Center.
Schindler, Kati, and Tilman Brück. (2011) "The Effects of Conflict on Fertility in Rwanda." Policy Research Working Paper no. 5715, Poverty Reduction and Economic Management Network, Gender and Development Unit, The World Bank.
Segall, Malcolm. (1977) "Health and National Liberation in the People's Republic of Mozambique." *International Journal of Health Services* 7 (2): 319–325.

Shapiro, David, and Tesfayi Gebreselassie. (2009) "Fertility Transition in Sub-Saharan Africa: Falling and Stalling." *African Population Studies* 22 (2): 3–23.

Silva, Romesh, and Patrick Ball. (2008) "The Demography of Conflict-Related Mortality in Timor-Leste (1974–1999): Reflections on Empirical Quantitative Measurement of Civilian Killings, Disappearances, and Famine-Related Deaths." In *Statistical Methods for Human Rights*, ed. J. Asher, D. Banks and F.J. Scheuren, 117–139. New York: Springer.

Singh, Kavita, Unni Karunakara, Gilbert Burnham, and Kenneth Hill. (2005) "Using Indirect Methods to Understand the Impact of Forced Migration on Long-Term Under-Five Mortality." *Journal of Biosocial Sciences* 37:741–760.

Sullivan, Jeremiah M. (1972) "Models for the Estimation of the Probability of Dying between Birth and Exact Ages of Early Childhood." *Population Studies* 26 (1): 79–97.

Trussell, T. James. (1975) "A Re-Estimation of the Multiplying Factors for Brass Technique for Determining Childhood Survivorship Rates." *Population Studies* 29 (1): 97–108.

United Nations. (1981) *National Experience in the Formulation and Implementation of Population Policy, 1960–1980: Mozambique*. New York: Department of International and Social Affairs.

United Nations. (1983) *Manual X: Indirect Techniques for Demographic Estimation*. New York: United Nations.

Urdinola, B. Piedad. (2003) "Does Political Violence Affect Infant Mortality? The Colombian Case." Presented at IUSSP Seminar on the Demography of Conflict and Violence, Oslo, Norway, November 8–11.

Verwimp, Philip. (2004) "Death and Survival during the 1994 Genocide in Rwanda." *Population Studies* 58 (2): 233–245.

Woldemicael, Gebremariam. (2008) "Recent Fertility Decline in Eritrea: Is It a Conflict-Led Transition?" *Demographic Research* 18 (2): 27–58.

Young, Lance S. (1991) *Mozambique's Sixteen-Year Bloody Civil War*. New York: USAF.

17 Population Policies in Sub-Saharan Africa
Evolution, Achievements, and Challenges

John Kekovole and Clifford O. Odimegwu

1 INTRODUCTION

This chapter provides a review of the road sub-Saharan African (SSA) countries have traveled in their endeavor to formulate population policies under diverse political, socioeconomic, and social-cultural environments, their achievements and challenges. Population policy has both narrow and broader perspectives in definition and content (Weeks 2001; Odimegwu and Oyedokun 2001). The narrow definition tends to focus on socioeconomic policy making and planning. The broader definition includes not only the factors that directly influence population processes but also all the social and economic measures that exercise either direct or indirect influence over population size, characteristics, and processes of fertility, mortality, and migration. Thus the scope of population policy includes population size, population growth rate, fertility and mortality levels, nuptiality, migration, age-sex structure, human resources utilization, and population quality (United Nations 1994; Oucho, Akwara, and Ayiemba 1995; Tarver 1996; Odimegwu and Oyedokun 2001).

Like many other developing countries, population policies aimed at reducing population growth as a component of overall development agenda were initially regarded inappropriate by many countries in the region as they were thought to undermine pro-natal attitudes embedded in cultural survival strategies (Odimegwu and Oyedokun 2001; African Development Bank 2012). However, countries in the SSA region have enacted different population policies following global historical evolution of population policy development. Thus in SSA, population policy formulation is continuously evolving and has been influenced by international consensus, changing economic scenarios, political and social environment, and research.

In the 1960s and 1970s, population was not considered as a problem in most countries in the subcontinent. The main concern then was the attainment of political independence from their colonial masters. Population size was considered as a sign of power. They did not at that time acknowledge the impact of population dynamics on socioeconomic development. The only countries that had population polices aimed at reducing population growth rates during this period were Egypt, Ghana, Kenya, Mauritius, Morocco, and Tunisia (African Development Bank 2000; Odimegwu and Oyedokun 2001; Oucho, Akwara, and Ayiemba 1995). Although the need to build indigenous capacity in data collection, analysis, and utilization of the findings in the formulation and implementation of national socioeconomic development plans was acknowledged, attitudes on population issues remained unchanged (UNECA 1995).

At the time of the 1974 World Population Conference held in Bucharest, African countries were pro-natalist and were of the opinion that socioeconomic development could take care of all population-related problems. They aligned themselves with the phrase "development is the best contraceptive." At the second African Population Conference held in Arusha, Tanzania, in 1984, African governments recognized that population was a central component in formulating and implementing policies and programs for accelerated socioeconomic development. This led to the adoption of the popular Kilimanjaro Plan of Action (KPA) for Africa Population and Self-Reliant Development. It emphasized the importance of population in social and economic development and noted that family planning was a health and human rights issue (Oucho, Akwara, and Ayiemba 1995; Odimegwu and Oyedokun 2001). The adoption of the plan of action brought a significant change in attitudes regarding the need for population policies in Africa, with governments becoming more concerned about rapid population growth and its associated problems.

The third African Population Conference held in Dakar, Senegal, in 1992 adopted the Dakar/Ngor Declaration on Population, Family and Sustainable Development. This conference reviewed the efforts of governments in Africa in implementing the KPA recommendations. The conference noted that despite increased number of explicit population policies formulated in most countries in the region since the adoption of KPA, fertility levels in the region were still high and other population problems remained unsolved.

The Dakar/Ngor Declaration, acknowledging the indispensable role of population and development framework for formulating viable development strategies, addressed the following issues: population, sustainable economic growth, and development; family, fertility, and family planning; mortality, morbidity, and AIDS; urbanization, migration, and physical planning; refugees, displaced persons, children, youth, women in development; data collection and analysis; and so on (UNECA 1995, African Development Bank 2000; Odimegwu and Oyedokun 2001). This declaration provided the basis for African governments' commitment to population policies and programs such that at the Mexico International Conference on Population in 1984, they all changed their position from "development is the best contraceptive" to the need to integrate population issues into development planning. Family planning programs and provision of modern contraception were strongly advocated as the right of all couples and individuals. Looking at this historical trend, it is clear that from the 1960 till 1993 the main focus of population policies globally was population control.

This changed when International Conference on Population and Development (ICPD) was held in Cairo, Egypt, in 1994 (African Development Bank 2000). Governments adopted a comprehensive framework that covered a broad cocktail of issues ranging from population growth, migration, reproductive health, maternal and child health, gender empowerment, education, and family. There was emphasis on reproductive health, which implied a comprehensive approach to women's health and well-being that includes fertility, infertility, contraception, abortion, childbearing, maternal morbidity and mortality, sexuality, sexually transmitted infections, menstruation and menopause, child survival, and male reproductive health (Lane, 2000). This change in focus has been reflected in population policies of most countries in the subregion. For instance, the basis of South African Population Policy of 1998 was the 1994 ICPD Program of Action (Department of Social Welfare 1998) while Nigeria, among other countries, formulated new population policies reflecting the new global approach to population and development issues, with a focus on reproductive health care.

2 THE ROLE OF DATA COLLECTION ACTIVITIES

Data collection activities played a crucial role in providing insights into the magnitude of the challenges countries were faced with in achieving their development goals and future consequences. There have been five rounds of censuses in the subcontinent from 1965 to date. These include 1970 round of census, covering the period 1965–1974; 1980 round, spanning 1975–1984; 1990 round of censuses (1985–1994); 2000 round of censuses (1995–2004); and 2010 round of censuses (2005–2014) (United Nations Statistics Division 2013; Onsembe and Ntozi 2006).

The data collected in these censuses have enabled countries to know the size, composition, and distribution of their population and their determinants (fertility, mortality, and migration). The link to the amount of resources required to provide basic services—education, health, housing, and so on—has become clearer. A number of surveys have also been conducted. These include the World Fertility Surveys (WFS) and Demographic and Health Survey (DHS), which provided comparative statistics across various countries. According to Garenne (2011), another major development for demographic research has been the development of Demographic Surveillance Systems in many African countries. These sites have been influential in promoting in-depth, high-quality research. Vital registration systems, though weak in most countries are also being strengthened. However the database of this work is African censuses.

Table 17.1 Rounds of Population and Housing Census in Sub-Saharan Africa

Countries or Areas	1970 Round of Censuses (1965–1974)	1980 Round of Censuses (1975–1984)	1990 Round of Censuses (1985–1994)	2000 Round of Censuses (1995–2004)	2010 Round of Censuses (2005–2014)
AFRICA					
Angola	December 15, 1970	—	—	—	(July 16–August 18, 2013)
Benin	—	March 20–30, 1979	February 15, 1992	February 11, 2002	(2013)
Botswana	August 31, 1971	August 12–26, 1981	August 21, 1991	August 17–26, 2001	August 9–18, 2011
Burkina Faso	—	December 1–7, 1975	December 10–20, 1985	December 10, 1996	December 9–23, 2011
Burundi	—	August 15–16, 1979	August 16–30, 1990	—	August 16–31, 2008
Cameroon	—	April 9, 1976	April 10, 1987	—	November 11–30, 2005
Cape Verde	December 15, 1970	June 1–2, 1980	June 23, 1990	June 16–30, 2000	June 16–30, 2010
Central African Republic	—	December 8–22, 1975	December 8, 1988	December 8, 2003	(2013)
Chad	—	—	April 8, 1993	—	May 20–June 20, 2010
Comoros	July–September 1966	September 15, 1980	September 15, 1991	September 16–30, 2003	(2013)
Congo	February 7, 1974	December 22, 1984	November 20–December 5, 1994	June 6–July 30, 1996	April 28, 2007
Cote d'Ivoire	—	April 30, 1975	March 1, 1988	November 21–December 20, 1998	(March 2013)
Democratic Republic of the Congo	January 7, 1970 January 7, 1974	January 7, 1984	—	—	(2013)

Population Policies in Sub-Saharan Africa 307

Djibouti	1970–1971 March 17, 1967	January 3, 1983	—	May 29–June 12, 2009
Equatorial Guinea	September–October 1971	July 4–17, 1983	July 4, 1994	February 2002 (2013)
Ethiopia	—	May 9, 1984	October 11, 1994	May 29–June 7, 2007
Gabon	June 1, 1969–June 1970	August 1–31, 1980	July 1–31, 1993	December 2003 (2013)
Gambia	April 21, 1973	April 15, 1983	April 15, 1993	April 15, 2003 (April 15–May 15, 2013)
Ghana	March 1, 1970	March 11, 1984	—	March 26, 2000 September 26–October 10, 2010
Guinea Bissau	December 15, 1970	April 16–30, 1979	December 1, 1991	— March 15–29, 2009
Kenya	August 24–25, 1969	August 25, 1979	August 24, 1989	August 24, 1999 August 24–31, 2009
Lesotho	April 14–24, 1966	April 12, 1976	April 12, 1986	April 14, 1996 April 13–May 13, 2006
Liberia	February 1, 1974	February 1–14, 1984	—	— March 21–March 30, 2008
Libya Arab Jamahiriya	July 31, 1973	July 31, 1984	August 1, 1993	August 11, 1995 April 15–May 7, 2006
Madagascar	—	January 26–August 18, 1975	—	— (2013)
Malawi	August 9, 1966	September 20, 1977	September 1–21, 1987	September 1–21, 1998 June 8–28, 2008
Mali	—	December 1976	April 1–30, 1987	April 1–14, 1998 April 1–14, 2009
Mauritania	—	December 12, 1976–March 1977	April 5–20, 1988	November 1–15, 2000 (2013)

(continued)

Table 17.1 (continued)

Countries or Areas	1970 Round of Censuses (1965–1974)	1980 Round of Censuses (1975–1984)	1990 Round of Censuses (1985–1994)	2000 Round of Censuses (1995–2004)	2010 Round of Censuses (2005–2014)
Mauritius	June 30, 1972	July 2–3, 1983	July 1, 1990	July 2–3, 2000	July 1–14, 2011
Mozambique	December 15, 1970	—	February 5–June 17, 1990	February 7–June 18, 2000	February 1, 2011
Namibia	May 6, 1970	August 1, 1980	—	August 1–15, 1997	August 1–15, 2007
Niger	—	August 26, 1981	October 21, 1991	August 27–28, 2001	August 28–September 10, 2011
Nigeria	—	October 7–11–November 6, 1977	May 20–June 3, 1988	May 20, 2001	December 10–24, 2012
Reunion	October 16, 1974	—	November 26, 1991	—	March 21–27, 2006
Rwanda	—	March 9, 1982	March 15, 1990	March 8, 1999	January 1, 2006
Saint Helena ex. Dep.	July 24, 1966	August 15–16, 1978	August 15, 1991	August 16–30, 2002	August 16–30, 2012
Sao Tome and Principe	September 30, 1970	October 31, 1976	February 22, 1987	March 8, 1998	February 10, 2008
Senegal	—	August 31, 1981	August 4, 1991	August 25, 2001	May 13, 2012
Seychelles	May 5, 1971	April 16, 1976	May 27, 1988	December 8–22, 2002	(2013)
Sierra Leone	August 8, 1974	August 1, 1977	August 17, 1987	August 29, 1997	August 26–30, 2010
		—	August 26, 1994	August 22–26, 2002	
			December 15, 1985	December 4, 2004	(2014)

South Africa	May 6, 1970	May 6, 1980	March 5, 1985	October 9–10, 1996
	—	—	March 7, 1991	October 9–10, 2001	October 10–November 7, 2011
South Sudan	April 3, 1973	February 1, 1983	April 15, 1993	—	April 21–June 5, 2008
Swaziland	May 24, 1966	August 25, 1976	August 25, 1986	May 11–12, 1997	April 28–May 14, 2007
Togo	March 1–April 30, 1970	November 22, 1981	—	—	November 6–19, 2010
Tunisia	May 3, 1966	May 8, 1975	April 20, 1994	April 28, 2004	(April 2014)
Uganda	August 18, 1969–November 1974	January 18, 1980	January 12–19, 1991	September 12, 2002	(August 15, 2013)
United Republic of Tanzania	August 26, 1967	August 26, 1978	August 28, 1988	August 24–25, 2002	August 26, 2012
Zambia	August 22–30, 1969 August 26–September 6, 1974	July 25, 1980	August 20, 1990	October 25, 2000	October 16–November 5, 2010
Zimbabwe	April 21–November 11, 1969	August 18, 1982	August 18, 1992	August 17–27, 2002	August 18–27, 2012

Source: Onsembe and Ntozi (2006).

3 AFRICAN POPULATION AND DEVELOPMENT INDICATORS

Since the 1994 ICPD, global population program has received serious impetus from different countries and development partners. In SSA, every government has invested heavily in population and reproductive health programs with a view to achieving the broad objectives of the ICPD plan of action. Development partners have also invested heavily in the plan of action. SSA countries have reformulated both direct and indirect population and development policies to reflect this evolutionary trend in population policy (Table 17.2). The large majority of SSA countries provide direct government support for the distribution of family planning methods, while others make contraception available by supporting the activities of nongovernmental agencies.

African population is currently estimated at about one billion, with the population growth rate of between 2.3 and 2.5 percent. The current regional total fertility Rate (TFR) per woman of reproductive age (15–49 years) is estimated at 4.7 (United Nations Department of Economic and Social Affairs 2010; PRB 2012) with modern contraceptive prevalence rate for women in the same age category of 26 percent (less than 20 percent for middle and Western Africa) (United Nations Department of Economic and Social Affairs 2011; UNFPA/PRB 2010; PRB 2001;PRB 2012). The crude birthrate is estimated at 36 per 1,000 populations, crude death rate (CDR) at 11 per 1,000 population and infant mortality rate of 67 per 1,000 live births. The maternal mortality ratio still stands at a high of 885 deaths per 100,000 live births, infant mortality rate at 86 per 1,000 live births, under-five mortality rate at 145 per 1,000 live births and children under age 5 underweight of 28 percent. Gross primary school enrollment for males is still higher than that of females at 108 against 100 with that of secondary school enrollment of 35 as against 28 percent for females. The current overall HIV/AIDS prevalence among 15–49-year-olds stands at 5.3 (3.9 among males and 6.0 among females). For adolescent and young adults aged 15–24 years, the HIV/AIDS prevalence for males is 1.2 percent as opposed to 3.5 percent among females with the rate of childbearing among adolescents aged 15–19 being 36 percent. Gender equality index reveals that males are still advantaged compared with their female counterparts as shown by labor participation rate for males aged 15–64 of 87 percent, and that of females at 65 percent with 17 percent of the seats in parliament being held by African women. Gender parity index (GPI) (net primary enrollment) stands at 90 and that of (net secondary enrollment) at 77. The overall unmet need for family planning currently stands at 24 percent (the need for spacing exceeding the need for limiting at 15 percent as against 8 percent for limiting) (UN Department of Economic and Social Affairs 2002; UNFPA/PRB 2010).

The overall life expectancy at birth has increased from 52 years (51 years for males versus 53 years for females) in 2010 to 58 years (56 years

Table 17.2 Demographic Indicators for Major Subregions of Africa, 1997–2025

INDICATORS	AFRICA (f) 1997	AFRICA (f) 2025	WEST AFRICA (a) 1997	WEST AFRICA (a) 2025	CENTRAL AFRICA (b) 1997	CENTRAL AFRICA (b) 2025	EAST AFRICA (c) 1997	EAST AFRICA (c) 2025	SOUTHERN AFRICA (d) 1997	SOUTHERN AFRICA (d) 2025
POPULATION (IN MILLIONS)	758.4	1453.9	221.8	446.6	88.1	187.5	234.3	480.2	49.5	82.9
PERCENT URBAN (1995)	34.5	57.8	33.1	58.9	39.6n	64.7	22.4	48.0	55.6	74.2
DEPENDENCY RATIO (PER 100 AGED 0–14)	46	55.5	48.0	58.6	49.0	63.7	49.0	61.1	39.0	42.1
ANNUAL POP. GROWTH RATE (TOTAL 1995–2000)	2.7	1.85	2.9	1.93	3.4	2.1	2.7	2.06	2.3	1.27
ANN. POPULATION GROWTH RATE (URBAN)	4.3	2.98	4.9	3.11	4.9	3.07	5.3	3.6	3.3	1.86
TOTAL FETILITY RATE	5.3	3.05	6.0	3.14	6.0	3.46	5.9	33	3.9	2.44
INFANT MORTALITY RATE (PER 100)	86	48	90	54	92	50	99	52	50	26.0
LIFE EXPECTANCY AT BIRTH (BOTH SEX)	53.8	65.2	50	61.7	52.1	64.2	51.8	64.6	62.2	72.2
POPULATION DENSITY (Square Km)	24	52	35	86	13	27	36	82	18	29

Sources: United Nations (1989); UNFPA (1997); United Nations (1996).

for males and 59 years for females). Africa is having a relatively young age structure with 41 percent being under age 15, while 3 percent of its population is 65 years and over, and of the top nine countries in the world in terms of population increase between 2000 and 2050, 44.4 percent are from Africa (United Nations Department of Economic and Social Affairs 2010). The child dependency ratio is 80 percent compared with 5 percent old-age dependency ratio (UNFPA/PRB 2010; PRB 2012; African Development Bank 2012; United Nations 2012; United Nations Statistics Division 2013). Socioeconomic and health indicators indicate that 53 percent of the African population is receiving below $1.25 per day and only 58 percent have access to improved drinking water supply (Malmberg 2008).

4 DEMOGRAPHIC TRENDS IN SELECTED SUB-SAHARAN AFRICAN COUNTRIES PRE- AND POST-ICPD 1994 CAIRO CONFERENCE

Close to two decades after the ICPD in 1994, reproductive health programs have been established in all the countries, with rising contraceptive use among couples; fertility is declining in some of the countries while stalling in others; and child survival is improving. Regional conferences to review developments since the conference have reported increased awareness among policy makers of the concepts of reproductive health and reproductive rights, more political commitment; revised population policies to incorporate reproductive health and so on (United Nations 2003; PRB 2012).

The African Development Bank (2012), among other studies, has documented that the slow pace of fertility decline in SSA has implications for future demographic trends. Bulatao and Casterline (2001) noted that it implies a growing population in the coming decades with attendant adverse effects on the prospects of socioeconomic development. There is progress made in mortality reduction interventions. This is shown by reported declining trends in infant and child mortality. However, the figures shown in Table 17.3 indicate that a number of countries, particularly those in Southern African region (Botswana, Lesotho, Malawi, Mozambique, South Africa, Swaziland, and Zimbabwe), have experienced minimal declines because of the HIV/AIDS scourge. Botswana and Zimbabwe even recorded a decrease in expectation of life. A number of countries (Sierra Leone, Chad, Central Africa Republic, and Guinea-Bissau) have infant mortality rates above 100 per 1,000 live births. The figures also indicate that those countries that recorded contraceptive rates of 40 percent and higher have witnessed significant declines in fertility. In terms of migration and urbanization, there is an increase in the rate of urban growth, and this presents daunting challenges for development (African Union Social Affairs Department, 2006). However Chapter 8 of this volume shows that countries in the Central Africa region will be the least urbanized.

Table 17.3 Population Indicators for Some Selected African Countries Pre- and Post-Cairo ICPD of 1994

Selected African countries according to the period adopted population policy	Total Population (Both Sexes)		Annual Population Growth Rate (%)		Total Fertility Rate		Modern Contraceptive Use among Women Aged 15–49 Years (%)		Infant Mortality Rate (IMR) per 1,000 Live Births		Expectation of Life at Birth (Years)		Urban Population (%)	
	Pre-ICPD****	Post-ICPD****	Pre-ICPD (1985)	Post-ICPD (2009)	Pre-ICPD***	Post-ICPD*	Pre-ICPD	Post-ICPD*	Pre-ICPD***	Post-ICPD*	Pre-ICPD**	Post-ICPD*	Pre-ICPD[b]	Post-ICPD[c]
Pre-ICPD Adopters (1965–1989)														
Ghana	14,011,000	24,392,000	3.3	2.1	5.9	4.2	5f	17	84	47	54	64	33	51
Kenya	21,894,000	40,513,000	3.8	2.6	6.5	4.4	10o	39	67	47	59	62	17	22
Liberia	2,190,000	3,994,000	3.0	4.1	6.7	5.4	6b	10	164	83	48	56	40	61
Nigeria	92,731,000	158,423,000	2.7	2.3	6.6	5.6	1d	8	127	77	45	51	32	49
Senegal	6,818,000	12,434,000	2.9	2.6	6.9	5.0	2b	12	80	47	49	58	38	43
Sierra Leone	3,850,000	5,868,000	2.2	2.7	5.6	5.0	2s	6	154	109	42	47	32	38
Zambia	7,432,000	13,089,000	3.2	2.4	6.7	6.3	14j	27	103	88	52	48	40	36
ICPD Era Adopters (1990–1994)														
Burkina Faso	8,838,000	16,469,000	2.3	3.4	6.9	6.0	4g	15	111	65	46	55	12	20
Cameroon	11,494,000	19,599,000	2.9	2.3	6.1	5.1	1h	14	93	62	53	51	36	58
Chad	5,646,000	11,227,000	2.5	2.8	6.7	6.0	1j	2	129	128	49	49	20	27
Ethiopia	45,240,000	82,950,000	3.0	2.6	7.1	4.8	3l	27	127	59	43	59	11	17

(continued)

Table 17.3 (continued)

Selected African countries according to the period adopted population policy	Total Population (Both Sexes)		Annual Population Growth Rate (%)		Total Fertility Rate		Modern Contraceptive Use among Women Aged 15–49 Years (%)		Infant Mortality Rate (IMR) per 1,000 Live Births		Expectation of Life at Birth (Years)		Urban Population (%)	
	Pre-ICPD****	Post-ICPD*****	Pre-ICPD (1985)	Post-ICPD (2009)	Pre-ICPD***	Post-ICPD*	Pre-ICPD	Post-ICPD*	Pre-ICPD***	Post-ICPD*	Pre-ICPD**	Post-ICPD*	Pre-ICPD[b]	Post-ICPD[c]
Guinea	5,315,000	9,982,000	2.6	2.3	6.9	5.2	4[m]	4	145	89	45	54	27	35
Lesotho	1,580,000	2,171,000	2.6	0.9	5.1	3.2	2[p]	46	84	80	55	48	12	26
Madagascar	10,640,000	20,714,000	2.6	2.7	6.3	4.7	10[q]	28	110	43	49	66	21	30
Malawi	8,617,000	14,901,000	3.1	2.8	7.0	5.7	1[o]	42	143	66	46	53	10	19
Mali	8,379,000	15,370,000	1.8	2.4	7.1	6.3	1[r]	6	135	97	41	51	21	33
Niger	7,337,000	15,512,000	2.8	3.9	7.8	7.1	2[s]	5	155	81	40	58	15	17
Swaziland	802,000	1,186,000	3.1	1.3	6.1	3.5	17[f]	63	77	70	56	48	22	25
Tanzania	23,929,000	44,841,000	3.1	2.9	6.4	5.4	13[j]	26	101	51	51	57	17	26
Uganda	16,482,000	33,425,000	3.1	3.3	7.1	6.2	3[t]	26	108	54	50	53	9	13
Post-ICPD Adopters (1995–1999)														
Benin	4,494,000	8,850,000	2.9	3.2	6.9	5.4	1[d]	6[e]	120	81	51	56	31	42
Botswana	1,301,000	2,007,000	3.3	1.5	5.1	2.8	32[f]	42	54	44	61	51	27	60
Cape Verde	339,000	496,000	1.9	1.4	5.6	2.5	46[i]	57	54	24	63	73	32	60

Country	Population												
Central African Republic	2,808,000	2.9	1.9	5.9	4.6	3^g	9	109	101	49	48	36	39
Côte D'Ivoire	11,694,000	4.4	2.3	6.6	4.6	1^k	8	93	73	56	55	38	49
Guinea Bissau	977,000	1.9	2.2	6.7	5.1	4^n	6^a	145	103	41	48	22	30
Mauritania	1,892,000	2.7	2.4	6.1	4.5	0^k	8	81	74	54	58	35	41
Mozambique	13,336,000	1.9	2.3	6.3	5.9	5^l	11	143	86	43	52	17	38
Namibia	1,304,000	2.6	1.9	5.6	3.3	26^e	53	69	34	59	62	26	37
South Africa	35,197,000	2.5	1.0	4.0	2.4	48^f	60	53	38	58	54	49	61
Togo	3,476,000	3.7	2.5	6.6	4.7	3^f	13	97	78	56	62	27	43
Zimbabwe	9,852,000	3.9	0.3	5.7	4.1	27°	57	56	57	60	48	25	38

Note: Pre-ICPD refers to available data, for between 1985 and 1988, a date before 1994 (choice arbitrary) and post-ICPD refers to the most recent dates (2009–2010 and/or 2012) for which data are available. (a) Indicates estimate from UNFPA/PRB (2010) representing the data for 2006; (b) indicates estimate from United Nations Department of Economic and Social Affairs (2010) representing the data for 1986; (c) indicates estimate from United Nations Department of Economic and Social Affairs (2010) representing the data for 2009 unless otherwise stated; (d) indicates data for 1982; (e) indicates data for 2006; (f) indicates data for 1988; (g) indicates data for 1995; (h) indicates data for 1978; (i) indicates data for 1998; (j) indicates data for 1996–1997; (k) indicates data for 1981; (l) indicates data for 1997; (m) indicates data for 1999; (n) indicates data for 2000; (o) indicates data for 1984; (p) indicates data for 1977; (q) indicates data for 1997; (r) indicates data for 1987; (s) indicates data for 1992; (t) indicates data for 1988–1989.

Sources: ***Data extracted from United Nations Department of Economic and Social Affairs (2011).
*PRB (2012).
**The data are an estimate for 1985 if pre-ICPD and the most recent date (2009/2010) if post-ICPD as cited in United Nations Department of Economic and Social Affairs (2010).
***The estimate covers 1985–1990 periods.

Despite this noticeable progress, mistimed and unwanted births are still reported while modern family planning methods have remained unavailable to large numbers of couples in the subregion (Imasiku et al. 2013). The subregion is faced with a number of challenges, including HIV/AIDS pandemic, conflict, food insecurity, poverty, corruption, and debt burden.

5 CONCLUSION

There is no evidence to clearly state that those African countries that adopted national population policies early (between 1965 and 1989) had lower population growth rate when compared with their counterparts who gave their support much later. However, population growth rate has declined significantly in many of the countries in Southern African subregion, followed by East African countries, while the rate is still on the high side in Western and Central Africa. The results also suggest that fertility has been on the decline in many parts of Africa although the levels are still relatively high in many parts of SSA. Adoption of national population policies by African governments has not really translated to massive current use of modern contraception by women of reproductive ages. Infant mortality rate has declined generally in many parts of Africa, although with subregional variations. Also, expectation of life at birth has been improving over time with possibility of an increase, although it has been observed that it may take some time before the effect of improved health systems can be felt. On the issue of migration, rural–urban drift is still a common phenomenon in many parts of the African continent, and there is an indication that many of the governments in Africa are confused and clueless about likely interventions that could be adopted to stem the tide. International migrations of different types—asylum, human trafficking, and so on—are on the increase.

Clearly analysis of existing census data in SSA has shown decreasing infant mortality in combination with high, though declining fertility rates in some SSA countries. Different countries are at different stages of demographic transition. While mortality started to decline in the mid-twentieth century through public health interventions, total fertility has also started declining. The decline is faster in some sub-Saharan countries (for example, South Africa, Botswana), stalling in others (for example, Kenya), and there is a slow decline in others, such as Nigeria and Ghana. Overall fertility level is still very high, far from replacement fertility level. The relatively slow fertility decline in the subcontinent is confirmed by UN (2012; United Nations Statistics Division 2013) projections for the reduction of infant mortality rates.

There are some challenges in spite of the progress that has been made to date. With declining fertility in some countries and continuous growing population as a result of population momentum, existing scarce resources will be placed under much strain. The youthful population envisaged will be a challenge to most governments unless appropriate measures are taken to ensure that they are engaged in productive economic activities. The provision of social services will also be impacted. Urbanization will increase, and this will affect the ability of government institutions to cope with problems associated with this phenomenon. Some countries that currently have fertility rates close to replacement level will gradually experience an increase in the proportion of the population aged 60 years and above.

Most of the demographic information on sub-Saharan Africa is still obtained from the UN sources based on assumptions and projections. This is because most countries in the subregion do not make their census data available for intellectual research and analysis. It is clear that while huge resources are expended on undertaking censuses in the region, there has not been a commensurate effort to use the data generated for national development planning and development. To address all demographic and socioeconomic challenges confronting the region, governments should commit to utilizing the data collected in censuses in decision making as far as national development planning is concerned. (Teller and Hailemariam 2011).

In order to accelerate various demographic and development objectives, countries in the subcontinent have to review their population policies and programs and intensify actions on specific targets with a view to benefiting from the demographic dividend, especially in the post-2015 development era. The post-2015 development agenda should account for a progressively and rapidly aging SSA by promoting healthy aging and economic well-being in old age. A reinvigorated population policy should prioritize planning for future urban growth, including appropriate infrastructure and access to basic education, and health, including reproductive health and other services, so that countries in the region can reap the benefits of economies of scale and greater efficiency. It can also specify how to manage and incorporate demographic dynamics in national sustainable development policies. The issue of data quality and availability, provision of scientific evidence for policy dialogue and policy development, and, clearly, robust and defined policy relevant indicators should be given due attention.

REFERENCES

African Development Bank. (2000) "Policy on Population and Strategies for Implementation." AfDB *Policy Document*.
African Development Bank. (2012) "Africa's Demographic Trends. Briefing Notes for AfDB's Long Term Strategy." AfDB Policy Document, March.
African Union Social Affairs Department (2006) Population Dynamics: Implications for Achieving the Millennium Development Goals: The State of the African Population Report 2006, Addis Ababa, Ethiopia.
AfricaBulatao, Rudolf A., and John Casterline, eds. (2001) "Global Fertility Transition." In *Population and Development Review, Supplement to Vol. 27*.: 1–211 New York: Population Council.
Department of Social Welfare. (1998) "Population Policy for South Africa." White Paper. http://www.welfare.gov.za/documents.htm.

Garenne, Michel. (2011) "Fifty Years of Research in African Demography: Progress and Challenges." *African Population Studies* 25 (2): 151–167.

Imasiku, E., C.O. Odimegwu, D.N. Ononokpono, and S.A. Adedini. (2013) "Variations in Unmet Need for Contraception in Zambia." *Journal of Biosocial Science*.

Lane, S.D. (2000) "From Population Control to Reproductive Health: An Emerging Policy Agenda." *Social Science and Medicine* 39 (9): 1303–1314.

Malmberg, Bo (2008) *Demography and the Development Potential of Sub-Saharan Africa*. Stockholm: Department of Human Geography, Stockholm University.

Odimegwu, C., and A.O. Oyedokun. (2001) "Cairo Consensus: Revisiting the National Population Policy." In *Policy Issues in Nigeria and National Development*, ed. Z.S. Famisa and O. Adebayo, Ife Press, Nigeria.

Onsembe, Jason O., and James P.M. Ntozi. (2006) "The 2000 Round of Censuses in Africa: Achievements and Challenges." *African Statistical Journal* 3:11–28.

Oucho, J.O., P.A. Akwara, and E.H.O. Ayiemba. (1995) "African Population and Development Agenda: From Bucharest to Cairo and Beyond." *African Population Paper Series* 5.: 1- 65

Population Reference Bureau. (2001) *New Population Policies: Advancing Women's Health and Rights*. Population Bulletin, March 2001, Washington DC

Population Reference Bureau. (2012) *World Population Data Sheet*. Population Reference Bureau, Washington, DC.

Tarver, J.D. (1996). "Population Policies." In *The Demography of Africa*, ed. J.D. Tarver, 223–235. Praeger.

Teller, Charles, and Assefa Hailemariam. (2011) *The Demographic Transition and Development in Africa: The Unique Case of Ethiopia*. New York: Springer.

UNECA. (1995) "Proceedings on "Experts and NGOs Workshop on the Implementation of the Dakar/Ngor Declaration and the ICPD Programme of Action." June 6–9.

UNFPA (1997) *The State of the World Population*. New York: United Nations.

UNFPA/PRB. (2010) *Country Profiles for Population and Reproductive Health: Policy Developments and Indicators 2009/2010*. www.unfpa.org/public/countries. Accessed on Feb, 20, 2012

United Nations. (1994) *Programme of Action of the International Conference on Population and Development, ICPD*. New York: United Nations.

United Nations. (1996) *World Population Data Sheet*. New York: United Nations.

United Nations. (2003) *Fertility, Contraception and Population Policies*. New York: United Nations.

United Nations. (2012) *The State of the World Population*. New York: United Nations.

United Nations Department of Economic and Social Affairs. (2002) *Fertility, Contraception and Population Policies*. New York: United Nations.

United Nations Department of Economic and Social Affairs. (2010) *World Population Policies 2009*. New York: United Nations.

United Nations Statistics Division. (2013) *2010 World Population and Housing Census Programme. Demographic Statistics Section*. New York: United Nations.

Weeks, J.R. (2001) *Population and Development*. 9th ed. Belmont, CA: Wadsworth.

Contributors

Stephen Ayo Adebowale, PhD, has a doctor of philosophy degree in demography and social statistics. He has an interdisciplinary research experience, combining demography, epidemiology, and applied mathematics to improve the understanding of mechanisms underlying contemporary health and social problems. He has participated in numerous National and International Health Programs and Demographic Surveys. He is on the faculty of the Department of Epidemiology and Medical Statistics, Faculty of Public Health, College of Medicine, University of Ibadan, Ibadan, where he teaches Advanced Demographic Methods and Mathematical Demography. He is also the coordinator of the Medical Demography Unit at the same Faculty in Ibadan, Nigeria.

Sunday Adepoju Adedini, PhD, is a lecturer in the Department of Demography and Social Statistics, Obafemi Awolowo University, Nigeria. He obtained a PhD degree in demography and population studies in 2013 from the University of the Witwatersrand, South Africa, where he studied the effects of community contexts on infant and child survival using multilevel modelling. He is a recipient of a number of academic fellowships, including Fogarty Foundation Postdoctoral Fellowship, Consortium for Advanced Research Training in Africa (CARTA) PhD Fellowship, Wits University Postgraduate Merit Award, amongst others. Dr. Adedini has published extensively in many important journals in the fields of population and public health, including *Journal of Biosocial Science, Global Health Action, African Population Studies Journal, Ethnicity and Health, Culture, Health and Sexuality, Maternal and Child Health Journal, BMC Public Health* among others. His research focus is in the fields of maternal and child health and mortality studies.

Akanni Akinyemi, PhD, is a senior lecturer in the Department of Demography and Social Statistics at the Obafemi Awolowo University, Ile-Ife, Nigeria, where he obtained his PhD in 2006. He is currently a visiting researcher with the Africa Center for Migration and Society at the University of the Witwatersrand, South Africa. Dr. Akinyemi's research interests cut across migration studies, aging, and reproductive health. He is a recipient of many academic awards and fellowships, including the IUSSP Junior Demographer award in 2005, United Nations Institute of Aging in 2002, and DHS fellowship in 2010.

Carlos Arnaldo, PhD, is assistant professor of demography and deputy director for research of the Center for African Studies at the Eduardo Mondlane University, where he has been a lecturer and researcher since 1996. His research interests include demographic estimation, fertility and its proximate determinants, reproductive health, and HIV/AIDS. He has a PhD in demography (2003), a master's degree in population studies from the Australian National University, and an honors degree in geography from the Eduardo Mondlane University (Mozambique, 1996).

Nicole De Wet, PhD, is a lecturer in Demography and Population Studies at the University of the Witwatersrand, Johannesburg, South Africa. She obtained her doctorate degree in 2013 with her thesis focusing on the causes and determinants of adolescent mortality in South Africa. Nicole has published several articles in peer- review journals such as *African Population Studies, Global Health Action, The International Journal of Interdisciplinary Social and Community Studies* and the *Journal of Health and Social Behaviour*. Nicole's research interests are in the fields of health and mortality with a special focus on adolescents. Nicole is a recipient of the University of Michigan's African Presidential Scholars Programme (UMAPS) 2014 cohort where her focus is on furthering the study on adolescent health outcomes in South Africa.

Henry Victor Doctor, PhD, an associate research scientist at Columbia University, holds a doctoral degree in demography from the University of Pennsylvania, where he graduated in 2003. He has ten years of experience as a population scientist of which five years have been at the Universities of Malawi and the Western Cape. His research interests include mortality; health status and aging; living standards and health; fertility transitions; religion and demographic behavior; survey research design and implementation; demographic surveillance and longitudinal health research; and health systems operations research. Some of his published research has appeared in journals such as *AIDS, African Population Studies, African Journal of Reproductive Health, International Journal of Educational Development, Rural and Remote Health, Southern African Journal of Demography*, and *Studies in Family Planning*.

Esther W. Dungumaro, PhD, is a senior lecturer at the Institute of Development Studies and Demographic Training Unit, University of Dar es Salaam, Tanzania. She holds a doctoral degree in sociology from Japan University with a major in environmental issues and population. Among her important areas of teaching and research are demographic methods, reproductive health, family and households, and population and environment. Apart from teaching, supervision, and research, Dungumaro currently serves as the research and publication coordinator for the Institute of Development Studies at the University of Dar es Salaam.

Latifat D.G. Ibisomi, PhD, is on the faculty of Demography and Population Studies Program of the University of the Witwatersrand, Johannesburg, South Africa. She has worked in government, NGOs, international institutions, and academic institutions (including the National Population Commission, Nigeria, EU, UNICEF, African Population and Health Research Center). She now works with the Demography and Population Studies Program of University of the Witwatersrand. She has participated in many academic and specialized population, health, and development trainings, teaching, evaluations, conferences, and programs. She has published a number of peer-reviewed journal papers and has participated in writing a number of technical reports and in the compilation of the 2008 African Population Data Sheet. Her research interests are in the field of fertility and reproductive health.

N.B. Kandala, PhD, is currently a principal research fellow in health technology assessment at Warwick Medical School, Division of Health Sciences, Population and Evidence Group, University of Warwick. He obtained a PhD in statistics from the University of Munich (LMU) in Germany in 2001, where he studied the impact of the environment on child health using Bayesian nonparametric spatial methods. He has previously worked as a medical statistician at the University of Southampton and King's College London and was a Mellon Foundation fellow at the University of Montreal, Canada. His main research interests are in Bayesian statistical methods and their application to epidemiology and health. In particular, modeling and estimating the impact of the location (physical environment) on health indicators in sub-Saharan Africa, using large-scale household data and the analysis of longitudinal data. Kandala has published widely in high-impact peer-reviewed journals in both the field of statistics and health in diverse populations.

Lawrence Kazembe, PhD, is an associate professor with the University of Namibia. He joined the University of Namibia in 2012, having served in a similar position at the University of Malawi, Chancellor College. Much of his career has been at Chancellor College, since 1995, when he joined as a junior lecturer and rose to associate professorship rank in 2009. He has previously served as senior biostatistician at Malawi Liverpool Wellcome Trust Clinical Research Program in Blantyre, Malawi, in 2010–2012; as a research fellow at Medical Research Council of South Africa, Durban, in the Malaria Lead Research Program, 2005–2007. He has worked as a consultant statistician with Malaria Alert Center, College of Medicine, Blantyre-Malawi, since 2005. He has published extensively, with more than forty peer-reviewed publications in malaria research and population health. His main research interests are in Bayesian statistical modeling and spatial analysis with applications in population health.

John Kekovole, PhD, has PhD and MA degrees in demography from the University of Pennsylvania (US), an MSc in demography from London School of Economics and Political Science (UK), BPhil in economics from the University of Nairobi (Kenya), and BA (Hons) in economics and statistics from the University of Dar-es-Salaam (Tanzania). He is currently an executive manager in charge of population statistics at Statistics South Africa. He previously worked for Kenya's government for thirty years, during which time he had the responsibility of setting up an integrated sample survey program.

Yohannes Kinfu, PhD, is an alumnus of the Australian National University and the University of Ghana. He is currently a leader of the Nairobi Urban Health and Demographic Surveillance Site and head of the Urbanization and Well-being Research Program at the African Population and Health Research Center in Nairobi, Kenya. Prior to joining APHRC, he was a senior research fellow at the University of Queensland in Brisbane, Australia, and prior to that he worked as a statistician for the World Health Organization, Geneva. He was also a research fellow at the Australian National University in Canberra, Australia. Yohannes's research interests are in the areas of health demography, population economics, and mathematical and statistical modeling of population processes. He has published extensively in such areas as nutrition and poverty, fertility and migration, measurement of mortality and causes of death, inequity in health service coverage, and so on.

Bruno Masquelier, PhD, is an associate professor in demography at the University of Louvain-la-Neuve (UCL, Belgium). He obtained his PhD in demography from UCL in 2010 after a master's in sociology. His research agenda spans a broad array of demographic topics, from the estimation of adult mortality in countries lacking full-fledged vital registration systems to kinship resources for young children and older adults in Africa. He is currently involved in several research projects in Mali, Senegal, Cameroon, and Madagascar.

Chuks J. Mba, PhD, is the coordinator of the Mobilizing Regional Capacity Initiative Program of the Association of African Universities, Accra, Ghana. Before joining the AAU, he worked at the University of Ghana for twelve years, having attained the position of associate professor at the Regional Institute for Population Studies, University of Ghana, and

Legon, Ghana. A former deputy director at Regional Institute for Population Studies, Ghana; acting executive director of the Union for African Population Studies; a member of the Steering Committee of the African Research on Aging Network; and the deputy general secretary of Population Association of Ghana. He has written extensively in peer-reviewed journals and contributed to reports and book chapters. His research interests include population aging, sexual and reproductive health, HIV/AIDS, and population policies and programs.

Clifford O. Odimegwu, PhD, currently heads a regional demographic training program at the University of the Witwatersrand in Johannesburg, South Africa. A graduate of Imo State University, and Obafemi Awolowo University, Nigeria and Harvard School of Public Health, Boston, Massachusetts, US, his research interests focus on broad areas of demographic methodologies, reproductive health, and their development interlinkages. He has published widely on different aspects of technical and substantive demography. He is also the editor-in- chief of *African Population Studies* , the premier Journal of the Union for African Population Studies, and assistant editor of the *African Journal of Reproductive Health.*

Emmanuel Olagunju Amoo, PhD, is a lecturer in the Demography and Social Statistics Program of the Department of Economics and Development Studies in Covenant University Nigeria. He had his BSc and MSc in demography and social statistics from Obafemi Awolowo University, Ile-Ife, Nigeria, in 1993 and 1998, respectively. His research interests are in the areas of gender and reproductive health. He has authored and coauthored several articles on issues related to gender, adolescents, conjugal relationship, male reproductive health challenges, sexual behavior, and HIV/AIDS. His teaching fields are data collection and analysis, social statistics, and demographic techniques.

Collins Opiyo, PhD, is the director of population and social statistics at the Kenya National Bureau of Statistics in Nairobi, Kenya. He is currently on sabbatical and hired by the UNFPA as the resident chief technical advisor for the Namibia 2011 census. Before joining KNBS, he worked as an economist/statistician at the Central Bureau of Statistics. He is also a part-time lecturer at the University of Nairobi. Dr. Opiyo has worked and advised extensively in population censuses and demographic surveys implementation. He has published in such areas as childhood mortality, maternal and child health, fertility, population dynamics, and so on. He is a member of various professional organizations, including Population Association of Kenya, Union for African Population Studies, Population Association of America, American Public Health Association, and IUSSP. Collins holds a PhD and MA degrees from the University of

Pennsylvania, MPhil and MA degrees from the University of Ghana, and BSc in mathematics and physics from the Kenyatta University, Kenya.

Sunday Omoyeni, MSc, is a program officer with International Organization for Migration, Abuja, Nigeria. He completed his MSc in demography and social statistics at the Obafemi Awolowo University, Ile-Ife, Nigeria, in 2011. He has worked on issues related to family planning and fertility behavior of migrants in Nigeria. He is the recipient of the prestigious Aderanti Adepoju prize at the Obafemi Awolowo University.

Serai Daniel Rakgoasi, PhD, is a senior lecturer in the Department of Population Studies at the University of Botswana. He holds a bachelor's degree in a combined major of demography and economics (1992) from the University of Botswana; an MA in demography from Georgetown University, Washington, DC (1996); and a PhD from the University of the Witwatersrand, Johannesburg (2009). Dr Rakgoasi possesses a vast array of experience as a researcher and academic and has provided technical assistance in monitoring and evaluation to various government departments and development partners in Botswana, including the UNFPA, UNICEF, AED, ILO, and a number of local NGOs. Dr Rakgoasi's areas of research interest include applied demography and sexual and reproductive health, especially HIV/AIDS. His PhD thesis explored the role of men and masculinities in sexual and reproductive health in Botswana, with a focus on HIV/AIDS. Some of his research work has been published in renowned international academic and scholarly journals.

Gideon Rutaremwa, PhD, is formally trained as a demographer. He holds both a master's and PhD degree in demography from the University of Pennsylvania, Philadelphia, US. He also holds a master of philosophy and masters of arts in population studies from UNRIPS–University of Ghana at Legon. Dr. Rutaremwa is currently the director of the Center for Population and Applied Statistics at Makerere University, Uganda, and is also a senior lecturer at the Department of Population Studies at the same university. Dr. Rutaremwa takes keen interest in demographic research, training of demographers, social science research methods, data analysis, and in policy and program management and implementation. His current areas of research interest are in the fields of migration, behavioral aspects of HIV/AIDS, morbidity and mortality, fertility, nuptiality, population analysis and policy, child health, and reproductive health.

Abdramane B. Soura, PhD, is a statistician and demographer. He obtained his MA and PhD degrees in demography at the Catholic University of Louvain (Belgium). He also holds a statistics engineer degree from the

National School of Applied Economics (Senegal). He currently lectures at the University of Ouagadougou and has also been responsible for the Ouagadougou Demographic and Health Surveillance System since 2009. The Ouagadougou urban Demographic and Health Surveillance System is collecting and analyzing longitudinal data of eighty thousand individuals. Dr Soura's interests are in the domain of population and health, poverty and vulnerability, and contextual effects of social behaviors. He has published in areas such as childhood mortality, poverty, and health.

Marilyn Wamukoya, MPH, is a biostatistician and a statistical analyst at the African Population and Health Center, Nairobi, Kenya. She works with research scientists at the center in looking at demographic, health, and poverty dynamics in Africa, using a combination of longitudinal and cross-sectional data and analytical tools. Marilyn holds an MPH in biostatistics and environmental health.

Onipede Wusu, PhD, is currently a senior lecturer in the Demography and Social Statistics Program and head of the Department of Sociology in Covenant University, Ota, Nigeria. He holds graduate degrees in sociology with specialization in demography from the University of Ibadan, Nigeria. He has published in several national and international journals on the dynamics of population, sexual and reproductive health, and poverty.

Index

A
ACAP-IPUMS, 130
Access to Education, 194, 206
Activity rate, 162–164, 166–169, 171
Adebowale, S., 78
Adedini, S.A., 78, 97–98, 108, 316
Adolescent dependency, 200, 201
Adolescents, 192–205
Africa, East, 63, 67
   Horn of, 63
   Southern Africa, 62, 63, 65, 67, 73, 74
   West, 62, 63, 67, 71, 73, 74
African
   Development Bank, 303, 304, 305, 312
   Migration, 131, 135
   Regions, 133
   Union, 131, 155
      Social Affairs Department, 312
Age
   discrimination, 245
   falsification, 33
   group, 210, 205
   pyramid, 199
Age-sex
   accuracy index, 17, 30, 31
   data, 12, 13, 15, 17, 27, 33
   specific activity rate, 162, 168
   structure, 12, 24, 158–159, 162–163, 165, 168–169, 198
Age-specific fertility rates, 98, 107, 109
Age-structure, 198, 205
Akinyemi A., 130
Amoo, E.O., 192
Arnaldo, C., 284
Arriaga's method, 100

B
Bachi's index, 15–17, 19–23
Bayesian analysis, 38–39
BayesX, 43, 58
Birth
   histories, 285
   rate, 205, 234
Botswana, 63, 65, 69, 70
Brass
   P/F ratio technique, 99, 100
   Relational Gompertz model, 100
Brass, William, 62, 63, 64, 73, 286–287
Burkina Faso, 63, 69, 70, 73, 137

C
Caldwell JC, 115, 126, 127
Cape Verde, 63, 65, 69
Causes of death, 64, 70, 71, 72, 74, 75 (*see also* cause-specific mortality)
Central Africa, 134
Child
   health, 60, 61, 63 (*see also* child mortality, under-five mortality, U5MR)
   mortality, 61, 62, 64, 65, 66, 67, 71, 73, 74, 75, 36, 37, 38, 39, 41, 53, 54, 55 (*see also* child health; under-five mortality; U5MR)
Children dependency ratio, 200
Children-parent wealth flow, 195
Children's education, 196
Classical demographic transition, 193
Contraceptives, 236
Crude activity rate, 161

D
De facto, 239
De jure, 239

328   Index

Death rates, 234
Defective data, 32
Demographic
  analytical strategies, 203
  Bonus, 194
  change, 234, 245
  dividend, 194, 195
  Indicators, 311
  Policies, 205
  strategies, 205
  transition, 159, 193–195, 200, 205
  window, 194, 203
Dependency
  burden, 203, 204
  ratio, 197–198, 200–201
Development, 194–196, 200, 204
De Wet, N., 173
Digit
  avoidance, 18
  preference, 18, 246
Doctor, H.V., 234
Dungunmaro, E.W., 268

E

East Africa, 134, 135, 150
Economic
  active
    life, 158, 160, 164–169, 170
    population, 161, 163
  activities, 197
  burden, 192, 199, 200, 203
  theory, 196
  transformation, 194
Education policy, 197
Educational attainment, 197–198, 201–202
Egypt, 235, 238, 239–241, 244–245
Elderly
  dependants, 192
  population, 234, 236, 240, 245, 246
Employed, 196–198, 203, 206, 207
Employment, 196–198, 200, 202, 205, 206
Epidemiologic transition models, 60, 74
Ethiopia, 63, 67, 69, 70, 72, 75
Expectation of life, 159, 166
Expected age at death, 240

F

Female-Headed Households, 223–224
Fertility, 193, 194, 195, 200, 235, 244, 249
  decline, 97, 101–102, 108–109, 195
  rate, 286, 294, 298
  replacement level, , 97, 108–109
  stall, 97, 101, 108–109
  transition, 97, 108–109
Frailty, 38, 40, 55, 59
Frelimo, 288

G

Generalized epidemic, 238
Geo-additive survival model, 41
Genocide, 162–163, 165, 168–169, 170, 289, 292, 297, 298
Global economic crisis, 158
Gross
  Domestic Product, 235
  national income, 238
Guinea, 63, 69, 70, 72, 75, 238

H

Harwood-Lejeune, 113, 114, 127
hazard (rate/model), 39, 40, 44, 55–56
Health, 175–176, 185, 188–189
  and Demographic Surveillance System, 246
High
  dependency ratio, 205
  fertility, 200
HIV/AIDS, 58–59, 62, 63, 65, 66, 74, 160–161, 164, 167–169, 170, 287–288
  epidemic, 210–213, 215, 218–220, 223, 225, 227–232, 237
  prevalence, 238, 245
Household
  Composition, 176
  Female-headed, 173–185
  Male-headed, 173–174
  Nuclear, 173, 178–187
  Single-parent, 173, 180, 182, 185
  Size, 174–177, 179–180, 182–185, 188–189
  Structure, 173–174, 177–180
  type, 173, 175, 177, 179–180, 182, 184–185

I

Ibisomi, L., 173
INDETH
  model life table, 161, 164
  Network, 161, 246
Indirect estimations
  fertility, 97
  mortality, 78

Index 329

Indirect methods, 237, 286 (*see also* Indirect techniques)
International Conference on Population and Development (ICPD), 305
International Labour Organization, 203
International Organization for Migration, 130
IPUMS database, 210–211, 218–220, 229
IPUMS-international, 237

K
Kandala, N.B., 36
Kazembe L., 36
Kekovole, John, 1, 303–318
Kenya, 63, 67, 69, 70, 72–73, 75, 141, 143, 176, 178–186, 188, 197–206, 235, 238–241, 244, 245, 247
Kenya Kilimanjaro Plan of Action (KPA), Policies, 304
Kinfu, Y., 61, 64, 72

L
Labour force
  life table, 160
  participation, 158, 161, 168, 170
  structure, 158, 160, 168
  survey, 160
Labour theory of value, 160
Lane, SD, 305
Length
  of economically active life, 158, 170
  of working life, 159–160, 165–169, 170
Liberia, 137
Life
  expectancy, 159, 161, 166, 168–169, 170, 237–238, 240, 242, 245, 290
  tables, 237, 286, 288
Literacy, 201
Longevity, 234, 236–237 244–246
Longitudinal data, 246
Living arrangements, 211, 268, 219–220

M
Mba, J.C., 12–14, 23, 29, 33
Malawi, 63, 67, 69, 71, 73, 133, 175, 178–186, 188–189, 238–241, 244–245, 270, 272, 273, 274, 276, 282

Mali, 63, 69, 70, 71, 72, 73, 75, 133, 137, 178–186, 188–189, 236, 238–241, 244, 247
Markov chain Monte Carlo, 43, 58
Masquelier, B., 210
MDGs, 32
Median age, 237, 240
Medium variant, 247–249
Millennium Development Goal (MDG), 60, 64, 69, 237
Model life tables, 237
Mozambique, 63, 65, 67, 69, 70, 71, 73, 133
Multilevel analysis, 37
Multiple Indicator Cluster Surveys (MICS), 211, 228, 230
Myers/blended index, 12, 15–17, 19–23

N
Namibia, 63, 69, 71, 73, 141
Niger, 133, 192
Nigeria, 133, 192
Nuptiality Patterns, 113, 127
  Education level of attainment, 121
  Employment status, 117, 124
  Religious affiliation, 122
  Rural-urban differences, 122

O
Odimegwu, C., 97–98, 108, 303–318
Old-age dependency, 170
Omoyeni, S., 130
Opiyo, C., 61
Orphaned children, 210
Orphans, 210–230, 268, 269, 272, 273, 274, 275, 276–278, 280–282
Own-children method, 287, 288, 295

P
Parental survival, 210, 230
Pension systems, 245
Population
  aging, 234, 236–237, 243–245
  analysis, 207
    spreadsheets for excel, 198, 207 (*see also* PASEX)
  distribution, 130
  growth rate, 192, 238
  Indicators, 313
  pyramids, 23, 205, 193, 195, 198, 199
Prospective median age, 237

R

Rakgoasi, S.D., 251
Random effects, 40, 44, 45, 50, 56
Rate of natural increase, 192
Regional patterns, mortality, 67
  East African, 67
  Southern African, 67
  West-Eastern, 67
  Western African, 67
Renamo, 2288
Reproductive health, 193, 200
Retirement incentives, 245
Rounds of Population and Housing census, 306
Rural-Urban Migration, 133
Rutaremwa, G, 113
Rwanda, 41–47, 52, 54, 63, 67, 69, 71, 72, 75, 176, 178, 186, 238, 239–241, 244–245, 247, 270, 272, 273, 274, 276, 277, 278, 279

S

School attendances, 276, 278, 279
Sex ratio, 17–18, 25
  defined, 17
Semi-parametric additive predictor, 55
Senegal, 41–49, 52, 54, 63, 69, 71, 197–206, 238–239, 242, 244–245, 247, 270, 272
Sierra Leone, 63, 71, 72, 75, 137
Singulate Mean Age at Marriage SMAM, 116, 119, 120, 125
Single-Year Age Distributions, 18
Size of African labour force, 161
Structural adjustment program, 159, 162
South Africa, 63, 65, 69, 71, 72, 73, 75, 134, 149, 174, 176, 178–186, 188, 283, 270, 272, 273, 274, 280, 281, 282
Southern Africa, 270, 280, 281, 282
Soura, A.B., 210
Spatial
  analysis, 36, 38, 41
  correlated, 38, 40, 53
Standard population, 31
Stats SA, 98, 100, 108
Structured additive regression, 40, 54, 58
Survival status, 268, 271, 272, 273, 275, 276, 277, 278, 279, 281

T

Tanzania, 63, 67, 69, 71, 133, 141, 143, 176, 178–186, 188, 238–239, 242, 244, 248, 269, 270, 272, 273, 283
Theory of fertility, 193
Total dependency ratio, 200
Total fertility rate, 98, 101, 244
  by employment status, 105, 109
  by level of education, 104, 109
  by place of residence, 103, 108
Transition, also phase, 60, 65, 66, 71, 72, 73, 74

U

U5MR, 62, 63, 64, 65, 72, 73, 74, 75
  (see also child health; under-five mortality; child mortality)
Uganda, 41–54, 63, 67, 69, 71, 72, 75, 141, 143, 176, 178–186, 238, 239, 240, 242, 244, 248, 272, 273, 274, 275, 276, 278, 279, 280, 282–283
Under-five mortality, 69, 72, 285–287, 292–294, 297–298 (see also child mortality, child health, U5MR)
UNECA, 304
Unemployed, 198, 206, 207
Unemployment, 159, 167
UNFPA, 60, 73, 310, 311, 312
UNICEF, 60, 61, 210–211, 215, 227, 230
United Nations, 133, 134, 135, 303, 311, 312, 316
  Department of Economic and Social Affairs, 310, 312, 315
  Economic and Social Council, 253
  Joint score, 17–18
  Statistics Division, 305, 312, 316
University of Minnesota Population Centre, 132
Unobserved heterogeneity, 38
US Census Bureau, 100–101

V

Van de Walle, 113, 128

W

Wamukoya, M, 61
West Africa, 132, 133, 134, 135, 149, 270, 280, 282, 283
Whipples index, 16
WHO, 61, 62, 64

Working
  age, 200, 205
  population, 200, 205
  life tables, 159, 161, 164, 169, 170
  population, 159, 164, 166–167, 204
World Bank, 136
World Population Projections, 236, 238, 247–248
Wusu, O., 192

Y
Young adolescents, 197–205
  persons, 192–193, 199
  population, 203
Youth, 236, 246
Youthful population, 205

Z
Zimbabwe, 63, 69, 71, 141